Phenomenology of the Human Person

In this book, Robert Sokolowski argues that being a person means being involved with truth. He shows that human reason is established by syntactic composition in language, pictures, and actions and that we understand things when they are presented to us through syntax. Sokolowski highlights the role of the spoken word in human reason and examines the bodily and neurological basis for human experience. Drawing on Husserl and Aristotle, as well as Aquinas and Henry James, Sokolowski employs phenomenology in a highly original way in order to clarify what we are as human agents.

Robert Sokolowski is the Elizabeth Breckenridge Caldwell Professor of Philosophy at The Catholic University of America. Twice awarded research fellowships from the National Endowment for the Humanities, he has also served as a consultant at the Los Alamos National Laboratory and gave the twenty-sixth J. Robert Oppenheimer Lecture there in 1996. He has also served as visiting professor at the Graduate Faculty of the New School University, the University of Texas at Austin, Villanova, and Yale University. Dr. Sokolowski is the author of many books, including *Introduction to Phenomenology*, *Moral Action*, *The God of Faith and Reason*, *Presence and Absence*, and *Husserlian Meditations*.

Phenomenology of the Human Person

ROBERT SOKOLOWSKI

The Catholic University of America

CAMBRIDGE
UNIVERSITY PRESS

CAMBRIDGE UNIVERSITY PRESS
Cambridge, New York, Melbourne, Madrid, Cape Town, Singapore,
São Paulo, Delhi, Dubai, Tokyo, Mexico City

Cambridge University Press
32 Avenue of the Americas, New York, NY 10013-2473, USA

www.cambridge.org
Information on this title: www.cambridge.org/9780521717663

First published 2008
Reprinted 2008

A catalog record for this publication is available from the British Library.

Library of Congress Cataloging in Publication Data

Sokolowski, Robert.
Phenomenology of the human person / Robert Sokolowski.
p. cm.
Includes bibliographical references and index.
ISBN 978-0-521-88891-2 (hardback) – ISBN 978-0-521-71766-3 (pbk.)
1. Human beings. 2. Philosophical anthropology. 3. Phenomenology. I. Title.
BD450.S 5645   2008
128 – dc22   2007036951

ISBN 978-0-521-88891-2 Hardback
ISBN 978-0-521-71766-3 Paperback

To Kevin White
with thanks
for philosophical conversations

Philosophy thrives on confusion.
– John N. Findlay

Viam veritatis elegi.
– Psalm 119

Contents

Acknowledgments

This book was written over a long period of time, and I am grateful to many people for help along the way. I have often discussed its issues with my colleagues at The Catholic University of America and with friends elsewhere. My thanks are due to John B. Brough; David Burrell, C.S.C.; Richard Cobb-Stevens; Jean De Groot; Thérèse Druart; John Drummond; Michael Gorman; James Hart; V. Bradley Lewis; Daniel Maher; Guy Mansini, O.S.B.; Francis Martin; John C. McCarthy; Alfred and Maria Miller; Gaetano F. Molinari; Timothy Noone; Catherine Pickstock; Owen J. Sadlier, O.S.F.; James V. Schall, S.J.; John F. Smolko; Allen Vigneron; and John F. Wippel. Deans Jude P. Dougherty and Kurt Pritzl, O.P., helped me in administrative as well as philosophical ways. I am particularly grateful to Francis Slade for his guidance in philosophy, now and in the past, and I recall our friendship with Thomas Prufer. An earlier version of the manuscript was used as the basis for a graduate course at Catholic University in the fall of 2006, and my thanks are due to the students for their comments and suggestions, some of which I acknowledge in the notes.

Much of the book is the fruit of my continuing discussions with Kevin White, to whom it is dedicated. It contains a great number of his insights and formulations, as well as many thoughts I would not have come upon apart from our conversations.

Phenomenology of the Human Person

Introduction

The theme of this book is the human person. To make this subject more visible and easier to name, I wish to introduce the term "the agent of truth" as a synonym for "the human person." The phrase is also meant to be a paraphrase of the term "rational animal," the classical Latinate definition of human being. The book is an inquiry concerning the agent of truth.

The new term has two advantages over the old. First, it expands the meaning of thinking and truth. The word *rational* seems to limit thinking to calculation and inference, but the new phrase does not connote such a restriction. It encompasses all the forms of understanding, including those that go beyond language. Second, the term shows that attaining truth is an accomplishment and not merely passive reception. It speaks not just about reasoning but about success in reasoning, and so designates human being in terms of its highest achievement: the human person is defined by being engaged in truth, and human action is based on truth. I do not intend to *prove* that human beings are specified in this way (what sort of premises could I use?), but rather to describe, analytically, what our engagement in truth means. I hope to show, not to demonstrate, what we are as human persons.

We cannot help but take ourselves and one another as involved in truth, but what it means to be so implicated remains obscure to us. The aim of the book is to clarify what we all know is true.

The major inspirations for this book are Husserl and Aristotle. The study will emphasize the role of syntax in language and thinking. Human voicing becomes speech, and it becomes able to serve as a vehicle for thinking and the attainment of truth, when syntax is introduced into it. *Syntax* is a plain word for Husserl's technical term, *categoriality*.

My study of syntax and thinking will lead me to focus on predication, on "saying something about something," as the central activity in thinking, and it will also lead me to discuss the nature of definitions, in which we give the genus and specifying difference of things when we wish to show

1

what those things are. I will also discuss accidents and properties. These
are ancient philosophical issues, but I will not treat them in an antiquated
way. I will claim that predication and definition take place, not simply in
"the mind," but in human conversation. I will show that logical forms are
the residue of public, conversational activity. The form of predication, for
example, comes about when a speaker brings an entity into a conversation
and states something about it. Likewise, definitions occur when a speaker
makes a specifying distinction and explains what it is that he has introduced into the conversation. I would like to think of this book as a recapitulation of Porphyry and Boethius as well as Aristotle. I take into account
the modern turn to the subject, but I consider this subject as a participant
in the human conversation and not a solitary self. Many conundrums of
modern philosophy are dissolved by this simple expedient.

A central topic in the book is the issue of mental representation. When
we know things, do we in some way assimilate copies, forms, likenesses, or
images of them? What can such representations be, and how do they work?
To avoid the difficulties associated with mental representation, I have tried
to reformulate the problem. I claim that when we speak about things we
take in their intelligibility, which we capture and carry in the names that
we use, and that when we picture things we embody their intelligibility in
the images that we compose. When we make distinctions, the intelligibility
and necessity, the substance of things, shows up to us, and this disclosure
occurs within the framework set by syntax.

Although logical, linguistic, and pictorial syntax are the major themes
in this book, I also explore the kind of syntax that occurs in human action,
when one thing is done in view of another, when ends are distinguished
from purposes, and when my good and the goods of others are brought
into syntactical reciprocity in such phenomena as acts of justice and
friendship. I hope to show that the ends of things, their being at their best,
is part of what they are and part of their meaning. When things are given
names and thus entered into syntax and enlisted into language, what they
should be is part of what their names signify.

Since the study of the brain has become so prominent in contemporary
theories of mind, it seemed necessary to say something about the neurophysiology that underlies thinking and truth. I have, therefore, included
some brief chapters on the involvement of the human body, especially the
brain and nervous system, in human experience and understanding. I try
to show that human perception can be seen as the transformation of many
different kinds of ambient energy into the one kind of electrochemical
energy that is found in the activity of the nervous system and brain. The
energy activated in our neural networks is not just input; it can also
become output generated by the nervous system itself, and when this
occurs in certain ways it allows us to reactivate earlier experiences in
imagination and memory and to project ourselves into new situations. In

connection with this topic, I take the rather bold step of proposing an alternative way of thinking about mental imagery. I suggest that, instead of saying that the nervous system and brain construct internal images of things that are "out there," we think of the nervous system and brain as functioning like a lens. The neural activity involved in experiencing can be considered as "lensing" and not as imaging or picturing. The advantage of this change is that it counters our tendency to think of mental images or ideas as intervening between our minds and the things that we know. I hope to provide an alternative to representationalism in sensibility as well as in thinking.

The role of syntax in our experience, activity, and speech is the central theme in my analysis, but I begin the book with a particular syntactic form, which I call the "declarative" use of the first-person pronoun. It is the use we make of the word *I* and its analogues when we endorse or appropriate a particular exercise of our rational, syntactic powers, when, for example, we say, "I *know* she is coming," or "I *promise* I will be there." Such declaratives could not be used except on the foundation of another syntactic articulation, and they mention us precisely as actively engaged as agents of syntax or agents of truth. They designate us as persons in action, as acting rationally even as we utter the words. A topic associated with declaratives is what I call "veracity," which I define as the inclination toward truthfulness that defines us as human beings or persons and establishes us as responsible agents.

The issue of philosophical language is treated episodically at various stages in the book. I try to describe what is distinctive about philosophical speech. The study of philosophical discourse is my way of speaking about what Husserl calls the "transcendental, phenomenological attitude," the point of view that we adopt when we enter into philosophical reflection. Husserl has made an important contribution to philosophy by showing how the philosophical standpoint is different from the stance we take in prephilosophical experience and speech, in what he calls the "natural attitude." I have tried to amplify and concretize some of his ideas by formulating them in terms of philosophical speech instead of philosophical attitudes and reflection. I distinguish philosophical speech from other levels of speech (from standard language, scientific language, and declaratives); I describe it as the theorizing of the human conversation in all its amplitude, with the inclusion of the things that are brought into the conversation and correlated with it; I differentiate it from scientific discourse; and I treat it at greatest length in the last chapter of the book, where I distinguish the philosophical voice from the voice of the omniscient narrator in a work of fiction, and where I discuss how words have to be troped when they are brought into philosophical discourse. The distinctiveness of philosophical speech is especially important in the study of human knowledge, because the claim that we have mental images and mental representations is stated from the philosophical viewpoint. The terms used in such claims need to be taken philosophically, but they are often given meanings taken from the prephilosophical attitude, with the consequence that a radical disjunction is introduced between what is "inside" our minds and what is "outside" them.

I wish to describe the human person philosophically by clarifying what it means to be involved with truth. We enter into rationality when we introduce syntactic composition, whether verbal, pictorial, or practical, into experience. Such articulation allows us to converse with others and to reason with them, instead of resorting to violence or disengagement; it allows us to appropriate, by the use of declaratives, what we have articulated, and to raise questions not only about facts and about our purposes, but also about the ends that are inscribed in things. The use of words reveals the good and the best in what we name. Our philosophical exercise is itself a culmination of our rationality, not something alien to it. It brings to a kind of completion the truthfulness we enter into when we begin speaking with others.

PART I

THE FORM OF THINKING

1

Two Ways of Saying "I"

> One could express it this way: In a zoo there could be a sign, "This is a zebra"; but certainly not, "I know that this is a zebra." "I know" has meaning only when a person utters it. But then it does not matter whether the utterance is, "I know...," or "This is...."
>
> Ludwig Wittgenstein, *On Certainty*, §588

> My observation is a logical and not a psychological one.
>
> §447

My purpose is to clarify, philosophically, what human persons are. It is our rationality that makes us persons, and I wish to describe such rationality in action, to show how it is made manifest. If I succeed in doing so, I will have helped exhibit what is distinctive about human beings. I will begin, not by making general remarks or offering broad descriptions, but by targeting a particular human activity, something very definite, and using it as a wedge to open up the dimension of being that is proper to persons. The activity I will target is a special way in which we use the word *I* and its variants, a special way we use the first person, when we speak. Our rationality and hence our personhood come prominently to light in this usage. This phenomenon can then serve – if I may switch metaphors – as a bridgehead for the exploration of other ways in which our rationality appears.

We cannot show what we are as persons without also showing what it means for things to appear to us. Our rationality is not simply the power to have ideas, to calculate, and to draw inferences in our minds; our rationality is essentially a disclosure of things, and even reasoning serves ultimately to show forth what things are. Reasoning comes to rest in understanding. In order to discuss rationality, therefore, we must discuss the manifestation or the truth of things as it occurs in its various ways: in perception, thinking, remembering, picturing, quotation, and the like, as well as in practical agency and deliberation, since human conduct also involves a specific manner of displaying the world. Our treatment of the human person must also study the appearance of things, and all of this will begin with a treatment of the way we use the word *I*.

We must maintain a certain modesty as we discuss the human person. We will always remain mysterious to ourselves, but it is possible to shed light on this mystery, to bring out its dimensions and keep it from being confused with other things. I hope to provide glimpses that clarify, not mechanisms that explain.

How We Speak of Ourselves

We use three different terms to refer to ourselves: first, we call ourselves *human beings* or, in the generic sense of the word, *men*. Second, we speak of ourselves as *persons*. And third, we say that we are *selves*. These terms have been developed at various stages in the course of Western culture and philosophy.

The first term, *man*, is the most basic and spontaneous. It simply marks us out as one of the species of things in the world, one among the many kinds of being: there are minerals, plants, and animals, and among the animals there are bears, wolves, cats, and, finally, men.[1] We come to light as differentiated from the other kinds of animals and living things. The second term, *person*, was developed after the earlier term *man* and as a refinement of it.[2] The term

---

[1] See Robert Spaemann, *Personen: Versuche über den Unterschied zwischen 'etwas' und 'jemand'* (Stuttgart: Klett-Cotta, 1998), 17: "'Man' is first of all a concept of a biological species, and ancient and medieval philosophy numbered man among the *animalia*, the animals. Man is an *animal rationale*." By contrast: "Persons enjoy a special place among all the things that exist. Persons do not make up a natural kind" (p. 9).

[2] The Greek term *prosōpon*, as well as the Latin *persona*, signified a mask and hence a character in a play, a meaning retained in the phrase *dramatis personae*, the persons or characters in the drama. One must have already been aware of human beings in order to be able to designate "someone" as a character in a play. The person is not the actor but the agent represented by him. In Stoic and Academic thought, *persona* often designated the role one played in life, as opposed to one's nature. In medieval society a *persona* was someone with legal standing, a freeman and not a slave, or a legally recognized human being as opposed to a thing. This too is a qualification added to a human being, and it presupposes the difference between men and other living things. Such legal standing could even be extended to artificial persons, so long as they could take legal action. Medieval theologians emphasized the singularity of the person; personality was taken not just as an instance of a nature, but as the ability to have one's nature and to be responsible for the way one "owns" it. On the ancient and medieval senses of *person*, see Spaemann, *Personen*, 30–42.

The connection between personhood and representation surfaces in an original way in the political philosophy of Hobbes. He defines a person as someone whose words and actions can be considered either to be his own or to represent some other man or thing. See *Leviathan*, ed. Richard Tuck (New York: Cambridge University Press, 1996), Chapter 16, which is entitled "Of Persons, Authors, and Things Personated." The verb *to personate* is used to good effect by Hobbes. Representation is a defining property of the modern state as opposed to premodern political society. One might ask whether political representation is somehow related to epistemological representation in Hobbes's thought.

is more sophisticated, and arose in conjunction with theological and legal controversies. Its classical philosophical definition was given early in the 6th century by Boethius, who said that a person is an individual substance of a rational nature.[3] This definition highlights our rationality: a person is an individual being that is endowed with reason. The definition also leaves open the possibility that there may be persons who are not human beings (Boethius applied the term to the divine and the angelic); they too could be individual entities invested with a rational nature. In the legal context, there can be "persons" like corporations and states, which are entities that have a standing in the law and are recognized as agents. My discussion, however, will be limited to the human person. Finally, in addition to *man* and *person*, the third term we use to refer to ourselves is *the self*, and this term is very strange indeed. It could not have come into use except through some philosophical contrivance. How odd it is, even grammatically, to speak of "the self."[4] The linguistic strangeness of the term *the self* is matched by the oddity of the terms *the ego* and *the I*, which are often used as its synonyms. Under what normal circumstances would we ever refer to "the I"? Why have we not contrived to speak of "the he" or "the she" or "the they," or even "the you"? Furthermore, why should we reserve to ourselves the privilege of being "selves," when every entity shares in that distinction? Everything – a horse, a tree, a ruby, a molecule – is itself, and hence it is "a self," is it not? Why do we presume to take ourselves as "*the* selves," the paradigms of identity? We seem to claim for ourselves alone the identity that belongs to all beings. Is this not metaphysical arrogance?

We begin with the word *person* and what it signifies. Our procedure will be twofold. On the one hand, we will explore certain phenomena and certain activities that manifest human persons as such. One the other, we will try to deal with certain problems or perplexities, certain choke points that block our understanding of human persons and hence impede our understanding of ourselves. Some ideas act like conceptual acid and dissolve the person into impersonal forces, or disfigure the person into a caricature of himself. Dealing with such perplexities is not a waste of time, since unraveling the snags in our ideas is also a fresh registration of what we are trying to discover.

---

[3] Boethius's definition is found in "A Treatise against Eutyches and Nestorius," Chapter 3. See *The Theological Tractates and The Consolation of Philosophy*, trans. H. F. Stewart and E. K. Rand, Loeb Classical Library (Cambridge, MA: Harvard University Press, 1968), 84–5.

[4] See Charles Taylor, *Sources of the Self: The Making of the Modern Identity* (Cambridge, MA: Harvard University Press, 1989), 113: "It is probable that in every language there are resources for self-reference and descriptions of reflexive thought, action, attitude .... But this is not at all the same as making 'self' into a noun, preceded by a definite or indefinite article, speaking of 'the' self or 'a' self. This reflects something important which is peculiar to our modern sense of agency."

Informatives and Declaratives

The classical definition of persons tells us that they are individual entities
that possess reason. It is the power of reason that makes us persons. Even
when we use the word *person* in a less technical way, simply as a reminder
that the individual we call a person is a human being and should be
treated as such, we imply that the dignity he has and the respect he
deserves follow from his rationality. It is because he is rational that he must
be "treated as a person and not as a thing." But how is the rationality that
establishes us as persons manifested to us?

We might think that this rationality appears primarily in our ability to
calculate and draw inferences: we work out sums and solve equations; we
draw conclusions from premises; we examine various facts and make
inductions from them. We reason deductively and inductively. Our rationality is exhibited by such calculation and inference, but it would be wrong
to restrict reasoning to such mathematical and logical exercises. To limit it
in this way would make us think of ourselves as animals that have calcu-
lating machines or computers in their heads. In fact, reason is more widely
distributed in our being, and it is manifested in many other ways besides
calculation and inference.

Instead of concentrating on the power of reasoning, we begin by
examining the word we use to name ourselves, the word *I* and its variants,
such as *me* and *mine* and the plural forms. Our rationality is exhibited and
our personhood is made manifest in our very ability to use the first-person
pronoun. To show this, we must distinguish between two different ways in
which we use this term.

First, there is what I wish to call the *informational* use of the word *I*, in
which we simply name ourselves as we would name any other object that we
want to say something about. If someone asks, "Who in this room weighs
over 150 pounds?" and I say, "I do; I weigh over 150," or if in another
context I say, "I am now in Cherry Hill, New Jersey," or "I am hungry," I am
using the term in that informational way. I might just as well have said,
"Robert is in Cherry Hill, New Jersey," or "The man sitting at this table is
hungry." I could have expressed the same fact in third-person discourse.

In contrast with this informational use of the term *I*, we can distinguish
what I wish to call the *declarative* use of the word. Suppose I say, "I suspect
that you are cheating," or "I shall return," or "I must pay my debts," or
"I know that this is a zebra." These statements are not merely reports about
myself, as were the informational remarks we just examined. If I say, "I
distrust you," I do not merely state a fact about myself; rather, I declare
myself as distrusting you, and I thereby declare myself in my rational
agency. I engage myself in what I say. This usage of the term *I* expresses
me, the speaker, as a rational agent and hence as a person or an agent of

truth. Moreover, it expresses me as acting rationally here and now, in my present use of the word *I*. This usage does not *say* that I am a rational agent; it does not predicate rational agency of me; rather, it directly expresses me as acting as a rational agent when I use the term *I* and say, "I distrust you." It does not just inform you about me, but exhibits me in my personal agency. It shows and does not just tell.

The difference between the informational and the declarative use of the term *I* is rather subtle. Its subtlety is enhanced by the fact that one and the same sentence can be used in both ways. It would be possible, albeit somewhat unusual, for me to say, "I distrust you" and state it as a mere matter of fact. I might say something like this: "Well, after all that has happened, it should be no surprise that I distrust you and have done so for some time now." I would not be *declaring* my distrust at the moment, but simply *reporting* it to you as a bit of information. I would just be stating a fact about a permanent state I am in, and I would state it with as much detachment as if I were to say that I am six feet tall, or if I were telling you about someone else. However, when I say, "I distrust you," in a declarative manner, I am formally establishing or confirming that relationship. The declarative, "I distrust you," institutes or reasserts distrust, while the informational merely tells you of it. The declarative appropriates, whereas the informational reports.

Still another indication of the subtlety of the distinction lies in the fact that we might not be sure whether a given statement is informative or declarative. A statement like "I am in this room" seems obviously to be just informational, a mere assertion of fact, but it could also be used declaratively if the speaker were making a significant point and asserting himself in his rational agency. He might state it in the course of a heated argument about whether or not he is going to remain with us during a difficult time; when he declares, "I *am* in this room," he may state this fact in order to show that he has engaged himself to be there with us. He declares that he is in this room deliberately, through his rational agency, not as a mere matter of fact. Sometimes a speaker might deliberately play on the declarative ambiguity of a statement, on the fact that it could be taken either as informational or as declarative: the statement shimmers between seeming to be the one and seeming to be the other, as a patch of color may shift between looking orange and looking red, and we are left unsure what it really is. The speaker toys with the listener. Linda says, "Well, I am here, am I not?" and Sidney cannot tell whether she is only recording a fact or deliberately making a point about what she is intent on doing. Linda might hide behind the ambiguity. If Sidney takes the statement as declarative, she might run for cover and say that she was just mentioning her presence and stating an obvious fact; but if Sidney takes the statement as an ordinary bit of information, Linda might make it clear that she was really transmitting a message or sending a signal, that she was declaring herself in what she said. The difference lies not in the words that are uttered but in the way they are used.

We are making use of the first-person pronoun to explain what declaratives are, but our analysis could have been based on other linguistic structures appropriate to other languages, such as the first-person voice in Latin (*scio, opinor*). We could have used, in Thomas Prufer's words, "whatever sign design plays the same role in any other language," that is, whatever sign design is "produced in order to designate only the producer as a speaker, as using, in the act of producing the token, a language."[5] The designated language user is signified, of course, not just as making sounds but as thinking in the medium of the words he speaks.[6] He would not really be using the language if he were not thinking, at least to some degree.

Bringing Ourselves to Light

In the rest of this chapter, we will discuss the declaratives related to cognitive terms like *know* and *see*. In the next chapter, we will discuss the special kind of freedom that is associated with such cognition, and will explore the declarative use of the term *I* in regard to affective and promissory terms. We will also examine "existential" declaratives.

[5] Thomas Prufer, *Recapitulations: Essays in Philosophy* (Washington, DC: Catholic University of America Press, 1993), 60.

[6] The phrase "thinking in the medium of words" is from David Braine, who uses it often in his book *The Human Person: Animal and Spirit* (Notre Dame, IN: University of Notre Dame Press, 1992). I might observe that the difference between the declarative and the informational uses of the word *I* is analogous to the difference between the uses of *shall* and *will* that are recommended by English grammarians; see H. W. and F. G. Fowler, *The King's English* (Hertfordshire: Wordsworth Editions, 1993), 142–63. To express simple futurity ("the plain future"), according to these rules, one should use *shall* in the first person and *will* in the second and third person. To express a future marked by deliberation, obligation, permission, or menace ("the colored future," marked by someone's mood), one should use *will* in the first person and *shall* in the second and third. Thus, if I were to say, "I shall come at five o'clock," I would simply be telling you what is going to happen; this usage would be analogous to an informational use of the first-person pronoun. If I were to say, "I will be there when you need me," I would be stressing my deliberate intent to be there in the future, and this usage would be analogous to a declarative use of the first-person pronoun. The distinction between *shall* and *will* is neglected by many, but sometimes it must be followed. On entering an elevator one will often see a sign that says, "The elevator shall not be used in case of fire." This statement does not predict the future; the elevator might in fact be used by someone when a fire breaks out. One is being informed that it ought not be used. One would never (or one should never) see a sign that stated, "The elevator will not be used in case of fire." The person who affixed such a sign could never be sure. In scholarly writing, many authors use *shall* in the first paragraph of an essay, when they tell us what will be done in the course of their paper, but fail to comply with the distinction afterward. Using *shall* for the first person in spoken American English draws attention to itself.

One might claim that every statement we make, even those that do not involve the first-person singular, has a declarative character. If I say, "It is snowing outside," I am engaging my rationality by registering or reporting a state of affairs. Even in such third-person statements, in which I do not mention myself, I engage my power to reveal the truth of things. Are not such statements also declarative, and do they not reveal us as agents of truth? Why restrict the declarative usage to the first-person pronoun, to the use of the word *I* and its variants?

It is true that I deploy my reason whenever I speak thoughtfully about anything, even when I do not mention myself as the one who is speaking. But whatever may be implicit in a statement such as "It is snowing outside," in fact I do *not* mention myself when I speak in this way, and philosophically we must not overlook that absence. In the words I explicitly utter, I do not mention myself as the one who is making the claim. There is a difference between "It is snowing outside" and "I see that it is snowing outside," or "I know that it is snowing outside," or "I say that it is snowing outside." There is something definitive and climactic when I use the word *I* in the declarative manner. The introduction of subscripts may help us see this more clearly. When I use *I* as a declarative, I explicitly manifest$_d$ myself in the act of manifesting$_o$ the world. I catch myself in the act of disclosure and display myself in the act, and this manifesting$_d$, which brings me to light as an agent of truth, is different from the original manifesting$_o$, the ground-based manifestation$_o$, which brings something in the world to light but still leaves me in the shadows. Declaratives achieve a double disclosure: they express the kind of rational activity I am engaged in, and they express me as engaged in it. Admittedly, my bodily voice shows me up as the one who makes the initial statement, "It is snowing outside," but it is I myself, and not just my body or my voice, who declare myself as the one who acts truthfully when I say, "I see that it is snowing outside." My own responsibility is more explicitly engaged in the declarative usage. A statement like "I see that it is snowing outside" manifests us as persons-who-are-acting-as-such at the moment we say these words.

This declarative use of the word *I* does not merely say that I am making noises or uttering an English sentence. It does not just highlight me as a voicer of sounds or a speaker of certain words. It expresses me as making a truth claim, as exercising my reason, in the sounds that I make and the words that I utter. It shows$_d$ me up as showing$_o$ up part of the world, but when it does so, it does not make me to be one more part of the world that is being showed$_o$ up by me. In a sense that we will have to clarify, I stand "outside" the world when I show$_o$ up something in the world, just as the seeing eye stands outside the field of vision. I necessarily could not be part of what I show$_o$ up through my power of thoughtful disclosure, and this necessity is akin to logical necessity. It is part of what has been called transcendental, as opposed to formal, logic.[7] When I declare myself as showing$_o$ up part of the world, my declaration exhibits$_d$ me precisely as occupying that strange marginal, evanescent, and "unworldly" position. It mentions me as being at work as an agent of manifestation.

For this reason, my declarative statement is not a statement like the original one that expressed something in the world. It may look just like the original statement (first we have "It is snowing," which speaks about the world, then we have "I know it is snowing," which seems to say something about me and seems just to add one more worldly fact to the first one), but it really is not a statement of the same order. The declarative statement is more like an emphatic restatement of the original statement, along with the engagement and manifestation of the speaker who states and restates it. To say, "I know it is snowing," is really to restate, "It is snowing," but to do so with two important additives: I now specify the manner in which I register the fact that it is snowing (I know, suggest, believe, or doubt it), and I express myself as the agent of disclosure, the one responsible for manifesting the fact in question. Strictly speaking, nothing more than "It is snowing" is said about the world when I say, "I know it is snowing," but something new is said in another dimension on the margin of the world, and specifically on this particular edge that is me as an agent of truth in action; I am indexed as such.

Refinements

I should also note that the declarative verb *know* (or *suggest* or *believe* or *doubt*) really applies more to the state of affairs, "It is snowing," than to me: it specifies the modality in which the state of affairs is presented to me. It does not primarily say anything about me as an entity. It does not primarily report about my state of mind or my psychological processes. If it were to do so, it would become a report about my mental activity, an informational statement about myself in the world. It would lose its logical – and hence also its personal – force. It would "reduce" truth to psychology. However, even though the declarative is primarily about what is declared, it does mention me as the agent of such disclosure. There could not be a disclosure without me or someone like me there to achieve and receive it, and I am there not merely as a biological organism or a psychological center of consciousness, but as an agent of logic and verification. The way the thing

---

[7] See Edmund Husserl, *Formal and Transcendental Logic*, trans. Dorion Cairns (The Hague: Nijhoff, 1969). In the first part of the book, Husserl examines a number of formal systems. The second part of the book is entitled "From Formal to Transcendental Logic," and there Husserl integrates formal structures into the activity of pursuing and achieving truth. The analysis of such activity is called transcendental logic. Husserl shows how formal logic is "grounded" upon rational, subjective activity. He thereby shows how we are elevated into logic and truth.

disclosed is there "for" me or "in" me, and the way I am there as its dative, are metaphysically perplexing topics, and our study of the declarative is an attempt to address them. We cannot properly speak about the human person without taking up these issues.

The first and basic act is that in which I disclose$_o$ something in the world. This is an exercise of my reason, an exercise of my ability to be an agent of truth. The next step is to exhibit$_d$ and declare myself as so exercising my reason, as actually being at that moment an agent of truth. I could not execute this new disclosure$_d$ had the original disclosure$_o$ not taken place, but the new exhibition$_d$ is not merely a prolongation of the original. It does not just stuff more material into it or add another fact to it. It operates in another dimension, but one that was implicit and complicit in the first. It is the first explicit mention of the personal, which had already been at work in the original manifestation but did not speak of itself there. Opening the new dimension gives us a glimpse into what Kant called the kingdom of ends; it is the domain of persons, the space of reasons, the place where we see agents of truth carrying out, well or badly, for better or worse, the things that they can do. This new dimension flickers on the margin of the world manifested$_o$ in our original exercise of reason, and a multitude of possibilities are opened up within it that could not have been recognized or achieved before it came into view.

The declarative use of speech, furthermore, does not just speak *about* persons and activities in this new domain. It does not just apply personal predicates to rational entities that stand there before it. It does not just say, for example, that this person is making a choice, that another person is deliberating, and that still another knows the meaning of a certain phrase. All such statements would be merely informational, not declarative. The declarative use of speech is more concentrated than this: it captures and expresses me, the rational agent, right in the actual exercise of my reason. It is time-specific and indexical. It is a kind of pinnacle in the manifestation$_d$ of the person, the person at work here and now. It exhibits me exercising my power to be truthful. Without this concentrated registration of personhood, this paradigm of evidence, all other statements about persons would lose their meaning for us and would be reduced to statements about impersonal entities and processes. Without it, the very dimension of the personal would not have arisen for us. Declarative speech gives us the primary intuition of the personal in its actual presence, the rational in its actual exercise, and the original distinction of the person from his context.

To sharpen our grasp of the declarational use of the word *I*, let us say a bit more about the informational use of the term. It is possible for me to speak about my own opinions, and about myself as holding those opinions, in a merely informational way. I can refer to myself as the one who has a certain belief, and as I do so I need not be declaring myself as holding that belief. Just as I can say, "Audrey thinks it is snowing," I can sometimes say, without engagement and without declaration, "I think it is snowing." The same words that can be used for a declaration can also be used informationally, and because the same words can be used in both ways, the difference between the declarational and the informative can easily be masked. I use the words informationally when I merely report about myself and my beliefs. For example, I might say, "I expected, this morning, that the traffic would be very heavy; that is what I was thinking at that time." The *I* in my phrase, "I expected, this morning," is not being used declaratively but only informationally. The state of affairs, "the traffic will be very heavy," is not being actively asserted as I speak now, but only reported. I am speaking of myself as an agent of truth at some other time, not here and now, and I am not declaring myself here and now. I am not endorsing what I said then. I could even use the present tense in this informational manner: I could say that as a matter of course, "I know that traffic is generally heavy at seven o'clock in the morning." The informational use of the word *I* can thus be applied to opinions, choices, deliberations, and other exercises or products of reason, but it applies to them in what we could call a sedimented state, when they are not being actively appropriated or declared at the moment. It mentions the rational activity after it has fallen into a state of rest, after it has gone to sleep and lost its energy. Declarational speech, on the other hand, can only be used at the moment we achieve and appropriate an act of reason, and it expresses us precisely as both achieving and appropriating it. Declarational speech expresses us at work as agents of truth.

A declarative is an enhancement and an endorsement of a state of affairs. The focus is on the state of affairs and not the endorsement. If I say, in a declarative manner, "I know the house is for sale," or "I doubt that the house is for sale," what is being emphasized is the house's being for sale. That state of affairs is being specified, and its modality is being determined: it is definitely the case, it may be the case, it is doubtful that it is the case. It is true that the state of affairs is known, suspected, or doubtful *to me*, but I am not the center of focus; the state of affairs is. This point could be expressed graphically by printing the endorsed statement in italics; in a declarative, it would be appropriate to print, "I know this, *the house is for sale.*" In a declarative, we start off with a single fact, the house's being for sale, and we remain with that fact, but the same fact is underlined, endorsed, and enhanced, and its modality is specified.

In an informative statement, by contrast, the emphasis is on the first person and the verb that follows it. In an informative statement, we move on to a new fact. It is no longer the fact that the house is for sale that matters, but rather the fact that I know that it is for sale. We would now have to print the statement this way: "*I know* that the house is for sale." The informational use of the first person does not endorse the original fact but introduces a new, higher-level fact. This new fact, the fact that I know the house is for sale, may be significant in some way (another person may have to move quickly if he wants to buy the house), but it is a new fact that comes into play, not the original fact that is being brought into greater prominence by being registered as being displayed by someone. The informational use of the first person downgrades the original fact and makes it simply an ingredient in another, more complex fact, whereas the declarational use enhances the fact and makes it stand out all the more independently.

An Illustration

We are trying to describe how we show up as persons, and I am claiming that we do so in a crucial and irreplaceable way when we use the word *I* in a declarative manner. Our discussion has been formal and abstract; let us try to visualize the declarative usage more concretely. Imagine an auditorium in which fifteen people are seated. On the stage are two people lecturing about science and performing some experiments. It is an informal event, and some in the audience have brought their pets with them: two golden retrievers and one Lhasa apso. Video cameras and tape recorders have been set up. The audience, the dogs, the video cameras, and the tape recorders are all "taking in" what is occurring on stage, but they are taking it in in different ways. The video and tape recorders receive physical impressions, but they have no awareness and no self-awareness, and they exercise no responsibility. The dogs, panting and with their tongues aloll, also receive impressions, of a different kind, and they do have some self-awareness; they could even be said to be aware that they are perceiving what is happening on the stage (though they probably would not categorize it this way). The fifteen people receive impressions and enjoy self-consciousness, but they also have something more: they have the ability to declare themselves. They can use the word *I* to register themselves as receiving impressions and articulating or stating them. They enter into logic and evidencing, but they do not just receive and articulate; they can also declare that they do so. Any one of them might blurt out, "I know what's going on; the chemical reaction is starting up; I can see it." Furthermore, not only *can* they declare themselves, they do so all the time whenever they speak. Human speech is peppered with declaratives. If you listen to any conversation, hear any speech, or watch any movie, you will find the engaged sense of the word *I* appearing intermittently throughout. We are constantly mentioning ourselves as speaking and are repeatedly appropriating what we say, playing it off against what others are saying.

Declarations, with the kind of responsibility that they involve, can flash on and off in those fifteen human bodies in that room, but in nothing else: not in the dogs, the video cameras or tape recorders, the desks, carpets, walls, or ceiling, nor in the molecules that make up the air in the room or the cosmic particles that come wandering through it. The declarative can occur only in a living human body; even the dogs can't declare themselves (we would be startled and alarmed if they did). The dogs can see what is going on, but they can't say that they see what is going on. Only those fifteen human beings are persons, and their power of declaration reveals them as such. Our present task as philosophers is to describe what happens in such declarative speech, and to show that it is decisive in manifesting us as persons.

We are trying to perform this task by making a strategic distinction, between the declarative and the informational uses of the first-person pronoun and its variants. If someone were to disagree with my argument, he would imply that the distinction I am drawing, between the declarative and the informational, is unreal. He would claim that it is not genuine but merely verbal, a distinction without a difference. He would accuse me of making something out of nothing. To counter such a claim, I must bring out more clearly the truth and the significance of this distinction by sharpening our understanding of declarative uses of the word *I*. Our next step, therefore, will be to show how declarations are different from simple self-consciousness. Our further steps, in the next chapter, will be to explore other kinds of declaratives and to show how declarations express an elementary kind of freedom in the human person.

Declarations and Self-consciousness

The declarative use of the word *I* must be distinguished from simple self-consciousness. Because of the diversity of our senses, almost any experience we have, no matter how rudimentary, is accompanied by some self-awareness. If we are pressing against a chair, we also feel our legs stretched out, we hear sounds, we see parts of the room, we have a sour taste in our mouth. All these experiences emerge in one field, and any one of them is profiled against the others, so that any perceptual focus we might enjoy at any moment will be played off against a background, a "self," that accompanies it. Besides perceiving other things, and while perceiving other things, we also experience ourselves as carrying on the perception. Such self-consciousness is a biological and psychological phenomenon, and in itself it does not involve any logic or reasoning. It involves what the Aristotelian tradition calls the internal senses. Animals, at least the higher forms, certainly have some self-awareness. Insects and the lower forms of animals, with less diversity of perception and less parallel processing in their nervous systems, certainly have less self-consciousness, and perhaps they have none; does a spider feel anything when it is crushed?

Self-consciousness also accompanies our ascent into articulated thinking. When we go beyond perception and its attentional diversity, when we begin to insert syntax into what we experience – when we not only see the brown table but begin to register the fact that the table is brown – our activity is obviously escorted by self-awareness, by a pre-reflective sense that *we* are the ones registering that fact. This accompaniment, however, is still not a declaration. We may be more aware of ourselves when we register a state of affairs than when we merely perceive something, because we have to be more active when we engage in thinking: we must articulate the things that are there before us; we have to distinguish and unite parts and wholes in what is presented. Such distinction and unification are expressed in the syntax of our speech, which requires a greater initiative than perception does. Still, even if our self-awareness is increased, it is not yet declared until we make the further move of somehow actually *saying*, "I see that …," or "I now know that …," or the like. We have to make a move in public. It is not the case that some sort of unspoken declarative silently precedes the one we voice. Declaratives are different from self-consciousness; they involve more initiative than self-awareness does, even the self-awareness that attends our predications and other categorial acts. There is thoughtful, syntactic initiative in the straightforward registration of a fact ("The table is brown"), but it is still not the kind that explicitly puts *us* forward in what we say.

Declarative speech is more than self-consciousness and cannot be reduced to it. On the other hand, we must also avoid the opposite extreme. We must avoid thinking that a declarative statement like "I see that the table is brown" means that we have stepped back entirely from our initial registration and that we attribute or relate the registration to ourselves in a further, higher-level, cognitional registration. It is not the case that in a declaration we stand back and say, "Here is my perception and there I am, and this perception belongs to me." No; the declaration is closer to the original registration than this picture would suggest. The declaration is already latent in the self-awareness we have when we register; when the declarative is achieved, when we actually say, "I see that …," what we express is more than that self-awareness, and it is different from it, but, still, there is no break between the self-awareness and the declaration. To use a spatial metaphor, the declaration curls out of the initial syntactic registration and its accompanying self-awareness. It does not stand over against it. It completes the initial manifestation, but it completes it by drawing it into a new dimension. To return to our subscripts, the declarative showing$_d$ is on the cusp of the original showing$_o$. The declaration is so close to the original manifestation$_o$ that it seems to add nothing to it. Wittgenstein, in the epigraph we have used for our present chapter, says that the declarative is insignificant and can be eliminated without remainder; he says, "'I know' has meaning only when a person utters it. But then it does not matter whether the utterance is, 'I know …,' or 'This is … '." But Wittgenstein goes too far here: the difference between "I know" and "This is" does matter. It is true that the declarative is not a new statement of fact; it is *almost* only a restatement of the original, but it is a bit more than a mere restatement, and this added bit must not be overlooked; the declarative appropriates and enhances the original, and this is more than simply restating the original. The declaration comes between the first-order statement and a wholly reflective, second-order statement of fact.

A statement such as "I am sitting here watching the chemical reaction take place" is a full-fledged second-order statement of fact. It is an informational statement, and it is different from the declarative statement, "I see that the chemical reaction is taking place." The former is a new statement with its own truth value, but the latter is barely different from the original statement, "The chemical reaction is taking place." It is barely different, but it *is* different, and the difference is important. The declaration emphasizes and appropriates the original, whereas the original as such was not yet emphasized or appropriated, even though we were conscious of it while we made it.

Veracity

Before going on to discuss other kinds of declaratives, I wish to introduce a special term, *veracity*, into our vocabulary. I propose this word as the name for the human inclination to attain the truth of things. I will gradually develop the sense of this term in the course of this book, but I now enter it formally into our lexicon.

By *veracity* I do not mean a virtue; it is something more elementary. It is in us from the beginning. Veracity is the impulse toward truth, and the virtue of truthfulness is its proper cultivation. Veracity is the origin of both truthfulness and the various ways of failing to be truthful. Thus, lying, refusing to look at important facts, being careless or hasty in finding things out, and other ways of avoiding truth are perversions of veracity, but they are exercises of it. Curiosity is a frivolous employment of it. *Veracity* means practically the same thing as *rationality*, but it brings out the aspect of desire that is present in rationality, and it has the advantage of implying that there is something morally good in the fulfillment of this desire. It also suggests that we are good and deserving of some recognition simply because we are rational. Veracity is the desire for truth; it specifies us as human beings. It is not a passion or an emotion, but the inclination to be truthful. The passions are not the only desires we have, and reason is not just their servant; we also want to achieve the truth.

If we cultivate our rationality we become truthful, and if we frustrate it we become untruthful or dishonest (or merely pedantic), but it is not the case that truthfulness and dishonesty are two equivalent alternatives for us to pursue. It is not the case that we are defined by veracity (rationality) and that we can cultivate it in these two different ways. Being untruthful is not one of the ways of being successful as a human being. We can be happy as human beings only by cultivating our veracity into truthfulness, not by developing it into *either* truthfulness *or* Machiavellian dishonesty. And failing to develop our veracity is not just *one* of the ways we can be unsuccessful as human beings; it is *the* way in which we fail and make ourselves false, that is, unreal as what we are.

Veracity is the *eros* involved with rationality. It signifies the undifferentiated inclination: not just the desire for the truth of natural science, nor the penchant for moral truth or technical discovery, nor the proclivity toward mathematics or history, but the tendency toward truth as such, in any form, whether theoretic or practical. Even our abilities to calculate sums and draw complicated inferences are motivated by it. We are persons because we are rational, but our rationality is not merely a skill in finding things out; it also involves the *desire* to possess truth, and I wish to name this specific desire veracity. We are born with this desire and are carried along by it, willy-nilly. Stalin, Hitler, and Lord and Lady Macbeth were specified by veracity, but they made a mess of it. It is in us because of what we are, not because we have chosen it. It would be incoherent to say that it arises as the outcome of a choice, because we must be inclined to the truth if we are to make a choice. It is very deep in us, more basic than any particular desire or emotion, more elementary than any particular attempt to find things out, and more fundamental than any act of telling the truth to others. We are made human by it, and it is there in us to be developed well or badly. Our exercises of it are indicated by the declarative use of the first-person pronoun.

2

Further Kinds of Declaratives

The achievement of truth defines us as human beings, and it is not limited to our purely cognitional activities. It is involved in how we want things and in how we act, and declaratives also function in these other ways of being rational.

Emotive Declarations and Truth

We have focused on the relationship between declarative speech and cognitive terms like *see*, *know*, and *suspect*, but we can also speak declaratively when we say things like "I love (or hate) you," "I sympathize with you in your troubles," "I have confidence in you," or "I am angry with those people." In these statements also we express ourselves as exercising our reason at the moment when we say the words, but these phrases may seem at first glance to express emotive attitudes rather than cognitive states. The appearance is deceptive, however, because a human emotive state incorporates an opinion and is therefore an exercise of reason: if I am angry, it is because I believe that I or someone related to me has been insulted or dealt with unjustly, and if I hate someone, it is because I think that the person ought to be hated. If I have confidence in someone, it is because I judge the person to be trustworthy. Affective attitudes have an opinion built into them. My opinion may be wrong – often enough, under the pressure of emotion, we form incorrect judgments – but it still is an opinion, and it provides the basis for my affectivity. Strictly speaking, therefore, I do not primarily declare *my* hatred or love, but the detestability or lovableness of my target.

In fact, if my emotive response to someone were to be based merely on a feeling without any opinion, without any engagement of my rational power, then it would be expressed through a merely informational use of the word *I*. If I were to say, "I just don't like you," and if I were to concede that this feeling is not based on my judgment that you are not likeable, then my report would be merely a statement of fact about me and my emotive state. I am not taking rational responsibility for not liking you; I simply am wired that way: you make me sick, and that's a matter of fact about me, not a rational, "reactive" attitude on my part toward you.[1] My feeling would be a merely subjective condition, a purely visceral reaction, not an affect based on an understanding or a true exercise of reason. Any "opinion" it might be based on would be a projection, not a disclosure. In the case of such a nonrational feeling, I would have to follow up my informational remark that I don't like you with further information about myself, not about you: "Well, I don't like you, but, hey, it's not you, it's me. I'm just like that." I might go on to say that my feelings come, say, from something that happened in my early childhood, and I would thus reinforce the fact that my disliking you has nothing to do with any repellent features you may possess. All these statements would be informational, not declarative. I would not be truly appropriating any judgment about you if I were to say, "I don't like you." On the other hand, if I take responsibility for my "feelings," if I consider them not just as feelings but as attitudes that respond to the way the world shows up to me – I despise you because I judge that you are despicable and can give good reasons for my judgment – then the words are being used in a declarative manner, because they engage me as an agent of truth, even in my emotions. When I say, "I hate you," I imply that in my judgment you are hateful. "I hate" incorporates "I think."

It is for this reason that the targets of, say, anger or gratitude can be so disturbed or so delighted by those sentiments in others. If someone bears resentment toward me, I may be unhappy not only because I have an enemy prowling about, but also – and perhaps even more – because I might take as possibly true the opinion that underlies his resentment: perhaps I did treat him unjustly; perhaps I was cruel; perhaps I deserve his reaction. My rational assessment of myself is disturbed by his assessment of me; his "feeling" is all his own, but his opinion can be shared by me. If someone is grateful toward me, I may be pleased not only by the hope of future benefits in return, but also because his thanks reinforce the good opinion I have of myself.[2] It is the rational part of the attitude, rather than the emotional turbulence, that cuts the deepest.

---

[1] I take the term "reactive attitudes" from the 1962 essay by Peter F. Strawson, "Freedom and Resentment," which became the eponymous chapter in his book *Freedom and Resentment and Other Essays* (London: Methuen, 1974), 1–25. Reactive attitudes are our "uptake" of actions that we experience as having been done responsibly: gratitude in response to benevolent actions, for example, and resentment in response to malevolent ones. Reactive attitudes are the ground-level manner in which we "take in" such actions. Strawson's essay is a critique of determinism, and I know of no discussion of the problem that is superior to it.

[2] See Aristotle, *Nicomachean Ethics*, VIII 8, 1159a22–3, where Aristotle says that "those who desire honor from good men and from men who know are aiming at confirming their own

It is also the rational part of an emotion that causes us embarrassment when it becomes clear that our reaction was impulsive and mistaken. If I explode into outrage and then am shown that I am shouting at the wrong person, or that I made the wrong calculation and in fact the bill is correct, it suddenly becomes clear to me and to all the onlookers that the problem lies in my choleric nature and not in what I had been assessing as the state of the world. There was nothing there that called for such a response. The declaratives I had been uttering prove to be, not the words of a truly rational agent, but more like the voiced sounds of pleasure or pain, animal noises and not intelligent speech. It is mortifying to be caught out in this way, because we are shown to have been inadequate precisely in our rational judgment. We presented ourselves, with great fanfare, as supremely thoughtful, as remedying an appalling injustice, but then we were shown to have been merely explosive. The pretense of thought and justification is what gave such dramatic power to our declaration, but that apparent force turns out to be a humiliating weakness. It is a feeling we cannot control, a biased opinion we project onto a situation.

Personal Commitments and Truth

We have examined declarative speech in regard to cognitive expressions and emotional remarks. We now examine a third category, that of commitments such as "I will return," "I promise that I will pay," "I must defend my honor," and "We will always remember." If the first category dealt with cognition and the second with emotion, the third deals with acts of willing. The state of affairs expressed in the statement – that which is promised, obligated, decided, or bestowed – is one that is being brought about or will be brought about or should be brought about through my agency. In this category belong performatives, statements in which we directly effect what we declare: "I, Helen, take you, Donald, to be my husband"; "I declare this session closed"; "I christen this ship the USS *Nimitz*."

In such commitments, the state of affairs does not yet exist. Its coming into being depends on me. Because it does not yet exist and depends on me, it is one among several possibilities. Acts of cognition and emotional reactions respond to what has been and what is, but commitments look to the future, and they look to me for their actualization. My declared commitments, therefore, express how the future should be or will be or is being determined by my intervention. I am vividly at an intersection between past and future when I am engaged in such actions; I am at the switch, and it is my cognitive articulation of the world, my understanding, that lays out the possible futures that extend from that point on.

---

opinion of themselves." (Ross translation; unless otherwise noted, translations from Aristotle are my own.)

Furthermore, it is not only the world that will be determined by what I declare; I myself will be different if I follow through with the course of action I now register in words. I am about to determine my own future perfect, the way I will have been if I bring into actuality the proposition that I declare.[3]

In such declarations I dedicate myself to some course of action. It might seem, therefore, that in them *I* am the one who comes to the fore, much more than the state of affairs that is expressed in them. I am presented as the cause of the change or as the one who is obligated to act. I seem more important than, say, the honor as defended, the meeting as closed, or the ship as named, because I am the one who defends, declares, or christens. In fact, however, the primary emphasis remains on the objective correlative, on the part of the world affected by what I say. The articulated state of affairs remains dominant, just as it does in the case of cognitive and emotive declarations. When I initiate or commit myself to some action through my words, I do not act simply as a material efficient cause; I do not just knock things over; I act by virtue of what I understand as the way the world could be. My agency is subordinated to my reason. My action proceeds because I am able to present to myself something that is not yet but that could be. It is the world as known, as proposed or as propositional, that then becomes realized through my words and my subsequent actions. I act not simply as an efficient but also as a formal cause (a driving wind or flowing water does not act as a formal cause), and in this causation I am informed by the content of what I declare.

It is the rational part of my commitment that is emphasized, not my sheer act of willing: my act of choice or will is specified by *what* I understand is to be done. The state of affairs has to be "in my understanding" before it can become real in the world. It is true that *I* am declared as acting, but I am declared as being on the margin or on the cusp of what is being done. If I say, "I will return," what is primary is *my return*, not *my* return, and certainly not me now promising to return. I exhibit a future state of the world that depends on me, and I am endorsing that state; I exhibit the world and not myself. Just as *I know* or *I see* appropriates and enhances the state of affairs that I am aware of, so also *I promise* or *I will* endorses the thing that will be done, and it does so in the modality in which I commit myself to it: as promising, guaranteeing, vowing, giving, accepting, deciding, or performing.

But have we not gone too far? In the case of commitments, is there not an act of willing that should be given greater prominence than we have allowed? It may be true that when I say, "I know this is a zebra," I mention myself as somewhat marginal and as subordinated to the state of affairs

---

[3] On choice and the future perfect, see Robert Sokolowski, *Moral Action: A Phenomenological Study* (Bloomington: Indiana University Press, 1985), 160–2.

that I know. I merely appropriate what I have registered in my original statement, "This is a zebra." But when I say, "I promise to come" or "I will return," my act of promising seems like a new, full-fledged act, an initiating pulse or a spiritual shove added to "my coming" or "my returning." Here and now I seem to do something. I seem to execute the act of willing expressed in my speech, and this act seems to be more substantial than my simply knowing something. It seems like a definite act of free choice, an episode of decision. In response to this objection, however, I would still claim that the act of willing expressed in the declarative is subordinated to the understood content of the declaration. It is the rational content that makes the act of willing possible, and the act of willing is essentially the endorsement of that content.

Consider the appetites and aversions we have as simple animal organisms: we move toward water when we are thirsty, we pull back from a fire when we sense its heat. Even in such elementary responses, we have to be aware of the thing if we are to move toward or away from it, but so long as we are limited to the things we perceive or to things near the margin of what we perceive, our appetition is rather plain and our motions uncomplicated. Through our imagination and reason, however, our appetites become much more sophisticated. We can desire not only the water over there, but also "water that could be brought here by an aqueduct so that everyone would have enough to drink even in the summer and there would be enough for farmers to irrigate their fields." When *this* sort of complicated and distant thing is what we want, then our desire has become a rational appetite, that is, it has become a wish, but the wish is brought into being by the rationality that can present such a good to us. We now deal not just with satisfactions perceived in our environment, but with satisfactions that are imagined, understood, and wished for precisely as understood. We move from merely wanting to wishing.[4] It is because of the amplification brought about through our reason, which can propose things that are absent and things that do not yet exist, that our appetition can change from seeking what is ready to hand to seeking what can rationally be proposed: we begin to deliberate about means that will implement the distant purposes and ends that we have. Our wishing is enabled by our reason.

And we are free in regard to that state of affairs because, since it is rationally presented, there will be alternatives to it: we could use something else besides a viaduct to get the water, or we could give up on getting more water and live more austerely, or we could move someplace else where there is more rain. We can also hold all these other things in mind, since the purpose is so distant and the ways of achieving it so diverse. Furthermore, we must recall that there already is a kind of freedom

<hr>

[4] On the distinction between wanting and wishing, see Chapter 15 of this Volume.

present in cognitive declarations, a love of the truth that can be achieved well or badly. It is this deep freedom or veracity that is the root of freedom in our practical commitments. If we love the truth, then when we attempt to determine the future we will be moved to deliberate truthfully, that is, to consider carefully all the realistic alternatives, including those we may find distasteful, and to choose the alternative that is truly the best, all things considered, here and now. Our freedom is a function of our veracity; freedom does not mean arbitrary selection, but adherence to what is best. Freedom is wanting what is truly good, not imposing what we want. The act of willing, expressed in our declared commitment ("I take you," "I shall return," "I must pay"), is, therefore, an endorsement of the state of affairs proposed by our rational understanding, just as our declaration that "I know" or "I see" is an appropriation of the state of affairs that we have registered or reported. The act of willing is not a psychological episode that bursts out on its own; it is not an event that has its own substance apart from what it seconds. It cannot exist by itself, any more than an assent or an "I know" or an "It is true"; they all are attached to a propositional content.

As animals, we live in three dimensions: in awareness of things, in dispositions or feelings based on such awareness, and in the mobility provoked by such awareness and feeling. Reason elevates this triad into thinking, emotion, and will; we then live in a thoughtfully articulated world and not just a perceived environment. When reason is added to our animality, all three components are enhanced: we have not only perception but complex articulation and knowledge of things that are absent to us; not only feelings stimulated by our surroundings but worries and sorrows, tranquillities and delights based on things that we only conceive and may not even see; not only appetition in response to what is present but wishing for distant and even impossible things, and also deliberation about the things that we can attain. Furthermore, our reason does not just amplify our world; it also allows us to declare ourselves as engaged in all such activities. It allows us to mention our *I*, our *ego*, as cognizing, as disposed toward things, and as willing; one and the same "self" or "I" is at work in all three. When we declare ourselves, we mention ourselves as a whole, but we highlight our rationality, the specifying part in us. We mention ourselves in action as persons, as rational animals, who exist in a manner not reducible to the causalities in the natural world. We live in a kingdom of ends, which is opened up to us by the rationality that makes us human.

Existential Declaratives

Two examples of the declarative use of the word *I* will move us into a new kind of declarative, beyond the cognitive, emotive, and decisional forms we have examined so far.

In the movie *Papillon*, two men are exiled to the penal colony in French Guiana. The convict called Papillon, played by Steve McQueen, tries unsuccessfully to escape, with disastrous consequences. At the end of the movie he tries again. He studies the ocean currents near a cliff and discovers how they ebb and flow. He thinks that if he could dive off the cliff and catch the current in just the right way, he might be carried out to sea, and that he could ride the current to a nearby shore. He and his friend, played by Dustin Hoffman, stand at the top of the cliff, and at the right moment he throws a raft into the water and jumps down after it. For a minute there is nothing but violent, turbulent water, but then the man and the raft become visible on the surface, and his voice can be heard saying, "I'm still here."

There are many situations in life in which these words express a great accomplishment. To say "I'm still here" in this way is a declarative use of the word *I*. It is neither a cognitional nor an emotive use; it has some affinity with the dedicational use we described in the last section; but it should be distinguished from all three categories and called something like an existential use of the term. This usage is often found in religious language. When using an existential declarative, I do not promise or dedicate myself to any project in particular; I am just there for whatever may come and whatever needs to be seen or done, but *I am* still there, and I declare myself as such, as a dative, a person engaged in veracity. This is not a merely informational remark, like telling the Internal Revenue Service that I am still alive; it is an engagement and not a report. Moreover, *what* is still here? Not just any kind of thing, not just a man or this man, but "I," not a *what* but a *who*, not just something in the world but someone who has the world and is on its margin, as the seeing eye is at the edge of the field of vision and "owns" that view: "I'm still here."

The existential use of the word *I* is brought out in a moving passage at the end of Cormac McCarthy's *Cities of the Plain*, the concluding volume of his *The Border Trilogy*.[5] Bill Parham, now an elderly man, a cowboy and a drifter, is living with a family that has taken him in. One night he has a dream in which he sees his brother, who was killed a long time ago: "He dreamt that Boyd was in the room with him but he would not speak for all that he called out to him." Betty, the mother in the family, comes into the room to see what is wrong. "Mr Parham are you all right? – Yes mam. I'm sorry. I was dreamin, I reckon." She offers him some water, which he says he does not want. "Boyd was your brother. – Yes. He's been dead many a year. – You still miss him though. – Yes I do. All the time." They continue to talk for a while ("I'd give about anything to see him one more time"), and she offers him some water again, which he again declines. Then she

---

[5] The three volumes of *The Border Trilogy* are *All the Pretty Horses*, *The Crossing*, and *Cities of the Plain*.

rises to leave. "Betty, he said. – Yes. – I'm not what you think I am. I aint nothin. I dont know why you put up with me."[6]

Bill's phrase, "I aint nothin," is a double negative that is used to make a positive point. It signifies that he truly is nothing, that he is not a counter on the chessboard of life. He uses the first-person pronoun to disavow himself.

When Bill Parham says he "aint nothin," he is not referring simply to his body or to himself as a living human organism. They obviously are something and not nothing and do not need to be declared or undeclared. Rather, he is referring to what he expresses in his declarative use of the word *I*, just as Papillon does when he says, "I'm still here." This is the singularity that each of us expresses when we use the term *I* in a declarative manner, our person and not our nature. In fact, Bill's last three, abbreviated sentences perfectly exemplify the declarative use of the words *I* and *me*: first, "I'm not what you think I am"; second, "I aint nothin"; and third, "I dont know why you put up with me." Betty understands what he means, because she does not answer by saying that she knows *what* he is, as his first sentence suggested she might. Rather, she says, "Well, Mr Parham, I know who you are." Even more perceptively she adds, in response to his last sentence, "And I do know why." She does not respond to his second remark; what *could* she say?

Bill Parham's declaration of himself is buttressed by other elements that enter into personal identification: the invocation of a past and future life, familial relationships, memory, dreaming and waking, the overtones of childhood as a background for one's present state (his bedroom was like the one he slept in as a boy), Betty's maternal behavior and Bill's childlike response ("You go to sleep now. I'll see you in the morning. – Yes mam."), Bill's life embodied in his gnarled, scarred hands ("The ropy veins that bound them to his heart. There was map enough for men to read. There God's plenty of signs and wonders to make a landscape. To make a world."), the person needing and pleading to be acknowledged by others. What kind of nothing is it that he is not?[7]

Philosophical Declaratives

We have distinguished between the informational and declarative uses of the first-person pronoun, and we have further distinguished four kinds of declaratives: cognitional, emotive, dedicatory, and existential. The

---

[6] Cormac McCarthy, *Cities of the Plain* (New York: Vintage, 1998), 290–2. I am grateful to Jamie Spiering for clarifications about this passage.

[7] It would be interesting to examine the absence of declaratives in the text (but not the title) of Samuel Beckett's supremely minimalist play *Not I*, which is recited entirely in the third person and visually presents only the mouth of the woman who speaks: "whole body like gone ... just the mouth." See Samuel Beckett, *Collected Shorter Plays* (New York: Grove Weidenfeld, 1984), 220–2. The phrase just cited is used three times in the play.

declaratives, in various ways, exhibit$_d$ us as exercising our reason, as
manifesting$_o$ in some way or other some part of the world. There is one
more dimension that needs to be added before we close this chapter, the
philosophical declarative. We have, from the beginning of this book, also
spoken about ourselves as engaged in both the first-order manifestation$_o$
of the world and the declarative appropriation and exhibition$_d$ of that first-
order display. We, therefore, have been operating all along from beyond
both the first-level thinking and the declarative endorsement. We have
exhibited$_p$ and endorsed from yet another dimension, from the philosophical. When I began the first chapter of the book with the statement,
"My purpose is to clarify, philosophically, what human persons are," the I-
in-action that I declared through the term *my* was a philosophical first
person, not an ordinary declarative.

The self or the ego that knows things in the world is situated, dimen-
sionless, at the margin of the world, as the seeing eye is on the margin of
the field of vision. The self or ego that reflects philosophically is situated
on the margin of the margin, because it considers what it means for
someone to be on the margin of the world. The philosophical ego moves
into a kind of logical hyperspace; it is even more detached than the ego
that appropriates its own first-level acts of thinking. This transformation
into philosophy is an inevitability built into the life of reason. It is exqui-
sitely formal and ought not be diluted into a lesser kind of thinking. It
extends and completes our veracity, our wanting the truth of things. All
human beings, as they use language, are able to declare themselves as
thinking through language, and each of us can take a further step and
speak about what it is to declare ourselves and to have a world and to be
there in it. Such philosophical reflection is an approach to the whole of
things (everything prior to it is radically partial), and everyone has some
opinion about the whole, however it may be expressed. To have such an
opinion is part of our nature as rational animals. We need not now discuss
the special logic of philosophical declaratives; it is sufficient at the moment
to have marked it off from the other dimensions of reason and speech.

3

Linguistic Syntax and Human Reason

The human person acts as such, as a rational animal and as an agent of truth, especially in his use of language, when he thinks in the medium of words. We began our study of human rationality by focusing on the use of the word *I*, and specifically on the declarative form of such usage. Let us now locate declaratives within the wider employment of language. We can distinguish four levels in the way words are used.

Four Levels of Speech

The first level is prelinguistic or sublinguistic. Words can degenerate and can be used in a purely associative, sensory way, as part of a general reaction to a situation and a general expression of feeling. If I am in pain and say things like "Ow, stop, that hurts," I am really not making a formal statement about things. My "words" are not very different from moans or, if the experience is pleasant and the words are happy, cries of delight, as in "Wonderful! That's just great!" They are expressions of pain or pleasure, not statements that could be quoted or verified. I am not putting an articulated thought on record; I am engaged in voice and not in speech. Although I may be making sounds that could serve as words in another context, here they have been deconstructed or dismantled as words; they are serving as mere sounds and are not very much different from expletives or exclamations. Both their syntax and their phonemic structure have been watered down.

The second level is the normal use of words, when they are placed within sentences to make a statement of some sort, whether a registration or report of the way things are, a command, a promise, a warning, or the like. All of these statements display something: a statement of fact displays, say, the tree's being in bloom; a command displays what is to be done; a warning displays the situation that is said to be threatening or threatened. The grammatical articulation of words in the sentence corresponds to an articulated display of something in the world. This level of language is constituted by syntax: not only by the grammatical syntax of the words, but also by the logical syntax of meanings in a proposition and the ontological syntax of states of affairs. (We will later discuss the perplexing relationships between logical and ontological syntax, and between propositions and states of affairs.) The syntactical frame that comes into play on this level, and that differentiates this level from that of sounds of pleasure, pain, and feeling, also exerts pressure on the sounds themselves and changes them into words by structuring them internally, with phonemic patterns of consonants and vowels.[1]

The third level of language is that of declaratives, and it presupposes the second. Here the articulation that is achieved on the second level is appropriated by the one who achieved it. If on the second level I say, "The campaign is not going well for our side," on the third level I could say, "I think the campaign is not going well for our side," or "I know that it is not going well," or "I suspect that it is not going well," or "I deny that it is not going well." The situation is not just articulated; it is explicitly appropriated as being articulated, and the one who articulates declares himself, and he declares himself with the appropriate modality. We could not have the appropriation if the articulation had not been achieved, but the appropriation and declaration are not a mere repetition of the articulation. The declaration highlights me as the one who takes a stand, who expresses the state of affairs, and who does so at the very moment that the declaration is made. My thoughtful responsibility is put on record. On this level, "I" come to the surface, whereas on the second level the state of affairs comes to light. On the second level, I shine a spotlight on something in the world and bring out its parts and wholes; on the third level, I am manifested as the one who is holding and shining the spotlight and doing the articulation. However, I am manifested in a different way: I do not turn the spotlight on myself. I keep it trained on the state of affairs, but I also let you know that I am there doing this, that I am active as an agent of truth. If I were to turn the spotlight on myself, I would be using the word *I* in an informational, not a declarative manner.

The fourth level of language is the philosophical. It is the kind of discourse we carry out when we reflect on the three previous levels of language and the things that are manifested in them. Notice that on this level we do not just reflect on language and on the users of language; we also reflect on the entities that the exercises of language have displayed (we consider them precisely as being displayed), and we reflect on the

---

[1] Consonants and vowels make up the traditional dichotomy in speech sounds, but modern linguists distinguish between obstruents and sonorants. Obstruents involve a blockage or constriction of the flow of air over the vocal tract and are usually voiceless, while sonorants involve a free flow of air and are usually voiced.

speakers not only as users of language but also as carrying out the displays. We also take for granted, on this level, that we as the agents of truth or datives of manifestation have already come to light when we declared ourselves on the third level of speech. We now think about what happened on the third level, and correspondingly we must also think about what happened on the second and first levels as well. And we run into a problem with our vocabulary on this philosophical level. We have to take up the language that is normally tailored for displaying things; we must turn it around to let us display that display. We have to trope the words we use. We must engage appropriate metaphors and analogies, and we must be aware that we have shifted onto a new level of discourse; we must be careful lest what we describe now, the achievement of truth, get turned back – reduced – to a merely natural process, to one of the things described on the second level. It is from this fourth, philosophical level that we speak most systematically about appearances and their agents and datives, as well as about the things that appear.

Where Should Our Analysis of Speech Begin?

We began this book by discussing the third level of language use. In Chapter 1 we examined the declarative use of first-person pronouns. We entered the building on the third floor. Was this a good starting point? Should we not have begun on the second level, since it is simpler, or even on the first, since it is the most elementary? Should we not have begun with the primary elements of language and built up the more complex wholes from them? Should we not at least have begun with simple, direct sentences about the world, that is, on the second level, where we have not yet declared ourselves?

It would not have been appropriate to start on the second level (the first would have been even worse). The appropriate whole for language, the whole within which all the parts make sense, is the third level, the one on which "we" come to light as the ones who use the language. Right from the beginning, language involves the speaker as well as what is spoken about, and it involves the one speaker as standing out among many others. Speech is indexical from the start. It would have been a misleading abstraction to begin on the second level, with speech about the world but without declaratives. If we had started there, we would have been treating the second level as a putative whole, and would have had to try subsequently to introduce the speaker as a mere addendum to speech itself. Such a procedure would give the impression that one could discuss speech and language without taking it as someone's speech and someone's use of language. It would take speech as an impersonal occurrence. It would raise unsolvable problems, which would be unsolvable because they were badly formulated, not because they were profound. Instead of seeing language in its proper wholeness, we would have taken only a part of it and would have been forced to try to reconstitute the whole by artificial, ad hoc maneuvers, by contrivances. It would be like trying to reconstitute a living organism by starting with bones and flesh. The first and second levels make no sense except as located within the third, which gives us the proper whole for language. In it we find the language itself, its use, and the user who declares himself as using it. The owner of language, the one who uses it and can declare himself when it is used, is essential to language from the beginning, and even though he may not be explicitly expressed at the beginning, he is in fact there already. Every speech is somebody's speech and someone's responsibility, someone who has been taught to speak by others and now takes a position among others and occasionally registers that action by saying "I... ."

Furthermore, if we had begun our discussion, in this book, by focusing on the second level, by examining speech about the world without declaratives, and if we had remained on that level, we would have found that we could not account for our own presence as philosophical speakers. An abyss would have opened up between ourselves and what we are analyzing. We as philosophers, of course, would indeed have been there from the beginning; we would have been speaking from within the fourth level of discourse from the start of the book. But if all we talked about was what could be found on the second level, we would not be able to detect any agents of truth, any persons, on our radar screen. And if no declared "I's" came to light within what we were describing, how could we explain how we ourselves, as philosophers, could have come on the scene? Where could we have come from? In fact, the fourth, the philosophical level assumes that we have already appeared as agents of truth on the third, the declarative level. The fourth is parasitic on the third, and the third finds its completion in the fourth. In carrying out philosophical discourse we enhance the agency of truth that occurs on the third level, but that agency must already be there waiting to be enhanced. The philosophical *I* presupposes the declarative *I*. Without the declarative dimension there would be no philosophical problems. It is appropriate, therefore, that our philosophical analysis begin with the third level of language use, the one that contains declaratives.

If we tried to give a philosophical discussion of speech but limited ourselves to the second level of discourse, to speech about the world bereft of any declarative dimension, we would be trying to describe speech as an impersonal activity. We would be trying to describe speech as unappropriated. But there is no speech, no claim to truth, that is not someone's achievement, someone's exercise of truthful responsibility, and the human person comes to light precisely in such activity. The third level of language is therefore an appropriate starting point for the study of the human person and his use of language.

Language and Protolanguage

How do we get from cries, shrieks, purrs, and moans into language? What is it that shapes our sounds into meaningful speech? How do we get onto what we have distinguished as level two of language? I wish to follow the thought of Derek Bickerton and other linguists and say that it is syntax that makes the difference. Syntax changes animal cries and sounds into human speech.[2]

To show how this transformation happens, we can, with Bickerton, discuss a stage intermediate between animal sounds and language. He calls this stage protolanguage.[3] Protolanguage is speech deprived of syntax, or speech that has not attained syntax. It is what we call baby talk. In it the speaker indicates things, but only episodically. It consists of one, two, or several "names" strung together to show something, but it does not have any explicit grammar. It has something like semantics but no syntax. This kind of speech is spoken by children under about two years of age, and it is also found in adults who were deprived of language instruction when they were young. There are recorded cases of children who were kept isolated and who missed the window of opportunity to learn grammatical speech. Such unfortunate people are not able to make up the deficit later in life. Even as adults, they speak in the chopped, simple speech of protolanguage; they say such things as "Want milk," "Big elephant, long trunk," "Applesauce buy store," "I want Curtiss play piano."[4] Such a speaker "has acquired something other than full human language – an alternative means of communication that incorporates some features of language but rigorously excludes others."[5] A third instance of protolanguage occurs when any mature speaker loses his grip on the grammar of his language because of emotional distress, delirium, intoxication, or illness.[6] Finally, something analogous to protolanguage can be found in the kind of "speech" that can be learned by apes who are trained in human language.[7]

---

[2] See Derek Bickerton, *Language and Species* (Chicago: University of Chicago Press, 1990) and *Language and Human Behavior* (Seattle: University of Washington Press, 1995), and William H. Calvin and Derek Bickerton, *Lingua ex Machina: Reconciling Darwin and Chomsky with the Human Brain* (Cambridge, MA: MIT Press, 2000).

[3] Bickerton, *Language and Species*, Chapter 6, "The World of Protolanguage," 130–63.

[4] Ibid., 116.

[5] Ibid., 117.

[6] Ibid., 131: "We may spontaneously revert to this mode when sickness, fatigue, alcohol, or some other cause depresses our normal functioning." See also p. 124: "When persons who are ill, exhausted, drunk, or merely impatient speak in this fragmentary manner, they are simply using protolanguage rather than language, and indeed there should be nothing surprising in the fact that when we are below par in some way we may fall back on some more primitive mode of functioning."

[7] Bickerton includes the linguistic expressions of trained apes among the kinds of protolanguage; ibid., 122.

In addition to these four instances of protolanguage (the "speech" of small children, stunted speakers, disturbed speakers, and trained animals), there is a fifth type, and it is perhaps the most interesting of all. It occurs in what are called pidgins. Pidgins arise when people from two radically different language groups come together and attempt to speak with one another. No matter how fluent each speaker or group of speakers may be in their native tongues, all of them have to revert to protolanguage to communicate with one another. They speak in "languages" that have no grammar, and what they say sounds very much like baby talk. Pidgins arise most conspicuously when two such groups begin to live together, but something similar occurs to any of us when we are visitors in a country where we cannot speak the language at all; we too find ourselves talking in the way under-two-year-olds speak. What is especially interesting about pidgin languages is the fact that they are spoken only by the first generation of people who have come to live together. The very next generation (the children who grow up speaking within the community) installs grammar into the pidgin and turns it into a creole: a creole can be called "a nativized pidgin."[8] Nor is the grammar that arises almost spontaneously in this way a primitive grammar; it can be extremely complex and sophisticated. In one generation, protolanguage gives way to language.

Language is something entirely different from protolanguage. It is not the case that protolanguage is only a more primitive stage of language; it is something else, an alternative to language and not a simpler version of it: "The faculties of protolanguage and language are disjoint,"[9] Bickerton says, and "there can be no plausible intermediate stage between the two."[10] The difference between protolanguage and language is discrete and decisive: "Between protolanguage and language, we find nothing."[11] The major difference between them lies in the fact that language incorporates syntax and protolanguage does not: "Syntax is the magic key that unlocks the floodgates of language."[12] It is "the Rubicon."[13] Moreover, syntax is not just linear concatenation; what is special about it is its hierarchic and nesting structure: "The really crucial relationships in language are not horizontal but vertical."[14] Through syntax, phrases can be embedded inside other phrases, not just strung along one after the other. This embedding, this Russian-doll structure, permits the exquisite articulation

[8] Ibid., 169.
[9] Ibid., 118.
[10] Ibid., 165.
[11] Bickerton, *Language and Human Behavior*, 71.
[12] Calvin and Bickerton, *Lingua ex Machina*, 52.
[13] Bickerton, *Language and Human Behavior*, 65; cf. Calvin and Bickerton, *Lingua ex Machina*, 24: "In fact, as was apparent nearly two decades ago, the real rubicon, unpalatable though this may be to the philosophically minded, is syntax, not symbols."
[14] Calvin and Bickerton, *Lingua ex Machina*, 140.

that is radically different from the "one-by-one" sequencing of protolanguage. In protolanguage one might say, "I want Curtiss play piano," but in language one would say, "I would be pleased if Curtiss were to play the piano." Even the sentence "I want Curtiss to play the piano" is different from the protolinguistic utterance we just mentioned; the addition of the simple words *to* and *the* changes everything. Here, Curtiss's playing the piano does not just come after my wanting, as it does in protolanguage; it is now the state of affairs subordinated to my wanting. The phrase packages Curtiss's playing of the piano and makes it ingredient in another phrase; it does not just bring it to mind. In language, "phrases are not, as they might appear to be, strung together serially, like beads on a string. Phrases are like Chinese boxes, stacked inside one another."[15] And Bickerton quite rightly concludes this remark by saying, "The importance of this point can hardly be overestimated." In protolanguage we have sequences of ideas, but in language we have thoughts, and thoughts occur as embedded in larger thoughts. That possibility is what makes them thoughts and not just sequences of ideas. With speech we enter into what Jean-Pierre Changeux calls "the combinatorial explosion that results from the use of syntax."[16]

Whereas protolanguage has "words" that bring to mind only things, features, and processes, language abounds in words that are purely grammatical and hence do not name any object, feature, or activity as such: words like *the, without, nevertheless, is,* and *have* (as in "I have come," as opposed to "I have five dollars"). Such words have no obvious objective correlates, as nouns, verbs, and adjectives do, and as grammatical items, Bickerton says, they "cannot be defined ostensively."[17] They belong to the sinews or tendons of the language, and words like them arise only when grammatical articulation has come into play. Protolanguage does not employ such structural components: "There are no *thats*, no *tos*, no overt markers of subordination."[18] Protolanguage is associative and not categorial. Furthermore, the fact that language is constituted by a grammatical grid means that it can have invisible structural elements, which are not overtly expressed by a word or inflection or position; such elements are indeed at work in the sentence, and they exercise a grammatical force on other words, but we do not find them as explicit verbal parts in the phrase or sentence. They are called null elements, and they can be detected by an analysis of the other grammatical elements that

[15] Bickerton, *Language and Species*, 60.
[16] Jean-Pierre Changeux, *The Physiology of Truth: Neuroscience and Human Knowledge*, trans. M. B. DeBevoise (Cambridge, MA: The Belknap Press of Harvard University Press, 2004), 124. He also says that in language we make "infinite use of finite means." There is no limit to the "combinatory possibilities."
[17] Bickerton, *Language and Species*, 108.
[18] Ibid., 117.

are expressed.[19] By contrast, if a term seems to be missing in protolanguage, we do not look to the other "words" to discern what it is; rather, we must look to the real-world situation to discover what it might be.[20] In protolanguage, words are pasted right onto things; they are not interwoven or textured with other words. There are no texts in protolanguage because there is no syntax to weave its parts together.

Another important feature of language is that it can function in the absence of the things it is being used to describe. Protolanguage is a response to the presence of things; the significance of protolinguistic expressions depends very much on what is going on around the speaker: "Only hearing the utterance in context could indicate whether *Mike paint* meant *Mike paints* or *Mike's paint*, for example, or could determine who told whom that the door was locked."[21] Protolanguage adheres to its immediate situation. But in true language, the speaker can refer to things that are entirely absent, things decisively cut loose from the immediate setting. The speaker can refer to things that are far away, things that are irretrievably past, things that will come about in the future, things that cannot exist, and fictional things, and he can use other grammatical terms and subordinate phrases to disambiguate any statement that is unclear to his interlocutors. Using an apt metaphor, Bickerton speaks of "the oft-neglected but basic and crucial distinction between on-line and off-line thinking,"[22] and he says that protolanguage works only on-line, whereas language can function either on-line or off-line: protolanguage works in the presence of its objects, but language can work in both the presence and the absence of its targets. It is true that protolanguage may be used to indicate a want or a need, and hence to stretch into absence to some extent, but such usage pulls the thing it names into the present setting, since it implies that the speaker wants the thing to be here and now. There is incipient absence in protolanguage. It is much like the absence of the other side of an object in perception, but it is not an absence crisply disconnected from the present context. The absences in protolanguage are not sharp. There is no embedding of something absent into the present context, only a stretching of the present into the absent. In language, however, the speaker and listener can be "with" the thing in its pure and simple absence. And the two principal features of language – its hierarchic, stacked, grammatical structure and its ability to range over the

---

[19] Ibid., 63–4, 71–2. It would be interesting to compare the role of null elements in language with the use of the zero in arithmetic.

[20] Ibid., 111: "In full-blown language, such empty slots can always be interpreted on the basis of formal criteria, but here one can only guess or infer from the context who participates, or is requested to participate, in the actions."

[21] Ibid., 116.

[22] Bickerton, *Language and Human Behavior*, 90; see also p. 58, where he mentions "the essential distinction between what one might call *on-line thinking* and *off-line thinking*."

absent – are somehow related. How and why syntax and the mastery of presence and absence are connected in language is an important philosophical problem.

We have explored the distinction between protolanguage and language in order to define the nature of language. We took advantage of Bickerton's concept of protolanguage, not to examine protolanguage for its own sake, but to provide a foil for the definition of language. We found, with Bickerton, that it is syntax that makes the difference; with its formal structure and its power to nest, stack, and embed words and phrases, syntax establishes human speech. Human speech is the primary expression of human reason; as John Henry Newman says, the Greek word *logos* "stands both for *reason* and for *speech*, and it is difficult to say which it means more properly. It means both at once: why? because really they cannot be divided – because they are in a true sense one."[23] Trying to separate reason and speech is, Newman says, like trying to separate the convex and the concave in a curve, or light and illumination, or life and motion: "the vigorous and fertile intellect" finds in speech "its own double." Reason and speech can be distinguished but not separated. "Thought and speech are inseparable from each other,"[24] and thinking occurs in the medium of words.

But if reason is expressed paradigmatically in speech, then the human person, the agent of truth, is likewise expressed primarily in it. And if syntactic structure establishes language as such, then syntax is the most tangible presence of reason and the most palpable presence of the human person. When the human person declares himself by saying "I ... ," he brings himself to light precisely as the one who has articulated a part of the world through a statement, a warning, a promise, a command, or some other rational achievement, that is, as someone who has installed syntactic structures into his speech, his concepts, and the things he refers to. This personal aspect of syntax calls for further exploration, but first a few more refinements are needed in our treatment of Bickerton's theory of language.

Animal Cries and Calls

We have used protolanguage as a context and a foil for language. Let us turn briefly to something even more basic, to animal cries, calls, and symbols, and attempt to distinguish both protolanguage and language from that form of communication.

[23] John Henry Newman, *The Idea of a University* (Garden City, NY: Doubleday, 1959), Part 2, Discourse 2, §4, p. 270.
[24] Ibid., 269.

The cries, calls, and symbols in question are things like the warning cries of certain species of monkeys, the motions used by bees to convey the location of a food source, and dolphin sonar signals. Animal cries and symbols are different from the "words" of protolanguage and even more different from the words and sentences of language. For example, the vervet monkey of East Africa can utter three distinct alarm calls: one for pythons, one for eagles, and one for leopards.[25] The offspring must learn the significance of these calls. Each of the calls, however, always remains the same, and so do their referents: "All such systems have a fixed and finite number of topics on which information can be exchanged, whereas in language the list is open-ended, indeed infinite."[26] That is, the "lexicon" or "vocabulary" of animal symbolism is severely limited, whereas linguistic symbolism is unlimited and can range over anything at all. Even protolanguage is not confined a priori to any fixed topics, despite being linked to its environment. Furthermore, there is no composition among animal symbols or calls: "All such systems have a finite and indeed strictly limited number of ways in which message components can be combined, if they can be combined at all. In language the possibilities of combination, while governed by strict principles, are (potentially at least) infinite."[27] In protolanguage we may have mere concatenation, but there are no restrictions on what can be concatenated, so protolanguage also exhibits more flexibility than animal cries. And still further, the animal call introduces no absence into its usage: "With the vervet call, there is always a python there. At least, with one rare exception, the vervet genuinely believes there is a python there."[28] The "one rare exception" Bickerton refers to is that a vervet may use a call falsely in order to distract another monkey; but such a deception is only possible if the call practically always means that the threat is actually there. The monkey who hears the call would never turn to the one who made it and state the equivalent of,

---

[25] Bickerton, *Language and Species*, 12–15. See also Alasdair MacIntyre's discussion in *Dependent Rational Animals: Why Human Beings Need the Virtues* (Chicago: Open Court, 1999). MacIntyre cites studies that seem to indicate something analogous to syntax in the comprehension and communication of dolphins (pp. 27–8), but he concedes that animals lack the power, which human beings have, to reflect on their own motivations and to evaluate and compare them. Such reflective power would involve the kind of linguistic embedding Bickerton describes as a constituent of language; MacIntyre writes, "But this is insufficient for human rationality. What is needed in addition is the ability to construct sentences that contain as constituents either the sentences used to express the judgment about which the agent is reflecting or references to those sentences" (p. 54). He also distinguishes between "prelinguistic reasons for action and the types of reasons for action made possible only by the possession of language" (p. 51). Prelinguistic reasons for action could be correlated with protolanguage.
[26] Bickerton, *Language and Species*, 8.
[27] Ibid.
[28] Ibid., 13.

"Python? What about it?" The call is used to signal, not to name. Even protolanguage enjoys more flexibility, distance, and absence than this.

Higher animals trained by human beings can make use of protolanguage but not language because they cannot master syntax: "With trivial exceptions ... the vocabularies of apes are strictly limited to lexical items.... No evidence produced to date gives any support to the idea that apes could acquire syntax."[29] Likewise, there is no "nested embedding" of phrases or symbols in the use made by apes, only sequential patterns.[30] In another passage, Bickerton asks, "Why should apes be totally incapable of acquiring syntax?"[31] Syntax is the crucial element whose presence establishes human language. Syntax, with its part-and-whole structure, with its hierarchic nesting, is the tangible – or audible – expression of intelligence in speech.

Bickerton claims that protolanguage was used by prehuman ancestors and that evolutionary developments led to further changes in the brain and nervous system that made language possible. Protolanguage is therefore a relic of our evolutionary past. In protolanguage, enough "words" would have accumulated to provide the foundation upon which the syntactic structures would have been able to develop: "Syntax could not have come into existence until there was a sizable vocabulary whose units could be organized into complex structures." For this reason, Bickerton says that there was "first a stage in which there was lexicon without syntax, then a stage in which infinitely productive mechanisms emerged to create syntax as we know it."[32] He says, concisely, "Before there was syntax there was only semantics,"[33] and he refers to "the vocabulary-without-structuring stage of protolanguage."[34] Thus, protolanguage does indicate or "name" things, and hence it possesses semantics, but it is bereft of syntax.[35] It was necessary to have a critical mass of semantic resources before the structuring of syntax could be installed. Bickerton tries to discover what aspect of semantics could have given rise to syntax, but we need not follow him in this exploration, as interesting as it may be.

---

[29] Ibid., 108.
[30] Ibid., 109. For the term "nested embedding," see Calvin and Bickerton, *Lingua ex Machina*, 165.
[31] Bickerton, *Language and Human Behavior*, 117.
[32] Ibid., 51.
[33] Calvin and Bickerton, *Lingua ex Machina*, 50.
[34] Ibid., 59.
[35] I use scare quotes around the word *name*, because protolanguage does not have full-fledged names. Its "words" fall between mere signals and authentic names, which require syntax to be what they are.

Syntactic Engines and the Human Person

The emergence of syntax requires that a stock of "words" has already been collected in protolanguage. This is true of human evolution, and it is also true in the development of the individual speaker. The child has to pass through the babbling and baby talk of protolanguage before syntax can kick in. Protolanguage, in turn, must have developed from still more primitive cries and calls. The child cries and giggles before getting to baby talk or protolanguage. Language thus depends on the prior acquisition of protolanguage, which in turn depends on earlier vocalization.

But there is also a neurological requirement for the development of language. Syntax can arise in human speech only after certain changes have taken place in the human brain and nervous system. Bickerton uses an interesting expression to describe the neural structure that permits syntax: he speaks of the moment in evolution "when the syntactic engine came along"[36] and brought about the transition from protolanguage to language. At a certain point, the hominid line "had added to it a syntactic engine that would automatically construct propositions."[37] There occurred a change in the human organism that "turned the human brain into an inference engine powerful enough to make possible the totally unprecedented cultural explosion of the last fifty millennia."[38] The terms *syntactic engine* and *inference engine* are colorful, but they are also questionable. They suggest that the use of syntax is automatic, the work of impersonal organizations of neurons in the brain.

I would disagree with this suggestion. I would claim that behind the use of syntax there is not an engine but a responsible agent, not a *what* but a *who*. Syntax is used by the rational agent we described in Chapter 1, the agent who is expressed in declarative uses of the word *I* and perfected by the virtue of truthfulness. The *ability* to carry out syntactic articulation, in speech, concepts, and things, may require certain neural structures as its preconditions, but its actual *exercise* is the work of the human being. Moreover, it is the work of the whole human being, not a part of him. It is the work of the person, not the achievement of a part of the brain, or even of the entire brain, which is itself only one part of the whole organism. Brains do not think; people who have brains do. It is because the human person acts as a whole in matters of thinking and linguistic expression that he can declare, "I know," or "I think," or "I doubt"; if the brain or an engine in the brain did the thinking, the speaker would not say, "I think," but "My brain thinks," and he would relinquish his own responsibility. He could speak only informationally, not

---

[36] Calvin and Bickerton, *Lingua ex Machina*, 150.
[37] Bickerton, *Language and Species*, 222.
[38] Bickerton, *Language and Human Behavior*, 84.

declaratively, and strictly speaking he should not even say, "*My* brain thinks," but "It thinks" or "This brain thinks." It is the entire human being who exercises his rationality by articulating his speech, his concepts, and the things he knows, and he does so responsibly. This person or agent of truth is not just a part of the human being; he is the human being acting as a whole and acting, in principle, publicly. To say that syntax is generated by something we could call an engine is to imply that it arises rather mechanically from a part of the brain, and that therefore *we* do not think and speak in our structured language: a part of us does the thinking for us.

To develop this point further, I wish to use another text from Bickerton. In *Language and Human Behavior,* he makes an excellent remark concerning computer intelligence. Bickerton observes that there are people who think that computers possess some aspects of intelligence. They hold this opinion because they think that intelligence is "the ability to solve problems," and computers seem able to solve problems.[39] Bickerton disagrees with these opinions and claims that computers really do not exhibit intelligence. His reasons are expressed in a clever passage: "The problems animals solve, the problems we solve, are our *own* problems.... But the problems computers solve are not problems for computers. If I have a problem, it's my problem. If my computer has a problem, it's still my problem. Nothing is a problem for it, because it doesn't interact with the world. It just sits there and waits for me to give it *my* problems."[40] This text presents an elegant contrast between things that can have problems and those that cannot; we (and other animals) can have problems, but the computer cannot. Any problems the computer has have been given to it by me, and hence they are still my own. I believe that in this text, the phrases *our own problems* and *my problems* make use of the first-person declarative, because they express the desire and the responsibility we have to determine the true solution to the problems at hand. Bickerton is declaring himself in these terms. His text, like all texts, is an articulated work of reason, and such a work cannot arise without a responsible agent behind it, and sometimes the agent declares himself in what he says, as Bickerton does here. It would also follow, from what Bickerton says, that declaratives could not be attributed to or used by the computer; it could never declare on its own, "I have a problem," or refer to "my problems," because it does not syntactically articulate things through its own responsibility. Bickerton's text is a vivid illustration of the inevitability of declaratives in articulated speech.

---

[39] Ibid., 86.

[40] Ibid. The italics are in the original. I wish to note one further detail. Bickerton is correct in relating syntax and logical inference, when he speaks of syntactic engines and inference engines as though they were equivalent. The logical structures involved in reasoning from premises to conclusions are only an expansion of the syntactic structures that establish propositions in the first place. Both are versions of formal structure.

Although Bickerton does not attribute intelligence to computers, he does go on to endorse a mechanistic interpretation of thinking. He turns from computers to robots and says that "by virtue of acting in the real world, the robot commits itself to a type of existence similar to that which animals enjoy." He even says that "a robot could in principle seek nourishment, avoid danger, and perhaps even mate with other robots."[41] If this were to happen, "robots would come under exactly the same kinds of selective pressures as living creatures." It is hard to understand how a robot can "commit itself" to anything, let alone a "type of existence," but it seems that Bickerton here does accept the mechanistic understanding of intelligence that his engine metaphor suggests; robots are run by engines, and if they are not essentially different from living things, then living things, and presumably human beings as well, would also be run by something like engines. Human beings would not be agents of truth. Bickerton's next move is to claim that intelligence should not be defined as problem solving but as "a way of maintaining homeostasis," which is "the preservation of those conditions that are most favorable for the organism, the optimal achievable conditions for its survival and well-being."[42] He then says that human beings differ from animals primarily because men enjoy syntactically structured language and can think "off-line," that is, they can think in the absence of the things they refer to. Bickerton develops some remarkable insights about the use of language, but in the end the engine metaphor wins out; he describes earlier stages of human evolution in this way: "Having protolanguage without the syntactic engine was like having gasoline without an internal combustion engine; there was not much you could do with it except sit around and wait for the engine to be invented."[43] Such relapses into a mechanical understanding of human thinking are symptoms of a recurrent tension in Bickerton's work. On the one hand, he speaks about language as specific to human beings, but on the other he drains away the specifically human and personal dimension of language, its involvement in truth and in the responsibility associated with truth.[44]

Bickerton and Husserl

One of the major reasons I find Bickerton's theory of language attractive is that it blends so well with what Edmund Husserl says about speech and thinking. Bickerton says that it is syntax that brings about the difference

---

[41] Bickerton, *Language and Human Behavior*, 86–7.
[42] Ibid., 87.
[43] Ibid., 120.
[44] On human versus artificial intelligence, see Robert Sokolowski, "Natural and Artificial Intelligence," in Stephen R. Graubard, ed., *The Artificial Intelligence Debate: False Starts, Real Foundations* (Cambridge, MA: MIT Press, 1988), 45–64.

between human language and protolanguage, and Husserl says that it is what he calls *categoriality*, formal articulation, that specifies human understanding: he says that we "define understanding, as opposed to sensibility, as the capacity for categorial acts."[45] Categoriality is another name for syntax. In his first major work, *Logical Investigations*, published in 1900–01, Husserl describes the part-whole structure of language and asks what the grammatical parts of language could possibly refer to: he says we must "pay special attention to [the meanings] expressed by formal words such as 'the,' 'a,' 'some,' 'many,' 'few,' 'two,' 'is,' 'not,' 'which,' 'and,' 'or,' etc., and further expressed by the substantival and adjectival, singular and plural inflection of our words, etc."[46] He asks, "Are there parts and forms of perception corresponding to all parts and forms of meaning?"[47] That is, can we find something in the objects we perceive that corresponds to the grammatical dimension of speech? Husserl's answer is, "It is hopeless, even quite misguided, to look directly in perception for what could give fulfillment to our supplementary formal meanings."[48] Husserl would agree with Bickerton, therefore, that the grammatical terms and dimensions of language, the syntactic components of language, do not have objective correlates in the content of the things we perceive; Bickerton says that such parts of speech cannot be ostensively defined, and Husserl says, "The 'a' and the 'the,' the 'and' and the 'or,' the 'if' and the 'then,' the 'all' and the 'none,' the 'something' and the 'nothing,' ... all these are meaningful propositional elements, but we should look in vain for their objective correlates ... in the sphere of real objects."[49] They do not signify things, but serve primarily to link other parts of language into wholes. Bickerton's concept of the syntactic finds a striking parallel in Husserl's concept of the categorial.

Another point on which Husserl and Bickerton would agree is the claim that human speech allows us to refer not only to objects present to us but also to those that are absent; we can transcend our immediate environment. Bickerton formulates this by making a distinction between on-line and off-line thinking and claiming that through language human beings can think off-line, whereas protolanguage and animal cries are almost entirely limited to on-line thinking. One of the most pervasive and original themes in Husserl's *Logical Investigations* is the contrast between what he calls filled and empty intentions: filled intentions are those that present their targets in their actual presence, and empty intentions are directed

---

[45] Edmund Husserl, *Logical Investigations*, trans. J. N. Findlay, ed. Dermot Moran (New York: Routledge, 2001), volume 2, Investigation VI, §64, p. 315.
[46] Ibid., §40, p. 272.
[47] Ibid.
[48] Ibid., §42, p. 276.
[49] Ibid., §43, p. 278. For the passage from Bickerton, see note 17, to this chapter.

toward things in their absence. The absence in question might be the kind found in perception, such as the other side of the building or the inside of a closed box, or it might be a higher-level, articulated, categorial object, something we might be talking about that is a thousand miles away or a thousand years off in the future or the past.[50] The treatment of absence is one of the most important themes in phenomenology, which sees the ability to deal with the absent as one of the essential features of human reason. Phenomenology also explores the many different kinds of absence: the kind found in memory, the kind proper to spatial distance, the absence of the future and the past, the absence proper to misunderstanding and confusion, the kind that occurs in pictures, the kind that prompts desire or fear. The ability to think off-line opens up a whole range of specifically human phenomena – such as hope and anxiety – that are intimately associated with language and human reason.

Still another important theme in Husserl that has parallels in Bickerton is nominalization. An example of this phenomenon is the following. Suppose I say, "Harriet will be coming home tomorrow." This is an articulated assertion with its parts all spread out. It is the object of what Husserl calls a "many-rayed intention."[51] But I can compress what it asserts and make it into the object of a "single-rayed intention." I can say, "It is good that Harriet will be coming home tomorrow," or "I am glad that she is coming home," or "Because Harriet is coming home tomorrow, we must change our plans." I nominalize what is stated and make it part of a larger statement. Such nominalization exemplifies the Chinese-box embedding that Bickerton describes as one of the essential features of syntax and language. One phrase can be nested within another phrase, and the hierarchic stacking of such components of language is what makes human speech different from protolanguage.

In *Logical Investigations*, Husserl begins with an analysis of language, but he goes beyond it and describes the syntactic or categorial structure of thinking as well as that of speech. He goes from linguistic grammar to

---

[50] The theme of presence and absence in treated in *Logical Investigations* under the rubric of filled and empty intentions and the interweaving of identity and evidencing that goes on between them. Husserl treats this topic in regard to both sensory perception and intellectual intending. The entire Sixth Investigation discusses the issue, and it is also treated briefly in the First Investigation, §§9–21.

[51] Husserl discusses the transformation of the complex object of a "polythetic" act into the object of a "monothetic" act in *Ideas: General Introduction to Pure Phenomenology*, trans. W. R. Boyce Gibson (New York: Macmillan, 1931), §119, p. 336: "Every such many-rayed (polythetic) constitution of synthetic objectivities – which are essentially such that 'originally' we can be aware of them only synthetically – possesses the essential law-conforming possibility of transforming the many-rayed object of awareness into one that is simply one-rayed." The topic is also treated in *Logical Investigations*, Investigation V, §§34–36, and Investigation VI, §49.

intellectual activity. He also studies the relation of categorial thinking to the perception out of which it arises and the verification that it makes possible. I think that Husserl places categoriality or syntax into a richer philosophical context than Bickerton does, but Bickerton has more to say about the biological foundation for language, and he examines linguistic phenomena in greater detail.

4

The Person as the Agent of Syntax

Predication

It is a traditional doctrine in philosophy that predication or judgment is the central activity of reason. Aristotle calls it *apophansis,* and describes it with the cryptic phrase *ti kata tinos legetai,* "something is said of something."[1] In Kant's writings the term is *Urteil,* judgment; all acts of the understanding can be reduced to judgment. Bickerton agrees with this consensus and relates predication to syntax. He says, "If nouns and verbs are the most basic elements of syntax, then predication is its most basic act."[2] The most basic act in syntax, the most fundamental thing done in it and that without which nothing else can be done, is predication. Syntax is, of course, immensely rich and varied. There are in the world's languages untold forms of subordination, conjunction, correlation, reciprocity, reflexives and possessives, tenses and cases, adjectives and adverbs, infinitives and gerunds, but underlying all of them is the never-absent form of predication, in which something is said of something else. All the other forms dangle from this or crowd around it. The heart of syntax is predication.

Bickerton adds the further refinement that, in his linguistic theory, the subject and predicate themselves should be considered not as single words but as explicit or implicit phrases.[3] This is an interesting claim, and it would imply that even single words are latent combinations, hence syntactically structured in principle. Bickerton also says that each predication can give rise to further subdivisions and subpredications within each of its parts: these further articulations yield the Russian-doll, hierarchic cascade of phrases that constitutes language and rational articulation. He says that

---

[1] Ernst Tugendhat stresses the centrality of predication in Aristotle's metaphysics. He uses Aristotle's phrase as the title of his book: *Ti kata tinos: Eine Untersuchung zu Struktur und Ursprung Aristotelischer Grundbegriffe* (Freiburg: Verlag Karl Alber, 1958), 5–6. An earlier version of my Chapter 4 has been published as "Predication as Public Action," *Acta Philosophica: Rivista internazionale di filosofia* 14 (2005): 59–76.

[2] Derek Bickerton, *Language and Species* (Chicago: University of Chicago Press, 1990), 59.

[3] Bickerton develops his theory of "phrase structure" in *Language and Species,* 59–65.

"the overall pattern" of such predication "can be repeated for any other kind of phrase, and constitutes, so to speak, the very core of universal syntax."[4] He also says, "The subject-predicate distinction is perhaps the most basic in language."[5]

We wish to study where syntax comes from and how it is related both to reason and to the human person. In order to carry out this project, we will focus on predication because it is the central syntactic structure and action. We will begin with some preliminary remarks, and then examine two inadequate explanations of the origin of predication (and hence of syntax), the Kantian and the biological. These two will provide a foil for our treatment of Husserl's phenomenological description of how syntax arises from pre-predicative thinking. Finally, I will offer a modification of Husserl's analysis, which I believe will give a better account of the origins of syntax. The goal of this chapter is, not just to clarify the formal structure of syntax, but to show how syntax is the work of the human person, the rational agent.

Three Fields for Syntax

In the last chapter we spoke about syntactic structure in a rather undifferentiated way, but we must now distinguish three domains in which it occurs: in language, in concepts or propositions, and in things. There is grammatical structure in language; there is logical structure in concepts and propositions; and there is a formal ontological structure in the things we articulate and present to ourselves and to others. The grammatical ordering of language is correlated with the syntactic structuring of our concepts and propositions, and these in turn are correlated with some sort of formal structures in things. We have, therefore, three fields: the linguistic, the conceptual or propositional, and the ontological, and in each of them there is structure or syntax. In listing these three domains I follow Husserl, who differentiates grammatical syntax, formal apophansis, and formal ontology.[6]

The three domains must be distinguished from one another, but they are also interrelated, and their mutual involvements, which are very important philosophically, are difficult to determine. It would be useful to have a linguistic device to designate each of these three fields. Many writers, including Bickerton, use the following technique: linguistic units,

[4] Ibid., 61.
[5] Ibid., 97.
[6] See Edmund Husserl, *Formal and Transcendental Logic*, trans. Dorion Cairns (The Hague: Nijhoff, 1969). On the distinction and definitions of formal apophantics and formal ontology, see §§24–5, pp. 76–9. Some remarks about linguistic structure and content can be found in §§2–3, pp. 19–25, and in Appendix I.

words, are designated by means of italicized terms; concepts or propositions are designated by means of terms enclosed in single quotation
marks; and things are designated by means of terms without any markers.
Thus, *leopard* signifies the word that is the name of the animal; 'leopard'
signifies the concept; and leopard signifies the animal itself. One and
the same word – *leopard*, 'leopard,' and leopard – can signify in these
three different ways, and we who read the texts that incorporate such
signification must develop a certain flexibility if we are to correctly
interpret what we read. Suppose a man named Simon tells some people
that a leopard is loose in the neighborhood and that they should be
careful. Then, suppose I write to you, "Simon used the word *leopard* to warn
everyone that a leopard was in the area, and their concept of the beast,
their 'leopard,' led them to take the proper precautions." One word
means the same thing from three different angles: it signifies the thing, its
name, and its concept. I will conform to this convention of plain text,
italics, and single quotation marks, but on occasion I will use italics for
other purposes, such as emphasis.

These differences in the use of the term *leopard* do not show up to
Simon (the man in the story) nor to any of his interlocutors. All those
people are focused on the leopard that is prowling about somewhere.
The differences in the use of terms show up only to the person who
writes this sentence and to us who read it. They show up to someone who
takes a distance to the situation being described and to what is said in it,
not to someone who is involved in it, and this new, more distant
perspective must be taken into account when we try to give a philosophical explanation of the differences between the respective domains of
language, concepts, and things. These shifts in perspective might seem
like nothing, because they do not introduce any new objects into the
situation; they do not install an elephant or a tiger, or a hunter and his
rifle, or another leopard or a copy of one, into the world populated by
Simon, his friends, and the leopard, nor do they introduce any new
words; but the perspectives and their shifts are not *simply* nothing. They
install new dimensions, even though they do not introduce new things,
and it is precisely the introduction of new dimensions that establishes the
differences between things, concepts, and words, as we shall see. It is in
the maze brought about by such dimensions, perspectives, and shifts that
philosophical problems arise, and only by recognizing these differences
in aspect can we dissolve the problems. We cannot solve a philosophical
problem by introducing a new thing; we can do so only by resolving
a dimensional dispute.

The three domains of word, concept, and thing come vividly into play
when we are not sure whether something we are talking about truly exists.
Suppose, for example, we are not sure that there really is such an illness as
paranoia. In this instance, as Bickerton says, "there may be *paranoia* and

'paranoia,' but no paranoia."[7] In other cases we may know for certain that there is no objective correlate, and so we can say with confidence, "There are 'unicorns' and *unicorns*, but absolutely no unicorns."[8] In such instances there is a word and there is a concept, but there is no thing. How do we juggle words, concepts, and things, so that phenomena and differentiations like these can occur? What are words, concepts, and things? How is it that we can have a word and a concept for something that does not exist? Clearly, without words and syntax we could never intend such nonentities as unicorns; animals, presumably, do not refer to things they know not to exist. But how does such reference to the nonexistent take place, and how is syntax related to it? These are all issues that we will deal with as we go along, and they are important for understanding what a human person, a rational agent, is. But for the present our question remains simply, where does syntax come from?

Two Inadequate Explanations for Syntax: Kantian and Biological Nativism

Kant, of course, claims that the formal structures that make judgments possible are simply part of understanding as such. They are built into our understanding and are available before any experience: they are a priori. Experience triggers their activation. They organize our experience and raise it to intelligibility. The judgments we make about the world are rendered possible by the combination of perception and the pure categories of the understanding, which order the perceptual and imaginative givens into judgments. Kant gives a transcendental deduction of the concepts that must be acknowledged as the understanding's contribution to our experience of things. The categories of the understanding bestow the formal structures of quantity, quality, relation, and modality on our judgments. Each of these headings in turn contains three categories, for a total of twelve "original pure concepts of synthesis that the understanding contains within itself a priori."[9] Kant deduces these structures or concepts; obviously, we could not directly experience them in themselves. Instead, we as philosophers reason back toward them. We need to postulate them because, according to Kant, the necessary and universal character they bestow on our judgments could not have been caused in any other way. The logical syntax of propositions, therefore, arises from the a priori structure of the understanding. It comes from an intellectual source. We are made up of sensibility and understanding, and logical

---

[7] Bickerton, *Language and Species*, 33.

[8] Ibid.

[9] Immanuel Kant, *Critique of Pure Reason*, trans. Norman Kemp Smith (New York: St. Martin's Press, 1965), A 80, p. 113.

syntax comes from the understanding. It would follow, then, that the grammar of our spoken languages expresses the logical syntax of our judgments. Kant would not say we are *born* with these a priori categories, because being born is a bodily event, and for Kant reason belongs to another domain. However, for purposes of classification and comparison, perhaps we might be allowed to adopt a contemporary term and speak of Kantian nativism. The term *nativism* has been used in reference to the innate ideas introduced by Descartes and Leibniz, and these ideas too are not corporeal, so it may not be out of place to apply the term to Kant's categories as well.[10] They are forms we are endowed with insofar as we belong to the kingdom of ends.

At the other extreme from Kant we have a biological form of nativism, which turns to neuroscience and biology and attempts to discover the origins of logic and conceptual thinking in the structures of the brain. These structures in turn are explained by our genetic endowment. Our brains are said to contain an innate language faculty or a language module. Here too we have an appeal to an a priori origin, to forms that are given beforehand to experience and speech, but now the origin is located in the body and not in the understanding as distinct from the body. Such nativism claims that the power to generate formal structures is hard-wired in the brain. Noam Chomsky, for example, is said to have postulated a "dedicated 'Language Faculty,' a biologically-specified 'mental organ'" that "incorporates ... the principles of Universal Grammar."[11] The reason why such nativism must postulate an inborn biological capacity is the "poverty of stimulus argument": "There are items in our mental stock that cannot be accounted for on the empiricist model.... For there is nothing in experience from which they could be derived."[12] The fundamental, elementary grammar of a language, the basic syntax in thinking, cannot be explained by the experiences a child has had of well-formed sentences. Children know that certain verbal combinations are ungrammatical even before they have experienced them and before they have been told that these forms are inadmissible. They spontaneously know that these combinations are impossible. There must, therefore, be something innate in the human organism that permits it to recognize certain newly experienced or newly composed combinations as either acceptable or unacceptable. The proponent of nativism does not know where else such a capacity could come from. It does not come from experience or instruction, hence it must be inborn, and somehow biologically inborn, not part of our understanding, as Kant would have said. Of course,

---

[10] See Fiona Cowie, *What's Within? Nativism Reconsidered* (New York: Oxford University Press, 1999), 7–12.

[11] Ibid., ix.

[12] Ibid., 32.

children learn to speak different languages, but these differences result from local variations in the Universal Grammar that each human being is born with. Our native language faculty is described as "the inborn cognitive substrate that, in interaction with our linguistic experience, enables us to learn the grammar of our native tongue."[13] Both forms of nativism, the Kantian and the biological, explain syntactic form as innate in us, whether in our understanding or in our bodies as the origin of our minds.

Where Does Syntax Come From? Husserl's Reply

I wish to claim that in Husserl's phenomenology we can find a better solution to the origin of syntax and logical form than those offered by both biological nativism and Kantian philosophy. I will present Husserl's alternative in this section, and I will make an important modification to it in the next.

Husserl's explanation for the origin of formal structures is expressed most fully in his posthumously published work, *Experience and Judgment*, but the essentials of his doctrine are present even in his earliest work, *Logical Investigations*.[14] He tries to show how the formal, logical structures of thinking arise from perception; the subtitle of *Experience and Judgment* is *Investigations in a Genealogy of Logic*. The "genealogy" of logic is to be located not in something we are born with but in the way experience becomes transformed. Husserl describes the origin of syntactic form as follows.

When we perceive an object, we run through a manifold of aspects and profiles: we see the thing first from this side and then from that; we concentrate on the color; we pay attention to the hardness or softness; we turn the thing around and see other sides and aspects, and so on. In this manifold of appearances, however, we continuously experience all the aspects and profiles, all the views, as being "of" one and the same object. The multiple appearances are not single separate beads following one another; they are "threaded" by the identity continuing within them all. As Husserl puts it, "Each single percept in this series is already a percept of the thing. Whether I look at this book from above or below, from inside or outside, I always see *this book*. It is always one and the same thing."[15] The identity of the thing is implicitly presented in and through the

[13] Ibid., 241.

[14] Edmund Husserl, *Logical Investigations*, trans. J. N. Findlay, ed. Dermot Moran (New York: Routledge, 2001), and *Experience and Judgment: Investigations in a Genealogy of Logic*, trans. James S. Churchill and Karl Ameriks (Evanston, IL: Northwestern University Press, 1973). The core of Husserl's analysis in *Logical Investigations* can be found in Investigation VI, Chapter 6, "Sensuous and Categorial Intuition." In *Experience and Judgment*, see §24 and §§47–57.

[15] Husserl, *Logical Investigations*, volume 2, Investigation VI, §47, p. 284.

manifold. We do not focus on this identity; rather, we focus on some aspects or profiles, but all of them are experienced, not as isolated flashes or pressures, but as belonging to a single entity. As Husserl puts it, "An identification is performed, but no identity is meant."[16] The identity itself never shows up as one of these aspects or profiles; its way of being present is more implicit, but it does truly present itself. We do not have just color patches succeeding one another, but the blue and the gray of the object as we perceive it continuously. In fact, if we run into dissonances in the course of our experience – I saw the thing as green, and now the same area is showing up as blue – we recognize them as dissonant precisely because we assume that all the appearances belong to one and the same thing and that it cannot show up in such divergent ways if it is to remain identifiable as itself. If it is starting to look blue when it shouldn't, we might look more closely or try to see the thing in a better light.[17]

This sort of perception does not involve any syntax or logic. It is pre-logical and precategorial: "In the case before us perception is merely, as it were, extended."[18] Any discrepancy in it – the green ball suddenly starts to look blue – is a felt disharmony and not an explicit contradiction. This sort of prelogical, pre-predicative experiencing would, in fact, be suitable as the experience that is expressed in protolanguage. Both are continuous but not formally structured. One impression follows another, even when we are dealing with one and the same object. Short strings of protolinguistic "words" like "play checkers," "big drum," "daddy car," and "horse go"[19] are an appropriate and commensurate vocalization of continuous, prelogical experience. The various features we indicate are not radically distinguished one from another, nor is any feature explicitly distinguished from and then identified with the subject it belongs to. One impression flows into another, and one "word" flows into the next. Both the perception and the speech are precategorial or presyntactic. This is the

---

[16] Ibid., 285.

[17] The description of color perception I give in the text applies to inorganic bodies. Andrew Parker describes how the colors of animal surfaces change radically when seen from different angles; the same patch can look different as we move around the animal's body. See *Seven Deadly Colours: The Genius of Nature's Palette and How It Eluded Darwin* (London: The Free Press, 2005), 9, where he speaks about Monet's attempt to paint freshly killed game birds: "As Monet moved around the pheasants, parts of their bodies would vary from invisible to positively dazzling. Colours began to turn on and off – the birds looked quite different depending on where one stood in the room.... How could he reproduce this dynamic effect on canvas armed only with pigments that display the *same* effect when viewed from any direction?"

[18] Husserl, *Logical Investigations*, volume 2, Investigation VI, §47, pp. 284–5.

[19] Derek Bickerton, *Language and Human Behavior* (Seattle: University of Washington Press, 1995), 165; see also Stephen Pinker, *The Language Instinct: How the Mind Creates Language* (New York: William Morrow, 1994), 33–9, 292–3.

sort of experiencing and vocalization we have prior to the explicit discovery of things as substances, that is, as subjects of predication.[20]

Such continuous perception can, however, become a platform for the constitution of syntax and logic. What happens, according to Husserl, is that the continuous perception can come to an arrest as one particular feature of the thing attracts our attention and holds it. We focus, say, on the color of the thing. When we do this, the identity of the object, as well as the totality of the other aspects and profiles, still remain in the background. At this point of arrest, we have not yet moved into categoriality and logic, but we are on the verge of doing so; we are balanced between perception and thinking. This is a philosophically interesting state. We feel the form about to come into play, but it is not there yet. Thinking is about to be born, and an assertion is about to be made.

We make the move into categoriality and syntax when we do the following: we go back to the identity of the thing; we now focus on the identity and on the thing as a whole (we establish a subject, S, "the ball"), and we focus again on the feature in question – say, the color – but we now take it explicitly as a part of the whole (we establish a predicate, p, "is green"). When we do this, we do not just have more of the continuous perception of the thing; we do not just prolong the perceptual experience; rather, we now have a new beginning, a discrete new elevation into something structured, into the proposition or the state of affairs, "The ball is green." We have reached something that can be formalized as S is p. As Husserl puts it in *Logical Investigations*, "It is clear ... that the apprehension of a moment and of a part generally *as* a part of the whole in question, and, in particular, the apprehension of a sensuous feature *as* a feature, or of a sensuous form *as* a form, point to acts that are all founded.... This means that the sphere of 'sensibility' has been left, and that of 'understanding' entered."[21] We explicitly embed the feature in the thing, the predicate in the subject, and we now enter the game of

---

[20] I take the phrase "the discovery of things" from Wolfgang Rainer Mann, *The Discovery of Things: Aristotle's 'Categories' and Their Context* (Princeton, NJ: Princeton University Press, 2000). Mann argues that Aristotle "discovered" the substantiality of material objects, whereas Anaxagoras dissolved things into elements and Plato dissolved them into ideas. Speaking of Anaxagoras, he writes, "All cases of what we ordinarily take to be change are really instances of the generation or perishing of mixtures, in other words, instances of rearranging the eternal, elemental stuffs. And hence there also is nothing the 'thing' actually *is*. Whatever it 'is', it merely *becomes*." And then, speaking of Plato, he says, "Plato, it seems to me, has essentially this view of ordinary things. Indeed, as John Burnet noted in 1914, 'a particular thing is *nothing else* but the common meeting place of a number of predicates, each of which is an intelligible form'" (p. 125). Even in his later dialogues Plato says that "an ordinary thing will still not be anything *in and of itself,* it will still be whatever it is *by participation in something else*" (p. 183). These metaphysical and linguistic issues will occupy us later in this book.

[21] Husserl, *Logical Investigations*, volume 2, Investigation VI, §47, p. 286.

logical inclusion and exclusion, with all its refinements and syntactic complexities.

The syntactically structured whole is, on the one hand, immersed in perception and hence attached to the thing being perceived, but it also contains, on the other hand, an intellectual, syntactic form that is detachable from that particular experience and that particular object: it is a form, a part-and-whole structure, that could be achieved within any other object. The maneuver we have performed on the green ball, the transition from perception to categorial formation, could also be performed on other things besides the green ball: it could be executed on the blossoming tree, the fevered patient, the threatening burglar, or even something as grand as the inflationary economy or the busy borough of Brooklyn.

We, therefore, in our experience and thoughtful activity, have moved from a perception to an articulated opinion or position; we have reached something that enters into logic and the space of reasons. We achieve a proposition or a meaning, something that can be communicated and shared as the very same with other people (in contrast with a perception, which cannot be conveyed to others). We achieve something that can be confirmed, disconfirmed, adjusted, brought to greater distinctness, shown to be vague and contradictory, and the like. All the issues that logic deals with now come into play. According to Husserl, therefore, the proposition or the state of affairs, as a categorial object, does not come about when we impose an a priori form on experience; rather, it emerges from and within experience as a formal structure of parts and wholes. It arises in the way things can be presented to us: they can become articulated, their wholes and parts shaken out and their formal structure made explicit. If things did not present parts and wholes to us, predication and syntactic articulation could not occur; predication takes place between us and things, not within our own consciousness or within a subjective world. The formal structure S is p, the grid or template that arises in this exchange, can be detached from any particular experience and any particular state of affairs, but such a detachment yields something abstract, a pure form, something that calls for supplementation by content.

This is how Husserl describes the genealogy of logic and logical form. He shows how logical and syntactic structures arise when things are presented to us. We are relatively passive when we perceive – but even in perception there is an active dimension, since we have to be alert, direct our attention this way and that, and perceive carefully. Just "being awake (*Wachsein*)" is a cognitive accomplishment of the ego.[22] We are much more active, however, and active in a new way, when we rise to the level of

---

[22] See Husserl, *Experience and Judgment*, §17, p. 79. The title of this section is "Affection and the turning-toward of the ego. Receptivity as the lowest level of the activity of the ego."

categoriality, where we articulate a subject and predicate and state them publicly in a sentence. *We* are more engaged. We constitute something more energetically, and we take a position in the human conversation, a position for which we are responsible. At this point, a higher-level objectivity is established, which can remain an "abiding possession (*ein bleibender Besitz*)."[23] It can be detached from this situation and made present again in others. It becomes something like a piece of property or real estate, which can be transferred from one owner to another. Correlatively, I become more actualized in my cognitive life and hence more real. I become something like a property owner (I was not elevated to that status by mere perception); I now have my own opinions and have been able to document the way things are, and these opinions can be communicated to others. This higher status is reached through "the active position-takings of the ego [*die aktiven Stellungnahmen des Ich*] in the act of predicative judgment."[24]

Logical form or syntactic structure does not have to issue from inborn powers in our brains, nor does it have to come from a priori structures of the mind. It arises through an enhancement of perception, a lifting of perception into thought, by a new way of making things present to us. Of course, neurological structures are necessary as a condition for this to happen, but these neural structures do not simply provide a template that we impose on the thing we are experiencing.

We have followed Husserl's description of the manner in which pre-predicative experience becomes transformed, by a responsible, rational agent, into predication. I would like to comment on the relationship between Husserl's description of the genealogy of predication and Bickerton's remarks about the central importance of predication in syntax. At the beginning of this chapter we quoted Bickerton as saying that predication is the "most basic act" of syntax. The central achievement in articulated speech is to say something of something; all other syntactic structures depend on this fundamental assertion. If predication were not there, none of the other intricate patterns of syntax would be there either. We have just seen how Husserl describes the emergence of predication from perception; the book in which he gives the most extensive analysis of this transition is entitled *Experience and Judgment*, and the judgment in question is predication. He describes how judgments arise from experience. What I wish to claim at this point is that the structure of predication is itself an outstanding example of the hierarchic, Russian-doll, embedding architecture that Bickerton says is

---

[23] Ibid., §47, p. 199.

[24] Ibid., §66, p. 273. If we recall that one of the meanings of the Greek word *ousia* is property or real estate, we see how similar Aristotle's metaphysics of substance (*ousia*) is to Husserl's analysis of judgment. Even in English the word *substance* can mean real property.

the major structural feature of syntax. It is not the case that such embedding starts only after predication, that it happens only when one predicative phrase or clause is embedded in another. There is stacking in predication itself. Even if we were to take predication as a very simple structure, as a relationship between a simple subject and a simple predicate expressed by a simple noun and a verb, we would still have an embedding and the sharp part-and-whole structure that constitutes syntax, because we would have the subject (the ball) now being taken as the discrete whole within which the predicate (being green) is being stacked. Conversely, if the predicate were to become the focus of our attention, we might want to say that the subject is being subsumed under the predicate, but in this case too the judgment would be an instance of syntactic hierarchy. Even a simple predication is a manicured formal garden shaped by intelligence, not a spot in the jungle of protolanguage. Things now click into place, syntax is introduced, logic comes into play, consistency and contradiction become issues, things are put on record, communication over distances becomes possible, presence and absence become explicit dimensions of what we experience, and we emerge as speakers who can not only articulate a situation but also begin to declare ourselves. It is because of what we do when we articulate things that we can say that *we* have done it, that we have carried out or are carrying out a statement of the way things are.

A Variation on Husserl's Analysis

Husserl's description of the constitution of judgment or predication has the advantage of relating the knower directly to the thing known. When we predicate, we do not merely rearrange our mental representations of things; we allow the things themselves, the things given to perception, to appear in a new, more structured and articulated way.

However, I think that Husserl's analysis can be improved upon in one important respect. I believe that his analysis of how logic emerges from experience is a major advance in philosophical thinking, but I also think that his description does not take intersubjectivity sufficiently into account. He describes categorial articulation as though it were done by a solitary mind, which first perceives an object in a manifold of appearances and then moves upward into categorial form as it articulates and recognizes parts and wholes in things. This description is correct as far as it goes, but it would be more adequate if it took into account the fact that our spoken words, as well as the thoughtful articulation associated with them, occur first and foremost between interlocutors. Instead of describing categorial intuition as something my own mind accomplishes, we should describe it as something a speaker does for a listener. The formal structures of logic arise between two (or more) persons, not primarily in the mind of a single person by himself.[25] These structures arise in things as they are presented by and between the speaker and listener. That is where the genealogy of logic is located.

Husserl marks an advance over both Kantian and biological nativism because he "publicizes" both the work of the mind and logical form: he describes them as occurring not within a private consciousness but between the person and the thing known. I wish to increase this publicity. Logical form arises not only between the mind and the object, but also between two (or more) people who articulate the object in common. They do so by the use of syntactically structured speech.

Let us say that two people are perceiving one and the same object through the manifolds of appearances that each enjoys from his own perspective. Then, one of the persons draws the attention of the other (as well as his own) to the object as a whole, in its identity. He names the object and establishes a reference, for another as well as for himself. By using a name, he sets up the object as the subject, as the thing that is going to be articulated. He then uses another term, the predicate, to draw the interlocutor's attention to some feature of the object. By conjoining the subject and predicate terms by whatever resources their language provides, by coupling the words, the speaker discloses for his interlocutor the fact that, say, the plate of steel is cold. He brings this fact before them. This articulation might be a new, fresh registration for the speaker as well as for the listener. If it is a thoughtful registration, and not the mere repetition of an opinion the speaker thought through some time ago, then the steel is being displayed as cold for both the speaker and the listener. The speaker does think the fact through. His constitution of the state of affairs is done in the same way that Husserl describes it. The speaker, however, "installs" categoriality into the experience and the object not just for himself but for the other person as well, and perhaps primarily for the other person. He does so by uttering a sentence, such as "This plate of steel is really cold," and this single statement serves, simultaneously, as a display for the listener and a display for the speaker. The one stream of words, spoken by one and heard by the other, allows two minds to artic- ulate the same categorial object, the steel's being cold.

The formal structure of subject and predicate (S is p) arises, therefore, because the speaker focuses the mind of the listener first on the whole object in its identity as something to be articulated, and then on a part or

[25] Husserl recognizes the role of other speakers and conversation at the very beginning of *Logical Investigations*, when he introduces the phenomenon of linguistic expression in Investigation I, §§5–10, but he does not make use of that dimension when he describes categoriality in Investigation VI, Chapter 6, §§40–52. Predication and judgment have been separated in some versions of modern logic. See Wayne M. Martin, *Theories of Judgment: Psychology, Logic, Phenomenology* (New York: Cambridge University Press, 2006). The result is that judgment is even further removed from its conversational setting.

a feature of the object, in a manner that couples them. The formal structure arises between the speaker and the listener. This articulation is a public action mediated by the language available for the persons involved in the speech situation, with the special slants that the language will afford. Both speaker and listener are thinking in the medium of words, and they are thinking about the thing being articulated, not about words or concepts. This explanation does away with the need felt by proponents of biological nativism to postulate hard-wired formal patterns of syntax in the brain. The syntax of words and concepts does not arise because the speaker and the listener each bring a brain-based formal template to their experience or to their language. Rather, it arises because two people can be so related to a given object that one of them can focus their attention on that object as a whole and then focus their attention on an aspect of that object. These two activities are done out in the open, and the form is something that belongs first and foremost to the thing being targeted by the two activities. All this clicks into place in public; it is as public as a salute or a vote cast in an election or an act of pointing to something. It is categorially formed conduct, and it displays a categorially formed target; it is not just categorially formed consciousness. This explanation is obviously different from that of Kant, who did not appeal to a biological foundation for syntax, but who did appeal to ready-made rational forms that precede experience. The logical forms that arise here are not ready-mades in the mind. This explanation is also different from Husserl's, because my proposal begins with an intersubjective context for the establishment of formal structures, not with the single mind moving upward from perception to logical structure. The space of reasons is a public space.

Speakers Predicate for One Another

My claim is that there can be subjects and predicates, there can be predication, "the very core of universal syntax," because, through the use of words, an object can be brought before a speaker and listener as an object of reference, and an aspect of that object can be differentiated and registered in it. There can be predication because we can interact in certain ways, not because our minds or brains function privately or organically in certain ways. The public character of predication is brought out by the Latin etymology of the term. The word *praedicare*, which means "to make known, proclaim, declare," is made up of the adverb or preposition *prae*, "before, in the face of, in view of," and the verb *dicare*, "to show, to indicate."[26] To predicate is to let something

---

[26] *Oxford Latin Dictionary, ad loc. Praedicare*, to announce formally and publicly, is different from *praedicere*, to predict or foretell.

show up before an audience, and when this is done, as it normally is, in the medium of words, it is to speak out about something "before" others. The term *praedicare* can also mean to mention something in a special way, and so the modern term *predicate* can also mean an honorable mention, as in the German, when a vintage wine is dubbed "*Qualitätswein mit Prädikat.*" In this spirit, we might wish to say of someone that he has "gotten his predicate" when he has become notorious for having done something spectacular, whether grand or foolish. Displays like these do not occur in solitude.

What remains of Husserl's analysis in my own is the fact that categorial objects are indeed based on perceptual, precategorial ones, and also the fact that the part-and-whole structures in categorial activity are different from those in perception. The two kinds are related to one another, and the categorial, which is discrete and distinctly identifiable, is a further heightening or elevation of the perceptual, which is continuous and has blurred boundaries. I would hold on to everything that Husserl says, but I would locate it more clearly in an intersubjective context, and I would claim that the categorial forming, the elevation into logic, is the achievement not of a single mind but of one mind working with another, of one person working with another, and doing so in public. The categorial activity is really very simple: the speaker draws attention to the object as a whole, and he then draws attention to an aspect or feature of the object. The two "draws of attention" are not separate from one another; the first is a preparation for the second, and the second is "boxed" into the first. When a speaker utters a name of some sort, the listener waits for what is coming, for what is going to be said about the thing named. The naming of the subject involves an expectation; it is not a discrete, isolated, and independent utterance. Then, the term for the predicate is also not isolated and solitary and independent; it is joined with the subject even while having been differentiated from it, and the coupling of the two is an assertion or judgment. The judgment occurs in this two-step action between speaker and listener, in relation to the object.

We can isolate the form that comes about in this transaction; we can isolate *S* is *p* from this situation. The form can hold in any number of other situations. It can do so not because the brain has this inborn template that it will activate over and over again, nor because our reason is endowed with a priori forms into which it channels all our experience, but because this speaker – and any other human speaker, any other person – can perform the same maneuver in any other situation: any speaker can conjointly focus his listener's mind on the object as a whole and on some feature in that object. The syntactic form is the molted skin or carapace shed and left over, abstracted, from any number of such intelligent and public performances. It is true that the judgmental form, *S* is *p*, belongs to the state of affairs that is brought to light or to the proposition that is achieved, but it belongs to it as being disclosed in this double action of first targeting the thing (establishing the *S*) and then featuring it (establishing the *p*). The judgmental form is so elementary in our thinking because this action is the simplest kind of manifestation that one speaker can bring about for another, not because our brains or our minds are structured in a certain way. It is the primary move in the conversational game, and it shapes the physiology of our brain and nervous system. The conversational game, furthermore, can be played on the things we speak about because things do present themselves as wholes and in part, as subjects with features. The ontology of things lets our speech and our language come into play.

But, one might ask, does not each person also perform the categorial articulation in his own mind? Does not each person, in the privacy and immanence of his own thinking, also carry out the apperception or apprehension that both Husserl and Kant say takes place when reason "informs" perception and elevates it into the domain of thinking? If this action happens in each of our own minds, does it not have to be accounted for psychologically or even neurologically? Is it not the case that this action first happens in each of our own minds, and that it then gets projected outward? The weakness of this objection should be evident. If the transition from perception to thought happened in privacy and immanence, then communication would be impossible. How could we ever establish a common world? Instead, we start with what is public, and the apparent "psychological" or "privately mental" achievement of thinking is really an internalization of what is first and foremost a public activity. We go, in fact, from the outside to the inside, not the other way around. We do not go from solitude and interiority to publicness. Any private thinking, any personal and solitary insight – and obviously such things do exist – is the derivation from or the rehearsal for a public performance. It is the shadow of what we do in public. Solitary thinking is internalized conversation. We tend to think of speech as voiced thought ("thinking out loud"), but we should think of silent thinking as unvoiced speech.[27] The public performance is the dominant and paradigmatic one; it is not the symptom of something done wholly within ourselves. We do have to think; we do have to achieve the categorial articulation associated with the words we speak or hear. We do not conduct ourselves in a merely behavioral manner. But the mind and thinking are primarily public, not private, and of course they can be activated not only by two speakers but also by many.

The predicational form comes originally from the interaction between speaker and listener and not from the brain. We are disposed to interact with other people, and in that interaction one person can refer to an entity and then bring out something within it. It is that interaction or coupling of focus, which is an almost legal achievement and documentation, that

---

[27] My thanks to Zachary Foreman for this formulation.

installs a syntactic form. Without the public establishment of language, no logical achievements would be generated by the brain. Even protolanguage has to be taught. Without interactions and the impress they make on our psychic organism, the human being would be capable of only the most elementary responses to stimuli. Even contradiction is primarily a public thing. It is true that one proposition can contradict another, but the paradigmatic form of contra*diction* occurs when one speaker says something that annuls what another has said.

Confirmation: Children and the Meanings of Words

I wish to confirm this claim about the intersubjective origin of language and syntax by appealing to a book written by the psychologist Paul Bloom under the title *How Children Learn the Meanings of Words*.[28] This book is about words and names, and hence about semantics and not primarily about syntax, but what it says applies both to syntactically structured speech and to protolanguage.

Bloom argues against a widely held theory of how children learn names. It is often thought, he observes, that names are learned simply by association with the things they signify. According to this view, the child gets used to hearing a particular sound when a particular object appears, and suddenly or gradually the sound becomes the name of the object: "Children learn the meaning of *rabbit*, then, because the word is used when they are observing or thinking about rabbits."[29] But, according to Bloom, words are not learned in that way; rather, the child must experience the sound as being used by someone else to name the object. The child has to realize that another person's referential intent lies behind the word. The child does not just experience the word and the thing; he experiences another person using the word to signify the thing. Without this mediation of another person, sounds would not be taken as words.

The original learning of names is, therefore, intersubjective. The dimension of words involves the dimension of other persons and the cognitive initiatives they take. The sound is taken as a name only in this wider context. When a word is uttered, "young children will make the connection only if they have some warrant to believe that it is an act of naming – and for this, the speaker has to be present."[30] The need for referential intent prevails even in highly artificial situations. Bloom describes experiments in which a robot is made to interact in a random way with infants, by beeps and flashes of light. Even if the thing has no face, "babies will nonetheless follow its 'gaze' (the orientation of the front, reactive part of the robot), treating it

---

[28] Paul Bloom, *How Children Learn the Meanings of Words* (Cambridge, MA: MIT Press, 2000).
[29] Ibid., 56. Bloom entitles this section "The Associative Infant."
[30] Ibid., 64.

as if it were a person. But they will not do so if ... [the] robot fails to interact with them in a meaningful way."[31] The mere sound occurring with an object will not be taken as the name of the object. The full context for learning how to use names involves another speaker, who determines the situation by introducing words, and it is the presence of this other speaker and his intent that introduces the dimension of naming. The decisive element is the interaction between the persons.

Furthermore, the child does not merely watch and listen as words are introduced; the child begins to use the words himself. He not only recognizes the other speaker but realizes that he too is a speaker and can enter into the verbal exchanges. The child enters into the human conversation, and in this respect he is different from other animals, who are not members of the community of rational agents. As Bloom says, "Some dogs come to their owner when they are called, but no dogs make the inference that if they were to produce the same sound, their owner will obediently run to them."[32] Bloom quotes Michael Tomasello as saying, "Children use symbols, whereas other primates use signals," and he paraphrases his conclusion about primates: "They don't communicate about other entities; they don't *refer*."[33] Certainly, some animals sense that others are attending to something – as the neuroscientist William Calvin says, "Apes are quite good at picking up on what another is looking at"[34] – but they do not sense that others are referring to something in order to say something about it. Even pointing is a problem for them; chimpanzees in the wild "never show, offer, or point to objects for other chimpanzees," and although they can be taught "to point to direct their trainers to food, they never quite get the hang of it; when they see someone else point, they are mystified."[35] Pointing is a more bodily version of referring: when you point to something, you expect something to be said or done about it; pointing, like referring, leads the other person to reply, "Yes? What about it?" The other person waits for the predicate (indeed, a person is someone who *can* wait for a predicate). He waits for something to be said about the something that has been targeted. What the child enters into when he begins to point and then to symbolize is the activity of establishing a reference and then embedding a predicate within the referent; he enters into categorial predication, the use of syntax in speech, in reciprocity with other speakers.

---

[31] Ibid., 62.
[32] Ibid., 74.
[33] Ibid., 85.
[34] William H. Calvin and Derek Bickerton, *Lingua ex Machina: Reconciling Darwin and Chomsky with the Human Brain* (Cambridge, MA: MIT Press, 2000), 119.
[35] Bloom, *How Children Learn the Meanings of Words*, 85.

What Bloom says about the learning of words can apply to protolanguage as well as to language. Children need a reservoir of protonames before syntax can kick in; the speech of under-two-year-olds is a kind of playful identification of things, still waiting for the rule-governed combinatorics of grammar and syntax. And when syntax does start up, what happens is not simply the activation of a more complex neural system, but conduct between the speaker and the listener: the child suddenly realizes that the speaker can codify a state of affairs – by isolating a referent and highlighting a feature – and that he can do the same himself. He too can package the situation in speech. This step up into syntax also releases the child from being confined to what lies within the environment. Now statements can be made about what is absent, and off-line thinking can come into play. And of course, once the child engages in such verbal give-and-take, he can distinguish himself as a speaker from his interlocutors, and the stage is set for him to mention himself precisely as engaged in the categorial activity he is now part of, that is, the stage is set for his declarative use of the first-person pronoun.

People who use pidgin have already entered into syntactic structures in their own native languages and have established and declared themselves as speakers therein, so their use of "baby talk" is more impatient; they already know that these formal things are possible and know that they are regressing into a more primitive form of communication. But once the pidgin slips into creole, a new species of language is born, and all the essential resources of speech are available: "By the time children are about four, they have mastered just about all of the phonology, syntax, and morphology they are ever going to know, at least for their first language."[36]

The Ethics of Predication

The use of language, the use of words, names, and syntactic structures, is inherently intersubjective, and predication occurs not when we impose categories of understanding on experience, nor when the language faculty becomes activated, nor when our own experience progresses from perception to judgment, but when speakers bring things into focus and establish references for the audience and themselves, and then determine features in what they have isolated. Referential intent is essential for both words and syntax, and it occurs reciprocally between speakers and listeners.

In developing this claim, we have focused on the speaker, who is leading the listener into thinking, but the action of the listener is equally intersubjective. The listener has to have a certain elementary trust in the speaker in order to awaken into rationality, to grasp what is being referred

[36] Ibid., 12.

to and what is being said about it. This confidence is especially necessary in the early stages of our intellectual life, when attachment to the expressed mind of another shapes the powers of our own mind, and when trauma and fear can introduce a distrust that will deform the way things show up for us for the rest of our lives. If we were to suffer such injuries, we still might recover; later in life, our own cognitive energy, or perhaps the curative generosity of others, might succeed in healing our power of disclosure, but remedies are needed. The ability to return someone's gaze is an essential ingredient in becoming able to look thoughtfully at things and to articulate them. The "brilliant, bestial eyes" of feral children have not been prepared to accept an introduction to linguistic thinking, to letting the truth of things show up for them.[37] Such eyes are not receptive enough to permit an entrance into conversation.

The truthfulness at the heart of our own thinking, the responsible impulse toward evidence, is cultivated in this elementary interchange with others. When human beings disclose things, they do not act like impersonal drones or machines or solitary scouts. They themselves are embedded in relations with others, and their syntactic thinking starts up in these relationships, with all the emotive forces, anxieties, and attachments that come along with them. When we enter into the space of reason, we do not float up into a kind of distilled detachment that places us beyond human involvement. There is an ethics to disclosure; we have to want to be logical for others and for ourselves, and this wanting can be cultivated in either a virtuous or a vicious way. We give and receive in the world of thinking as well as in the more practical world, and we might even say that we give others the ability to know, by helping them bring this power into a healthy active state, one in which they will be eager to let things come to light. There is a distinctive kind of friendship and justice in our cognitive achievements.

Bernard Williams, in his book *Truth and Truthfulness*, describes two ways in which we exercise moral responsibility as speakers.[38] When I say something to you, I imply, first, that I am not lying, and second, that I have taken the appropriate steps to be sufficiently sure of what I am telling you. Any discourse implies what Williams calls the two "virtues" of truthfulness, Sincerity and Accuracy.[39] It is not enough for me to tell the truth: I must also have done whatever I needed to do in order to discover the things I am reporting, and different kinds of things demand different kinds of evidence.

---

[37] The phrase is from T. M. Luhrmann, "The Call of the Wild," *Times Literary Supplement* (January 25, 2002), review of Michael Newton, *Savage Girls and Wild Boys: A History of Feral Children* (London: Faber and Faber, 2002). See also Charles Maclean, *The Wolf Children* (New York: Hill and Wang, 1977).

[38] Bernard Williams, *Truth and Truthfulness: An Essay in Genealogy* (Princeton, NJ: Princeton University Press, 2002).

[39] Ibid., 11, 84–148.

My use of the first-person declarative – "I know ...," "I suspect ... " – is an explicit expression of this implied claim. It is easier to see this ethical dimension in human thinking if we realize that originally and essentially predication occurs between persons, not in a solitary mind that imposes logic on experience. I would like to go a step beyond Williams and speak about the common root behind both Sincerity and Accuracy. This common source is veracity, a concept we introduced at the end of Chapter 1: it is the elementary desire for truth that shows up in these two ways, in being honest in what we tell others and in being careful in what we disclose. When we are truthful, we not only exercise our own veracity but generously help others to develop theirs.

The ethical dimension of predication can be brought out by a lovely synonym that Michael Oakeshott has used for *judgment*. He uses the word *verdict*.[40] Its etymology is the Latin *vere dictum*, "something truly stated." *Verdict*, like *judgment*, signifies the conclusion of judicial deliberation, and it obviously names a public event, not just an interior mental act. It connotes something definite that can be announced to others and made into a part of a larger whole. A verdict, like a judgment, proclaims how a given entity is featured. It connotes careful consideration and honest statement, and it also evaluates the thing it decides about: it determines how the thing measures up to what it should be.

[40] Michael Oakeshott, *On Human Conduct* (Oxford: The Clarendon Press, 1975), 2.

5

Reason as Public

Quotation

We gain a number of philosophical advantages if we consider syntax as originating in an intersubjective exchange, not in an operation performed by and in a single mind.

Four Benefits of Taking Syntax as Intersubjective

First, we start off with an obvious realism in the use of language. We avoid the egocentric predicament. The very establishment of language occurs between two (or more) speakers, and both speakers are talking about a thing that is presented to them in common. Their speech focuses both of their minds first on the thing as a whole and then on some attribute that they articulate within the thing. It is precisely in this double disclosure carried on between speaker and listener that the thing shows up as a substance: as that which presents itself in and through a feature, and also as that which has an essential structure, something that belongs to it in itself, in contrast with things that belong to it accidentally. The thing shows up, in Aristotle's terms, both as a substrate and as "what it is for this thing to be," the two central meanings of substance.[1] We will clarify these dimensions of things when we examine the content of speech.

The speakers, therefore, do not operate on their private mental representations, but on the thing they present to one another, the thing they have in common. Mental representations are a deadly trap philosophically: if you start with them, you never get beyond them. They lock us into subjective isolation. The intersubjective approach we have been taking avoids the very notion of mental representations, because in it the words are used immediately by two people to refer to things and to formulate

---

[1] See Aristotle, *Metaphysics*, VII 3. Aristotle begins by presenting four meanings for *ousia*, but two later become the most important: substrate and the "what-it-was-to-be" or the essence of a thing. See also V 8, where the four meanings again give way to two.

them into their wholes and parts. Each person is rescued from solipsism by the other and each is placed in the direct presence of the object, because the thing is known by each as being presented not only to himself but also to the other, as well as to anyone who overhears or who is addressed later on. Since two minds originally articulate the thing together, the signification of the words being used could not be a private, mental meaning. It could only be the thing that is known.

There still remains the problem of how concepts fit into this picture. Bickerton, along with many cognitive scientists, often refers to mental representations or concepts as that which is immediately given to us. I believe that, despite his excellent treatment of syntax, he slips into philosophical confusion on this point. For example, when speaking about what words do, he writes, "They serve to focus your mind on some aspect of reality – or rather, I should say, of the picture of reality you carry about with you in your brain."[2] (He should have stayed with the first alternative.) He also says that "everything we or any other creatures perceive is a representation, and not in any sense naked reality itself," and he claims that impacts on the retina are transformed into information that is transferred electrochemically to the visual cortex, "where it is automatically reconstituted to provide a fairly, but not always completely, accurate simulacrum of what there is around us."[3] I think this description of perception and mental representation is clearly inadequate; I address the issue later on, and now merely stake out the claim that the first advantage of my intersubjective understanding of syntax is realism in the use of words.

The second advantage is that we are not obliged to add communication to the use of words. The communicative dimension is there from the beginning. There would be neither words nor syntax if people were not displaying something one to another. We use names to identify things for other people, and syntax is an articulation done with and for these others. It is not the case that in the beginning we form judgments privately, that we acquire bits of knowledge in our minds and assent to certain states of affairs, and only subsequently try to ship that knowledge into the minds of other people. There would be no syntactic articulation of things, concepts, or language for ourselves if we did not talk with one another; language is not a psychological but a public thing. Both syntax and the meaning of words come to us in public exchanges. Thinking by ourselves is a kind of conversation, and it is supported by language.

---

[2] William H. Calvin and Derek Bickerton, *Lingua ex Machina: Reconciling Darwin and Chomsky with the Human Brain* (Cambridge, MA: MIT Press, 2000), 15.

[3] Derek Bickerton, *Language and Species* (Chicago: University of Chicago Press, 1990), 17 (see also pp. 19, 21), and *Language and Human Behavior* (Seattle: University of Washington Press, 1995), 102, 115; Calvin and Bickerton, *Lingua ex Machina*, 118.

Of course, once language is established, there will be cases in which we have language-based insights on our own, without the help of any immediate interlocutor, but such solitary successes are entirely derived from the language we learned in more public situations. What happens in private thinking is that we pull this public exchange, with its formal structure, into ourselves. The solitary insight is not the default condition, and it is not the paradigm. To say that insights or judgments are first achieved privately and then communicated to others would be like saying that we first carry out a salute in our own minds, and this internal action is the real salute, the true one (because it is the salute we have "in our hearts"); the salute that we subsequently perform with our arm and hand, in the presence of the person who deserves to be saluted, would then be only a public expression of the real one in our minds. Such an internalist interpretation of salutes is obviously erroneous, and so is the analogous interpretation of the use of words.

Third, this intersubjective approach to syntax leads us easily and obviously into the declarative use of the first-person singular. If syntax arises when one speaker "packages" a situation for another when he raises the situation to the level of categoriality, then the speaker also emerges in that context as the agent, the one responsible for having done so; he emerges as *this* speaker over against *that* one. And what exactly has he done in this accomplishment? He has exercised a display, he has responsibly brought something to light. He has acted as an agent of truth. It is the thing they hold in common that he has displayed, but *he* is the one who has displayed it, and the listener and any onlookers cannot help but acknowledge the rational agency of that speaker. They can even call what he has said into question and ask him to justify what he has said. If it is appropriate, the speaker can and will declare himself as the one who has carried out that particular engagement of truth. In his articulation, he has not intervened in the world in a bodily way: he has not chopped down a tree or heaped up a pile of stones (although he *has* made some noises); he has merely displayed something within the frames supplied by grammatical and logical syntax, and this kind of achievement is proper to persons, to rational agents.

The speaker has, furthermore, not done something that occurs only very rarely; people disclose things all the time; the activity has been carried out throughout the millennial history of what Michael Oakeshott has called the human conversation: "As civilized human beings, we are the inheritors, neither of an inquiry about ourselves and the world, nor of an accumulating body of information, but of a conversation, begun in the primeval forests and extended and made more articulate in the course of centuries. It is a conversation which goes on both in public and within each of ourselves."[4] Oakeshott says that through our education "we learn

---

[4] Michael Oakeshott, "The Voice of Poetry in the Conversation of Mankind," in his *Rationalism in Politics*, new and expanded edition (Indianapolis, IN: Liberty Press, 1991), 490–1.

to recognize the voices," that is, we become able to discern who is declaring himself in the discourse and the various ways he can do so, and we also learn when and how to intervene in the discussion ourselves; we learn "to distinguish the proper occasions of utterance ..., and acquire the intellectual and moral habits appropriate to conversation." This human exchange locates us, together with what we say and do, in the human community or the kingdom of ends: "And it is this conversation which, in the end, gives place and character to every human activity and utterance." That is, the conversation embeds us and all our words and actions in its overarching syntax, and it surpasses any other human achievement: "This conversation is not only the greatest but also the most hardly sustained of all the accomplishments of mankind." The conversa-tion acts as a preservative for human disclosures: there are uncountable manifestations stored in our books and records, and many more that have simply settled into our unwritten common beliefs, but all of them are the residue of acts of disclosure that have established the human tradition. Each of these disclosures, moreover, no matter how trivial it might seem, has a moral tone to it. If it is done honestly, it is a successful exercise of the veracity that is the emblem of the human person.

Fourth, this intersubjective approach to syntax permits an enrichment of what can be included in formal logic. Traditionally, logical form is said to include only those elements that are essential for predication and implication, those elements that are a precondition for truth values. Frege, for example, excludes from logic features like concession, which is expressed by a word like *however*. He says that this feature belongs to the coloring (*Färbung*), the scent (*Duft*), the illumination (*Beleuchtung*), or the mood (*Stimmung*) of a statement, because it affects only a subjective reaction and has no impact on truth value or logical consistency.[5] Thus, if I were to say to someone, "Pauline came in the morning. She left, however, early in the afternoon," the logical formalization of these statements would reduce the *however* to a simple *and*, to a plain conjunction, because the *however* would not affect the truth value of the two statements and their combination. The statements, as far as truth and logical form are concerned, should be boiled down to: "Pauline came in the morning. She left early in the afternoon." But something seems to be lost in this reduction; there is an element of meaning in the original that has been deleted from the simplified transformation. What is lost is the sense that

---

[5] See Gottlob Frege, "Thoughts," trans. Peter Geach and R. H. Stoothoff, in *Collected Papers on Mathematics, Logic, and Philosophy*, ed. Brian McGuinness (New York: Basil Blackwell, 1984), 356–7, and "A Brief Survey of My Logical Doctrines," in *Posthumous Writings*, ed. Hans Hermes et al. (Chicago: University of Chicago Press, 1979), 197. Michael Dummett criticizes Frege on this topic; see *Frege: Philosophy of Language* (London: Duckworth, 1973), 83–9.

the first sentence arouses a certain expectation in the listener – if Pauline came early in the morning, one would expect her to stay for a while – and the *however* cancels that anticipation. Implied in the concessive conjunctive is the sense, "You expect her to stay longer, but she did not; she left early in the afternoon."

This dimension in the original statement can be dispensed with if we consider judgments just as combinations of concepts that are present to a single mind, combinations that can be verified and tested for consistency. But if the statement is achieved between two speakers, the expectations of the listener and the attitude of the speaker toward the listener cannot be dismissed. We have to take them into account in our speech and also in our verifications. The adverb *moreover* would be another example. In straight formal logic it would not need to be taken into account as far as the truth value of the statements is concerned, but in the logic between interlocutors it has the sense, "You might think we're finished, but in fact there is more." In the sentence, "Jason won the game; moreover, he won it by several points," the speaker does not just report two facts; the second is not just one more fact, but an emphatic addition to the first, and such an emphasis makes sense only between interlocutors, not in the plain unfolding of assertions by themselves. More kinds of logical operators come into play if the intersubjective dimension of syntax is taken into account. The complexities of grammar – subordinate clauses, prepositional phrases, reversals of order, each with its own emphasis and nuance – are ways in which we adjust the presentation of things for the benefit of those to whom they are being manifested by what we say. There is a melody in syntax that enhances disclosure. Speech is not just a code to be cracked.

Reprise

A long, complicated sentence, as well as the proposition it expresses, exhibits syntactic form. The hierarchic embedding typical of syntax is realized in subordinate clauses, verb forms that take many arguments, adverbs and adjectives, prepositional phrases, conjunctions and alternations. Phrases are nested within other phrases, and yet all this complexity is synthesized into one statement with a beginning and an end. The complexity can go far beyond the individual sentence or proposition. A paragraph or an argument, even a long text or a lengthy conversation, are complex wholes in which hierarchic stacking is achieved. The complex structure of a book, for example, has judgments embedded within paragraphs, paragraphs boxed within chapters, and chapters nested within sections, and all this is situated within the book as a whole, which in turn is played off against other books, as well as political constitutions, laws, contracts, instructions, messages, and the like, and all such linguistic entities are finally nested within the conversation of mankind. There is no predetermined limit to the complexity that can be reached. However, turning back from the complex to the more elementary, even the simplest predication, made up of subject and predicate, is also a syntactic whole, with its own hierarchic, embedded structure. All these works of reason are qualitatively different from the flattened and nonhierarchic rhythm of protolanguage, which, as Bickerton observes, is "endlessly, monotonously unstructured and analytically uninteresting."[6] The discrete articulation of intelligence rides on the waves of continuous perception and its protolinguistic verbalizing, but it rises above them into the crisp world of syntactic structure.

The intricate syntactic patterns of speech are peppered with declarative uses of first-person pronouns. The person who articulates things and situations also intermittently signals his own presence and responsibility as the one who does the articulating and arrives at the verdicts. He not only codifies states of affairs but also manifests himself, in his speech, as the one responsible for the codifying, with the modality proper to that particular assertion. He not only says, "We have to change our strategy and get more support from the farm states," but also says, "I think [or I know, or I suspect] that we have to change our strategy and start getting more support from the farm states." The speaker draws attention to himself precisely as speaking and judging, as an actualized agent of truth. He does so, moreover, in response to other persons who take positions over against his own, sometimes in agreement, sometimes in contradiction. Although individuals might be the ones who stake out a claim, the claim itself, if it is a matter of truth, is ultimately what engenders assent; the speakers, listeners, and onlookers are all ultimately led by the truth of the things said, not simply by the authority of the one who says them, although at times the only way we can get to the truth of things is by provisionally acknowledging the authority of the one who we judge does know and is honest in his statements.[7]

A Special Instance of Syntactic Form: Quotation

A particularly important instance of the embedded stacking found in syntax is the phenomenon of quotation. Among all the stacked arguments, sentences, phrases, and forms of speech, we find some phrases in which the words are not those of the speaker who is organizing this speech, but the words and articulations of another speaker who is being brought into this speech. Structurally, a quotation is embedded: it is located within

[6] Bickerton, *Language and Human Behavior*, 51.
[7] Yves R. Simon develops the kind of authority that comes into play in regard to cognitional matters as opposed to practical ones. He calls this the authority of the witness. See *A General Theory of Authority* (Notre Dame, IN: University of Notre Dame Press, 1980), 84–131.

a larger statement, but it is not like an ordinary subordinate clause. What is peculiar about it is the fact that although it is spoken by me, it is spoken by me as being stated by someone else. I allow someone else to take over my voice and to speak through me. I as the speaker who quotes become something of a ventriloquist, or, more accurately, the reverse of a ventriloquist: whereas a ventriloquist projects his own speech into the mouth of a dummy, I, the person quoting, permit someone else's speech to come to life in my own mouth. I make myself, so to speak, into the dummy for someone else, and I do so precisely as an active speaker, not as a wooden puppet. I actively quote someone else. The power to quote is an eminent form of rationality, a particularly refined exercise of syntactic structure, because it not only articulates a situation into a categorial whole but also, within that articulation, introduces another structuring that is not the speaker's own, but a segmentation, a part-and-whole actualization, that has been achieved by someone else with another point of view. This stacking of what is given to and articulated by another mind within the speech that expresses my own mind is a particularly sophisticated form of embedding. Within the world as it appears to me I insert a part of the world as it appears to someone else. Other animals do not quote one another; a dog's bark is essentially his own, never the voicing of what another dog has said. Topper can never, alas, tell us what Brandy has barked.

Furthermore, the modality of the quoted passage can be different from the modality that the current speaker would attribute to it. I can quote a statement of someone else that I do not believe; I can say, "Andrea says James is suffering from pneumonia, but I don't think he is." In such quotation I present a prospect that is someone else's and not my own, but I also differ as regards the truth of that prospect, and I say so; I present what I think is not the case. I embed within my own speech not just a statement made by someone else, but a statement that I would not assert on my own. I distinguish not only my mind from the quoted person's mind, but also the truth value of what the other person says from the truth value of what I say. Such intricacy of presentation and differentiation could never be achieved without syntactic form and the kind of stacking it makes possible in speech.

Quotation cannot take place in protolanguage. As we have seen earlier, a phrase like "Mike paint" might mean that Mike should paint, that Mike is covered with paint, that the paint is Mike's, or many other things. The protolinguistic "phrases" are so underdetermined, so wedded to the situation in which they are uttered, and so tied to the wishes of the speaker who verbalizes them that when they are repeated later on their truth value and even their meaning can hardly be reinstated. Repeating them in another context is less like quotation and more like imitating a giggle or a moan. They do not articulate a situation into a state of affairs, and so they cannot be repeated as doing so in another speech context. And suppose that the "speaker" who tried to quote them would himself be speaking only in protolanguage; how would he be able to show that "what comes next" should be taken as a quotation and not as a continuation of his own verbalizing? If we who are speaking in syntactic language try to quote someone speaking in protolanguage, we have an enormous advantage because of the structure of our discourse; in fact, the quoted proto-linguistic "phrases" are surreptitiously drawn into the structure and stacking of our own speech; they show up more or less as shabby cousins at our formal garden party. But try to quote within the resources of proto-language itself, and try to quote someone who is also speaking protolan-guage; you will find that the two major elements of language are unavailable. You would not have the structural resources of embedding (how could you tell that the quoted phrase is not a continuation of your own continuous speech?), and you would not have the resources of dis-placement, of being able to refer explicitly to things in their absence (how could you tell that what you say next manifests a part of the world that is not being given now to you and your interlocutors?). These deficiencies of protolanguage in regard to quotation bring out, by contrast, the special characteristics of language and its power of quotation.

Quotation in speech is something like painting a picture of another picture. In quotation I syntactically package a part of the world (I say, "Andrea claims ... "), and syntactically within that package I embed another articulation, another packaging (this: "Jim is sick"). Within the world as it appears to me I enclose a part of the world as it appeared to someone else, and I flag it as such, as appearing to that particular other dative.

How is quotation related to declaratives? Quotation is the contrary of declaration. In declaratives we appropriate what we have said and take responsibility for saying it, but in quotation we disappropriate what we are about to say – we imply, "The phrase that follows is *not* necessarily my conviction; *she* is the one who said it" – and we place the responsibility for its articulation onto someone else, whom we identify to a greater or lesser degree, and we do all this even as *we* say the words in question and articulate the state of affairs that they signify. We, of course, as the ones who carry out the quotation, can declare ourselves as doing so. We can say, "*I know* that Andrea said Jim is suffering from pneumonia." We can take explicit responsibility for stacking the quotation within our own speech, and for presenting Andrea as a speaker who has the world showing up to her in a specific way (as containing Jim suffering from pneumonia).

It is obvious and noncontroversial that the speaker who does the quoting can use a declarative; but what about the speaker he is quoting? Can there be a declarative element in what is said about him? If I say, "I know that Greta thinks the market will go up," is the term "Greta thinks," or a substitute like "she thinks," being used just informationally? Certainly there would be no problem with saying that it is being used just informationally. I could just be reporting what Greta thinks, just telling you a fact about her and the world she inhabits. But this might not be a sufficient interpretation; there might be a bit more to it than this. There might be a trace of her declarations in what I say about her, if I am presenting her precisely as an active agent of truth. I might lend her a kind of declarative force when I seriously quote her. Obviously, she herself is not declaring herself through my speech, but I might be allowing her to perform a kind of resuscitated declaration if I am taking her statement seriously as a manifestation of truth that she truly would have appropriated at some other time and place. Our use of language is so complex in its stacking that not only the words of other people but even their manifestations of the world, and their appropriations of those disclosures, can be brought to a kind of cognitive life in me as speaking now, if I quote what they say and think. In this manner, Homer can come to life again, and so can Plato and Aristotle, Seneca and St. Augustine, Shakespeare, Milton, and Samuel Johnson, and even some person unknown to us who a thousand years ago wrote a letter that we read and quote now. This is what it means to have a mind and to be a person, a rational animal: that our thoughts can come to life again, and we ourselves can be echoed, in the minds and speech of others. Human life is intellectual as well as biological. All this is made possible by syntactic structures and the kind of life they bring us into. A third-person declarative within a quotation is obviously different from a current first-person declarative, but both belong to the same linguistic category.

To clarify the category they belong to, let us recall the four levels of speech we distinguished at the beginning of Chapter 3: first, the prelinguistic or protolinguistic level; second, the standard use of words to articulate something in the world; third, the first-person declarative; and fourth, the philosophical level of discourse. The declarative level is that on which we appropriate what we articulated on the second level, and of course we can appropriate only what we ourselves have asserted or do assert. But we can also mirror someone else's appropriation, and we do so when we quote them. That other speaker manifested himself as a person when he stated – and perhaps appropriated, in his first person – the way the world seemed to him, and we now mirror him as so acting; but we do so as persons ourselves, and so we embed in our discourse and declaration someone else's discourse and declaration. Suppose we say, "I know that James doubted that there would be any snow on the weekend." James's doubting may or may not have been declared by James himself in the original situation, but both he and his doubting now come to life in my speech, and so does the state of affairs that he doubts (that there will be snow on the weekend); the state of affairs is articulated in a doubly nested way within my speech. In fact, without such a state of affairs there would be nothing for the speakers to articulate, and hence there would be no logical space for the speakers and their declaratives. This state of affairs is nested in my speech as appearing to someone other than me. As the one who quotes, I can not only entertain and present the articulated state of affairs that James is responsible for bringing to light; I can also entertain and present, to my present interlocutors, James's activity as an agent of truth. I can mirror his declarations and the activities that lie behind them.

An Example of Quotation Taken from Antiquity

This revival of the mind of someone else in the mind of a current speaker is brought out in a vivid and colorful way in a biography of St. Augustine, written by his contemporary Possidius, bishop of Calamensis.[8] At the close of the biography, Possidius writes about Augustine's death and reflects on his accomplishments. He says that Augustine left behind not only a large number of clerics and many monasteries, but also whole libraries filled with his writings, which would bear witness to what he was. In these writings, Possidius says, Augustine will live on and be encountered by the faithful: *in his semper vivere a fidelibus invenitur*. Then he quotes a couplet from an unnamed secular poet. The poet had given instructions that he should be buried in a public place, and that his epitaph should read:

> Vivere post obitum vatem vis nosse viator,
> Quod legis ecce loquor, vox tua nempe mea est.
>
> Traveler, know that the poet lives beyond his death;
> What you read, behold, I speak; for your voice is truly my own.

The passerby reads the epitaph, probably aloud, and the dead poet takes over that living voice to come to life again. It is not just the sounds that the poet composed that are revived, but more importantly the thing thought, the way the world showed up to him, the state of affairs he registers. Through the written and read words, the world is disclosed to the traveler in the same way that it was disclosed to the poet, and so the poet's mind and minding remain active, in the minding of another, even after his death.

In the biography, Possidius goes on to say that Augustine's life and his outstanding virtues are manifest in his writings. Those who read Augustine's works will see this, and will derive great benefit. But, he says, an even greater benefit accrues to those who, like himself, were able to hear and see Augustine in his actual presence, speaking in the Church. Possidius closes by asking his own readers – *qui haec scripta legetis* – to join him in thanking and blessing God because he was given the understanding to formulate these things in his biography of Augustine, to record them

---

[8] Possidius, *Vita Sancti Aurelii Augustini*, Migne, *Patrologia Latina*, volume 32, col. 64.

"for the knowledge of men both present and absent, those both of the present time and the future; *ut haec in notitiam et praesentium et absentium praesentis temporis et futuri hominum.*"[9] Language, in its hierarchic structure, straddles the present and the absent.

Possidius thus speaks to his readers and imitates the poet who wishes to come to life in the mind of those who read his epitaph. This unnamed poet's couplet is embedded within Possidius's text, and the poet's address to his reader is embedded within Possidius's address to us who read him. The stacking, this hierarchic power of language, is not just a matter of verbal phrases, but of speakers and listeners as well. To bring the whole thing to closure, Possidius draws our attention to the fact that his own writing straddles both the present and the absent, the contemporary and the future (the future that is our present, as we read his words, now that he himself has slipped into the past). Since Possidius is a Christian, he concludes his biography with a request that we pray with him and for him (*et mecum ac pro me oretis*), so that he might imitate that man with whom he passed almost forty years "without any bitter dissension at all, *absque amara ulla dissensione,*" and that he might, with Augustine, enjoy the promises made by almighty God. This eschatological conclusion sets the widest context that Possidius can conceive.

But the Russian-doll stacking has still more dimensions to it, because I now in my writing, and you the reader in your reading, take in both Possidius's text and the unnamed poet's couplet, as well as the personae of the biographer and the poet. They and their texts are stacked within my discourse and the text you read, and as I use the declarative now to speak about my writing, my context is for the moment the dominant and most concrete. When you in turn read this, it will be your context that comes to the fore. Writing and reading can be intensely private versions of the human conversation, but their public dimensions and origins should not be forgotten. In these intricate and multiple ways our own minds share in the minds of others, and our declarations are never absolute, never isolated and independent of declarations and articulations that have been achieved or will be achieved by others. None of our thinking is without an element of recapitulation.[10] Such is the complexity that can develop from

---

[9] Possidius, *Vita Sancti Augustini*, col. 65. The passage of poetry that I use here was used by Thomas Prufer in "A Reading of Augustine's *Confessions*, Book X," in his *Recapitulations: Essays in Philosophy* (Washington, DC: Catholic University of America Press, 1993), 27.

[10] See Thomas Prufer's volume, *Recapitulations*. It seems to me that 'recapitulation' is a better category to use than 'hermeneutics' or 'interpretation' when we speak about the thought of one person or one age as coming to life again in another. *Hermeneutics* as used in modern speech is burdened by much epistemological freight. *Recapitulation* is a fresh word, and it connotes public activities and syntactical action. To recapitulate is to repeat, but also to select, to summarize, and to put into hierarchic order, with the more important distinguished from the less. We place the old material into new chapters or headings,

those simple predications that originally occur between two minds. As human persons, we owe our rational life to those who have shared with us their thoughts, the way the world appeared to them.

And finally, there is a special twist to all this stacking, because we are not only reading and quoting other people; we are also thinking philosophically about them. We are taking a special kind of distance as we look at these quotations and declarations. We examine all these persons and activities, along with what they display, from a philosophical point of view, and so we further embed all this in a still more distinctive way.

capitula. To sum up is to compute and hence to present an understanding of what is at issue; this aspect of computation is expressed by the colloquialism, "That doesn't compute," which is said when something does not make sense; it does not add up. When something is said to be recapitulated, it is obvious that it is still there in the recapitulation, but it is also obvious that it has been abridged, rearranged, and inevitably slanted. By contrast, when something is said to be interpreted, we might doubt that the thing has survived the interpretation. We might suspect that it has gotten lost in translation and dissolved into perspectives. A text could not be lost in recapitulation, but it obviously is not simply repeated. I think, for example, it is more perspicuous to say that I have, in this book, recapitulated Bickerton's work than that I have interpreted it. Finally, it would be interesting to compare the concept of recapitulation to Michael Oakeshott's concept of abridgment, which deals with the adaptations of political traditions and forms. See Michael Oakeshott, "Political Education," in *Rationalism and Politics*, 55: "If ... the English manner of politics is to be planted elsewhere in the world, it is perhaps appropriate that it should first be abridged into something called 'democracy' before it is packed up and shipped abroad."

6

Grammatical Signals and Veracity

We have shown how human rationality is exhibited in the syntactic compositions that human beings introduce into their discourse. Such syntax occurs most palpably in the strings of words that are spoken or written. When it occurs in speech, in the use of language, it is called grammar. But syntax is also present in the meanings or concepts or propositions that are woven into the words, and there it can be called logical grammar or logical syntax. Finally, syntax also occurs in the things that are being presented: if I articulate a tree as blossoming, I distinguish between the tree and its blossoming, the thing and its feature, and I compose them into a formulated whole. The tree is presented or manifested in its whole and parts. Here we might speak of ontological syntax or perhaps of the formal relations between a thing and its various attributes.[1] I have already said that the most troublesome of these three fields for syntax is that of meanings, concepts, or propositions, and I now repeat my promise to explain later on what that domain is.[2]

What I wish to examine in this chapter is the special way in which the grammar of speech is related to the cognitive activities of the speaker and listener. In earlier chapters we discussed the various parts of speech and showed how grammar allows us to embed some phrases within others and to organize them hierarchically. All this dealt with the content of our discourse, with what is being said or displayed. Now we turn to the activity of saying and displaying, to the acts of the speaker and listener.

It might seem at first glance that when we make this transition, going from what is said or displayed to the activities of saying and displaying, we

---

[1] Husserl speaks of formal ontology, which he describes as "an ontology (an a priori theory of objects), though a formal one, relating to the pure modes of anything-whatever." It examines the "*Ableitungsgestalten des Etwas überhaupt.*" See *Formal and Transcendental Logic*, trans. Dorion Cairns (The Hague: Martinus Nijhoff, 1969), §24, pp. 77–8.

[2] The issue will be treated later in Chapters 8, 10, and 11.

will be moving from grammar and logic to psychology, because we will now be looking at the mental actions, the psychic performances of the speaker and listener. And if we do turn to something psychological, the danger seems to arise that we will fall prey to psychologism, which is the reduction of the hard-and-fast laws of logic to the more flexible, empirical laws of the habits and performances of the mind. But we can avoid this danger and eschew psychologism. In fact, our discussion of this topic will, I hope, clarify the perplexing relationship between logic and psychology, the issue that John Macnamara has, in the title of his book, called *A Border Dispute.*[3]

How Grammar Signals the Speaker's Acts of Thinking

We begin with actual speech, which, as always, gives us a more tangible way of discussing thinking. We distinguish, within words, between the grammatical dimension and the material, semantic dimension. The word *sidewalk* has both dimensions: its formal, grammatical aspect is its being a noun, and its material aspect is its content, its signifying sidewalks. The word *jump* has the grammatical aspect of being either a verb or a noun, and it has the semantic aspect of signifying a certain bodily motion. The words *and* and *is* seem to be almost purely grammatical and formal; there seems to be practically no content or substance that they designate, certainly nothing like sidewalks or jumping. Such words seem to be exhausted in their activity of linking words, and they seem to have no semantics. A word like *have* in the phrase *I have come* also seems to be purely formal and grammatical, without material content. Prepositions, like *with* and *after*, and conjunctions, like *unless* and *although*, also seem to be largely grammatical. The grammatical dimension can show up in separate words, such as those we have just enumerated, but it can also appear in the inflection of words, such as the nominative or dative case, the future or past tense, and the passive participle. It can also show up in the position of words in a sentence. The point we wish to make is that the grammatical dimension of words can be distinguished from their semantic content, even though both dimensions, the syntax and the semantics, pervade any statement we may make.

It seems clear that the nonformal, material part of words serves to name things, such as sidewalks, jumps, trees, houses, and ships. The grammatical, formal part of words seems not to name anything, but seems only to establish links with other words. Grammatical parts of speech seem to be the sheepdogs of language, gathering the flock into the patterns that are appropriate for the statement that needs to be made. However, besides this syntactic task of coordinating words into sentences, grammatical terms

---

[3] See John Macnamara, *A Border Dispute: The Place of Logic in Psychology* (Cambridge, MA: MIT Press, 1986).

and aspects do in fact accomplish something else. They do not just organize words. They also signal to the listener that the speaker is performing
an intellectual act. If a speaker, Molly, says of her two dogs, "Topper and
Brandy are getting hungry," the phrase *Topper and Brandy* includes the
grammatical conjunction *and*, and this term signals to the listener, Chad,
that Molly is conjoining Topper and Brandy. Also, the verbal form of the
sentence, the form of predication expressed especially in the word *are*,
signals that the speaker is distinguishing between Topper-and-Brandy on
the one hand and their feature of becoming hungry on the other, and is
manifesting the pair of dogs in that way. For simplicity's sake we shall stay
with the conjunction, but we keep in mind that a lot of syntactic action,
a lot of cognitive fireworks, goes on in every sentence, no matter how plain
the sentence might seem.

If Molly says *Topper and Brandy*, and if she thinks through what she is
saying, she conjoins Topper and Brandy. She "collects" them into a single
complex subject. She takes the two as one. She could not have performed
this action had she not been graduated from protolanguage to language,
with its syntactic possibilities, but the action of conjoining is not reducible
merely to the linguistic accomplishment of joining two names. Besides
joining the words, she has also joined Topper and Brandy; indeed, she
conjoins Topper and Brandy, for herself and for her audience, precisely by
conjoining the two names. She and her listener think Topper and Brandy
together. Topper and Brandy are presented together. Molly has not done
anything bodily to them: she has not put them into the same kennel, or
placed them next to one another; she has done something spiritual and
rational, she has simply conjoined them, taken the two as one.[4] She has
performed a categorial act that collects two things.

I note in passing that it would be wrong to say that Molly conjoins only
'Topper' and 'Brandy,' her concepts or ideas of the two beasts; to say this
would hurl us into the representational pit with no hope of escape. Once
we say that we intellectually process only our concepts, we will never be
able to say that we know anything about any real things. Molly conjoins the
two real dogs, Topper and Brandy, not merely her ideas of them. This
topic will occupy us, as promised, when we explore the status of concepts
and propositions.

Let us suppose that Molly is talking with Chad when she says the words
"Topper and Brandy are getting hungry." Her use of the word *and*, flanked
by *Topper* and *Brandy*, communicates something to Chad. On the one

---

[4] The theme of taking two as one has been developed by both Jacob Klein and Hans-Georg
Gadamer, who find it in the doctrine of Plato that Aristotle described under the rubric of
the One and the Indeterminate Dyad. See Robert Sokolowski, *Presence and Absence: A
Philosophical Investigation of Language and Being* (Bloomington: Indiana University Press,
1978), Chapter 15, for a discussion of both Klein and Gadamer.

hand, her use of the words communicates "Topper and Brandy together." Her spoken words are used to express the two dogs taken together. But, on the other hand, because Molly is the one who uses the word *and*, her use of the word also signals to Chad that she, Molly, is the one who conjoins the two dogs. Molly uses the grammatical word *and* to signal that she is thinking, and in this case her thinking is the act of conjoining. Molly does not *say* that she is conjoining Topper and Brandy; her communication of her mental action is more implicit than that. Rather, her use of the word *and* makes the point simply by signaling, not by expressing or asserting. Both Molly and Chad are focused on the two dogs, and yet, while thinking about the dogs, Chad also appreciates, out of the corner of his eye, so to speak, that it is Molly who is taking the intellectual lead here and performing the thoughtful operation. Chad knows that Molly is speaking because he picks up the signal in the word *and*, and thanks to the syntactic structure of speech, he acknowledges Molly as a rational animal, a human person, who is actively exercising her rationality as she says the word *and* and uses all the other grammatical terms in her speech. Molly's personhood shines through the signaling action of the grammar of her speech.

I should also add that it is not necessary that Molly "feel" anything special when she conjoins Topper and Brandy. Her intellectual, logical act of conjoining is not something she is conscious of in the way she might be conscious of a pain in her shoulder. Of course, she knows that she is conjoining, but she is not conscious of this act in the sense that she would be aware of some sort of psychological *qualia*, some mental feelings. Her act of conjoining is not something given to her through inner perception. It is not something that she could "look" at in any way at all. Rather, she is aware of it as something she does publicly as she uses words in a certain way while being attentive to things, to Topper and Brandy.

I have taken this notion of signaling from Husserl's *Logical Investigations*.[5] In that work, Husserl says that the words that we speak perform two functions: they *express* a state of affairs (in this case, the fact that the two dogs are getting hungry), and they also *indicate* a cognitive action on the part of the speaker. Husserl introduces the distinction between expression and indication at the very beginning of the first Logical Investigation. In my opinion, this valuable philosophical doctrine has not been sufficiently exploited by commentators on his work. I believe that this distinction, and

---

[5] See Edmund Husserl, *Logical Investigations*, trans. J. N. Findlay, ed. Dermot Moran (New York: Routledge, 2001), volume 1, Investigation I, §§2–4, pp. 183–7. See also Robert Sokolowski, "La grammaire comme signal de la pensée," trans. Jocelyn Benoist, in *Husserl: La représentation vide*, ed. Jocelyn Benoist and J.-F. Courtine (Paris: Presses universitaires de France, 2003), 97–108, and "Semiotics in Husserl's *Logical Investigations*," in *One Hundred Years of Phenomenology*, ed. Dan Zahavi and Frederik Stjernfelt (Dordrecht and Boston: Kluwer, 2002), 171–83.

especially the concept of indication or signaling, can be of great service to the theory of language and to semiotics generally, because it draws our attention to the activity of the person who is carrying out an act of communication. It reminds us that there cannot be a speech or a message without a user of language behind it, without someone who is acting as a thoughtful speaker. Husserl shows that we communicate not only a state of affairs, which is *expressed* in the words we use, but also our own activity of speaking and thinking, which is *indicated* or *signaled* by the same words. Our words indicate and specify to our listeners what Husserl calls the "categorial activity," the acts of intelligence or reason, that we perform while we speak. I also think that this concept of indication can be developed in ways that Husserl himself did not explore, as I hope to show in the rest of this chapter.

It should also be noted that when a speaker moves into a declarative use of the first person, when, for example, Molly says, "I know that Topper and Brandy are getting hungry," she is sanctioning the cognitive actions that her use of grammatical terms has signaled. The person whose actions were indicated by the grammar of a sentence is now more directly mentioned by the use of the first-person pronoun.

False Signals and Complex Signals

It is specifically the grammar of our speech that signals the intellectual activity behind our words. The grammar of living speech, tangible and obvious and noncontroversial as it is, gives us a handle by which we can "perceive," as immediately as is possible, the mind and the actual thinking of another person. There is no better or more direct access to someone's mind; this is as good as it gets. We may also get at the person's mind more indirectly, by seeing what he does and figuring out his motivations, intentions, and plans, for example, or by diagnosing his facial expressions or his emotive states, or by getting a sense of his character, but all such approaches, important and accurate as they may be, are less immediate than the approach through the grammar of his speech, which directly signals his mind in action. All these other ways of interpreting the mind of a person presume that the entity in question does have a mind, and this is what the grammar of his speech indicates. If an animal were to use grammar in its sounds or gestures to indicate syntactic, categorial actions, we would have to say that it was thinking.

But the grammar of our speech truly signals our rational activity only if our speech is thoughtful. We must be thinking while we speak. In fact, much of our speech is not really thought through as it is being uttered. In much of what we say, we merely repeat phrases, clichés, and clots of words that are not really being chosen as we utter them. Furthermore, it is normal that we should speak this way; we cannot think through everything we say. But sometimes we should be thinking through what we say, and still may fail to do so; we merely repeat the slogan, or we daydream while we talk and let the associative pull of words lead us on to other words. We really are not *saying* what we are saying. We fall into vague, inauthentic speech. Sometimes we may be trying to talk about very complicated things that are beyond us, things that we cannot handle, and so we fall back on routine phrases and hope that we will not stray far from the mark. We may be expressing sequences of ideas but not coherent thoughts. In such cases, obviously, the grammatical parts of our speech do not truly signal any thinking.

However, because they still remain grammatical expressions, and because grammar as such does signal rational actions, our listeners may take it for granted that we know what we are talking about, and they may take us seriously. They may, naively, try to follow our "thought." But as we continue to speak, we get more and more tangled up, our argument gets more and more scrambled, and we fall into more and more incoherence and contradiction (we unsay what we said earlier).[6] At the extreme, we may even fall into grammatical incongruity. At some point our listeners may finally realize that they should not take us seriously; they write us off, and they may be quite incensed because they were taken in by us; we seemed at first to know what we were talking about. These very failures in speech bear witness to the fact that the grammar of our discourse does in principle indicate or signal that we are thinking as we speak.

And think of how much grammar there is in what we say. Even a simple statement, "Topper and Brandy are getting hungry," contains a conjunction in the subject phrase, and this dual subject then becomes the substrate for a predication. In this simple statement, two acts of intelligence, a conjoining and then a predication, have to be performed, and they are signaled by the grammatical terms *and* and *are*. The words are formulated, furthermore, as nouns, verbs, or adjectives by the syntax of the sentence. This sentence would, in turn, normally be embedded in many more statements, with far more conjunctions, prepositions, complex verb forms, adverbs and adjectives, subordinations, gerunds and infinitives, and the like. As these grammatical elements flash on and off, they signal the thinking that is going on behind them. Acts of thinking of the most complex sort are always going on as we speak, and they are being actively signaled, with almost electronic velocity and abundance, by the grammatical complexities in the words we use. Think of someone uttering a very long, complicated German sentence, with everyone waiting expectantly to get to the end: will it be a negation, so that everything we are hearing now must, after all, be canceled? Or will it end with an *auf* or an *ab*, and only then inform us whether everything goes into forward or into reverse?

---

[6] See Sokolowski, *Presence and Absence*, 79–86.

The embedding stacking, the hierarchic, Chinese-box structures of syntax, occurs not only in the words we utter but also in the acts of thinking, of differentiating and identifying, that are being carried out as we speak. We stack our acts of reason as well as our phrases. And it is not a misnomer to say that our thinking is almost electronic in its speed, since both chemistry and electricity are at work in our brains as we speak and think about what we are saying.

The transition from protolanguage to language and syntax marks the transition from the higher forms of sensibility to rational activity. The best access we have to intelligence in action is the syntax of language, which signals that activity as occurring as the words are being spoken. Mind is made present in the syntax of speech. Thinking occurs in the medium of words.

The rational, categorial action is most immediately and vividly made present when the speaker actively chooses his words as he speaks. In that case, the grammar in the words signals the actions that are being performed there and then. Sometimes, however, there is a delay between the intellectual action and the signal: if I thoughtfully write a speech at one time and read it before an audience later on, I may, as I read it, let my mind wander, or I may pay attention to my tone of voice rather than to the content of the speech, but still the rational actions being signaled by my words were my own at an earlier time, and my audience picks them up as mine. I am saying and endorsing them now, precisely as my own. I can relax and read because my thinking has been done, but the audience has to strain to keep up with what I say. And sometimes, as we have seen, there is no real thinking behind the signals but only confusion or incapacity, and the verbal signals are fake; they seem to indicate intelligence where none exists.

In Chapter 4 we showed that syntactic action is public. Predication is an activity in which a speaker draws attention to an object; while holding that focus in place, he draws attention to an aspect of the same object; and by uttering some syntactic term, he clips the two together. All the attention – that of the speaker and that of all the listeners – is focused on the objects being articulated, but the same term that clips the object and feature together also signals that the speaker has done this, that it was his doing, and that it was his authority that differentiated and identified the state of affairs. If the speaker were to conjoin two things, his use of the word *and* would hold them together for inspection and determination, but the same word would also signal that *he* had conjoined. The things being thought – the objects being predicated or conjoined – are displayed publicly, but the thinking of the speaker is also being displayed publicly, not by being expressed but by being signaled.

When a speaker goes a step further and declares himself by using the first-person pronoun, he draws attention to himself as the one who performed the acts that are signaled by the grammar of his speech. Even then, however, the focus of both speaker and listener is directed toward the thing being displayed. If Molly says, "I suspect that Topper and Brandy are getting hungry," both she and Chad are still concerned with Topper and Brandy and their condition, even though Molly's activity of articulating them has been signaled by the grammar of her sentence and endorsed by her use of the declarative.

The grammar of words is lodged deeply in our minds. It shapes our minds and their activity, and when we speak, the grammar of the sentences we utter spreads our minds out into the open. This exposure of our minds, through the grammar of our speech, manifests our thinking more directly than any sort of brain scan could do. When we hear the grammar of a speech, we get as deeply into a person's mind as we are ever going to get. The speaker may try to conceal his thinking by telling lies, by using a grammar alien to that of his true thoughts, but no one can lie all the time, and the way a person thinks will show up sooner or later, at one time or another, in the words that he speaks.

How Grammar Signals the Listener to Think

Husserl helps us see that words can signal the intellectual, categorial activities of a speaker. He does not, however, notice another kind of signaling that the same words also carry out. Besides signaling that the speaker is thinking, the words the speaker voices also signal to the listener to carry out the same intellectual activities himself. If Molly says *Topper and Brandy*, and if the word *and* indicates her act of conjoining, it is also true that Chad, who hears her speak, is also being signaled by the same *and* to perform a conjunction himself. He too, as he hears the words, collects Topper and Brandy and takes the two as one. He does not just hear Molly as conjoining; he, also, simultaneously, conjoins (if he didn't conjoin, he couldn't hear Molly as conjoining), and then he predicates. He as the listener performs all the other categorial activities that are signaled in Molly's subsequent speech. The word *and* signals Molly's performance, but the very same word, publicly spoken and heard between Molly and Chad, signals to Chad to achieve a similar performance. Husserl, in *Logical Investigations*, recognizes that the word indicates Molly's rational action, but he does not consider the fact that the same word prompts Chad to think as well.

It is the public word, the sound reverberating between Molly and Chad, the word chosen and spoken by Molly, that does all this. The word is not an acoustic image in Molly and another acoustic image in Chad. Words are not psychological things; they happen *en plein air*, out there where the sound waves move. The one sound signals in two directions: it signals that something is occurring in Molly, and it signals for something to occur in Chad. It signals in two ways: to make manifest and to prompt; it signals *that,* and it signals *to.* All the categorial activity in the speaker and listener and perhaps in crowds of listeners, all that thinking, clusters around the single sound and its grammatical structure. If one man is addressing a multitude, the one flow of grammatically ordered words, the one articulated wave of sound, signals that the speaker is thinking, and it signals everyone in that crowd to think, to articulate the world, in the same way. The one stream of sound is the basis for a chorus of thinking.

Grammatical indications are a special kind of signal. When we react to normal signals, we have to go through two stages: first, we must perceive the signal as a signal, and, second, we must perform the action that is being signaled. The two activities are distinct. Suppose the signal is a gunshot to start a race. The runners in the race have to do two things: they must first hear the gunshot and take it as the signal to start, and they must, secondly, begin running. The running is different from hearing the signal and taking it as a signal. In a school, the closing bell is obeyed not just by hearing the bell but by closing the books, putting down the chalk, and leaving the room. In football, the referee's whistle is obeyed not just by hearing the whistle but by stopping the run or letting go of the player you have tackled. In normal signals, there is a difference between perceiving the signal as such and obeying it.

In the case of grammatical signals, these two aspects collapse into one. If Chad hears the word *and* and understands it – if he does not take it as just a rushing sound – he has conjoined the two things flanking the conjunction. He does not first hear and understand the word, and only subsequently perform the rational act of conjoining two things. His very understanding of the word is a conjoining. He obeys the signal precisely by understanding it, not by doing something other than understanding it. Molly, by saying *and,* gets Chad to conjoin just by hearing her speak, not by doing anything beyond hearing her speak. Chad conjoins Topper and Brandy, he takes them as one and exercises that categorial performance immediately upon hearing and understanding the word *and* in Molly's phrase *Topper and Brandy.* The word *and,* spoken between Molly and Chad, signals that Molly is conjoining, and at the same time it gets Chad to conjoin as well. Our mental activity is not an internal performance detached from the perception of the word that signals it. Our intellectual action is not like the running of the race, which is different from and detachable from hearing the starter's pistol shot. If the mental act of conjoining *were* different from understanding the word *and,* we would again be locked into an internal mentalism. Instead, the mental performance is precisely the understanding we have of the publicly spoken word *and.* Our minds are working "out there" as much as are the words.

How Grammar Gets into a Listener's Mind

Because words are such a special kind of signal, different from normal signals like bells and whistles, the speaker's mind, as we have seen, is immediately manifested in his speech. Minding is precisely the performance of categorial activity, and such activity is displayed for all to see – or to hear – in the grammatical aspects of speech. However, it is also true that the speaker gets very deeply into the mind of the listener through the grammar of his, the speaker's, words. The speaker's words immediately shape the mind of the listener, and the mind of the listener is laid open, in the act of listening, to receive what the speaker says. The speaker, after all, is the one governing the situation. He is the controlling verbal authority. He is the one sending the signals and expressing part of the world. Because the very understanding of the grammatical signals is itself the accomplishment of the thought, as soon as the speaker speaks and the listener listens, the thinking that the speaker conveys *has been installed* in the listener's mind. It is almost as though the listener is forced to think the thought the speaker expresses; he immediately thinks the world in a certain way. The speaker, for the moment, shapes the mind of the listener by the words he speaks, and specifically through the grammatical dimension of those words. The listener can escape thinking the thought only by covering his ears (and the reader by averting his eyes).

The ability to hear grammar is to the mind as the retinal surface of the eye is to the brain. The retina is not a medium that leads to the brain; it is not like the eardrum or the surface of the skin, where an impulse must go through something else to get to the neurons that are connected to the brain. The retina is the exposure of the optic nerve; it is the brain itself opening up or unfolding, and what strikes the retina is already inside the neural system, already, in a sense, inside the brain. Likewise, the grammar in the words we hear already shapes our minds. The grammar is not a signal that commands us to do something else. Just grasping the words in their grammar is having the thought and being inside the mind.

This immediacy is brought out in a particularly vivid way when the speaker says something that the listener finds repulsive or something he strongly disagrees with. Even if the listener does not assent to the statement being made, *he does have the thought* as soon as the speaker states it. The listener, moreover, not only has the thought as something inserted from outside into him; he himself achieves the thought, he actively thinks it, under the sway of what the speaker is saying. The listener cannot just look at the thought from afar, he cannot look at it as not his own, as the runner in a race can just hear the pistol shot but decide not to start running. In the understanding of words, the listener cannot help but achieve the thought, even though he may immediately deny the truth of it and abhor the thought itself.

This immediate insertion of thoughts into the minds of others, through the grammar of speech, is the reason why people sometimes get very angry when they hear someone saying something that they, the listeners, vehemently dislike. Suppose Sidney says something grievously insulting about Albert's parents or siblings, or his religion, or his hometown. Albert may flare up in anger just at the statement, because he feels debased by having achieved the thought itself, even if he knows it is not true; there is no way he cannot have had the thought once he hears Sidney say the words that he uttered. Albert has indeed formulated the thought; he is contaminated and even humiliated by having had to think it, and all this has happened because of the words that Sidney uttered. It's not just that Sidney has this opinion and may act on it or that the opinion may be spread around and may influence others in their actions; it's that by expressing it he gets Albert – and perhaps others – to think it as well. There is a certain degradation in just hearing yourself or something that is yours being put down. It takes a great deal of maturity, ego strength, and diplomatic sophistication to hear someone say something that we detest and to maintain our equilibrium even as we express our disagreement and respond appropriately; and sometimes the thought is so offensive that the listener will bristle even if he is the perfect diplomat.

We have emphasized the situation in which the speaker leads the listener to think a repugnant thought, but the opposite also occurs. Because the speaker gets so deeply into the thinking of the listener, it is also possible for him to elevate the listener's mind and enable him to think in a way he never could have thought on his own. William Shakespeare, for example, has raised the thinking of countless people by the grammar of his written words. He has made it possible for them to have insights that they could not have achieved through their own strength. Their minds have been activated by him and his grammatical signals. When we listen to people we wish to learn from or read their words, we trust them and entrust our minds to them. We let them lead us. We want their grammatical signals to shape our minds by activating them into thinking; we want them to enable us to see the world as it has appeared to them. Such people serve as authorities for us, witnesses to the truth, and without their help we would never have achieved the thoughts they formulated for us. Their syntactic action builds up our own minds, as we think the thoughts that first are theirs but then become our own.

In our study of the signaling function of words, we have been discussing the direct interaction between speaker and listener, the push and pull that occurs between their respective activities of thinking. Each thinks in his own mind, but both do so through the single stream of words that are produced by whoever is speaking. And we must recall the other dimension of this speech, the expressive: the speaker and listener do not normally interact just face to face; both of them are focused on the part of the world, on the things and situations that are being expressed through the words as the activities of thinking are being signaled. Both are focused on, say, Topper and Brandy as being hungry, on inflation as spiraling out of control, on the Redskins as winning or losing a game, on the tree as blossoming. Just as there is only one stream of speech, so there is only one situation being manifested to both speaker and listener. The speaker and the listener do their own individual thinking, but they think the same thing. They share in one and the same truth that is manifested to both of them. In this respect they have a world or a truth in common, even as their possession of that one common truth is individualized. Many classical philosophers have shown that truth is a common possession, that it can be shared by many without being diminished for each, but the study of grammar and its signaling and expressive functions sheds further light on how this common possession of truth can occur.

The speaker and listener exchange places in a conversation, and the one stream of words signals two thoughtful perspectives on one and the same state of affairs. The two conversationalists, Molly and Chad, reciprocally articulate the world. Each occasionally mentions herself or himself as the one who is for the moment leading the interaction; each uses the first-person singular to declare himself as the one who says, thinks, knows, suspects, or doubts what is being said. Each highlights his own achievement from time to time and appropriates and takes responsibility for the evidencing that is taking place. When the first-person declarative is used in this way, the one who is listening also appreciates more delicately that he is at the moment a hearer and not a speaker, and that despite the one stream of sound and the one state of affairs being disclosed they are truly two minds and not one. The otherness and the individuality of the persons are brought to the fore, each with his or her own veracity.

Veracity and Truthfulness

At the close of this chapter, I wish to discuss a final topic that pertains to the formal analysis of speech. At the end of Chapter 1 we introduced the theme of veracity, and at the close of Chapter 4 we examined the distinction that Bernard Williams makes between Sincerity and Accuracy.[7] He describes them as the two "virtues" of truthfulness, two ways in which we can be truthful. The first, Sincerity, is the disposition to be honest, to say what we believe to be the case. It resists the temptations to lie, dissemble, or mislead. This is the most obvious sense in which people are said to be truthful. The second, Accuracy, is the disposition to take the appropriate steps to determine the truth in question. It resists the

---

[7] Bernard Williams, *Truth and Truthfulness: An Essay in Genealogy* (Princeton, NJ: Princeton University Press, 2002).

temptations of indolence, bias, partisanship, and wishful thinking. The two virtues, furthermore, are interconnected. We could not, strictly speaking, be disposed to lie to others and yet be seriously committed to discovering the truth for ourselves; a failure in Accuracy is, in fact, a kind of failure in Sincerity toward ourselves.[8] Vices opposed to each of these virtues will bleed into the other.

Whenever we speak we engage these two virtues. What Williams says about the historian can be said about anyone who presents something to someone: "He comes before the public as one who tells the truth, and he needs its virtues."[9] When we say something, we do not have to make a separate declaration that we *are* telling someone the truth; our very use of speech in making a report or registration implies that we are honestly telling others what we think to be the case. It also implies that we have been responsible enough in the matter in question to have determined how things stand: we imply that we are dependable enough to *have* an opinion, and so to have the ability and the authority to say what is the case. We may have looked into the matter for ourselves, we may have learned from others, from people we trust (and even in this case, we have to be responsible enough to know whom to trust), or we may have drawn inferences from other things that we know to be true. Just saying something thus involves a double moral claim: that I am telling you what I think is the truth, and that I am responsible enough to have carefully determined the truth. You can trust me in both ways. When I make use of grammatical signals, therefore, I indicate the intellectual actions that I perform, but I also implicate the two moral dimensions of this act: that I am being honest and that I have been accurate. Williams also observes, at the end of his book, that "in some form or other, they [the virtues of truth] are bound to keep going as long as human beings communicate."[10]

Williams speaks about Sincerity and Accuracy in regard to speech, but the same virtues are present in other symbolic forms, such as depiction. If a painter paints a portrait or a landscape, his "picturing act," like a speech act, again implies two things: that this *is* how he sees the subject, and that he is authoritative enough to have something to say about it; he is reasonably intelligent and has thought sufficiently and carefully enough about this matter to have an artistic "opinion" about it, to bring something of the subject to light. The painter implicitly claims that if the viewer will open his eyes and his mind to this painting, this visual syntactic composition, he will take in what is being said in the painting. He also

---

[8] Ibid., 126: "But when we consider, as we shall in this chapter, the further development of Accuracy that consists in the desire for truth 'for its own sake' – the passion for *getting it right* – then we must remember equally the role of Sincerity in one's dealings with oneself."
[9] Ibid., 251.
[10] Ibid., 268–9.

claims, implicitly, that he, the painter, does have something to say and that he has said it honestly. Even if he is being ironic, he must be honest in his irony.

Williams considers Sincerity and Accuracy to be the two kinds of truthfulness, but we can dig a bit deeper and inquire into the origin of truthfulness, an origin that I have introduced as veracity, the inclination to truth that defines us as human beings and persons.

Human beings are rational animals by nature. We are born to exercise intelligence, and this activity is specific to us; it defines us. Our reason unfolds by nature, spontaneously and from within, even though it needs the help of others to come to itself. It does not have to be artificially forced on us as, for example, the form of a table is imposed on wood. Still, to put it this way runs a risk. We might think of human reason as unfolding in the way the human body grows, as the cells of the body divide, or as the impulse to eat and drink develops on its own. All these things occur without any thinking or willing on our part. They simply come about when the circumstances are appropriate. The early stages of our own cognitive life also evolve without any special moral engagement.

But truthfulness does not occur without the active intervention of other human beings, and it also does not occur without our "wanting" it. There is an intrinsic connection between the flowering of veracity and the presence of human freedom or responsibility. The awakening and growth of truthfulness calls for our personal involvement; in fact, it *is* our personal involvement. Discovering the truth has something morally good about it (this observation does not just say something about truth; it also says something about morality and its relationship to truth). Wanting to be truthful, veracity, is praiseworthy, and not wanting it, or wanting not to be truthful, is blameworthy. The unfolding of our reason is at the heart of our own identity and self, and it is not an automatic emergence. It is more fundamental than any particular assertion or inquiry. Furthermore, besides being at the core of our reports and registrations, it underlies all our practical conduct, whether in *poiēsis* or *praxis*, whether in making or acting. Truthfulness is an issue in the practical order as much as in the more theoretic, and our veracity, our disposition to face the truth, expands into both domains. It expresses itself in the two forms of Sincerity and Accuracy, but it is prior to both.

The orientation toward truth is a natural inclination, but to say only this does not differentiate it sufficiently from other natural impulses, such as those toward nourishment or warmth. Veracity is an inclination that needs to be wanted. In fact, specifically human wanting is constituted precisely by the presence of veracity. The other inclinations that we have are somewhat prehuman; they are made human by their involvement in truthfulness. This inclination to be rational is not an indifferent impulse; it is not geared to either truth or falsity, to either one or the other or to both. It is an inclination toward the truth of things and of ourselves, and as such it is good in a way that underlies more specific forms of ethical goodness. The kind of truth we are talking about, furthermore, is not just the confirmation of propositions. It is not just finding out whether this or that statement is indeed true. Rather, it is the establishment of any and all statements in the first place, that is, it is the articulation of things in their presentation. It includes the disclosure of things. Letting things come to light is more original as a form of truth than is the verification of a given proposition. Things come to light paradigmatically in verbal articulation, as we think in the medium of words, but they also come to light in imaging and music, as well as in the fabrication of things and in human moral conduct. For example, when a person gives something to eat to someone who is hungry, he not only performs a good deed but also reveals something about the world; he discloses something of what food can be, something that might not show up when we just consume some food or just speak about food.[11]

Reason as Autonomous but Not Automatic

The use of the word *reason* in the phrase "the development of reason" might make us think that our cognition will gradually "find things out" rather automatically, as a machine might gather data about the wind and weather. The use of the words *truthfulness* and *veracity* makes it easier to see that there is something moral, something engaging our responsibility, in this development. It is not the case that our reason gathers in various truths in an impersonal manner, and that our responsibility starts up only after such acquisitions have taken place. It is not the case that our freedom comes into play only after our reason has lined up various alternatives for us to consider. The very disclosure of things, the initial manifestation that makes the options available, depends on our responsiveness to the way things are: am I willing to let things appear, or do I force them into showing up as I wish? Would I be willing to forgo the truth of things? What kind of agent of truth am I?

Our responsiveness to the truth of things lies deeper than any specific choices that we make. It opens up the possibility of deliberation and choice. This veracity, with all the forms of responsibility that are associated with it, does not emerge automatically; it is not the product of evolution. Our way of being is different from that of nature, and our appearance within nature cannot be accounted for simply in terms of a natural

---

[11] On the levels of significance and hence of truth in food, see Leon R. Kass, *The Hungry Soul: Eating and the Perfecting of Our Nature* (Chicago: University of Chicago Press, 1999). Kass shows that there is a biological truth to food, a truth of human "dining" that must be distinguished from mere feeding, and also a religious truth in eating.

process. Robert Spaemann uses the metaphor of "awakening" to describe how truthfulness arises; we are free because we are awakened to reason, and yet we ourselves bear responsibility for this awakening. This manifestation of rationality is not something we carry out as a particular deed: "The original awakening can in no way be taken as the subject's own achievement. It is, rather, constitutive for personhood."[12] He speaks of "awakening to reason" (*Erwachen zur Vernunft*) and "awakening to reality" (*Erwachen zur Wirklichkeit*), which I would consider two correlated ways of expressing veracity.[13]

Some people are particularly powerful agents and datives of manifestation. Because of what they have disclosed, they make it possible for others, even for vast multitudes, to be more rational and to live more thoughtful lives. Their declaratives carry more weight than those of most people. Homer, Dante, and Shakespeare, to say nothing of Plato and Aristotle, were much more able than most people to bring things to light. They did not just determine whether certain claims were or were not true; rather, they manifested certain things that had been either concealed or obscure. To do so, they must have been not just excellent stylists of language but thinkers; that is, they excelled in veracity. Their ability was not something they contrived; their veracity was a gift, and there is something almost shamanistic about it, but it was also something that they "wanted" to have, something they appropriated or made their own, since it would not have been there at all had they not made it theirs. It did not occur automatically in them, nor was it an external gift that they could have given away to someone else. It was not the result of a method that they could teach. The reverence many people have for scientists is an acknowledgment of the goodness of truth; scientists are often considered to be better than most people because in their very profession they are supposed to serve and cultivate truthfulness. Their value is not just utilitarian but also exemplary. They are esteemed not just because they help cure diseases and make life easier, but also because they are dedicated to displaying the way the world is, and in being so dedicated they also show, by implication, what human beings are and what they should be, agents of truth.

People who fail in their exercise of veracity, on the other hand, are disordered not just in regard to one or another passion, but in regard to what makes them human. In fact, other vices and weaknesses, such as intemperance and cowardice, are also failures in veracity. A tyrant is a more comprehensive failure, and, as Plato shows, his worst crime is that

---

[12] Robert Spaemann, *Glück und Wohlwollen: Versuch über Ethik* (Stuttgart: Klett-Cotta, 1998), 189.

[13] Ibid., 125, 129–30, 138, 141. On p. 116, he defines human reason: "Consciousness is life that has come to itself. But reason (*Vernunft*) is nothing other than fully awakened consciousness."

he turns his own fantasies into a public nightmare.[14] It is this corruption of veracity that makes the tyrant into what Richard Hassing has said is probably the greatest malady in humankind.[15] Certainly, the most demoralizing aspect of living under regimes like that of the former Soviet Union is the unremitting, comprehensive falsehood one must continually endure. As George Orwell has shown, modern tyranny is complete only when the subjects are willing to disavow their own exercise of truthfulness, and to say that the four fingers being held up in front of them are not necessarily four, but that they could be three, or five, or four, or even all of these at once, depending on what the Party says they are. As the tyrannical O'Brien says to Winston in *1984*, "The thought is all we care about," and, "When finally you surrender to us, it must be of your own free will."[16]

Veracity is a disposition we are born with. It remains to be actualized. It is activated, with the help of others, when we articulate things, that is, when we compose things syntactically into manifestation. The grammar of our speech signals these activations of our truthfulness, and our declaratives confirm and appropriate them.

---

[14] Plato, *Republic* IX, 574e–575a, 576b–e. Aristotle says that the tyrant loves the flatterer, not the truthful advisor: *Politics*, V 11, 1313b39–1314a1.

[15] The remark was made by Richard Hassing in a lecture entitled "The Question of Self-Reference in *Nicomachean Ethics VI*." He cites Thomas Aquinas: "Just as it is a most excellent thing (*optimum est*) for someone to use power well in ruling over many, so also it is most evil (*pessimum*) if he uses it badly." *Summa theologiae* I II, q. 2, a. 4, ad 2. The lecture was given at the Catholic University of America on December 5, 2003.

[16] George Orwell, *1984* (New York: Signet Classics, 1961), 209–10.

PART II

THE CONTENT OF THINKING

7

The Content of What Is Said

Essentials and Accidentals

We have been discussing the activity of human reason and hence of the human person, and most of what we have been saying has been related to the syntactical parts of speech. We have used the syntax of speech as a window through which we can get a philosophical look into the human person. The formal aspects of language elevate the voicing of pleasure and pain and the "speech" of protolanguage into human speech, and thus mark the presence of reason. But the formal aspects of language, obviously, do not subsist on their own; they are *only* formal. They are always set off against the content of speech; the syntax of language is played off against its semantics, just as consonants are played off against vowels. We now turn, therefore, to the material that is shaped by syntax, to the content encased by form. We turn to what is expressed, not by grammar, but by the rest of speech, by its nongrammatical dimensions or what we might call its lexicon: not by terms like *and* and *therefore* and *is*, but by terms like *tree* and *automobile, leopard* and *horse*.

Human reason works in this domain as well; it carries out differentiations within the content of what is said. It is not the case that reason's only work is to impose syntactic structures on undifferentiated, monochromatic contents or simple ideas. The differences that are introduced into the contents, however, can be activated only because we have entered into the domain of syntax. Formal syntax enables us to make explicit distinctions between and within the kinds of things.

The Object's Intelligibility Appears, but It Needs Syntax to Be Presented

Suppose Henry and Jane are standing before a tree, and Henry says to Jane, "This oak tree is very old." The tree, as it turns out, has been there, in the yard behind their house, for over a century. When Henry does this, he has not just turned Jane's attention to the tree, as a vervet monkey might turn the attention of his fellow creatures to a snake that has entered their environment. If this were all that Henry wanted to do, he would have just said, "Look," or he would have pointed, or simply uttered a cry. All such gestures would have been signals or demonstratives, not expressions, and Jane would have been left to her own resources to deal with the tree. Henry does turn Jane's attention to the tree ("This oak tree . . ."), but he does so in order to prepare the tree for a predication that he is going to specify, and he accomplishes it by finishing the sentence (". . . is very old"). When Jane hears the first part of the sentence, she does not simply react to the oak tree, as the monkey might react to a snake; she just waits to hear what Henry has to say about it. She begins the articulation and waits for it to be finished.

When something like this happens, it is not just the *tree* that shows up, but also the *intelligibility* of the tree. The minds of both Henry and Jane, not just their sensibilities, are responding to the tree. The tree shows up to the monkey, but the intelligibility of the tree shows up to Jane. The tree is being presented and understood in a certain way, as being very old (as well as being an oak). Henry and Jane are not just processing information in their respective brains; they together are displaying the tree; their activity is being guided by the single stream of words that are being pronounced, and what they do is as public as voting in an election. The intelligibility of things shows up in public, not in the silent processing of our brains.

Obviously this particular registration does not exhaust the understand-ability of the thing. The oak tree can be registered in countless more ways, through innumerably more sentences. Any particular registration is only one disclosure, which is always in a context and almost always preceded and followed by other manifestations. It is part of a conversation. All the further registrations bring out more of what is latent in the thing designated when Henry says, "this oak tree." Once the tree is named, it becomes a reservoir of appearances that can be captured in further articulation.

But all these disclosures could be accomplished only within syntactic frames and their corresponding syntactic actions. It is only because the tree has become enfolded and unfolded in syntax that its intelligibility comes to light, that what it is becomes manifest, and that such a multitude of articulations becomes possible. The tree should be grateful to the power of syntax, because without syntax it would not have been enabled to show itself for what it is; without syntax it could not have become poetically or theoretically displayed; it would have continued to sleep in obscurity. It would not have come to light. Of course, without the presence of human beings and the syntax they introduce, the tree could still have been dis-played, say, to the wolves that prowl around it and the squirrels that climb its branches, but these creatures do not let the intelligibility of the tree come forward. They let the tree come forward, but not its intelligibility. Only the magic wand of speech lets that happen, and only the agent of disclosure can wave the wand.

The tree shows up to the rational creature, to man, in more ways than in speech: the forester and the farmer know the tree in ways that they might not be able to express in words. The lumberjack will have a lot of "know-how" about the tree that he could communicate to someone else only by training, not necessarily by speech. Such nonverbal acquaintance with the tree does bring out something of what the tree is; it will bring out some essentials that never reach the stage of verbal expression. But still, these other forms of acquaintance participate in intelligence only if they too acquire a kind of practical syntax, an ability to do *this* in view of *that* (or this instead of that), a sense that this procedure is related to that one, and such practical embedding can be achieved only by participation in the paradigmatic use of syntax in language. Speech fixes formal structure. It is only because the agent has entered into linguistic syntax that his other practices can become syntactic as well. Without linguistic syntax as the exemplar, the other forms of conduct remain mere routines, the practical analogue of protolanguage; they may show proto-intelligence, but they do not rise to the level of thoughtful action. Language is the primary place for syntax and the disclosures it makes possible. Other rational activities are analogous to speech. Speech, *logos*, is the eponymous use of reason.

Essentials and Accidentals Come into Play

Once an object is captured into syntactic form, countless other syntactic possibilities arise. Many more things can be said about the object; the thing can be manifested or grasped in many other guises. But besides this expansion into more and more syntactic articulation, something else also happens: when the object is elevated into syntax, a distinction starts to appear between what is essential to the thing and what is merely accidental. A distinction arises between what the thing is in itself (the *very* tree), and what it just happens to be but might not be (even while remaining itself). The two consequences, furthermore, are interrelated. It is only in the multiplicity of articulations that the essentials and the accidentals come to be sorted out. It is not the case that the essentials of a thing are given to us as single, discrete manifestations, all by themselves, and that the accidentals come only afterward, just tagging along. We do not have independent views of essentials; we do not extract them, like some sort of template, from things. Rather, the essentials of a thing are given to us only in and through a multiplicity of syntactic assertions and activities and only in contrast with the accidentals. As Anthony Burgess has one of his characters say, "Don't try and ... enter a world of visions and no syntax."[1]

---

[1] Anthony Burgess, *Enderby Outside*, in *The Complete Enderby* (New York: Carroll and Graf, 1996), 369.

How does this disclosure of the essential come about? We must approach the problem in an oblique manner. As philosophers, we cannot speak simply and directly about essentials. We are not the primary recipients of the essentials of things. To work out the difference between essentials and accidentals philosophically, we must expand our attention and consider not only the thing being disclosed but also the people who are speaking about the thing.[2] To use a term from Husserl, we must examine the noetic-noematic correlation; but while Husserl considers this topic primarily in regard to a single consciousness and its objects, we will work with people conversing about things.[3]

Suppose a topic is introduced and people discuss it. They go on saying more and more about it. Gradually or suddenly, the people involved in the conversation come to recognize a difference between those who know what they are talking about, who know what the thing truly is and what belongs to it in itself, and those who seem to wander all over the place, who show by what they say (and by what they do) that they are confusing the thing with something else, or that they are confusing what the thing necessarily is with what it just happens to be. The first group of speakers have grasped the essentials of the thing, but the second have not. It is not even necessary that the speakers in the first group be able to define the thing in question; their very ability to speak insightfully about it as they go on talking shows that the essentials of the thing have appeared to them. It shows that the essentials are there bubbling beneath the surface of what they say. Something has happened to them that hasn't happened to the others.

But what has happened to them? What is it that appears to those who speak with authority about a topic, but remains concealed from those who speak nebulously about it? In the one case, the specific intelligibility of the thing has shown up to the speakers; in the other case it has not. How does this occur? What has happened in the first instance, and what is missing in the second?

I think it is insufficient to say that the form of the thing in question has been received in the minds of the speakers who seem to know what they are talking about, and that the thing now exists cognitively in their minds as well as entitatively in the world.[4] The appeal to a cognitive existence of

---

[2] Plato, as a philosopher, does this as well. He considers not just the forms of things but also the people who know the forms, whether implicitly or explicitly. Socrates talks with people who have opinions about things and who grasp some of the essentials but usually not enough of them, and Plato in turn writes about both Socrates and these people. It is not the case that essentials show up only to Socrates or only to Plato.

[3] On the correlation between object and subject as the theme of philosophy, see Edmund Husserl, *The Crisis of European Sciences and Transcendental Phenomenology*, trans. David Carr (Evanston, IL: Northwestern University Press, 1970), §§46–50.

[4] The doctrine that the knower becomes identified with what is known, that things can enjoy both a real and a cognitional existence, and that such identity and existence are brought about by the thing's form being received immaterially in the knower, is a central theme in

things is more a restatement of the problem than a clarification of it. I believe that this explanation short-circuits the problem and puts our philosophical minds at ease when they should continue to search for greater resolution. It seems to be an answer, but in fact the words used in it are so tailor-made for this problem that they merely reformulate it. What this solution says is simply that the essentials of the thing become present to the mind of the knower because the form of the thing begins to be present, cognitively, in the knower. I think that this explanation does not say enough, and I wish to offer an alternative philosophical description.

When Henry says, "This oak tree is very old," the essentials of both "tree" and "old" are functioning in his speech, and if Jane is up to the issue at hand, the essences are functioning for her also, as she responds and speaks about the topic herself. All the various things Henry and Jane say and all the actions they carry out make sense and cohere with one another because they know what they are talking about. But suppose Jane were to say, "I can tell it's very old; look how wrinkled it is." Her remark would show that she does not grasp the essentials of the tree; being wrinkled does not signify old age in trees, as it does in human beings. Henry would start to wonder how much else of what he's said has been in vain.

People make irrelevant statements, and it is hard to know how to respond to them. "Knowing what we are talking about" does not just require that we be informed about a lot of facts; the essentials latent in those facts must have been registered with us as well, and whether or not they have been registered shows up as we go on talking about the thing. There are times when we go on to formulate the essence in itself, that is, when we attempt to formulate a definition and say explicitly what the thing is, but this achievement comes only after we have grasped the essentials in the multitude of manifestations we have brought about concerning the thing in question. The definition does not come first; it involves a further reflection on what we have experienced and what we have come to know.

Aristotelian and Scholastic metaphysics of knowledge. The doctrine is true, but it is not an *explanation* of knowledge; it is, rather, an expression of it, and it should more clearly be presented as such. For example, Joseph Owens writes: "The twofold existence – real and cognitional – that a sensible thing can have *explains* how the same thing exists in the real world outside cognition and is simultaneously present within one's awareness through thoroughgoing cognitional identity with the percipient or knower [my italics]." *Cognition: An Epistemological Inquiry* (Houston, TX: Center for Thomistic Studies, 1992), 39–40. In another passage he says, "You may speak technically and say that the form received has made you be cognitionally the distant object itself" (p. 200). I certainly agree that a thing can exist both as itself and as known, but I do not think that this possibility *explains* how the thing is identifiable in both modes. The statement just says that such dualities occur, just as one might observe that things can both be themselves and be pictured. We are philosophically enlightened when we formulate such truths about beings, pictures, and knowers, but we have not thereby explained how knowledge or picturing occur. We simply have a deeper appreciation of what it is.

The Accidental Mind

Let us illustrate the difference between knowing and not knowing what a thing is. Consider the way "being a professor" shows up to the facile and perhaps to the popular mind. (We limit ourselves to the male professor.) Some decades ago it would have involved being clothed in a tweed jacket with elbow patches, smoking a pipe, wearing horned-rimmed glasses, standing at a lectern, and being loquacious, with much hemming and hawing. For a while afterward it would have involved wearing jeans and an open-collar shirt, definitely not smoking, and excitedly trying to raise people's consciousness. All these features are obviously peripheral or accidental to being a professor, but many people take them to be properties, not accidents; movies and television dramas often make such presentations. The essence of being a professor – knowing a particular field and helping others acquire such knowledge and understanding – does not lie behind such manifestations; only the accidentals are presented. The predicates are merely piled on, and there is no depth to what is said. Similar confusion about essentials can occur in regard to being a soldier, being an artist, being a lawyer, and being a father or mother, as well as about being a living thing, being an economic transaction, and being a political society. In some television sitcoms, for example, physicians are identifiable only because they wear white coats and utter quasi-medical words. Nothing substantial is disclosed about them specifically as physicians; they are involved in emotional exchanges and actions that could be related about anyone at all.[5]

People lost in accidentality are not simply ignorant of the thing in question. Sheer ignorance is not a problem; when we are just ignorant of an issue that is raised, we know that we do not know. What is dangerous and misleading is the unselfconscious confusion of accidentals with essentials. Confused persons don't know that they don't know, but they use the names and the words associated with the things they are talking about, and so they seem to know or at least think they know what the things are. Mixing essentials with accidentals leads to more than just embarrassment in speech; it can be lethal in life. Consider its effects, for example, when people are being recruited into a particular career or community, getting married, or joining a political cause; they might be attracted by peripherals that will eventually, but inevitably, disappear from the involvement itself. No one knows the full sense of things one enters into, but one must have at least a glimpse of what is essential if the engagement is to succeed.

[5] The phenomenon has been noticed by others. See Richard Webb's review of the movie *Sunshine*, in *Nature* 446 (April 5, 2007), 615: "Science is handled pleasingly well in *Sunshine*. Scientific vocabulary is not flung about with the gay, context-free abandon that is traditional in such circumstances... . The gratifying (if somewhat surprising) result is a scientist on the silver screen who seems manifestly sane."

The distinction between the essential and the accidental does not show up in the syntax of our speech. It belongs to the content of what we say and not to its form. Things would be so much easier if this distinction could somehow be made visible in our grammatical form, because then we could hand it on to others. We could signal that something is essential or relevant and not merely peripheral. But, alas, the distinction cannot be so easily conveyed; the essential and the accidental cannot be tagged by a part of the syntax. Each of us has to "get the point" on his own, and we can do so only on the basis of our own experience and insight, which no one can supply for us. If someone were to *tell* us that this or that point is essential, we might *believe* that it is so, but we would still not understand it as such. The essential would not show up to us as essential, and we would not be reliable in our further dealings with the thing in question.

The essentials of things are not expressed in the syntax of speech, but the manifestation of essentials can happen only when syntax comes into play. Even the failure to grasp the essentials, the failure exhibited by the person who can't speak clearly about the thing in question, could not happen without syntax. Only because such a person has entered into the game of syntactic apprehension can he make a fool of himself and confuse the accidental and superficial with the essential. You have to be playing the game in order to be able to lose it.

We do not have a choice about this distinction; we could not say, "Well, you may want to distinguish between essentials and accidentals, but I'm not going to do so. I don't want to get into that way of speaking. It's not my way of doing things." If we tried to avoid entangling ourselves in the essentials of things, we would no longer be speaking as human agents and no one would take us seriously. Such a speaker would be no more than a chatterbox. The activation of mind that we call speaking brings this distinction with it, and it does so ineluctably.

In fact, there is something incoherent about a statement like "I choose not to distinguish between essentials and accidentals." This is not the kind of thing that is subject to our choice. We don't *decide* to be blinded in this way; having or not having the ability to distinguish between essentials and accidentals occurs prior to our choices and makes them possible. We are chatterboxes not by choice but more by our individual nature. There may be a kind of wanting that is involved in this distinction, but it is more elementary than choice. It is a failure in veracity.

The distinction between essentials and accidentals is manifested first to intelligent people, not specifically to philosophers. Philosophers come later and reflect on how the difference arises. They can clarify the difference and contemplate it, but they must first trust the insight of thoughtful people, who let the substance of things show up in contrast with the coincidentals. Without the prior phenomenon of sound opinion, philosophy would not have anything on which to reflect. As Husserl puts it, the "natural attitude" precedes the "phenomenological attitude" and provides it with its field of inquiry.

Properties and Essence

We need to refine our discussion of what occurs when we distinguish essentials from accidentals. The essentials must be subdivided into two parts: the properties of a thing and what the thing is (its essence, what it is for the thing to be). People who are able to discriminate the essentials of a thing or a situation know some of the properties of the thing, and they also know something of its essence or definition. Our term *the essentials*, therefore, encompasses two forms, *properties* and *essence*. For clarity, and because spatial display helps us to take things in, we could diagram these points in the following way. At first we distinguish between essentials and accidentals:

Accidentals
Essentials

Then we subdivide the essentials into properties and essence:

Accidentals	
Essentials=	Properties
	Essence, what the thing is

And all these things – the accidentals, the properties, and the essence – come to light in and through syntactic form. They do not present themselves except through compositions.

The distinction between properties and essence introduces what we could call a third dimension, depth, into the manifestation of a thing. The essence and its parts are not just additional properties. Imagine the accidents and the properties as mapped onto a two-dimensional surface; the essence or substance would then be placed into a third dimension, one that underlies the other two. The essence of things stands "beneath" or "behind" the properties and accidents, and the properties "flow from" it. The words *beneath, behind,* and *flow from* are normally used in a spatial sense, but they are now being used metaphorically to express a logical and ontological relationship. We have to open up a new, third dimension because the essence is the root of the properties and explains them; it is not just annexed to them as yet another property.

For example, being able to laugh or smile is a property of human beings as rational animals. As John Milton puts it, "For smiles from reason flow, / to brute deny'd."[6] If being able to smile is a property of human

---

[6] John Milton, *Paradise Lost*, Book IX, lines 239–40.

beings, it is because human beings are rational entities. We explain their power to smile by their rationality; we do not explain their rationality by their power to smile. We cannot, however, explain why they are rational; that is simply what they are, and it would be pointless to look for an explanation. We can't ask why human beings are rational animals, but we can ask why they can smile. Properties can be explained, but essences are simply understood. Rationality makes human beings what they are, and it explains why they can smile and why they have their other properties, such as being able to speak and to engage in political life.

We can smile because we are rational animals. What kind of *because* is this? How does our essence or definition explain our properties?

We do not enjoy direct access to the essence of a thing. The essence, what the thing is, is presented not by itself but only in and through the properties that flow from it. It would be wrong to say, however, that we *first* collect a lot of properties and only *subsequently* infer that they flow from an essence. Properties and essence come together. We would not know that certain phenomena are properties unless we also had an inkling of the essence of the thing and had begun to take the thing as one, as an instance of a kind. Certain activities and features become known as proper, as somehow per se and not just as accidental, concomitantly with their being taken as the properties of a thing that has a nature. The essence of a thing does not show up as one of the properties, but we get a hint of it as soon as we start to appreciate certain phenomena as properties and not just as accidental conjunctions. The grasp of essentials is thus a split achievement, a contact with both properties and essence, and it is played off against the awareness of the accidental.

This concomitant manifestation of both properties and essence is best illustrated by cases in which an intelligibility dawns on us. Suppose you work with a group of people, and you find various events taking place among them. Suddenly you begin to suspect that something is going on; there have been too many striking "coincidences," too many things have shaped up in odd ways. Strange things have happened. You begin to suspect that a plan is being executed. This "chance" meeting, that "random" remark, this unexpected proposal – all these things show, let us say, that your coworkers are trying to get this friend of theirs hired as manager. The events are not coincidental after all; rather, they are properties, and properties of a thing, a thing of a certain kind, which in this case is a bureaucratic maneuver. The events, which first seemed to be a mere congeries of accidentals, are gradually or suddenly interpreted as properties, and concomitantly the thing, something unitary, begins to show up for what it is. Something one, a something, is going on; it is being presented and consolidated here and now.[7] This is how essences are

---

[7] On the conjunction between being and one (between "something" and "something one"), see Aristotle, *Metaphysics*, IV 2, 1003b22–1005a18.

manifested to us, as the root and entity, the substance or *ousia*, within and behind what we concomitantly recognize as properties. We "see" the essence or nature only through the properties, but we do not see it as a property.

Of course, we can also turn toward the thing itself and give it a name – a maneuver, a power play – and we can go on to speak about the thing itself and perhaps try to spell out its definition. We can target its intelligibility. But this thing, in its essence, is not originally and directly given by itself; it can be given only within its properties, its per se attributes.

In other words: once we start to distinguish essentials from coincidentals, once we start to distinguish between properties and accidentals, we also begin to identify a "one" or an "entity" behind the properties as that from which they flow. We might be wrong, of course; we might be paranoid or hasty in seeing a pattern of properties; there may, in fact, be nothing behind the "properties" we thought we were perceiving; they may, in fact, not be properties at all. They might be only accidental, just a heap of coincidences with nothing behind or beneath them as their substance. But when we are wrong in this way, we err specifically in respect to the kind of intellectual performance in which one discovers properties and simultaneously gets a hint of an essence that can be named. This formal structure is at work whenever we use a word with content, that is, whenever we engage our vocabulary. All this could happen only within the domain of syntax, to a being that enjoyed the power to constitute syntax and predication: an agent of truth, a rational animal, a human person.

The Importance of the Shape of Things

Our discussion of properties will become more focused if we turn our attention to a particularly important property, the shape of a thing.[8] A thing's shape is the most significant indication of what the thing is; it is the shape that first and foremost tells us that we are dealing with, say, an elephant or a tree, a man or a giraffe, a car or a leopard. By shape I mean not only the spatial configuration of parts, the static silhouette, so to speak, but also the size of the thing, and I also include the thing in motion, in which the shape is dynamic and not rigid: the thing moves in a certain way. The discussion of shape means that we are considering individual material things, which are the paradigms of things, and not such less tangible entities as a bureaucratic maneuver or a vote in an election. Even when we deal with intangible things, however, we may try to give them a shape by using a diagram or an image, which bodies forth or figures out the thing we are trying to understand.

---

[8] I am grateful to Kevin White for bringing to my mind the philosophical importance of the shape of things.

The shape of a material substance is a property of it, but it is not just one property among many. It is the property that establishes the space where all the other properties will occur; they all "take their place" within the shape of the thing. But the shape of the thing is still not the substance of the thing. As a property it points to something more elementary than itself; it points to the thing in its kind, in its essence or nature. To be able to distinguish the shape of the thing from the thing, to see the shape as a property, is an enormous intellectual accomplishment. We could even say that it is the birth of intelligence, because it is correlated with the manifestation of the intelligible. Certainly, children and animals already recognize things by virtue of their shapes, both their generic shapes and their individualized forms, but to see the shape of a thing as a property and hence as derivative is to become able to identify the thing in itself, the thing as it offers itself to intellectual definition and recognition, which is the thing as a referent of discourse and a subject of predication, the thing "behind" the shape. The shape of a thing is very basic to it, but it is not ultimate; the thing itself is more ultimate than the shape, and if we come to see the shape as only a property, we come to appreciate what the thing is in itself, what it can be defined as being.

As a property, the shape of a thing is "caused" by what the thing is. This is most clearly seen in living things, but it is not exclusive to them. A living thing shapes itself because of the kind of thing it is: a giraffe gives itself a long neck, a spider develops eight legs, and a man forms a face, hands, and opposable thumbs. The shape of a thing is not imposed on it from outside; it is generated by the thing itself. The thing itself grows into its own form.[9] In this respect, a natural substance differs from an artifact. An artifact is shaped by things that are aggregated into it from outside – the automobile's metal, rubber, plastic, and fabrics are brought together and assembled into the thing, and even a bird's nest is put together from outside – but a living thing spreads and shapes itself from within. It takes raw materials into itself and generates its own parts and configuration. Even nonliving natural things shape themselves. Crystals, for example, are not planned and arranged by anything outside themselves, but compose themselves into the patterns they show forth to the chemist and physicist, as well as to the person who admires a diamond or a ruby.

The shape of a natural thing, therefore, "flows" from the thing itself, but in a more fundamental way than do the thing's other properties, such

---

[9] On living things as bringing about their own matter, see Robert Sokolowski, "Soul and the Transcendence of the Human Person," in *Christian Faith and Human Understanding: Studies in the Eucharist, Trinity, and the Human Person* (Washington, DC: Catholic University of America Press, 2006), 155–7. On the way natural forces and mathematical laws combine in biological shapes, see the classic work by D'Arcy Wentworth Thompson, *On Growth and Form* (New York: Dover, 1992).

as its color, which needs the shape for the surface that it fills, or its activities, such as stalking or speaking, which are carried on by the formed entity and could not occur without the bodily shape. It is true that many properties and their activations go beyond the bodily envelope of the entity (hunting prey is not just the animal in motion, but relates to the prey itself and the environment, and speaking is speaking to someone), but such actions are still centered in the shape of the thing. The shape, therefore, is fundamental to the entity and the activity of the thing, and it is also fundamental to the thing's disclosure: it is the first property that is shown. We recognize what a thing is first and foremost by its shape.

But we have to see the shape as *only* the shape of the thing. It is only a property and not what the thing is in itself. The shape is not ultimate but derivative. There is something beyond the shape, and this something is not another shape: it is the thing in its whatness, that which Aristotle would call the entity or substance. We could, with Jacob Klein, call it the look of the thing, but it is the "look" that is "seen" not by vision but by the mind.[10] It is hard for us to think about this principle or origin, because, led by our imagination, we tend to posit it as yet another shape, albeit a ghostly one. Even the classical names for it, *forma, species, morphē*, and *eidos*, suggest that it is like a shape. But it is an identity of another sort, one that is the target of the names that we use when we speak of it: it is the leopard, the tree, the man, or the automobile, and all these things are not their respective shapes but that of which the shape is the property. It is the thing or substance itself, taken as a whole. The thing's shape can also seem to be the whole of the thing, but in fact it is only a part.

The shape is not static. It is continuously active, both as it establishes itself in the growth of the thing and as it shifts in the movements of the thing: the animal modifies its shape in one way as it grows and in another way as it runs. In being continuously activated, the shape is different from other properties, which are not always brought to actualization. A human being always maintains the human shape, adjusted to the circumstances, but he does not always smile, speak, carry on political activity, or fabricate things. Even when the other properties are only latent, however, even when they are in repose, they find their home within the shape of the thing. But the shape is not their origin; we have to see the shape as

---

[10] See Jacob Klein, "About Plato's *Philebus*," in *Lectures and Essays*, ed. Robert B. Williamson and Elliott Zuckerman (Annapolis, MD: St. John's College Press, 1985), 315: "But when we consider intelligibles, the *eidē* of things, the 'invisible looks,' which can be encountered only in speech (*en logōi*), and each one of which is one and unique, the 'one and many' problem becomes extremely perplexing." See also "Speech, Its Strength and Its Weaknesses," ibid., 371, as well as *Plato's Trilogy* (Chicago: University of Chicago Press, 1977), 45–55, 69. Klein says that Plato examines how the various "looks" are linked with one another in an arithmetic structure. I would like to consider my appeal to syntax as another attempt to develop this ancient Platonic and Aristotelian theme.

penultimate, not ultimate. The activities come not from the shape but from the thing as a whole, even though they reside in the space marked out by the shape.

Properties as Potential and Manifold within the Shape of a Thing

The involvement of the shape of a thing makes it easier for us to speak about all the other properties a thing has, and especially to discuss in what sense the properties are powers or potentialities and how they become actualized. When we are acquainted with a thing, we do not just recognize the features it presents at any given moment; it is equally important that we know what *else* the thing is capable of and how else it can appear. When we recognize a leopard, we do not know merely its shape and its spots; we know that it will run after prey and that it will digest the food that it eats, even though it may not be doing these things when we perceive it. The powers or potentialities are paramount in the thing and in our thinking about it. Recognizing what the thing is, is precisely the formulation of a definition that gives the root for all of these powers, potential and actualized, known and unknown. But the shape plays a strategic role here: the shape is that crucial property that is always activated to some degree, the power that is never just a potentiality but always somewhat actualized. Material things are never without some shape, which provides the haven where all the other powers can reside ("spirits" are so spooky because they seem to have the powers without the shape). Still, as basic as it may be, the shape *is not* the thing, nor is it the root of the other properties the thing has; the shape is only one property of the thing.

When we name things – when Henry says to Jane, "This oak tree … " – we name them on the basis of the thing's shape, but we do not name the shape; we name the tree that is "behind" and "within" the shape; we name the substance or the entity of the thing, that from which the shape flows, and the predicates that we distinguish are said of the thing, not of its shape, even though they are found within the thing's shape. Language introduces this distinction between the shape of the thing and the thing. The property that is foremost in allowing us to name things is the shape; all the other properties, such as the ability to grow, to sprout leaves, and to absorb nutrients, to do all the things that trees do, reside within the shape but flow from the nature of the tree, from what it is. The name that we use, *oak tree*, names this nature, even though we have no direct access to it apart from the properties that flow from it.

Moreover, when we do name the tree, we may have registered a few of its properties, but there will always be others that we have not yet become acquainted with. No inventory of properties of any thing can be exhaustive; there will always be more to learn about the thing in itself, more essentials to register and accidentals to notice. The thing always retains a potential of disclosure, and hence the thing always remains somewhat mysterious and unknown. To know fully the essence of a thing, we would have to be able to predict everything the thing could be, in all the contexts into which it might be placed; how could we ever acquire such a wholesale grasp of what the thing is? To name a thing is to begin an adventure in manifestation, not to conclude it; to think that the properties that now give us access to the thing is all that the thing can be is to close our minds to everything else the thing can disclose. And yet we do grasp the properties of things, and we do know something of their essentials. Any property at all is sufficient to give us a glimpse of the essence itself, the thing as what it is, and the discovery of new properties does not cancel the ones that were known before. Such a registration of a property, any property, is sufficient to pin down the thing as an object of reference and a thing named and somewhat defined, and in the case of material objects it is the shape that serves as the preeminent property that permits such identification.

The Move into Geometric Abstraction

Once we are able to see the shape of the thing as merely a property, we become able to see the thing as being an individual of a certain kind or species. The "definition" of the thing in terms of its essence becomes an issue for us; the thing is now recognized as being there as an entity "behind" the shape in the special sense of the preposition or adverb *behind*, the sense the term has when it is used to speak of the way in which a thing is behind or beneath its properties and accidents. Consider how perplexing this sense of the word *behind* is, or, for that matter, this sense of the word *beneath*.[11] It is a "logical" and not a spatial sense, but it is very easy to take the word in its more normal spatial sense, and when we take it this way, we are inevitably led to imagine the thing as yet another shape behind or beneath this spatial shape; this new, deeper shape would be the form of being, say, an elephant or a tree. But the entity, the *ousia* of the elephant or the tree, is not another shape; it is simply that of which the shape is a property, and that from which the shape and the other properties flow.

Only when the thing is distinguished from its shape can the *substantial* "shape," the form or the *eidos*, become differentiated from the spatial form that the thing enjoys, its spatial shape. Only when this distinction comes into play is there something there that has an essence and a definition. Seeing the shape as a property and not as the thing itself is a crucial step in knowing what the objective correlatives of our judgments

---

[11] In linguistic development, prepositions tend first to have a spatial meaning, then a temporal one, and finally a causative sense, and subsequently they take on a logical and then a philosophical sense. See Robert Sokolowski, *Presence and Absence: A Philosophical Investigation of Language and Being* (Bloomington: Indiana University Press, 1978), 122–8.

are, because the subjects of our judgments are things in their substance and not their shapes.

The shape is not ultimate. It is possible for us, however, to carry out an important intellectual move in which we begin to focus on the shape itself, apart from the entity of which it is the shape. When we do this, we begin to take things geometrically and not predicationally. Shapes alone become our concern, and we become fascinated by what can be done with them (not what *we* can do with them, as though it were just a matter of our subjective capabilities, but what can be done with them, the possibilities that they have in themselves and that they lend to us). Shapes can be reconfigured into other kinds of shapes; they can be compared to one another; and we can discover the rules by which these procedures are done. Some parts of a given shape can be mathematically related to other parts. A world of shapes can be constituted. This world can become infinitely complex and interesting, and what we discover can be used to our great advantage. The correlations (equations) that can be determined in it are endless. But the very fascination of this world brings with it a temptation, since we can forget that the shapes we are investigating are only properties. We can begin to take them as the things themselves.

Husserl claims that such a transformation occurred at the birth of modern science. We began to focus on shapes (*Gestalten*), and we projected them into idealized geometric shapes (*Limesgestalten*). This procedure gave us a heightened power of identification and precision, and we began to interpret the lived world (*Lebenswelt*) in terms of the "garb of ideas" (*Ideenkleid*) that we tried to clothe it with. Nature became idealized and much more subject to our technological exploitation.[12] It acquired that extreme precision that it must have if it is to serve us well; as Harvey C. Mansfield observes, "For human purposes nature needs to be supplied with more exactness than it has by itself."[13] Material things were not definable entities any longer but became, in Descartes' term, *res extensae*.[14]

If the world of shapes becomes the "bottom line" for us, and if we no longer see shapes as properties of things, we lose the world of things as

---

[12] The scientific "geometrization" and "mathematization" of the world has been described by Edmund Husserl in *The Crisis of European Sciences*, §9; for the German terms mentioned in my text, see pp. 26, 29, 51. See also Robert Sokolowski, "Measurement," in his *Pictures, Quotations, and Distinctions: Fourteen Essays in Phenomenology* (Notre Dame, IN: University of Notre Dame Press, 1992), 139–54.

[13] Harvey C. Mansfield, *Manliness* (New Haven, CT: Yale University Press, 2006), 211.

[14] Descartes does not consider the shape of things to be ultimate; it remains a property or an accident, but the only thing beneath it is extension. The shape is not a property of an entity with a definition, but a temporary condition of extended matter. Substances, with their form and definition, no longer come between sheer matter and the properties such as shape, color, and motion, and things no longer have ends apart from the uses to which we put them.

entities that have other properties that flow from them. We also lose the
world of things that have essences. The entity "beneath" the shape is not
there any longer to be the "owner" of the "properties" or the "things
owned" that we articulate in it. Material things no longer show up as
"ones," as beings that have an identity and a definition. The deepest
identity that we now acknowledge is that of shapes, but these shapes
simply move around and into one another. The only real and original
properties that things in the world can still possess are what Locke called
the primary qualities, such as solidity, extension, figure, number, rest,
and motion. The other features, the secondary qualities such as heat,
color, taste, and sound, become ideas in our minds that do not resemble
anything in things.[15] When we go this far, we do not simply abstract the
geometrical aspect of things from the things as wholes; we reduce the
thing to its mathematical aspect, which is now no longer an aspect but
the whole itself.

When this transformation occurs, it is not just the ontological status of
the thing that is changed. The nature of human judgment and the human
mind changes as well. Judgments, which we have described as the most
basic syntactic performance, are no longer the true display of things. We
have taken judging to be the public activity in which a speaker establishes
a reference to an object (he brings, *refert*, the thing into prominence before
himself and his audience) and then says something about it; he publicizes
the thing. But if the thing is not really the entity from which the properties
flow, if the thing is really a patch of extended matter, then the act of
judging becomes displaced as the primary act of manifestation. Judgments
are replaced by equations, and we have measurements but no verdicts. To
take a phrase from David Lachterman, "equations are substituted for
propositions."[16] The only "truly" public mind becomes the geometric or
ultimately the mathematical mind, the mind of the mathematical physicist,
who describes the correlations among the spatial parts of things and the
transformations of their shapes. Pythagoras displaces Aristotle.

If the mathematical analysis of the world is the ultimately true one, then
the other way of describing things becomes merely our subjective
arrangement of our own ideas. Predication and judgment lose their
primacy in the intellectual life; they are said to reflect merely the

---

[15] Husserl, *The Crisis of European Sciences*, 36: "What we experienced, in prescientific life, as
    colors, tones, warmth, and weight belonging to the things themselves ... indicates in
    terms of physics, of course, tone-vibrations, warmth-vibrations, i.e., pure events in the
    world of shapes. This universal indication is taken for granted today as unquestionable."
    See also, p. 37: "Everything which manifests itself as real through the specific sense-
    qualities must have its mathematical index in events belonging to the sphere of shapes
    (*Gestaltsphäre*)."
[16] David Rapport Lachterman, *The Ethics of Geometry: A Genealogy of Modernity* (New York:
    Routledge, 1989), 157.

vocabulary our society has developed or the way we choose to configure our own images and thoughts. The world becomes "carved up" according to our interests and customs, according to the significance we project onto things, and not according to the way things are. This fall into relativism takes place because our focus on the world of shapes and the geometric world has canceled the place of judgment in the life of the mind. Shapes are not relativized, but judgments are. The mind becomes mathematical (at first geometric, at a later stage algebraic) and not predicational. Classical logic is replaced by Frege's logic, and the "laws of nature" replace things and their essences and properties.

The transformation of the world of things into the "true" world of mathematical physics has a long and intricate history, which has been narrated and interpreted by many people.[17] It is a basic element in the establishment of modernity. It has led to the spectacular successes of modern science, but it also lies behind the threats to human self-understanding that modern science, technology, and bureaucracy bring. Because of this transformation, "things" are no longer there, and "we" are no longer there either, not in the way we think we ought to be around, as agents of truth who can judge the way things are. There is no role for declaratives in mathematical equations. The transformation of the world into a mathematical world is not an isolated philosophical issue (no philosophical issue can ever be isolated, since philosophy as such is the inquiry into the widest context of things); it is related to political philosophy and philosophical anthropology, as well as to ethics and logic. The two antagonistic camps in this controversy are the ancients and the moderns, represented by Aristotle and premodern thinkers on the one hand and by figures ranging from Machiavelli to Nietzsche on the other. The philosophical desideratum is not simply to return to Aristotle but to restore the validity of what he describes within the context set by the great transformation brought about by modern thought, and one of the elements in such a restoration is the recovery of the publicness of the mind that executes judgments. Along with this restoration of mind is the rediscovery of things as having essences, properties, and ends, which govern the purposes we set for ourselves.[18] It is not philosophically wrong

---

[17] Besides Husserl's *The Crisis of European Sciences* and Lachterman's *The Ethics of Geometry*, see Jacob Klein, "The World of Physics and the 'Natural' World," in *Lectures and Essays*, 1–34, and *Greek Mathematical Thought and the Origin of Algebra*, trans. Eva Brann (Cambridge, MA: MIT Press, 1968).

[18] On the distinction between human purposes and natural ends, see Francis Slade, "On the Ontological Priority of Ends and Its Relevance to the Narrative Arts," in *Beauty, Art, and the Polis*, ed. Alice Ramos (Washington, DC: Catholic University of America Press, 2000), 58–69, and "Ends and Purposes," in *Final Causality in Nature and Human Affairs*, ed. Richard Hassing (Washington, DC: Catholic University of America Press, 1997), 83–5. I have used the distinction in my essay "What Is Natural Law? Human Purposes and Natural

to focus on the mathematical dimension of things, but it *is* wrong to forget that this dimension is only an aspect of an entity, not the thing itself. Equations remain subordinate to judgments, and the shape of things is their property but not their substance. Let us, then, go back to the kind of world in which there are not just shapes but also entities, which enjoy both properties and a definition.

Ends," in *Christian Faith and Human Understanding,* 214–33, and in a lecture, "Discovery and Obligation in Natural Law," to be published in a volume edited by Holger Zaborowski at the Catholic University of America Press.

8

Properties and Accidents Reveal What Things Are

We turn back to the distinction between accidentals and essentials, and more specifically to the distinctions among accidentals, properties, and essences. We have seen that the essentials of things must be distinguished into their properties and their essences, and both of these must be differentiated from the accidentals that occur to things and are predicated about them. More needs to be said about these three dimensions of speech and the interactions among them.

Step One: Predicating Accidentals

All three of these components – the accidentals, the properties, and the essences – can be predicated of things, but they are predicated of them in different ways. For that reason, they have classically been called the "predicables." Thus, we might say to someone, "Susan was smiling when she entered the room." In this case, we predicate "smiling when she entered the room" *accidentally* of Susan. Susan was smiling at that moment, but she might have been scowling or glaring instead. If we were to say, "But remember: Susan is capable of smiling," we would probably be predicating the power to smile as a *property* of Susan. In the antique terminology, we would be saying that she is risible. (If we were reporting this as a mere fact, however, perhaps as the fact that she can now smile again after having been grieving for a month, the predication would be accidental; we would not be reporting on what she is essentially capable of doing, but on what she is now able to do in these circumstances.) Finally, if we were to say, "Susan, after all, is a rational being," we would be predicating "being rational" as part of what she is and not just as a property that she has. The feature would be declared as part of her *essence* or *definition*. It is not something that she is capable of but something that she is. Predication, therefore, is not univocal. It can occur in any of these three ways.

When we converse with others, most of our statements are of the first kind, accidental predications. The predication of accidentals is informative because the accidental does not necessarily "go with" the thing in question, and people have to be advised whether or not the feature does in fact belong to it. There is nothing odd about an accidental predication; it is the default manner of saying something about something. There is something odd, however, about the other two. Thus, in my previous paragraph, I had to add the phrases "but remember" and "after all" to the second and third examples in order to make them plausible. There is nothing unusual about telling someone that Susan was smiling at a certain moment, but there is something peculiar about observing that she is capable of laughter or that she is rational. Normally we do not say such things, nor do we need to say them. If the listener knows who and what Susan is, he would not need to be told about her properties and essence. Still, sometimes it is necessary to say such things, and it will be philosophically important for us to determine when the necessity arises.

We might be tempted to think that accidents, properties, and essences are to be explored in ontology, in the science of being. They seem to be different kinds of features of things. They do in fact belong to things, but they show up as such ontological features in our speech and through its syntax. They are correlated with different kinds of activities on the part of people engaged in discourse. They belong not just to ontology but also to what we could call the theory of judgment or the phenomenology of speaking and thinking. Exploring the differences among accidentals, properties, and essences will not only clarify the way things are; it will also clarify what speech is, what we are as agents of disclosure, and how we are actualized in our discourse. The contrasts among accidents, properties, and essences, furthermore, are not to be correlated simply with human "consciousness," but with conversation. They show up primarily not to a single mind but to minds activated in the reciprocities of speech.

We are trying to examine how things show up in syntactic speech. We should mention at the start that our inquiry ought not to focus just on single judgments. Judgments don't normally occur one by one. Each judgment is indeed a unit, but it is a unit within a larger whole. In order to give a philosophical analysis of judgment we must focus on a whole conversation, a series of judgments that gradually unfold the thing in question. A conversation or a discourse is the proper whole within which the judgment can be philosophically understood. True, we sometimes do make a single statement, but this is unusual and should not be taken as the standard. If we focus on a single judgment, we lose all the flexibility and nuance that are in play when things are made to show up through speech. As we proceed in our analysis, we may take single judgments as our examples, but we need to remember that any particular judgment belongs to a series of reciprocal statements made in conversation.

Step Two: Moving On to Properties

When we speak, we bring something before ourselves and our inter-locutors and we say something about it. Normally, we say something that is accidental to the thing. We inform our interlocutor about the thing; we say, for example, "Anselm was smiling as he spoke to the class." In this speech, Anselm is manifested as featured in a certain way at a certain time.

Standard predications serve to disclose an object as having some acci-dental feature. Every such feature, however, is nested within a property: Anselm was smiling, but he was able to do so because as a human being he has the property of risibility, which can be actualized in different ways or not activated at all. We might also have said that Anselm was *not* smiling; being risible belongs to him essentially and always, but smiling does not.

Each accidental predication specifies a property. The property itself, however, is not stated in the predication. If Helen says, "Anselm was smiling," she does not have to add, "and he is risible." She assumes that her interlocutors know about this property and do not need to be informed about it. Smiling is, after all, just one of the activations of the power we call risibility, and if we are familiar with the actuality then we must have a sense of the potentiality behind it. The property remains unstated when the accidental is declared. When we highlight a feature we do so, necessarily, against a background that is unstated. The background property *could* become declared in our speech, but its way of coming to light is different from that of the accidental nested within it, and the way a speaker declares a property to someone is different from the way he declares an accidental. He also treats the listener differently.

The fact that all accidental features are given as nested within a property shows that predications have a certain "depth." They have two dimensions and not just one. They are not confined to the dimension of the predicate that has been stated. Even to say something simple, such as "The box is green," makes the assumption that the box has the property of being colored, but no one normally feels obliged to tell another person that boxes are colored. If you know what a box is, you would know that it is colored, because being colored is a property of being a box and of any spatial, material object. You would not, however, necessarily know that it is green, because being green might or might not belong to it. If a speaker were to pull back and say that the box is colored, it would be more to remind the interlocutor of what he already knows (or should know, or was presumed to know), not to inform him about the box and its properties.

A property is a potentiality or a power, and it can be realized in mul-titudinous ways. Bodies have shape, but any given body has an indefinite range of figure and size. Human beings are risible, but they can go from grins to belly laughs, from a giggle to a guffaw. If properties "flow" from the essence of a thing, they each in turn issue in a waterfall of possible accidentals.[1] Any time we use a word to designate a feature of a thing, we surreptitiously invoke the distinction between potentiality and actuality. We predicate the feature, but we do so against the unspoken background of the potentiality, and we at least implicitly know both of them, the feature and the property. The potential and the actual are not just dimensions of things but also dimensions at work in our speech. They function within the contents that are ordered by the syntax of our statements.

It would be wrong, therefore, to think of predicates as mere labels that we attach to features (or to ideas we have of features). They are not one-dimensional. They select a feature within a range of options located within the property that underlies the feature, and we need to specify the feature because there are so many other ways in which the property could have been actualized. This selection is made possible not just by the virtualities of the language; it is not just that English gives us a range of words to designate the various kinds of risibility (laugh, chuckle, snicker, giggle, chortle, titter, smile, grin, sneer, guffaw); English gives us these possible choices in vocabulary because we can be engaged in a continuum of actualizations of our risibility. Some of them have become encoded in the language, but there are a lot of variants that do not have distinct names, such as the kind of laugh that comes between a sneer and a giggle. Acci-dental predicates, therefore, implicate a property as the potentiality behind them.

Step Three: Moving On to the Essence

The property itself, however, is not at the bottom of what comes to light in speech. The property is nested within something still deeper, the essence or the definition of the thing, but it is nested within it in a manner dif-ferent from the way an accidental feature is nested within the property. The property is not a specification and actualization of the essence (as "smiling" specifies and actualizes "risibility"). The property is different from the essence and yet it "flows" from the essence as from its "source."

But these terms are metaphors. Can we say more about how the prop-erties are related to the essence? How do the properties and the essence come to light when we speak? We have already seen, in Chapter 7, that our awareness of properties gives us an implicit glimpse of the essence from which they flow; properties and essence are given concomitantly. Let us examine how.

Whenever we predicate something of something, the something about which we say it serves as a kind of receiver. It is like a tub or a basket, that in

[1] I am grateful to Joshua Maroof for this image.

which the accident and the property are to be placed. To use the classical term, it is a substrate, that which "lies beneath" the features we designate as its predicates.[2] But these formulations are also metaphorical, because predication has nothing spatial about it and the entity that underlies the accidents and properties is obviously not really a tub or a basket. Predication is a logical maneuver and not a spatial one. Still, we do use such spatial terms when we speak about predication, and they do seem to tell us something. Metaphors will not mislead us if we know that they are metaphors. Can we unpack them?

Predication is a public performance. When we predicate we do two things. First, we bring something into the center of our conversation, and, second, we declare something about what we have introduced. Our first move, bringing something into the discussion, is done in view of the second. We bring the thing forward in order to say something about it, not to eat it, not even just to look at it. We bring it forward to bring it to light through syntactic articulation. When we introduce the entity (by saying something like "This ..." or "The sleeping dog ..."), our interlocutor waits for us to complete our statement. If we were to stop there, if we were to say or indicate nothing more, he would wait for a moment and would then say, "So? What about it?" No matter how pragmatic the context of our speech may be, there is something simply contemplative about each predication.

And obviously, to bring something into the conversation, to "haul it into court" for judgment, does not necessarily mean that we bodily toss it out in front of us and our interlocutors. Sometimes we do point something out; sometimes we do take the thing out of a box and place it before the others; but most of the time we speak about things that are absent. Normally, we converse about what is *not* there before us. That we can do so is remarkable, and it shows the power of speech to master absence. It also shows how nonspatial and nonbodily our identifications and predications are.

So the first step is to introduce an entity into the conversation, to establish a reference. But bringing an entity into the conversation may be quite complicated, and it may stand in need of two or three steps. Sometimes we simply mention the thing's proper name, or we use a common noun or a descriptive phrase, and the thing has been successfully entered. At other times, however, we may have to delimit or define the thing we are bringing into the discussion. We may not have made it clear to our interlocutor what we are talking about, so we need to make a further explanation before we can say anything about the thing. The thing is not yet adequately there; we need to specify the topic, and the conversation is

---

[2] When Aristotle discusses the meanings of entity or substance (*ousia*) in *Metaphysics*, VII 3, he first examines substance as substrate, as *hypokeimenon*, because that is the sense that is most obvious to us. He moves on, however, to substance as essence as being more primary.

put on hold for a moment until the thing is entered and the discussion can go on.

When we do specify what we are talking about, we have not yet said anything about it. Rather, we have simply defined it, and definition is not the normal kind of predication, in which we state something informative about a subject. Aristotle himself tells us that knowing the nature of a thing is different from predication, but he does not mention the conversational context in which the distinction can most evidently be seen.[3] Definition simply introduces something into the conversation, while predication articulates some feature belonging to the thing we have successfully introduced. We are dealing with two different moves in the conversational game.

Suppose that we try to introduce something into the conversation and the interlocutor does not know what we are talking about. We begin to define the thing we have introduced. To define something, we must start with something that we do not need to define, so we start with the genus, which is not just an ontological dimension of the thing in question but a dimension that the interlocutor is familiar with. We cannot speak of a genus entirely apart from the conversational setting in which it is presented as such. Suppose that we are in the middle of a conversation and we want to speak about aardvarks; we say something like, "Well, consider aardvarks; they come pretty much in one size... ." But our interlocutor has no idea what they are (a form of Dutch cottage cheese? a kind of potato?), so he interrupts us and says, "Wait a minute; what are you talking about?" He cannot identify what we have tossed into the conversation, so all the predications we would go on to make about it, all the features we would drop on it, all the accidentals we would state about it, would be pointless. They would be left suspended, hanging in the air with no substrate to come down on.

So we respond to our interlocutor's question by interrupting our conversation; we stop predicating and back up from the thing we want to introduce; we move back to a genus, to a genus that the interlocutor knows: "It's an animal. You know, of course, what an animal is." Once we are assured that the interlocutor knows the genus, we begin to specify it: "It's an animal that lives in Africa; it's nocturnal and about five feet long; it's like a pig with a long snout, large ears, and a long tongue; it burrows in the ground, and it eats termites. That's what an aardvark is." These features are given not as predications but as specifications, as parts of a definition. They are being used merely to establish a reference, to enter an entity into the conversation, not to continue the conversation itself. We have interrupted the predicational drift of the conversation in order to clarify, by a definition, the thing that we are introducing into the discussion.

[3] Aristotle, *De Anima*, III 6, 430b26–30.

In this case of the aardvark, the specifications were properties of the thing. In other, more elegant cases, the specification can be carried out by simply giving the difference that identifies this kind of thing in contrast with other things. In such cases we would give the "specific difference," and we would have a purer kind of definition, in which we were able to provide the genus and difference: "You don't know what an oligarchy is? It's a political form (you know what *that* is) in which the wealthy rule." Such a specification of a genus by means of a "difference" is the paradigmatic form of definition. The "rule of the wealthy" is not a property of an oligarchy but its substance, its defining difference. The rule of the rich does not flow from oligarchy but defines it.[4] There are, however, many instances in which we cannot determine the difference; what sort of genus and difference can one give for aardvarks? In such cases, we define by giving some of the properties that distinguish the entity, not by giving its specific difference.

How can we get an elegant definition, one made up of genus and difference? By making a distinction, which is to say, by bringing out a difference. More specifically, it can be done by making *the* strategic distinction that differentiates this kind of thing from all other kinds. The distinction would differentiate the thing from its proximate things, those with which it is likely to be confused. Whenever we make a distinction, we are implicitly defining a thing. To speak somewhat redundantly, we are specifying a species. We are differentiating the thing within an encompassing genus, and we are doing it for someone, in order to carry on a conversation. We may not spell out the entire definition for our interlocutor; we may not declare the genus and the difference; most of the time the genus is left unspoken because it can be taken for granted.[5] It is the context or the horizon within which we specify what we want to introduce into the conversation. But there has to be a genus if the distinction is to have friction and give us a grip on things.[6]

When we, in our philosophical analysis, speak of something unknown as being introduced into the conversation, we are not talking about the unfamiliarity of a *word*, but the unfamiliarity of a *thing*. If it is the word that is unfamiliar, the speaker could always provide a synonym; but if

---

[4] Presenting a definition as though it were an accident can be exploited in jokes: "There is one positive thing you can say about money: it's a good medium of exchange." Money is not *a* medium of exchange; it *is* the medium of exchange.

[5] The genus is like the major premise in an enthymeme, the syllogism appropriate to rhetorical argument. The major premise in an enthymeme does not need to be stated because it is the expression of an opinion that everyone shares. To state it would be to state the obvious. The genus also does not normally need to be stated, but it becomes necessary to mention it when we must define something and need to back up into the genus in order to get a starting point for the definition.

[6] On the importance of the genus as a setting for distinctions, see Robert Sokolowski, "Making Distinctions," in his *Pictures, Quotations, and Distinctions: Fourteen Essays in Phenomenology* (Notre Dame, IN: University of Notre Dame Press, 1992), 66–9, 75, 82–5, 88.

the interlocutor is unfamiliar with the thing, then no synonym will help. It is then that an explanation by means of genus and difference is needed. The fact that one is using a genus and difference is a sign that one is explaining a thing and not just a word.

A Remark about Our Method

We must interrupt the discussion of our three predicables (the accidental, the property, and the parts of the essence or definition) to make some remarks about the method we have been following. We have been treating these three dimensions as they arise in human speech, and more specifically in human conversation. We might be inclined to discuss the three in a more purely metaphysical way and to think of accidents, properties, and essences simply as aspects of being, apart from any human involvement. Some things are substances, others are properties of substances, and still others are just accidents. The accidents don't count for much ontologically; they have a very feeble hold on being and are practically nothing, but the other two kinds of beings, substances and properties, are more robust. All three dimensions, the weak and the strong, belong to things in themselves.

Have we, in our analysis, diluted the metaphysical import of accidents, properties, and essences? Have we "relativized" them by connecting them to the human conversation? Have we made them into dimensions that arise only when we project human thinking into being? Not at all; what we have done is to bring out the subjective conditions that allow the objective distinctions to be disclosed.

When we converse with other speakers, we talk about things. We articulate them syntactically, and, as we have claimed in Chapter 5, the formal structure of syntax is a residue of public conversation. As we articulate things syntactically, we allow the distinctions between accidents, properties, and essences to come to light. The syntactic form serves as a kind of frame within which the difference between accidentals and essentials comes forward in the contents of what is being presented, and this occurs as we turn to one another in conversation. These differences are not just read off things in themselves; they arise when things become phenomena and legomena, but both phenomena and legomena involve accidentals being contrasted with essentials. There are no conversations or manifestations in which these differences do not come into play, in which we do not distinguish between people who know what they are speaking about and people who are lost in coincidentals and talk without understanding.

The differences in question do not just arise over against a single mind that exercises different kinds of intentionalities toward things. They arise over against people engaged in conversation, telling things to one another and introducing different entities into the conversation. The various intentional acts are not just rays that emanate from our brains (from someplace behind our eyes) and stretch toward things; they are accomplishments in our conversation. A definition, for example, is not merely a combination of words that somehow matches the way the thing is put together; it is a successful entering of an entity into a conversation.

Consider how a dictionary can be understood from this perspective. In this view, the many definitions in a dictionary are not so many verbal representations of things in the world; they are, rather, so many potential entrants in the human conversation, so many things waiting to be called into the exchanges between one speaker and another. When we look up a dictionary definition, we do so not simply to bring a form into our minds but to be able to say something to someone about something. We discover the things that *are*, but as they are for speakers.

I would like to use some Husserlian terminology to clarify the place of human conversation in distinguishing among essences, properties, and accidents. In his phenomenology, Husserl wishes to give two kinds of analyses, "noetic" and "noematic." A noetic analysis focuses on intentional acts, such as perception, memory, and categorial articulation, and it tries to describe their structures and relationships. A noematic analysis focuses on the objective correlate to the noetic intentions: it describes the perceived object as perceived, the remembered object as remembered, the categorially articulated object (a state of affairs) as articulated. In his analyses, however, Husserl primarily works with the solitary person and his consciousness; he analyzes "my" mind as carrying out these various intentionalities and disclosing the objects that are given in different ways to me.

But "I" as engaged in thinking am not actualized as "me" except as played off against another speaker in discourse. As stated in Chapter 4, I wish to offer an improvement on Husserl's descriptions. I would have the noetic analysis focus not on a single mind but on the persons engaged in conversation. From this perspective, a predication is not just my mind rising from perception to intellectual articulation, but one speaker manifesting an object to another by saying something about it and thus bringing out one of its features. The state of affairs correlated with an activity of judging is, therefore, not just a state of affairs over against me and my own consciousness, but a state of affairs, a phenomenon and a legomenon, articulated by one speaker for another. A genus is not just an overarching background for a differentiation I want to make in my own experience of a thing; it is the setting that the conversationalists are both familiar with, the setting within which I as one speaker can bring out for another the difference between *this* thing and *that*.

We can clarify this adjustment by looking to a doctrine that Husserl develops in *Cartesian Meditations* and in his other writings on intersubjectivity. An important step in his analysis is to reach what he calls the "sphere of ownness" (*Eigenheitssphäre*).[7] He proposes that we try, imaginatively, to think away any dimension of other minds. This "reduction to the sphere of ownness" is not like the factual removal of other persons (in that case, the *sense* of other persons would remain, but nobody would be there). We are to abstract from the very dimension of other persons, and see what would be left in our experiencing, as well as in the world given to our experiencing. This residue would be the sphere of ownness. Husserl claims that in this sphere we would still have a world with permanent bodies in it. Our own body would stand out as different from the others (we would still "hold sway" in it); we would still experience spatial mobility and kinesthesia. Husserl knows that we could never exist in this way – the sphere of ownness is an abstraction, not a concrete possibility – but he undertakes this philosophical maneuver in order to show what is added to this abstract sphere when other persons come into play. It is a device that he uses to clarify intersubjectivity and the experiencing associated with it, and to show that his philosophy is not solipsistic.[8]

But Husserl seems to imply that categorial intentionalities could be imagined to occur in the sphere of ownness. He does not make a special point of this, but he does not deny it either, and he does explicitly say that there are "eidetic objectivities" within the sphere of owness.[9] I would claim, however, that categorial forms and syntactically shaped experience could not be thought to occur in the sphere of ownness, because such syntax is the deposit of conversational action, and such activities could not occur without the presence, in principle, of other speakers.

In adjusting Husserl's thought in this way, I do not merely *add* the domain of conversation to the solitary consciousness; rather, the categorial level belongs first and foremost to the intersubjective exchange, not to the single mind. To discuss thinking, with its use of syntax, we must start with conversation. The noematic structures are constituted in this context, not in the solitary consciousness, and their structure can only be understood as correlated with the noetic intentionalities of human conversation. We do at times engage in private cogitation, but such solitude is the marginal instance and the aberrant situation. What Husserl describes is the extreme case and not the normal.

---

[7] Edmund Husserl, *Cartesian Meditations*, trans. Dorion Cairns (The Hague: Martinus Nijhoff, 1977), §§44–8, pp. 92–106.

[8] Husserl's purpose in developing the theme of the sphere of ownness is often overlooked. He observes that the tone of his transcendental philosophy might make people think they are being led into solipsism, and he wishes to counter that impression. The reduction to the sphere of ownness is not a dive into solitude but part of an argument that shows that we and our minds are not solitary. See ibid., §42, p. 89, and §62, p. 150, where he says, "The illusion of a solipsism is dissolved."

[9] Ibid., §47, p. 105.

One more point needs to be made concerning genus and difference as parts of definitions. In scholastic philosophy, the notions 'genus' and 'difference' are said to be "second intentions." They are not predicated directly of things themselves, as "first intentions" are. Genus and difference are predicated of things as known by us, as conceptualized or as present "in the mind." They arise when the intellect reflects on itself and on what it contains.[10] Here again, I would like to change the emphasis and publicize these issues; I would claim that "first intentions" are primarily said of those things given to the participants in conversation, and "second intentions" are the dimensions that arise when things are reflectively considered as spoken about and known by the conversants. Genus and difference should not be treated philosophically by considering a single mind and examining how it articulates things and reflects on itself; they come forth primarily when one speaker attempts to introduce a new topic into his conversation with other speakers. He appeals to a generic background and makes the strategic distinction that defines the thing in question for his interlocutors.[11]

Properties and Essences as Mysterious and Obscure

The dynamic and differentiated interplay among essence, property, and accident occurs in regard to every name. It is not just full-fledged substances like trees and horses that have essences, properties, and accidents. Any thing that is nameable in any way engages these dimensions. Traffic, for example, is not a full-fledged substance, but it can be named and articulated in the manner we have described. If a speaker says, "Traffic ...," the part of the

---

[10] See, for example, Robert W. Schmidt, S.J., *The Domain of Logic according to Saint Thomas Aquinas* (The Hague: Martinus Nijhoff, 1966), 127: "Logic is concerned with the nature under the aspect of these intentions which follow its existence in the intellect and not under that of the existence which it has in external reality." See also p. 128: "There is nothing in reality directly corresponding to logical intentions such as those of genus and species." In this understanding, a genus appears when the intellect reflects upon its mode of knowing and upon what it contains within itself; a second intention, such as a genus or species, "presupposes a reflection upon the act of understanding and the concept or term of that act" (p. 119). In other words, the mind sees that it understands a genus as containing a variety of species. This relation of genus to species is a feature primarily of the way the intellect understands things, not immediately of the way things exist, and, therefore, the word *genus* expresses a second and not a first intention. Second intentions have only a remote and mediated foundation in things. This analysis of genus and species is indeed illuminating, but I think it is better still to think of them in terms of a conversation, not just in terms of a single intellect and its reflective capabilities.

[11] In fact, Schmidt quotes Aquinas as saying that dialectics and sophistics, which discuss argumentation and speeches, examine such things as genus and species (ibid., 128). Aquinas says this in his commentary on Aristotle's *Metaphysics*, where he paraphrases Aristotle. I should also mention that Schmidt says that the terminology of first and second intentions is used only marginally by Aquinas himself; see p. 123, n. 90.

world designated by that word enters into the conversation, and we wait to hear what the speaker is going to say about it: "... is very heavy on I-66 at this time." And this accidental predication is nested within the property that flows from traffic, namely, that traffic can be more or less intense at any given moment. Every traffic report, every weather report engages our intelligence in this differentiated way. We can introduce the words *color* or *azure* or *monthly rent* into the conversation, and each of them will bring out a part of the world that has a definable essence with properties flowing from it and accidentals nested in them.

The three layers of accident, property, and essence might seem simplistic and obvious, but that is because we have been using a standard and familiar example: Anselm is smiling, his smiling is based on his risibility, and this property flows from his rationality. But take a more obscure case. Sylvia is selling her valuable furniture and using the money to help Jasper, who is in desperate straits. This is an accidental predication: she is at this moment selling these things to help that person. The activity can be rather clearly described, but what is the property behind this event? What is going on? Is it simply an admirable instance of benevolence? Is it family loyalty? Is it a need to make restitution? Perhaps it is none of these but some other unknown property and potentiality, one of the things that people do that we may find hard to name. The question may remain open; we may never know exactly what is going on. And if the property is shadowy, so is the essence from which it flows. Sylvia is a human being, a rational animal, and her conduct is, therefore, one of the ways in which a human being can act – but how and why? What is it in human nature that is the source of such ways of acting? How does this property, the possibility of this sort of activity, "flow" from being human? What is human being, if this kind of thing flows from it? What is Sylvia, and what are we?

For that matter, even the connection between risibility and human rationality is not all that easy to understand. What is it about rationality that makes us capable of smiling? And what is risibility, that it can be activated in both a joyful laugh and a cruel smile? The familiarity of the example masks the obscurity of the issue.

If our words register anything at all, we can be sure that the forms of accident, property, and essence will be there behind what we name, but in many cases we may not know specifically what the properties and the essence are. We have the syntax and are able to make accidental predications; we can give an approximate description of what is going on; but we don't know what is really happening. We cannot easily identify what the "deeper" parts of the situation are, the properties and the essence, and yet we do know that there *are* properties and that they flow from an essence that *is* there, obscure as the properties and the essence may be. The evidential force of our words witnesses to the reality of the thing. This is where the "depth" between accidents and properties, and between properties and essence, becomes more than just a trivial and obvious move into another dimension.

Artists exploit these differences. They call up auras of mystery and hidden depths. They hint at things that are hard to name directly. T. S. Eliot, toward the end of *East Coker*, mentions, parenthetically, "The evening with the photograph album." This poem, like all of the *Four Quartets*, is about the way we, as human beings, exist both in and out of time. We exist in such a way that we are caught up in the current flow of time, but we can also have the past (as well as the future) immediately present to us.[12] We can even occasionally touch something that seems neither past, present, nor future. In the passage from *East Coker*, Eliot has just contrasted "the evening under starlight" with "the evening under lamplight," and he describes us spending the evening under lamplight with the photograph album; we look back at ourselves pictured in time past, and we do so in the present, in the glowing light of a human artifact. This predicate is highly accidental. It even depends on there being photograph albums and lamps, a situation that was in play only in the late nineteenth and most of the twentieth century, in certain parts of the world. (Would we now look at images on a computer monitor? Does this change make us less nostalgic, or are we nostalgic in another way? Can human beings arrive at something like dreamtime after they have constructed electric lights?) What is the human property behind the accident of looking at photographs under lamplight? And from what part of our essence does this property flow? What are we, that we can and need to do such a thing?

Eliot tries to lead us to the answer, or to tease it out of us, and he tries to do so through the accidental predication of ourselves enjoying the photograph album. But in order for such an artistic construction to work, the accident that is brought to mind has to be the right one, and it must be set in a proper context; it has to be the kind of predication that awakens our minds and makes it possible for us to glimpse the property in which the

---

[12] We have seen that the involvement of syntax differentiates rational from nonrational experiencing. Rational creatures also have a distinct kind of temporality. The "meanings" or "propositions" they achieve are omnitemporal. A proposition or an equation, for example, recurs as identically the same at different moments of time (it is always the very same Pythagorean theorem each time we think or speak of it). It is also possible for intellectual beings to make their past or their future present to themselves in a way that nonrational creatures cannot. I who remember can experience my past self as the same as my present self. Also, rational beings are capable of reminiscence and not just of memory. In both these ways, in entertaining ideal significations and in exercising rational memory, intellectual or spiritual beings can achieve identifications that transcend bodily time and motion. The temporality of intellectual beings was recognized in medieval philosophy and theology; it was called *aevum* and was considered intermediate between time and eternity. I am grateful to Cornelius O'Brien for bringing the relevance of *aevum* to my attention.

accident is nested. It must also lead us on further, beyond the property to the essence, whether or not we can spell it out. The accident is explicitly stated, but the property and the essence are insinuated. The writer has to know which episode to describe; the painter has to know which expression to sketch; the sculptor has to know which pose to capture. The artist must choose his incident.

Lear behaves in one way toward Goneril and Regan and in another toward Cordelia; what is the human property that is being activated in this "accidental" event, and what is the nature of the fatherhood – or the human nature – that lies behind the potentiality? Cleopatra arrives in gilded, scented splendor; everybody in town rushes to see her, leaving Antony behind, sitting alone in the marketplace: vision, scent, attraction, desire, isolation – all in their combination a property that flows from our human nature. What is human being, that it gives rise to such possibilities?

A particular artistic achievement, if it is successful, has such a twofold depth: we move beyond the accidental statement to the property behind it (to the potentiality that this accident actualizes), and from there to the essence from which the potentiality flows. These are two different kinds of depth. The same formal steps occur not only in artistic constructs but also in natural inquiry. A lion stalks and brings down a zebra; what animal property does this incident actualize, and what are animals that they do such things? This compound boils at this temperature, and that compound boils at that; what are these compounds, that they act and react in that way?

We know the three dimensions of accident, property, and essence together. We do not know them separately one by one; they are three dimensions of one insight, and they come as a package. The accidental predicate is grasped against the background of the property, and the property in turn is understood as flowing from the nature of the thing, the correlative of the name that we use to identify the subject we are speaking about. Every time we predicate something of anything, all three dimensions are at work. In one respect, the accidental is the weakest of all these forms of being, because it comes and goes and does not flow necessarily from the entity itself, as the properties do; but in another respect, the accidental is the clearest and the truest of the three, because as we declare it we know it actually occurs, whatever it may signify. We *have* looked at the pictures in the photograph album, whatever property this action engages and whatever part of our nature it reveals. The incident becomes ineluctable once it occurs, however contingent it may have been.

Distinctions as Specifying the Essence

We must clarify in particular the presentation of the essence. We might especially need to be reminded that the essence presents itself to us only in conjunction with the properties and accidents. In traditional scholastic thought, we are told that the "first act of the intellect" is to grasp the essence of a thing. The second act is judgment, in which the intellect "composes and divides"; that is, it asserts the existence of what we have conceived and articulates accidents and properties. The third act is reasoning, in which we move from one judgment to another and establish conclusions. Following Aristotle, Aquinas calls the first act of the mind the "grasp of indivisibles," and says that it is prior to the activities of both defining and judging.[13] This grasp seems to provide the raw material for the other acts of reason.

In the analysis we have given, however, the essence is not presented by itself; it comes to light only "behind" or "beneath" or "within" the properties and their actualization in accidents. In our philosophical analysis we do not begin with the "first act" of the intellect; we begin by considering the third act, reasoning, or, as we have formulated it, the reciprocal reasoning that is conversation. The grasp of an indivisible cannot be examined by itself, as emerging simply from sense experience; it must be understood in the setting provided by conversation and the predications that make it up, both of which are structured by syntax. But once we are given the phenomenon of conversation, we do find within it such a thing as the grasp of an indivisible or the presentation of an essence or a kind, and this indivisible is presented to us as that from which the properties and the accidents flow.

The presentation of the essence involves the making of distinctions. Andrew is an automobile salesman. Amelia, his friend, is visiting his dealership. She has been watching his behavior and listening to his comments about people who come into the showroom. He is friendly and attentive to some people, and he speaks well of them; he is inconsiderate and abrupt with others and speaks badly about them. Later, Amelia says to Andrew, "I don't understand why you treat some of your customers in one way and others so differently. Why is your conduct so inconsistent?" Andrew replies, "It's not inconsistent at all. They are different kinds of people. Some are shopping and others are just browsing. Browsing is not shopping. I don't waste time with browsers, and, furthermore, I don't like them very much." A similar story could be told about real estate agents or computer salesmen. Amelia may not have been able to see a difference between the two kinds of people, but Andrew, as an experienced salesman, immediately picks up clues – properties expressed in accidents – that tell him whether he is dealing with a browser or a shopper.

---

[13] Thomas Aquinas, *Summa theologiae*, I q. 85, a. 8. See also article 3, where Aquinas speaks eloquently of vagueness in our knowledge; we first know things "sub quadam confusione" until we articulate parts and wholes.

Before Andrew made his distinction, Amelia was experiencing and describing all the visitors to the showroom as customers. She saw Andrew treating these customers in two different ways. For her, his conduct did not add up. It was not consistent. It went in two different directions when, she thought, it should go in one. Andrew seemed to articulate properties that conflicted with one another, but Amelia was looking for cohesion. She was trying to apply all the accidents and properties to one kind of thing, but Andrew was speaking and acting in regard to two.

So Andrew made a distinction, and as he did so, a new essence, a new kind of thing, the browser, manifested itself to Amelia. She had been treating everyone globally as a customer, but now she distinguished the genus (people coming into the showroom) into two species (shoppers and browsers). The genus had to be there as the setting within which the distinction could be made, but it became activated as a genus when the two species, each with its special difference, were articulated within it. Now the properties have been placed into two tubs, not one, and Andrew no longer seems inconsistent.

Of the many things involved in this procedure, the one that interests us most is the fact that an indivisible (the browser) has been presented to the intellect of Amelia. The difference that defines the browser is the manner in which he investigates. He looks idly at the cars and equipment, without any serious intent to buy, whereas the shopper is looking as a step toward buying. The shopper has an intention under which his visit is ordered and he is busy, while the browser is a *flâneur*. A synonym for *browser* is *window shopper*, which is an elegant concept: we can see what is in the store window, but we cannot pick it up and buy it, so our "shopping" is bound to be idle.

The browser is definable by a genus and difference; he belongs to a species or a kind, and through all the conversational discourse between Andrew and Amelia, through all the properties and accidentals that come to light, and finally through the distinction that is made, this species becomes present to Amelia's mind. The species could not become present to her just by itself in an isolated "first act of the intellect," segregated from the various predications and the conversation in which it was embedded.

How We Grasp Indivisibles

The browser is an indivisible, an *adiaireton* or *asyntheton*, because he is the origin of a number of properties that are realized in accidental ways. One of his properties is, for example, his tempo. This property is activated in this particular browser at this moment by the way he drifts casually from one model of car to another, a fact that is grimly noted and stated by Andrew ("He's wasting my time"). But the browser's indivisibility is even more sharply brought out for Amelia when he is distinguished from the shopper, when his "kind" is distinguished from its neighboring "kind." It is when Andrew says that browsing is not shopping that the indivisible browser is truly registered for Amelia. At that moment the essence enters her intellect.

The essence of browsing has entered her mind, and all its associated properties fall into place. The assorted properties and their more immediate phenomena now make sense. But this does not mean that Amelia has fabricated some sort of new hypothesis or postulated some new kind of entity separate from the phenomena she had already noticed; rather, the phenomena are now simply seen as belonging to one thing and as being the potentialities of that one thing. They are now taken as the way that one thing can essentially act and react. The phenomena take on a cohesion as belonging to one being. The phenomena are not mere accidents or coincidences; rather, they belong, through their properties, to browsing, and browsing is shown up as being an entity. It is something that *is* and does not merely seem to be. The properties themselves, therefore, also *are*, but they are in a derivative way. There is a single entity on which they depend for their being, and the truth and density of browsing, its reality, is warranted by the fact that there is something that browsing necessarily *is not*, namely shopping. Because it necessarily is not something else, it necessarily is what it is, and the properties that flow from it truly are as well. What we are describing is what Aristotle presents in Books 7 to 9 of the *Metaphysics*, where he shows how the entity or substance of things shows up in our speech.

Another service that distinctions perform is to pin down the significance of a word in a particular conversation. Practically every name in a language has multiple meanings, which might be either purely equivocal or related by analogy to one another. Even the word *browser* has more than one meaning. It can, nowadays, refer to a kind of computer software as well as to someone looking at merchandise. In its primary meaning, browsing is contrasted with grazing, and in two ways: in one distinction, browsing is done by wildlife and grazing by livestock; in the other, browsers nibble on leaves, bark, and stems, while grazers feed on grass and other vegetation close to the ground. Andrew, in the automobile showroom, would not distinguish his browsers from grazers or word processors, but from shoppers, and his specifying distinction determines which of the multiple meanings is at play in the current conversation. And besides using the term in one of its standard, acceptable ways, a speaker might use it metaphorically to bring out an entity that may not yet have its own name.

We have said that the presentation of the essence brings coherence to the properties and accidents, and allows us to understand them as "flowing" from the entity in question. To say that things fall into place this way, however, is not to say that we now somehow understand *how* the properties flow from the thing, as though we had discovered the mechanism in the entity that generates these properties. If we suddenly realize that we are dealing with a browser and not a shopper, we come to know *why* the person is moving around slowly and carelessly and we stop expecting him to act otherwise, but we do not know what it is in his makeup that generates these properties. All we know is that these properties belong to this kind of thing. That is the kind of thing it is.

Dual Usage of a Name: Individual and Kind

A name can be used to signify either a particular individual or an abstraction, and the use of the name can oscillate between the two designations. Thus, Andrew might grimly say to Amelia, "The browser is now looking at the SUVs," and he would be speaking about the man who is wandering over from the convertibles to the SUVs. Andrew might also say, "If you are not careful, the browser will chew up a lot of your time." As he said this, he would probably be speaking about the browser as such and browsers in general; he is waxing philosophical about the life of a car salesman.

But this second statement is ambiguous; Andrew might possibly be using it to refer to the annoying visitor and not to the species. The ambiguity is inevitable, because any name used to identify an individual also connotes a kind (even a proper name will generally connote a male or female person or a certain kind of thing, such as *Rover* or *Tabby*). The word *browser* might be used to denote this man, but then it would identify him not just as a man but as a browser, and it might also be used to denote the species, and in doing so it would connote this individual as well as all the instances of that kind.[14]

There are interesting flexibilities that come along with this dual usage. We might use the word to identify the individual and then to predicate some accidentals of him as an individual of that kind: "That browser is the slowest one I've ever seen; he's been here an hour." The predicate stems from the man's essence as a browser. But we might also use the word just to establish a reference to the individual and then say something about him that stems from other parts of his nature, from one of the genera that encompass his being a browser: "That browser has three children." He has offspring not as a browser but as a human being or, perhaps, as a mammal.[15] We would more likely state this as, "That man browsing over there has three children." A given word is like a lens that can be tilted this way and that, and it would direct our focus in correspondingly different ways. Its focus can oscillate between the *tode* and the *ti*.

---

[14] My remarks in this section are an attempt to deal with "the problem of universals." I treat it not simply as an ontological or an epistemological problem ("How can an individual concept have universal reference?"), but as an issue that arises in the way words can be used, to signify either the thing or the kind.

[15] On establishing a reference by formulating a description, see Robert Sokolowski, "Referring," in *Pictures, Quotations, and Distinctions*, 189, 196–8, 202.

Not all listeners will be able to follow when the use of a word fluctuates between signifying the individual and the kind. Some will be unable to generalize and will just take in the individual signification. Shakespeare tells the story about Antony and Cleopatra and also directs our minds toward seduction and infatuation as such, but some hearers will remain fascinated only by the story, not by the kinds of things or the essences that are instantiated in it. Such listeners might be intrigued by the events that are narrated in a story but may not be able to catch the moral, although they would probably sense that something more than the mere incident is at play. The story seems to be "deep" in a way they cannot quite grasp.

Another feature of names is that the use of any name engages universality, and it does so either explicitly or implicitly. When a name is used, either it *designates* an essence (as distinct from the properties that flow from it and the accidents that actualize the properties) or it *connotes* that essence. If Andrew uses the word *browser* to designate the kind, he specifically leaves out of focus whether the browser is young or old, tall or short, male or female. Precisely because these features are left out, the term is universal, because it can be applied to a browser with any such characteristics. When the intellect abstracts 'browser,' it does not take it away from such potential features, but merely leaves them undetermined. Then, the term can always be put back into a setting in which some of its features are specified. The name is then used in a given situation to refer to *this* browser with *these* accidents, and in this case it would be used in a particular way, but because it always connotes the kind and does not just designate this thing, the universal always hovers in the background and the name can always be adjusted to a universal use. The speaker shows whether he is engaging the universal or the particular use by what he says before and after this utterance of the word.

When speakers use names in these two ways, they are not using options they have set for themselves. The flexibility we have between designating individuals and designating kinds is not a human convention about words that we agreed upon at some moment in the distant past. It is a possibility given to all human beings by the things that they know and bring to light in speech. It is not *we* who decide that we will speak about individuals and kinds, but things that lend themselves to such discourse.

The thing may present itself, but it still speaks to and through us, and we confirm this fact from time to time by the declarative use of the first-person pronoun. This usage shows not only that we have introduced syntax into the sounds we make and the things we disclose, but also that we are responsible for the essentials and definitions that – if we have been successful – have been registered in what we say. Such usage expresses a certain authorial confidence and satisfaction in the verdicts we have made.

9

Knowing Things in Their Absence

Pictures, Imagination, and Words

In the last two chapters we have explored several dimensions of the content of speech, but one topic has remained largely undiscussed and must be approached now: the fact that we also speak about things when they are not bodily present. In Chapter 7 we used as our paradigm the case of two people, Henry and Jane, speaking to each other about an oak tree that is present to both of them; Henry points it out and says something about it. But most of our speech and conversation is about things that are not present: about what we did last week or what we will do tomorrow, about Tokyo or Buenos Aires, Napoleon or Charlemagne, quarks or the center of the sun. The names that designate things before us can also be used to designate things that are absent. An essential strength of speech and thinking is that they can reach into the absent as well as respond to what is present. The ability to deal with the absent is a constitutive element in rationality. One of the important philosophical discoveries of Edmund Husserl was the role of absence in human experience, thinking, and expression. We can distinguish four ways in which absence enters into our experience and thinking.

1. The Absence Inherent in Perception

Even the direct presence of things involves some absence. When Henry and Jane see the oak tree, they each see it only from one side and from one angle, but they also "see," in an extended sense of seeing, the other sides, the ones they would directly see if they moved around the object. Also, while seeing the tree they can anticipate touching it and hearing it rustle in the wind, as well as other ways of perceiving it. They never experience just one detached profile of the tree; they see the tree itself, and the tree includes all the other perceivable sides, aspects, and profiles that it can offer them as they continue their experience of it. These other sides, aspects, and profiles are indeed absent, in one sense of absence, in comparison to the view that

Henry and Jane each enjoy at any moment, but such an absence is minimal; all these other dimensions are co-perceived in the overall experience of the tree; they are just around the corner. The perceptions carried out by Henry and Jane are continuous, and so are the dimensions that they perceive as they explore the thing; the interplay of presence and absence forms a continuum. But if Henry and Jane were to walk away from the tree, so that the tree was no longer present within their perceptual field, the continuum would have been severed and a more discrete and definitive kind of absence would have come into play, one different from that of the "other sides" that accompany perception. The tree is now entirely absent, and its various appearances are no longer continuous with whatever new perceptions Henry and Jane are enjoying. The thing is gone and not just profiled.

2. The Absence Involved in Picturing

This more radical kind of absence can be somewhat overcome by a picture of the tree. Henry and Jane cannot experience the tree any longer, but they can look at its picture. Suppose they have a photograph of the oak tree and begin to talk about it; the tree is now pictorially present to them. Two kinds of intentionality are possible as they look at the picture: they might talk about the *photograph*, or they might talk about the *tree*. In the first case, they might discuss the shading of blacks and whites in the picture, or the crisp lines, or the fidelity of the image. But while looking at the same photograph they could also speak about the tree itself, not about the picture: "I never realized that the tree reached out so far over our neighbor's yard"; "Notice how few leaves there are on this branch; I wonder if there is something wrong with it. Should we remove the branch?" Henry and Jane are looking at the picture, but they are talking about the tree, even though the tree is miles away from them. They are talking about the tree through its presence in the picture. That they can do so is a presentational possibility of great importance. It involves a mixture of intentionalities (the pictorial presence combined with the verbal intending of the absent) that deserves close philosophical scrutiny.

In the examples I have given, what Henry and Jane say about the tree is rather prosaic, mere matters of fact or items of information (that the tree extends over the neighbor's yard and that one of the branches seems to lack leaves). But pictures do not just convey information; they are also able to bring to light a deeper intelligibility; they can show what the thing is. Henry and Jane might discover and express to one another not just matters of fact but something more profound about the tree, something that belongs to it by its own nature and some of its deeper properties. They might, through the photograph, appreciate how the tree brings shade and form and repose to their residence, or how the tree gives a sense of continuity through the generations of people who have lived near it, or how a tree can remain an identity as it grows and develops its shape. Some of the essentials of a tree might show up more vividly in a picture or a painting than in the tree itself as it is perceived. Suppose Henry and Jane express such things to one another as they look fondly at the tree in the photograph. They would be talking not about the picture but about the tree in the picture, and they would be talking about the tree not as it is in the picture but as it is in itself. The photograph would have enabled them to speak with some depth about the tree, perhaps about trees as such, maybe even about the essence of tree. If the photograph had been taken by a skilled and thoughtful photographer, it might have been deliberately framed or conceived in such a way as to bring out precisely the essentials of what it is to be a tree. And, certainly, a good painting would bring out the essentials and the intelligibilities of its subject and make them visible to the thoughtful viewer. The viewer may be looking at a picture, but he could be thinking and speaking about *the* tree or about *this* tree, or he might be thinking and speaking about political leadership as such and not just about Winston Churchill.

Pictures allow such complex intentionalities to occur. We can speak about something absent, and we can do so by virtue of its pictorial presence. What Henry and Jane have thus understood about the tree or about trees through a depiction would then flow back, by what Thomas Prufer has called reflux, into their lived experience of that tree and trees in general, just as a portrait or a depiction in a drama would flow back into life and give it form and significance.[1] In fact, we may learn more about trees and about life through their depictions than through our own experience. The intelligence of the person who made the picture, the photographer or the painter, may show forth more about the subject than we have been able to see in our untutored perceptions. The intelligibility of the thing may be more vividly disclosed in the image than in the thing itself. What is gained in the absence associated with pictures blends back into the presences given in direct experience. It can flow back into experience in this way because we have, all along, been dealing with one

---

[1] Thomas Prufer, "Providence and Imitation: Sophocles' *Oedipus Rex* and Aristotle's *Poetics*," in his *Recapitulations: Essays in Philosophy* (Washington, DC: Catholic University of America Press, 1993), 18–19. On the manner in which an entity becomes presented through its image, see p. 14: "The limiting and tightening by means of the imitating work fit the action imitated in and through the work for contemplation which delights." Also see p. 19: "The imitated action is heightened and sharpened by the imitation into being more truly itself than it would be if it were not imitated and thus made available for contemplation in and through the transforming imitation." The intelligibility of the thing shines more brightly through the imitation, and it remains the intelligibility of the thing. The image is not another thing. Prufer's digest of the story of Oedipus, at the beginning of this essay, is a paradigm of recapitulation.

and the same thing in its presence and its absence: things are identities in presence and absence.[2]

Pictures can enrich life, but they can also mislead. We might begin to live in mere picturing, in movies or novels, for example, or in television. A farmer or a soldier might laugh at the fanciful depiction of farming or warfare in a film, but others might take the picture seriously and may even make decisions based on the way the thing is presented. The reflux of art into life may submerge life for a while, until the real thing's insistence finally breaks through. Such unrealistic depictions, however, are only part of the story, and they should not make us cynical about depiction. There also are true images that condense the thing and truthfully present its intelligibility. Even the most unromantic farmer or soldier will rejoice if he sees a thoughtful depiction of the thing he knows, one that truly brings out its essentials. The illusory and the authentic portrayal, as well as the reflux that deceives and the one that confirms, are all made possible by the dimensional, presentational difference, the interplay between thing and image. The thing is itself in both its presence and its absence.

We have this flexibility toward pictures, by which we can intend either the picture or the thing depicted, because we use words and can bring them to bear on pictures and on what is pictured in them. Picturing alone would not make the intelligibility of the thing present to us; we need the support of words in picturing just as we do in perception. Wording and picturing are a joint venture for human beings. Henry and Jane can intend either the tree in the photograph or the tree itself because they can use the word *oak tree* while responding to the picture. They can even use the word *this* in these two ways. It is the blend of the two intentionalities, the pictorial and the verbal, that makes such variation possible.

In fact, a kind of syntax is at work in pictures, and it allows the intelligibility of what is depicted to be visible and nameable in them. Pictures are made to be works of intelligence by their compositional form, which also enables them to convey a "content," just as the grammatical form of speech signals intelligence and allows an intelligibility to be distinguished and thus made manifest. Pictures have to be structurally composed by their makers and syntactically "read" by their viewers. When we look at the parts of a painting, for example, we recognize both combinatory successes and "grammatical" incompatibilities. The composition of images in paintings is analogous to the syntactic composition of words in speech; the composition of lines and colors is analogous to that of consonants and vowels; and both pictures and speech exhibit rhythms or cadences that are proper

---

[2] Names target things across presence and absence. See Robert Sokolowski, *Presence and Absence: A Philosophical Investigation of Language and Being* (Bloomington: Indiana University Press, 1978), 26–31.

to each of these modes of presentation.[3] Composition works in both words and pictures, and the intelligibility of things is made manifest in each.

3. The Absence Involved in Imagination

Still another way of dealing with absence is through imagination, which in some respects is like picturing but in many important ways is very different from it. Certainly, we have something like internal "images"; we dream and daydream, and as we do so we obviously have something like a moving picture or a recording going on inside us, but it is *only* something like a real image; it is not a standard picture.[4] Imagination does not involve our looking at an internal screen, even though people usually talk about it as if it did. Imagination is more like reliving an experience than seeing a reproduction of what was experienced. Imagination reenacts an experience; it does not copy the thing that was experienced. As Catherine Abell and Gregory Currie put it, "The image of the tiger is not a tiger-like entity inside the head … but the experience as of seeing a tiger."[5] Currie and Ian Ravenscroft say that imagination is "perception-like," and that imagination "simulates" perception.[6] Imagination is *like* a perception, but it is not really a perception, and, more specifically, it is not the perception of an object that is a picture of another thing. When I visualize something, I do not see anything; I only *seem* to see it, and I seem to see *it*, not something like it.

Imagination is the reenactment of an experience, and as such it involves displacing ourselves into two selves: the present self, alive here and now in the present, the one that slips into daydreaming, and the "past" or "other" self that is involved in the activity we are imagining. Every human

---

[3] For the analogies between speech and pictures, see Robert Sokolowski, "Visual Intelligence in Painting," *The Review of Metaphysics* 59 (2005): 333–54. An amusing conjunction of syntax and pictures can be found in a whimsical poem by William Combe that was very popular in the 19th century, *The Tour of Dr. Syntax in Search of the Picturesque.* The poem was accompanied by caricatures by Thomas Rowlandson, so syntax and pictures are found in both the title and the text. The poem was published as a book in 1812, after having been serialized in a British magazine from 1809 to 1811, and it was occasionally republished (along with two subsequent "tours" by the pedantic Dr. Syntax) up to the early 20th century.

[4] Two valuable recent books on imagination are Colin McGinn, *Mindsight: Image, Dream, Meaning* (Cambridge, MA: Harvard University Press, 2004), and Gregory Currie and Ian Ravenscroft, *Recreative Minds: Imagination in Philosophy and Psychology* (New York: Oxford University Press, 2002). Among the many recent psychological studies of imagination in children, one might mention Paul L. Harris, *The Work of the Imagination* (New York: Blackwell, 2000).

[5] Catherine Abell and Gregory Currie, "Internal and External Pictures," *Philosophical Psychology* 12 (1999): 438.

[6] Currie and Ravenscroft, *Recreative Minds*, 11. On "simulation theory" and the "simulation programme," see pp. 49–70.

person is a displaced person in this way. If imagination is perception-like and if it simulates a perception, then it simulates perceiving, and it must also simulate a perceiver. In fact, it does simulate a perceiver, but not just anyone at all; it simulates none other than me (who else?), the same one who is engaged here and now in imagining something. It is always me that I find displaced in my memories and imaginations; how disturbing it would be to find someone else. The special character of such displacement or *Versetzung* has been elaborated by Husserl in his analyses of inner time consciousness and intersubjectivity, as well as by other writers in phenomenology, who have articulated the different kinds of identifications and identities that come about in these experiences.[7]

I here and now can be reliving myself engaged in something there and then, and, strictly speaking, "I" am the identity between these two guises of myself. Looking at a picture hanging on a wall does not involve any such personal displacement; when I look at a picture I am there simply as the viewing self, the one standing in the museum here and now, but in imagination I am there in two guises, as the imagining self here and now and as the imagined self there and then. I imagine not just a scene but myself as engaged in the scene, or at least as there perceiving the scene. When I look at a picture, by contrast, I do not displace myself into the scene depicted in it; I do not enroll myself among the people who are pictured.[8]

The experience of personal identity depends on such imaginative displacement, which can occur in different modes. I might imagine myself memorially, as I relive something that I was engaged in some time ago; I might imagine myself in anticipation, as I try on several actions I might perform in the future; and I might imagine myself in a pure dream world, a never-never land, without memory or anticipation. Furthermore, because imagination involves a displacement of the self, I imagine myself not just as an inert object but as acting and responding in the world I imagine, and so imagination engages me an actor. I imagine myself as doing something, or at least as seeing or hearing something. In standard picturing, however,

---

[7] Eduard Marbach gives a fine survey of Husserl's doctrine of the identity of the ego over time and its relation to the lived body; he also notes some of the unfinished elements in Husserl's ideas. See *Das Problem des Ich in der Phänomenologie Husserls* (The Hague: Martinus Nijhoff, 1974), 298–339. A particularly good discussion of personal identity in the displacements of memory and imagination can be found in Theodor Conrad, *Zur Wesenslehre des psychischen Lebens und Erlebens* (The Hague: Martinus Nijhoff, 1968). After treating the experience of being displaced (*Versetztseinserlebnisse*), Conrad examines anticipation (*das Vor-Erleben*), dreams, and "inner speaking and inner hearing."

[8] One of the finest literary expressions of the displacement of self and the reflux of art on life can be found in Henry James, *The Ambassadors*, Book 11, Chapter 3, where Strether makes an excursion into the countryside outside Paris and interprets his present activity in terms of a French landscape painting he had seen when he was young. See Sokolowski, "Visual Intelligence in Painting," 348–9.

I do not picture myself doing anything in the landscape that I see hanging on the wall; I am there simply as a viewer, not as a simulated agent. And finally, imagination involves a full-body displacement. Vision may be the most dominant sense engaged in our imaginings, but it is not the only sense; we also hear, touch, move, and interact imaginatively, and we might even be able to taste and smell. We displace ourselves entirely into the imagined context. By contrast, when I see a picture, only my seeing is involved (and perhaps my hearing, in the case of movies or staged depictions); my other senses go on experiencing the present and not the depicted world. I eat real and not depicted popcorn at the movies; I chew real gum at the opera.

Suppose, then, that Henry and Jane have traveled far away from the oak tree and that they do not have any pictures of it. They still can talk about the tree, and it is very likely that they will activate some sort of mental imaging of it as they do so. Sometimes they can even get information or confirm information about the tree by calling up an image. Recently a friend and I went to a movie. About an hour after we left the theater we were talking about the excursion, and one of us asked, "Is the movie popular? The theater was full when we were there, but what about the next show? Was there a crowd waiting outside?" We agreed that there were not many people waiting for the next show, and both of us did imaginatively "call up" the scene we experienced as we were leaving the theater. I recalled myself walking through the lobby, pushing open the door, and going into the street; and I remembered that I saw only a handful of people waiting to go in. I noticed that fact as I left the theater, and I visualized it again as we talked about it later. I would not have been able, on the basis of my imagination, to *count* how many people were there, but I knew definitely that there wasn't a crowd. I can also reenact that same perception as I write these words now, even though it is getting blurred over time. Another example that shows that we can learn from our imaging is given by Stephen Stich and Shaun Nichols. Suppose, they say, that someone were to ask you how many windows there are in your home; how would you answer? "Almost everyone reports that they *imagine* themselves walking from room to room, counting the windows as they go."[9]

Such memorial imaging is notoriously unreliable. Witnesses to an accident, for example, often have different memories of what happened, and what they remember may well be shaped by the questions put to them by others or by their own opinions about what they should be remembering, but these problems of accuracy do not matter for the point at hand; the main thing philosophically is the opening of the new dimension, the fact that we do recover the past experience in memory and imagination, and

---

[9] Stephen Stich and Shaun Nichols, "Folk Psychology: Simulation or Tacit Theory?," *Mind and Language* 7 (1992): 55.

that we relive what we lived before. We call it up and displace ourselves into that other dimension even as we live in the immediate present. Our memories may be unreliable, but they are unreliable precisely in regard to a past that we reenact imaginatively. And of course there is some kind of neurological activity in the brain that underlies such recall, some sort of reactivation of what happened physiologically when we first experienced the event. This neurological activity goes on in the present, but the experience itself is given as past, and hence as absent from the world in which we presently live.

Our present environment is continually flooding us with sensory and neurological input; mental imagery is neurological output, generated from within, and yet it is nested within the contemporary input.[10] Our neurophysiology allows us to become duplicated and displaced within ourselves (even as we are situated within our larger, "external" environment), and, thanks to our syntactic powers, we are also able to "manage" this inward displacement to some extent. We can, through reminiscence, control what happens here. Such control over our imagination is related to syntactic structure.

Imagination can occur when two people are speaking with one another, but it can also occur in solitude. It is more vivid and noticeable when we are alone. We can and often do reminisce, anticipate, and daydream all by ourselves, and as we do so we normally activate our use of language. There is such a thing as solitary speaking, and it is an important aspect of human speech. To clarify it, we must make a distinction in regard to such "internal" speech.

A. Two Kinds of Speech in Imagination

Since the beginning of this book, we have emphasized the publicity of speech and the thinking that takes place in it. We have underscored the fact that the standard and paradigmatic exercise of language takes place reciprocally between speakers, when one person establishes a target of reference for the other and says something about it. But there is also internal or solitary speech, the kind we carry on in imagination, when we are alone, or when we "leave" the company of others and drift into daydreams, even while remaining in their bodily presence. Such private speech is not primary; it is derived from public discourse. Private speech is internalized conversation; conversation is not externalized internal speech. But, obviously, solitary speaking does occur, and much of our thinking takes place in it. It is what Plato describes as the soul's conversation with itself.[11]

---

[10] On input and output, see Abell and Currie, "Internal and External Pictures," 431 and 438.
[11] Plato, *Theaetetus*, 189e–190c, and *Sophist*, 263e–264a.

This internal speech can occur under two different forms. First, we might imagine that we are speaking with someone else. Just as I can imagine myself walking through the lobby of a theater, I can imagine myself talking with someone about something. Second, however, I can also carry on real, not imagined, speech while I imagine a scene. I might imagine the oak tree swaying in the wind, against a dark sky, and may begin to formulate some words about the scene and perhaps make some statements about it. Such speech may be choppy and grammatically unformed, but it is an authentic use of language. If I imagine myself going from room to room in my house to count the number of windows, I am probably counting not within my imagined scene but here and now, "outside" the scene, even though I count silently. I am counting outside the self who is going from room to room. In this second case, when I speak about the oak tree or count the windows, I do not imagine myself speaking; I actually do speak, with or to myself. I use language to articulate what is being presented imaginatively to me. I engage in syntactic display and try to manage what is going on. Even though it is done in solitude, it is real, not imaginary, speech, but it is about what is being imagined. It is something like the speech that goes on when we write a letter to someone (in the present case, however, the recipient is undetermined; it is, perhaps, more like writing a book than a letter). We distinguish, therefore, between imagined speaking and real but internal speaking attached to imagination.[12]

These two forms of speaking can be correlated with the two aspects of the self that work in imagination. The imagined speech is carried on by my imagined self (I might imagine myself complaining to my employer about my working conditions), but the "real" speech is carried on by my imagining self (I might be trying to figure out how to deal with an irascible person the next time I meet him, or I might be trying to figure out the significance of a particular scene). The first kind of speech is inside my imagined scene, the second is outside it, and it is being carried on by me now as I try to think about what I am imagining. In the latter case, I need not be speaking out loud, although I might do so; I might blurt out the words, or I might start mumbling or at least move my lips and tongue. Normally I would be speaking internally and silently, but even though silent the speech is real and not fantasized. It is like the speech I carry out when I read a book. I am not displaced into another guise of myself when I carry on such speaking. Rather, in this silent speech I am actively trying to come to terms with what I am living through in imagination, memory, or anticipation; I am trying to get clear about it and trying to articulate it for myself.

---

[12] Suppose I imagine someone speaking to me. Do I imagine him speaking to my imagined self or to my contemporary self? Probably the latter. Also, I could respond to the speaker in one of two ways: imaginatively or truly.

In other words, real speech can take place internally, and we can appreciate it more clearly by distinguishing it, as we have just done, from speech carried out inside an imagined scene. To speak internally about what I imagine is something like speaking about a picture, something like Henry's and Jane's talking about the picture of the oak tree. The major difference is that in fantasy I am speaking about what I experience in the displaced manner proper to imagination. The distinction we have made can be presented as follows:

1. imagined speech, and
2. real but silent speech.

B. A Further Subdivision

One more distinction must be introduced into this complicated situation. We can subdivide the second item we have just distinguished. Suppose I am carrying out real but internal speech about something I am imagining (I am, for example, trying to puzzle out what happened in an event that disturbed me). Such speech can be subdivided into two kinds. I can direct my speech toward one of two targets. (a) I might speak about the event as being imagined, as being present in my imaginative presentation. I might note how insistent the memory is, how vivid, or how unpleasant and frightening. But (b) I might also speak about the *thing* in the imagination: not the thing as it is imagined but the thing itself, that which is imagined. When I imaginatively count the windows in my house, I count the windows themselves. This distinction is the same as the one we can make in regard to a picture or photograph. Henry and Jane might talk about the photograph of the tree, the tree as it is in the photograph, but they might also talk about the tree itself, as they do when they notice that the tree extends over the neighbor's yard or that one of the branches seems to be withered, or when they begin to reflect more generally on the nature of trees as such or on their complexity as living organisms.

To fill out the outline we have just made, we can now schematize the four uses of language that can occur in regard to imagination. We distinguish between:

1. imagined speech, and
2. real but silent speech, which in turn can be:
   a. about the image or the thing as being imagined, or
   b. about the thing itself (through its image), whether the individual or the kind.

The last of these forms of silent discourse, the one in which we speak about the thing itself, deserves special attention. In it we have real (not imaginary) speech directed toward an imagined target, but directed toward the target itself, not the target as imagined. For example, suppose that I have been insulted by someone. I keep going over the incident in my imagination, in my memory, and I feel much resentment. I reenact the scene in which the person reviled me in the presence of others. Using my own internal speech, I try to articulate the scene for myself, to bring out something of its meaning, to bring out, as much as I can, its intelligibility, that is, its properties and its nature. As I do so, I am articulating not just my imagination or my memory; I am articulating the event that happened when that person insulted me. I am articulating something past and absent, something that occurred a week ago, but something that is being kept alive in my imaginational memory (just as Henry and Jane may be articulating the oak tree itself as they look at its photograph). I am trying to capture in syntax something that is present to me only through an imagined displacement. The combination of real internal speech blended with an imagined scene makes it possible for us to deal with the absent, and even to articulate the absent. When we articulate this echo of the thing that reverberates in our imagination, we articulate the thing itself, because the echo is a special kind of presence of the thing itself.

As in viewing a picture, it is possible to use an imaginary scene to register not simply information about the thing in question but the intelligibility of the thing. If we are imagining or remembering an insult, we can bring out some of its incidental details, but we can also come to realize, more fundamentally, "what an insult is" or, to use Aristotle's phrase, "what it is to be an insult" or "what it is for an insult to be." The essentials of things can come to light for us if we think while we imagine, and such thinking is done by letting words, with their syntactic force, play on the surface of the imagined thing. The combination of real speech, whether internal or external, with an imagined presence lets the essence of things come to light. The essentials of things can come into view for us only through the mediation of this union of phantasm and speech. We need the distance that imagination or picturing affords if we are to grasp what things are in their essence. The pictures that we have taken in will shape the way we experience the world, but our imaginative presentations will exercise an even more intimate reflux, because they blend directly with the perceptions we have of the thing in question. Even pictures that we have seen will affect our experience by way of the imaginations we have of them.

I would suggest that this grasp of the thing's intelligibility, as I have described it, is related to what ancient and medieval thinkers were aiming at when they spoke of the "agent intellect" as illuminating the phantasm, thereby allowing the "intelligible species" to be abstracted from the phantasm and received into the "passive intellect." In my description, the power to abstract needs the concurrence of syntactic structures as it works on the phantasm and makes an intelligibility present to us. Our ability to constitute syntax enables the intellectual "look" of the thing to shine through the imaginative presence that the thing enjoys in our internal sensibility. The intelligibility of the thing then becomes the content of the formal, syntactic structure of our speech. We will have more to say about the Aristotelian and medieval theory of knowledge in Chapters 17 and 18.[13]

The thinking we have described can be done in solitude and privacy, but it can achieve great public effects if this internal speech and imagination are expressed in poetry of one form or another, whether in sonnets, dramas, or novels, or in paintings or music. The novelist sitting at his typewriter or word processor is not responding to his perceptible surroundings. If he were, he would write only about computers, desks, and windows. He is articulating an imagined life as he expresses his words on the monitor, and he is in the first stages of making what he imagines public. The combination of intelligibility and imagery that the writer has worked out on his own, the insight he has achieved in this joining of words and phantasms, becomes spoken and declared for others, as his speech returns to its normal place in the conversation of mankind. The speech that began in intercourse with others does take up residence in the writer's internal life, but the domicile is only temporary, and it certainly is not primary; the speech is meant to revert to the public space where it belongs.

4. The Absence of Intelligibility

One more form of dealing with the absent must be mentioned. We have so far discussed three kinds of absence: the marginal type that accompanies perception, the kind involved in pictures, and the kind involved in imagination (including memory and anticipation). These are all grades of bodily, perceptual absence. In each of them, some sort of sensible presence, whether in the external or the internal senses, serves as a foothold for what is absent. The thing retains some sort of representational presence, at least in a picture or an imagination. These degrees of absence are accompanied by the use of words, which bring out specific aspects of what we perceive, picture, or imagine. The words are played off against the thing in its degrees of bodily presence and absence.

All along in this analysis, we have been speaking not only about the thing but also about the intelligibility of the thing. We have observed that we might, for example, understand the tree better in its pictorial or imaginative presentation than in its actual presence, even though all three forms of presentation can convey something of the intelligibility of the tree to us. The intelligibility of the tree is the target of the words used by people who speak about the tree. The intelligibility of the tree begins to appear when we appreciate certain features (expressed in predicates) as being properties, that is, when the difference between the essentials and the accidentals comes to light for us as we speak syntactically about

---

[13] I would also suggest that this grasp of intelligibility is related to Husserl's process of "imaginative variation," through which we achieve "eidetic intuitions."

the thing. This disclosure, obviously, occurs in the medium of speech. Furthermore, people who speak about the tree and appreciate its intelligibility, people to whom the difference between the accidental and the essential has become manifest, can also turn away from the normal activity of registering and reporting properties or accidents and begin to define the thing, to spell out the nature of its specific difference; they can begin to distinguish the thing from other things that are like it, and when they do so they are no longer predicating further properties of it. When they define the thing they get to the root of its properties.

But the intelligibility of the thing does not arise only when the full predication of properties, the full execution of a judgment, takes place; it can occur even before that. The intelligibility of the thing starts to appear as soon as we establish a verbal reference to the thing in question. As soon as we say, "The oak tree …," or "George Washington …," as soon as we name the thing and set it up as a target of discourse, we begin to await what is going to be said about it, that is, we await the unfolding of the thing's intelligibility, of what it is and of what it can be understood to be. The mere use of a name (as opposed to a signal) begins to target not just the thing but the intelligibility of the thing. Any single predicate, whatever we declare about the thing, unfolds one of the thing's features or relationships and engages one of its properties, and it can do so only because the thing has already been named and thereby held up for disclosure. Furthermore, any predication leaves open the possibility of still further things to be said, further features to be unpacked. Even if we say everything we know or everything anyone knows about the thing, there will still remain the possibility of other disclosures as new contexts come into play. So the intelligibility of the thing comes into view in response to the words we use to speak about the thing: the tree is unfolded as healthy, as old, as large, as made up of certain chemical compounds, as reproducing its kind in certain ways, and so on, and all these manifestations show what the tree can be understood to be, that is, they show its understandability and its being, what it is and what it can be. The simple name of the tree, *oak tree*, refers to the tree as having this power of disclosure. When a name is used, the first step in the disclosure of intelligibility has taken place; to name a thing is to bring it and its intelligibility to mind; it is not just to bump into the thing.

The thing's intelligibility comes to presence in such discourse, both in simple naming and in predicating or judging, in declaring something about the thing. But it is also possible that the intelligibility of the tree does *not* come to light, that it remains hidden or absent even though intended. Absence functions not only in regard to the bodily presence of the thing, but also in regard to the thing's understandability. What are the kinds of absence that can occur in regard to the thing's intelligibility? We will speak about four forms of such absence: vagueness, nominalization, reporting, and the experiencing that does not yet involve a name.

A. *Vagueness*

Sometimes we use words and think we use them correctly, but in fact we do not understand what they mean. Husserl describes this phenomenon as the vague use of words.[14] We may be familiar with the word *tree*, and we may be acquainted with trees, but we may still fail to understand both the word and the tree (these are not two understandings but one). We do use the word *tree*, and seem therefore to target the tree, but what we go on to say about it shows that the intelligibility of the tree has not appeared to us; the tree is present to us, but the intelligibility of trees remains absent. The name is used by association, not with logical insight, and other people, those who do understand trees, will see that we use the word but do not know what we are talking about. It is true that we would probably need to recognize at least the shape of the tree, and so we would need to grasp at least that much of the tree's intelligibility and to know at least that property; without that much of an inkling of what it is, we probably could not use the name at all. But if we are speaking vaguely, we would know practically nothing more of its essentials. We might, for example, expect it to bleed if someone cut it, or we might expect it to reproduce by generating little trees inside itself (these are far-fetched possibilities, but they help make the point).

Because we have the word and the thing but not the intelligibility, our speech about the tree is unstable. We may in fact say something true about trees, but this happens more by accident than by knowledge. We may have heard people say things about trees and might repeat what they say; or we might just take a chance and manage to say something true; but as we continue to speak about trees, the inadequacy of our knowledge becomes obvious to anyone who knows anything about trees. The specific intelligibility of trees is absent to us. It is not that we are altogether ignorant of trees; we are indeed trying to think and speak about them, and we are using what seem to us to be the appropriate names and predicates that belong to this thing, but we use the words vaguely, without thinking and without insight into what the thing is. *This* intelligibility is not there for us; *this* specific understandability – not just any one at all, but the one belonging to trees – is absent to our minds.[15]

My example of the intelligibility of trees is, as I have conceded, rather far-fetched. It is hard to imagine anyone with any intelligence and even a minimal acquaintance with trees being so entirely devoid of insight into what trees are. But it is much easier to imagine that people use words like

---

[14] Edmund Husserl, *Formal and Transcendental Logic*, trans. Dorion Cairns (The Hague: Martinus Nijhoff, 1969), §16, pp. 56–62.

[15] I deliberately say that the intelligibility is absent *to* our minds and not absent *from* our minds; the latter suggests total ignorance, while the former says that I try to intend the thing but do not succeed in doing so.

democracy, politics, freedom, and *happiness,* or even *atom* or *electricity,* in a vague
way.[16] The phenomenon often occurs when academics pretend to know
something about quantum mechanics or Gödel's Theorem. Such vague
usage sometimes embarrasses the user. Often enough we want to impress
others with our "knowledge"; we want to "fake it" for some reason or other.
We say a few things and may, by accident, seem to have gotten them right,
but then, as we try to hold forth further, our inadequacy to the thing, the
absence of the thing's intelligibility to our minds, shows up more and
more. This inadequacy shows up most vividly in the vagueness of our
syntactic articulation of the thing, but it is also present in our very naming
of the thing, in our use of a vocabulary. It is not just the syntax that has
been vaguely executed; the name has been vaguely used as well. The
content as well as the form of our speech is inadequate. We do not possess
the *eidos* of the thing in question.

Such an absence of intelligibility is a public phenomenon. It occurs in
the same public domain as the judgments we make for and before one
another, and it is dependent on the vocabulary that we have as a resource.
A speaker can be profoundly confused about democracy precisely because
there is a word, *democracy,* floating around in his linguistic environment,
being used by many people. He enters into conversation with them and,
very likely, his use of this term and others related to it will be vague at the
start. If he is insightful and willing to take in the way things are, his use of
the word and others associated with it will become more distinct and clear,
but if he lacks insight or does not want to learn, his usage may remain
confused for the rest of his life. The intelligibility behind the term
democracy, the intelligibility in democracy, will remain absent to him even
as he seems to make it present.

The vague use of words may seem to be a trivial issue. It might seem to
be a marginal topic, dealing with people who either do not have insight or
do not wish to have it. One might say that philosophy should not spend
much time with such cases; it should concentrate on true insight, not on
this kind of failure. Why pay attention to people who are mindless? But

---

[16] The vagueness might not infect just the single speaker; it might be the case that the whole
community is using a word vaguely, in such a way that the term cannot present anything real
for consistent and coherent articulation. The word *democracy,* for example, as used in
modern political discourse, might be problematic. Aristotle does name something definite
by his use of the term; he names a certain political configuration of human beings. But an
argument can be made that the modern use of the term, influenced by such thinkers as
Hobbes and Locke, does not name anything real, that it is a philosophical construct, that
incoherences and contradictions emerge sooner or later as the term is used, even in
questions about policy. The word *sovereignty* is even more problematic. It does not mean the
ruling part of a political society, which is an identifiable thing. Philosophical argumentation
amounts to an effort to determine whether a given word is capable of naming something,
that is, whether the use of the term is inherently infected with vagueness.

unless we have a sense of the failure, how can we describe the success? Unless we have a sense of the absence of an intelligibility, how can we determine the corresponding presence? The vague exercise of speech is a precious commodity for philosophers. It should be cherished. It is that against which insight must be contrasted, that from which it must be distinguished. It would not be profitable to play insight off against sheer ignorance, such as the kind we find in people who are entirely unaware of the topic at hand. Rather, vagueness in thinking and in the use of words is the proper "other" against which insight must be distinguished. Such vagueness was dramatically described at the beginning of philosophy in Plato's dialogues, which involve people who speak without knowing what they are talking about, and where Socrates is defined precisely as the one who gets them to try to overcome their vagueness and to speak distinctly about things.

The phenomenon of vagueness can be clarified by the use of some Aristotelian terms. Aristotle distinguishes two kinds of potentiality in regard to the exercise of knowledge. Consider the knowledge involved in biology. First, someone who has never learned any biology at all (say, a young child) is "potentially" a biologist in one sense. He can learn biology; he has the potential to become a biologist in a way that an animal does not. Second, someone who has learned biology but is not currently exercising his knowledge is "in potency" in another sense; he is a biologist, but he is not activated as such at the moment; he is, instead, sleeping or swimming.[17] The vague use of words is different from both of these possibilities and their actualization; it comes between them. Consider someone who is not intellectually able to learn biology but is trying to do so. The person in question would have acquired the words, and he would use them in his speech, and so he would seem to be thinking biologically, but as he tries to exercise his "knowledge" it shows up as not being knowledge at all. He has the words but not the understanding, which is beyond him. His use of the words is a counterfeit, not a real expression of the intelligibility in question. The presence of the words masks the absence of understanding. A person speaking vaguely would be like a biologist who is inebriated and who therefore exercises his knowledge in a confused way.[18] It is also true, of course, that someone speaking vaguely can use the

[17] The two kinds of potentiality are discussed in *De Anima* II 5, 417a21–b2. Aristotle does not speak specifically about biology, but simply about knowledge, and in one passage he specifies the knowledge as grammatical (linguistic).

[18] In *Nicomachean Ethics* VII 3, 1147a10–24 and b6–12, Aristotle discusses *akrasia* or moral weakness, in which the agent is overcome by his passions and, therefore, fails to act. He compares the akratic agent to a person who is reciting the verses of Empedocles while intoxicated; the speaker uses the words but does not know what he is saying, and the weak agent tries to act rationally but succumbs to passion. In both cases, reason loses its grip on the action. On *akrasia* as a failure to act, see VII 10, 1152a9: "The incontinent man is not

first-person declarative, but to those who know him he uses it with little authority. The declarative is used as vaguely as the expression it endorses, and when we use it in this way we, paradoxically, disqualify ourselves as speakers.

To overcome vagueness is to achieve what Husserl calls distinctness (*Deutlichkeit*).[19] The distinct use of words shows that an insight has occurred to us, that we have taken in the intelligibility of the thing being named. The specific difference of the thing has been disclosed to us; we have gotten clear about it. Sometimes this achievement is possible if we take the proper care, but sometimes it is beyond us; the material is just too difficult for us to take in. If we do take it in, however, the achievement is shown by the fact that our subsequent discourse avoids incoherence and contradiction and reveals the relevant properties of things. But such an accomplishment always rides on the possibility of vagueness, which remains as a kind of matrix or substrate from which distinctness emerges and into which it can descend.

B. Nominalization

The phenomenon we have just described, the vague use of names and syntax, is one type of the absence of intelligibility. It is a deficiency in our intellectual life. There is another kind of absence of intelligibility that is not a deficiency but an achievement; it is a higher-level accomplishment of thinking. It occurs when we "nominalize" an intellectual, syntactic articulation. In vagueness we implicitly strive for distinctness but have not reached it; in nominalization we have reached distinctness and go beyond it.

Suppose that we have articulated an object; we have brought out the fact that the tree is swaying. Having done this, we can move on and make this fact itself a target of reference; we can say, "This [this fact] ...," and go on to say something about it: "... shows that the wind is very strong." We can treat an articulated state of affairs as an object of reference. When we do so, the articulated fact is no longer being articulated; we focus on it, as Husserl says, in a "one-rayed" act, whereas when we articulated it we dealt with it in a "many-rayed" act.[20] This particular intelligibility of the thing (this state of affairs) is, therefore, absent to the mind, but absent because it has become ingredient in a higher-level fact. It is now being taken for granted, not slurred over, as it is in vagueness. It is good that we can package our articulations in this way. If we could not do so, we would be

---

an agent, *ho d'akratēs ou praktikos*" (Ross translation modified). In VII 3, 1147a21–2, Aristotle compares akratic agents to people who are just learning a science but have not yet mastered it; such persons "can string together its phrases, but do not yet know it." This would be another instance of vagueness, one that can be corrected by further study.

[19] Husserl, *Formal and Transcendental Logic*, §16, pp. 60–1.

[20] Edmund Husserl, *Ideas: General Introduction to Pure Phenomenology*, trans. W. R. Boyce Gibson (New York: Macmillan, 1931), §§118–19, pp. 333–7.

reduced to merely saying one plain fact after another: "The tree is swaying," "The sky is cloudy," "The wind is blowing." There would be no hierarchic structure in our speech. The possibility of nominalizing our articulated facts is one element that makes possible the tiered, Russian-doll structure of speech that, as we have seen, is a constitutive feature of human language.

When we package an articulated thing and make it ingredient in further articulations, the intelligible power, the field of force exercised by the packaged content of our speech, continues to work on what we are saying now as we progress further in our discourse. We might find that one of our later statements is at odds with what we compressed in a nominalization, either by contradicting it or by being incoherent in relation to it; but we could discover such a discrepancy only if the original intelligibility were still at work for us, still exercising its syntactic and semantic force. The fact that we see this discrepancy shows how different nominalization is from vagueness, because in vagueness we succumb to inconsistency and incoherence but do not realize that we are doing so. In this case, we are aware of it and try to correct it. We know that we have gone wrong somewhere and try to find out where. The "lower-level" articulations, therefore, remain in force, but they still are not the immediate object of focus, and hence they are somewhat absent, but in a way different from that of vagueness.

C. Reporting

There is a third use of words in which the correspondent intelligibility is absent: it occurs when words are used merely to report what we think or what we know. We say what we think, but we do not think it through as we say it. Our report is somewhat mechanical and routine. In Husserl's terms, we speak the words but do not carry out the "categorial intuition" belonging to them. A vivid example of such reporting happens when we read, to an audience, something that we composed and thought through at an earlier time, when we wrote it. As we read it aloud we might pay attention to the sounds, intonation, and tempo, but we do not necessarily register what we are reading, even though we accept it as our own. Our declarative appropriations of what we say are authentic. Another instance of such absence of understanding would occur when we merely report our opinion about a given topic to someone else. Our audience or our interlocutor would have to think our statements through, and so in that respect the intelligibility does become present, but for us it is merely latent, asleep, as it were. We do not allow its intellectual force to be activated for ourselves, even though it may be publicly activated.

In nominalization we move beyond the proposition but let it continue exercising its energy; in the present case, we merely report what we think. We have, however, thought it through earlier, and we still possess it as a conviction, so this case is also different from vagueness, in which the thing has not been thought through at all.

D. *The Unnamed*

The last three forms of absence we have discussed, vagueness, nominalization, and merely verbal reports, are all carried on through the explicit use of words. In the first the words are confused; in the second they are supercharged; in the third they are relaxed. The final kind of absence of intelligibility that we discuss does not begin with words. It begins with pre-predicative experience that is reaching upward and looking for a word; we suspect that there is an intelligibility in what we are experiencing; we get an inkling of something going on; but we do not know what it is, and we do not know if there really is anything there at all. Is there a "one" that calls for a name, is there a "something" that has properties, is there an "entity" (an *ousia*) that can be defined, or are we dealing with a heap of accidentals? We suspect there is an intelligibility, but it hasn't yet presented itself to us, so it remains absent and intended as such, not because we are thinking confusedly, or because we are not paying attention to the thing, or because we are entirely ignorant of it. We are not careless but extremely thoughtful, because we know we do not yet know and we do not wish to commit ourselves until we have the right word. Things have not yet clicked into their syntactic place; what we are dealing with is so far nameless but, presumably, nameable. We are looking for a name, or at least a metaphor or an analogy, and are trying to achieve a thought, whereas in vagueness we have the name but not the thought. Here we ask, "What's this?," but we are not sure that there truly is a "this" for which there can be a "what." We might be dealing with a material object of some sort ("Is this just a hillock, or is it a burial site?") or with a situation ("Are they plotting something, or were these events merely coincidental?").

The use of declaratives in this situation is very interesting. We use the word *I* specifically to show that we do *not* know what is going on: "I can't figure this out. This does not add up for me." We appropriate our cognitive distress. We succeed in expressing our lack of success in understanding, and we do so within the conversation in which we are engaged. This recognition of our dilemma is itself a high cognitive achievement.

What Happens When an Insight Occurs?

Suppose that we go from a vague use of a name to a distinct one: we achieve the thought, we understand something of the thing being named, and the intelligibility of the thing clicks into place for us. Or suppose that we go from an uncertain experience of a thing to an insight into what it is, into some of its essentials. From that point on, we become capable of speaking coherently, consistently, and informatively about the thing in question. We become capable of using the appropriate words effectively, and we also become capable of dealing with the thing, of responding to its mode of being and acting. We have been changed; but how? What happens to us when such an insight occurs? How can we describe the event philosophically?

It seems inescapable that the only way to "explain" what has happened is to say that some sort of representation of the thing has taken up an existence in us: a copy, a similitude, a concept of the thing starts to exist in our minds, it springs into being in our intellects, and the words we utter from then on express this representation, this meaning that exists in us. But if we try to explain the phenomenon this way, a great danger arises. We become inclined to distinguish all too sharply between the concept in our minds and the thing of which it is a representation. We might think that the words we utter publicly express our concepts, the meanings in our minds, but not the thing, or at least not primarily the thing. We begin to distinguish between the expression of the *meaning* and the expression of the *thing*. Such a distinction is problematic and highly misleading. It is far better, philosophically, to say that the expression of any sort of meaning or concept is precisely the expression of the thing in question, and not the expression of a representation of the thing. It is the expression of the thing and of what the thing is. The understanding of a name is also the understanding of what the name designates; these are not two understandings but one.

And yet we do want to say that *we* have been changed when we come to know an object or a situation, that the object or situation does somehow exist in us, in our minds. We have become qualified to speak truthfully about the thing and to act appropriately toward it. We have somehow become "adequated" to the thing; we have been made adequate to deal with it. We have assimilated what it is. How can we account for this change without positing a duplicate thing, a representation, that would threaten to stand between the thing and us? We might say that the thing exists in one way in the world and in another way in us (it exists "cognitively" in the mind), but this is more a statement of the problem than a resolution or clarification of it. What is cognitive existence? How are the meaning in our minds and the nature of the thing related? In what sense are they "two," and in what sense are they "one"? Some sort of distinction seems legitimate here, but what kind of distinction?

Several points must be kept in mind as we try to deal with this persistent philosophical problem. First, it would be better if we did not focus simply on the simple, elementary parts of the problem. We should not speak about the thing and the concept just by themselves, as though we had the thing "out there" all by itself and had somehow extracted or abstracted a concept from it. We should, instead, look to the rich syntactic context in which such cognition takes place. We should look to judgments with their syntax, and we should move even beyond single judgments to the whole network of syntactic structure that occurs in arguments, proofs, and conversations. It is within such complex syntactic patterns that things are "taken in" intellectually. It is not the case that we have a simple abstraction of a thing's concept just by itself and that we add syntax to it. Rather, only within the context set by syntax do we let the intelligibilities of things become manifest to us. Furthermore, the syntax in question is not used, first and foremost, to articulate ideas in our minds; it articulates and illuminates, first and foremost, the things we are experiencing.

The second thing to keep in mind is the fact that the paradigmatic use of syntax, and the insight into what a thing is, occurs in public conversation, not in isolation. The model is found in people speaking with one another, not in solitary meditation.

Third, we should also be aware of the perspective from which we are speaking when we posit concepts and other such mental representations. We are not speaking with others in standard, ground-level, world-oriented conversation. Rather, we are speaking from the philosophical standpoint, from the perspective we have when we reflect not only on what we are saying, but also on the fact that we declare ourselves, and confirm or deny what we or others have said. We are speaking *about* truthfulness, not engaging in a normal exercise of it, and we need to remember that our language is adjusted when we move into this dimension. Words like *inside, outside,* and *likeness* take on new shades of meaning.

Finally, we must remember the strategic and indispensable role of the word or the name. The intelligibility of the thing becomes present when the name is found, when the right word, whether literal or metaphoric, comes to mind, fully alive and distinctly used within its syntactic frame. The intelligibility crystalizes around the word, which is its carrier.

10

Mental Representations

Our next challenge is to determine whether we need to appeal to mental representations of some sort when we speak, philosophically, about language, communication, knowledge, and truth. The unquestionable phenomenon is that we use words to name things and that we syntactically articulate the way things appear. When we try to explain how this happens, and how we can be right or wrong in what we say, must we postulate in our minds some sort of mental entity, some sort of meaning, concept, or proposition, that corresponds to the things we speak about? What do our words express: do they express the things we speak about or these mental entities? Are we forced to posit these mental intermediaries, or can we somehow speak philosophically about cognition without invoking them?

Mental Representations are Problematic

Such mental representations or mental entities are troublesome things, for two basic reasons. First, it is hard to say what sort of things they are. They never present themselves to us directly. We don't experience them, even when we reflect on our experiencing. We do know that there is something like internal imaging, which we obviously experience in dreaming and daydreaming, but we never directly experience our "thoughts" or mental representations or meanings. We have to posit them philosophically because we don't know how else we can account for knowing and speaking about things; they seem needed as a kind of bridge that links our minds to the objects that we know, and they seem to be what is behind our words; they seem to be the "meaning" that makes the sounds we utter to be words. They are hypothetical constructs, and we attribute to them precisely the features we need them to have if we are to "explain" how we can know things in the world. They are tailor-made for this task, and hence they seem more like contrivances than real entities.

But perhaps the problem lies not in the process of human knowing and speaking but in some deficiency in our description of what knowledge and speech are. Could we speak philosophically about knowledge without needing to posit mental representations? Such a description would certainly be leaner and cleaner than the one that forces us to postulate entities that we never encounter and that seem to have such peculiar properties.

The second reason why such mental representations are problematic is that they threaten to become taken as the things we directly know. They are originally posited as intermediaries between us and the things we think about, but surreptitiously and almost inevitably we begin talking about them as the direct targets of our awareness. We begin to say that our words primarily express our "ideas" and only secondarily the things we speak about. We tend to interpret even perception as the viewing of internal images; Husserl calls this an "almost ineradicable error, *ein schier unausrottbarer Irrtum.*"[1] These proclivities make us think that our minds are enclosed, self-regarding spheres, and we wonder how on earth we can ever get outside ourselves. The development of sciences of the brain reinforces this tendency to postulate mental representations; if there are such entities, then perhaps we could map them onto the brain and thus explain how our thoughts come to be and what they "really" are, namely, a certain activity of our brain cells that have been stimulated by the thing outside us.

We then wind up trying to explain how we can ever go beyond our own concepts; how do we even know there is a world out there? We seem to be imprisoned in the cabinet of our own minds, and yet the walls of this cabinet are imperceptible and unimaginable; *we* posit them, and they seem to be the strangest kind of thing. The very entities that were supposed to explain knowledge turn out to make knowledge of the "extra-mental world" problematic. We get tangled up in our own shoelaces, in a problem of our own making.

Misleading, illusory philosophical problems arise. We raise questions that are not real questions but that look like real ones, and we find it impossible to "answer" them: "You mean that you can't even prove that there is a real world beyond our ideas? If you can't do that, what good is philosophy?" This is the epistemological problem that so besets modern philosophy. The impression is given that we cannot do anything in philosophy until we first have proved that we can really know the real, "extra-mental" world.[2] Getting caught up in such bizarre problems distracts us

---

[1] Edmund Husserl, *Logical Investigations*, trans. J. N. Findlay, ed. Dermot Moran (New York: Routledge, 2001), volume 2, Investigation V, Appendix to §11 and §20, p. 125. See John B. Brough, "Translator's Introduction," in Edmund Husserl, *Phantasy, Image Consciousness, and Memory (1898–1925)* (Dordrecht: Springer, 2005), lii.

[2] The very term "extra-mental" is problematic. What is it opposed to and defined against? The "intra-mental" world? What could *that* be?

from real philosophical insights, and it also gives a bad name to philosophy. No one *really* thinks that we are locked into our brains or our minds or our mental representations, but if people are asked about this issue they find it hard to avoid falling into the egocentric trap, so they simply do not talk about it and give up on what they think philosophy to be.

Problems in Modern Philosophy

The history of early modern thought, with its "way of ideas," bears witness to the fact that once we start talking about mental representations, even in the most sophisticated way, we are in danger of concluding that what we really and directly know are those representations, not the things themselves. We begin to think that our thoughts are something like the images we experience when we dream or daydream, except that the mental representatives, the thoughts, are more transparent and ethereal.

If we imitate David Hume and begin our philosophical inquiry with this problem of "ideas," we will inevitably accompany him into the final section of the first book of his *A Treatise of Human Nature*, where he gives us a memorable description of someone who has tried to make the turn into philosophy but has done it wrongly: "I am first affrighted and confounded with that forlorn solitude, in which I am plac'd in my philosophy, and fancy myself some strange uncouth monster, who not being able to mingle and unite in society, has been expell'd all human commerce, and left utterly abandoned and desolate."[3] This is philosophical detachment run wild but beautifully described, with pathos and existential declaratives. The problem of speaking with others arises: "I call upon others to join me, in order to make a company apart; but no one will hearken to me. Every one keeps at a distance, and dreads that storm, which beats upon me from every side." This is Plato's Eleatic Stranger with a vengeance, a foreigner not just to Athens but to the whole human race: "Where am I, or what?"[4]

Hume has tried to enter the transcendental, phenomenological attitude but has done so without the subtlety and distinction that it requires. His only way of validating the natural attitude, therefore, is simply to rejoin it and to drop his philosophical questioning, not to contemplate the natural attitude and its world sympathetically: "Most fortunately it happens, that since reason is incapable of dispelling these clouds, nature herself suffices to that purpose, and cures me of this philosophical melancholy and delirium, either by relaxing this bent of mind, or by some avocation, and lively impression of my senses, which obliterate all these chimeras." He gets over philosophy by relaxing into the natural attitude with his friends: "I dine, I play a game of

---

[3] David Hume, *A Treatise of Human Nature*, ed. L. A. Selby-Bigge (Oxford: The Clarendon Press, 1960), 264.
[4] Ibid., 269.

back-gammon, I converse, and am merry with my friends." At this point, he retains no fondness for philosophy but is glad to have been relieved of it: "And when after three or four hours' amusement, I wou'd return to these speculations, they appear so cold, and strain'd, and ridiculous, that I cannot find in my heart to enter into them any farther."

Hume's reason goes off the tracks because he, poor man, starts with a doctrine of what one might call mental representations ("perceptions," which he divides into "impressions" and "ideas," which differ only in their vivacity), and also because he has no way of showing that philosophical reflection continues the trajectory of natural reasoning even as it takes a distance from it. He cannot show that there is continuity as well as difference between natural language and philosophical speech. He has not had the benefit of Husserl's analyses of the transcendental reduction. In fact, it need not and should not be upsetting to enter into philosophy; philosophy liberates and attracts, it does not sequester the person who practices it; entering into philosophy does not make us lose anything but gives us a new and fascinating perspective on the whole, no matter how incomplete our grasp of that whole may be.[5] Nor need we abandon philosophy when we recover the natural attitude; it always remains a concern and an illumination on the margin of things and of ourselves. There is such a thing as the philosophical life, and it does have something to think about. It confirms and refines the identities and differences that occur in our pre-philosophical lives, and it does so from a new angle, with a new perspective, and with its appropriate modification of language.

It is highly regrettable that the British Empiricists contaminate their philosophy by beginning with mental representations. Both Hume's *Treatise* and John Locke's *An Essay concerning Human Understanding* are marvelous works of metaphysics. They discuss such prototypical themes as identity and difference, substance and relations, parts and wholes, causes and effects, chance and existence, and seeming and being. They make many wonderful observations, but they spoil it all by claiming that everything they say applies only to the walls of the cabinet of their minds, to ideas, impressions, or perceptions, not to the being of things. What a sad waste of philosophical talent! If we could use something like a philosophical virus scan to clear away the distorting subjectivism

---

[5] The entry into the dimension of philosophy is analogous to our entry into the game of language. As soon as we name something, its entire intelligibility is being designated even if we have only a feeble grasp of it. As soon as we shift from the natural attitude into philosophy, we have the entire philosophical world given to us. The turn to philosophy opens a prospect. The whole "promised land" is there, even if we have only glimpsed it and cannot yet make out the features of its landscape. See Edmund Husserl, *Ideas: General Introduction to Pure Phenomenology*, trans. W. R. Boyce Gibson (New York: Macmillan, 1931), "Author's Preface to the English Edition," 29: "The author sees the infinite open country of the true philosophy, the 'promised land' on which he himself will never set foot."

infecting these writings, we would be left with metaphysical treatises that compared favorably to the classics of that genre.

There is a natural melancholy that affects reflective people. Aristotle asks, "Why is it that all men who have become outstanding in philosophy, statesmanship, poetry or the arts are melancholic?" After citing several examples, he continues: "In later times also there have been Empedocles, Plato, Socrates, and many other well-known men. The same is true of most of those who have dealt with poetry."[6] This despondency can be dealt with by customary remedies, but it is made pathological and Nietzschean when it is reinforced by the doctrine of ideas, which locks us into ourselves with no hope of exit.

My attempt to deal with the problem of mental representations is also an attempt to restore the authentic philosophy latent in the British Empiricists and to overcome the disjunction between what Hume calls "the ancient philosophy" and "the modern philosophy."[7] The dichotomy between the modern and the premodern must be surmounted if we are to return to philosophy as such and escape a historicized counterfeit. Furthermore, it is not only metaphysics that is at stake, but also philosophical anthropology, the understanding of ourselves not as isolated, autonomous thinkers and actors but as datives of manifestation and agents of truth, who by nature live in community and can declare ourselves within it.

Speaking about Appearances

The chief reason why we tend to go astray in the "way of ideas" is that it is extremely difficult to speak coherently about the appearances or the presences of things. Our language is geared toward speaking about things. Our use of language generates a great variety of appearances. Speech makes things show up in many different ways. The legomena, the things being said, introduce many dimensions of phenomena, things becoming manifest. Once language has done its work, we become able to speak about appearances as well as about things, but, sadly, we inevitably tend to make the appearances into further things that are just like the things we originally talked about. Speaking about appearances requires metaphysical subtlety and sophistication, but we often come up short in these qualities. We tend to flatten appearances out and reduce them simply to more things. For example, even something as simple as the color of an object,

---

[6] Aristotle, *Problems*, trans. W. S. Hett, Loeb Classical Library (Cambridge, MA: Harvard University Press, 1957), vol. 2, Problem XXX, 953a10–32. Most of the *Problemata* are not from Aristotle himself, but both Plutarch and Cicero claim that this particular question does come from him. I have amended the translation slightly.

[7] Hume, *A Treatise of Human Nature*, 219, 225.

which is one of the ways an object appears to us, becomes reduced in many analyses to an entity that is generated in our eyes and brains, something caused by the thing and not one of its manifestations. A meaning or a concept or a thought also becomes something in our "minds" or ultimately in our brains, and it is likewise separated from the thing of which it is the meaning or concept or thought. Instead of being the thing's appearance to our thinking, it becomes another thing in us.

To avoid such philosophical dead ends, we will try to sidle into the problem of meanings, concepts, and thoughts by working through several stages in the philosophical description of appearances. We have to learn to be flexible in these matters; we have to train ourselves for some fancy footwork as we negotiate our way through manifestation.

1. The first step is a brief analysis of pictures, such as photographs and paintings. Pictures are good things to start with in phenomenology, because we are far less inclined to "subjectivize" them. We know that the picture is there on the wall. It is made up of the paper and the chemical stains on it, or the canvas and the paint. We are less inclined to say that there is nothing but canvas and paint hanging on the wall, with the real picture being in our heads. We are quite happy to admit that the picture is, purely and simply, out there.

A curious kind of identity occurs in pictures. A picture does not simply present something that looks like the thing depicted. The thing pictured is not just similar to the thing itself. It is identically and individually the same, not just similar. Suppose I have a picture of Dwight D. Eisenhower on my desk. The figure in the picture *is* Dwight Eisenhower himself (as pictured). It is not merely similar to Eisenhower, as his brother or son, or someone else from Kansas who happens to look like him might be. Dwight Eisenhower's brother is similar to him, but he is not a picture of him. Similarity alone does not make something a picture. Picturing involves individual identity, not just similarity.

But, you may say, the picture really is not Dwight Eisenhower; he has been dead for many a year. The picture *is* really only a piece of paper. Of course, the two are different entities, different substances; but when we take them that way, we are not taking them as picture and pictured. We are taking them just as things. Once we get into the logic of pictures and appearances, something else happens, and we have to report the phenomenon as it is, not as we would wish it to be. In the metaphysics of picturing, in the metaphysics of this kind of appearance, the thing pictured and Dwight Eisenhower are identically the same. The picture presents or represents that man; it does not present something just similar to him.

We should also note that the picturing relationship is one-sided. The photograph pictures Eisenhower, but Eisenhower does not picture the photograph. This is another way in which picturing differs from mere similarity, which is a reciprocal relationship. If Dwight Eisenhower's brother is similar to him, he also is similar to his brother, but Eisenhower is not a picture of his image. Why not? I cannot give you a reason, but I know that it could not be otherwise. Neither can I give you a reason why things have predicates, but I know that they do have them when they are spoken about. Such necessities are involved in the metaphysics of appearance.

We should also note that picturing is an exhibition of intelligence or reason. To depict something is not just to copy it but to identify it and to think about it. It does not just make the thing present; it also brings out what that thing is. For example, the remarkably beautiful prehistoric cave paintings found in Lasceau, Altamira, and Chauvet are exercises in intelligence. They do not just identify the animals and men that they depict; they also display them and bring out what they are, and they succeeded in doing so even at a time when human beings had not yet discovered or invented writing. A picture is like a predication in that it identifies a subject and brings out something essential about it, even when it explicitly just mentions something accidental; it brings out the properties of the thing as lying behind the accidental feature. Not just paintings but even photographs can do this, because it takes intelligence and insight to position the subject properly and to capture it in its significant profile.

Why are we engaging in this discussion of pictures? Because we wish to shed light on how "thoughts" are related to things. We are aiming at the conclusion that somehow a thought of a thing is identical to the thing of which it is the thought. In order to come to this conclusion, we need to elaborate the logic and metaphysics of appearance and the various kinds of identities that can occur within appearances, and we are starting with pictures because they are the most tangible and hence most graspable of all the forms of appearance. We want to show that identity is seen to be very complex once we start thinking about its various dimensions. We want to avoid an oversimplified understanding of identity and difference. To this end, we move on to the next stage in our analysis of the dimensions of appearance.

2. The second stage is mental imaging, such as the kind that occurs when we visually remember or imagine something. Identities occur here as well, but in a way different from that of pictures. We have spoken about mental images in the previous chapter, and now discuss the topic further.

I was a student in Washington, D.C., in January 1957, when Dwight Eisenhower was inaugurated as president of the United States for his second term. A friend and I, both of us from Connecticut, went down to the House Office Building and got tickets for the inauguration from our representative. It was not hard to do in those days. The inauguration was held outdoors on the east side of the Capitol. We sat in the stands that were set up to the left of the inauguration platform. I visually remember Eisenhower being inaugurated, and I can call up the memory anytime I wish. I can't seem to remember the trip downtown to the event. Did we take a trolley? We must have, but I don't remember it. I presume, however, that if something were to trigger my memory this event also could come back to me. It probably is stored there in my brain (what is "it"?). But I certainly do remember seeing Eisenhower being sworn in, and I have often recalled that event as I write and revise these words.

Each time that I do so, the Eisenhower that I remember is the Eisenhower that was inaugurated as president at that moment. He is identically the same, and not only the same individual but the same man being sworn in. I recall the man involved in the event at that time; I do not recover only the man. Furthermore, I also recover and reenact my own experiencing of that event. I represent myself (to myself) as the viewer and participant there and then. I install a distinction between myself now as I remember that event and myself then, the remembered self engaged in what is (or was) going on. When I do so, there is, obviously, a certain pattern of activity going on now in my brain, and this activity is a purely contemporary thing, a chemical and electrical process. It could be measured and registered scientifically, and there is nothing "past" about it. But what is presented to me is Dwight Eisenhower, there and then, being inaugurated as president, and me watching the occurrence, along with my friend. My personal identity is very much involved with the particular treasury of remembrances that are stored in me, which I can call up when I wish, and which sometimes surface, with greater or less obscurity, with greater or less urgency and force, on their own.

We might be inclined to say that what occurs in such remembering is the internal viewing of something like a picture, a mental image. But picturing is very different in its presentational logic from remembering and imagining. In picturing, I do not represent myself as viewing the picture. I do not engage in any displacement. I simply look at the object on the wall that I take in as a picture. In remembering, by contrast, I remember myself there and then as well as the event I participated in and the things involved in that event. Sheer phantasy involves the same kind of displacement that remembering does, except that the things and events imagined, and my own imagined, displaced self, are not recalled as being in any particular place or time in the past. We are dislocated and distemporalized, unlocated and untimed. The displacement, *Versetzung*, that occurs in imagination and memory can take on various forms.

The point I wish to make is that a certain range of identities occurs in remembering and imagining, both on the side of the objects and events presented and on the side of the person engaged in the activity, and these identities are different from the kind that occurs in a photograph or painting, when, say, Dwight Eisenhower is presented in his individuality. The identities are of different kinds, and each kind has its own type of manifold of appearances.

Before closing this treatment of memory and imagination, we should bring out a particular difference in the identities constituted in them. A remembered identity is still public, even though our individual slants on it may be private. There is a truth to it that can be determined. One can ask whether there was snow on the ground when Eisenhower was inaugurated, and if I don't remember I can ask my friend about it or consult a newspaper. But purely imaginary objects, figments constructed in phantasy, are purely private. As John B. Brough says in commenting on Husserl, "My centaur is mine; the other's centaur is his. Even if they are perfectly alike, they are not individually the same."[8] Such objects are "not intersubjectively available." Much of our conscious life, including our memories, is geared toward public identities that we can identify and reidentify with others, but phantasy introduces a dimension that can draw us into isolation and privacy, with identities that only we can recognize, many of them fragmentary and obscure, and since this dimension always hovers around our public life and often bleeds into it, there will always be aspects in us that others find hard to comprehend. We ourselves do not want to sink too deeply into such identities; we need to come up for air and hold on to the more familiar identities that we share with others. Still, the private aspects and objects, with their interwoven resentments and delights, can bring an original illumination on the way things are, because they themselves are a reaction to the things we have experienced and can even become reidentified with them, mapped onto them.

3. Our next step is to move to the kind of identification and identity that occurs when we speak about something, as opposed to picturing or imagining it. This is yet another kind of intentionality. Suppose that instead of seeing a picture of Eisenhower or remembering seeing him at some time and place I simply use his name in a sentence. I say, for example, "Eisenhower was very successful in World War II in managing the Anglo-American alliance, but he was not a great battlefield general; he could not 'read' the Normandy battle; he did not have a 'grip' on the battlefield, and he had no training or experience in maneuvering great armies, as the German and Russian generals did."[9] I need neither pictures nor imagination for this statement to be successful. Any images that come to mind

---

[8] Brough, "Translator's Introduction," in Husserl, *Phantasy, Image Consciousness, and Memory*, xliii.

[9] See Max Hastings, *Overlord: D-Day and the Battle for Normandy* (New York: Simon and Schuster, 1984), 240, and *Armageddon: The Battle for Germany, 1944–1945* (New York: Knopf, 2004), 26–8.

are purely accidental. As I speak this sentence and you hear it, you and I may entertain an image of Eisenhower sitting in a jeep or talking with Field Marshal Montgomery, but any other image would suffice (an image of a map of the Normandy beachhead might come to mind). For that matter, there might be no image at all and the words could still do their work.

What identity is presented when the word "Eisenhower ..." is uttered? Not simply the identity of Eisenhower, but his intelligibility as well. His intelligibility: that is, what can be understood about him. The name calls up Eisenhower as a subject of predication, Eisenhower as that which is to be unfolded in speech. In the sentence that I stated in my previous paragraph, Eisenhower is unfolded and manifested as a general. I could also have spoken about his birth, youth, and education, and then he would be unfolded and understood as a human being and as a member of a family. Any entity can be manifested and hence made to be understood in regard to what it is, that is, in regard to its essence and the properties that flow from it. Things as intelligible, as capable of being unpacked and manifested, are the targets of our thinking when we begin to use words. We use the name to fasten on the thing and to enlist it into syntax, and the syntactic articulation that follows brings out what we were aiming at with the initial use of the name. The name is used to introduce the entity into our conversation, and such an introduction puts forth the entity as a thing to be intellectually unfolded: the understandability of the entity is brought forward.

To pin down the manner in which a name identifies an intelligibility as well as a thing, let us contrast the name with something that seems very close to it: a sound used as a mere signal to bring the thing in question to mind. A mere signal is not yet a name, even though the sounds may be the same. The same sound can be used in two different ways. Suppose I saw Eisenhower and were to say, "Ike!" Or suppose Eisenhower walks into the room, and I nudge you and say, "Ike!" This sound is not being used as a name; it is not the beginning of a sentence. It does not hold Eisenhower up for predication. It does not target his intelligibility. It just draws our attention to him. The same effect could have been achieved by the sound "Look!" or by an orchestra playing *Hail to the Chief.* The sound is merely associated with Eisenhower; it does not name him. A different intentionality is at play. This associated sound, this exclamation, furthermore, does not designate or identify the intelligiblity of Eisenhower; it just brings *him* to mind, not his understandability.

But the name, as a step in syntactic articulation, does designate the object's intelligibility and not just the object. Syntax is precisely the frame in which intelligible content is disclosed, and a name identifies *that* intelligibility in particular. (Where we speak of intelligibility, the ancients would have spoken of form or *eidos*, but we would do well to avoid those terms for the moment.)

A picture contains something like an artificial embodiment of an intelligibility, but a word "contains" or carries only the intelligibility and the identity of the thing, not any embodiment. Words are more ethereal than pictures. They contain just the thing's intelligibility, which they have lifted off from some particular embodiment. Words do their work in contrast with pictures, imaginations, and perceptions. They can be brought back and applied to pictures, imaginations, and perceived things, but they can also work in the absence of such presentations. Words function with syntax, when they are used to unfold what the things are; they are used to unfold the intelligibility that they contain. And we cannot speak philosophically about words and what they do except in conjunction with picturing, imagining, and perceiving, because words work only in conjunction with these other ways of intending.

You might complain that you do not like this talk about intelligibility as that which is contained in the name of a thing. Intelligibility sounds so intangible, so obscure and mysterious. You might prefer something definite, a particular *thing* that somehow is the target and objective correlate of the word. But to say that a word is correlated with a particular definite entity (such as a "meaning" or a "concept") would not do justice to words. Words are not just signals; they do not just bring things to mind. They present a thing as to be thoughtfully unfolded; that is, they present the thing in its understandability and speakability, as an exprimend, something to be expressed; they can do so because along with the words comes the armature of linguistic syntax with all its resources; the content associated with syntax is the thing in its intelligibility.

Identifying an Intelligibility in Public, in Presence and Absence

Still, it is hard to get a handle on what it means to identify an intelligibility. We are less troubled when we try to describe how we identify an object that is given to us in perception. We see the thing from this side and that, at this time and that, and it is always the same object. We identify and reidentify it. Even the identity found in pictures, as perplexing as it may be, is still rather tolerable: we do see and we must admit that the picture depicts Eisenhower himself; it is not just similar to him. The identity in remembering and imagination is more complicated, but, again, it is rather tangible. We have at least the obscure mental image. Furthermore, we know where to locate the identity in all these cases. The identity of the perceived object is in the object itself; its oneness is associated with its being. The identity of the picture and the thing pictured is in the image itself. The identity of the remembered or imagined event, as well as the identity of me as remembered or imagined and me as remembering or imagining, are all somehow "in me."

But what is this curious identity of the intelligibility of the object, and where are we to locate it? Obviously, the intelligibility of Eisenhower is first and foremost found in Eisenhower himself. He is the thing that we want to understand. In fact, he himself was born intelligible, and his parents, his community, and his own actions have made him intelligible in further ways. Much can be said and displayed about him. His wife, his relatives, and his colleagues all knew and understood him, to varying degrees.

But Eisenhower's intelligibility can be available even when Eisenhower himself is not. It can be present and identified even in his absence. We don't even have to remember him in order to understand him. We don't need to have pictures of him in order to understand him, but they would help. (We have no photographs of the prophet Daniel, and yet we understand him to some degree; we can say something about him. Artists have constructed pictures of Daniel, but in this case the pictures come from the intelligibility that we possess of him in our words; the picture is not the primary source of the understanding.) The intelligibility of a thing can be presented and identified even when the thing is not present and identifiable, neither in its body nor in its image. Names and words, with their syntax, make this intelligibility present. They somehow detach the intelligibility from the thing. The detachment gives flexibility, power, and range to our reason, but it also brings its own dangers; we might be inclined not only to distinguish the intelligibility from the thing, but also to separate the two and make the intelligibility something that floats away apart from things. The understandability belongs first and foremost in the things that are understandable, even though it can be thought of by itself, when it becomes an understanding.

The Location of Intelligibility

Suppose we bring a certain intelligibility to light. Suppose we do understand something. Where is this understanding to be located? Is it inside us, the way our memories and imaginations are, with their identities and identifications? Yes and no. The British historian Max Hastings has an understanding of Eisenhower. He is old enough to have seen Eisenhower and to be able to remember him, but his understanding need not rest on his memory; Hastings also has some understanding of Napoleon, whom he has never seen and obviously does not remember. But through his studies and writings concerning World War II, Max Hastings has an extensive and authoritative understanding of Eisenhower. I also have some understanding of Eisenhower, but it is far less informed and less exact than that of Hastings. Despite the differences in depth, both our understandings are of Eisenhower (that is why I can compare my understanding with that of Hastings). The intelligibility embodied in Eisenhower is present to both of us and somehow "in" both of us. It, the very same intelligibility, is also present to and "in" countless other datives of manifestation. This understanding can be embodied in pictures, but in principle it can be pictureless.

The intelligibility, one and the same, somehow hangs around the words we use. If we did not use words, with their syntax, the intelligibility in things would not be identified and displayed. It would not have come to light. Words conjure up its presence. Intelligibility is potential, not actual, and there would be no understanding if there were no words and people to use them. The active use of words shows (signals) that understanding has taken place, and it allows this understanding to occur "in" others. It makes the intelligibility present to others.

I would like to locate the intelligibility of Eisenhower not just "in" Max Hastings and me, but in the human conversation. The human conversation is not a bubble made up of mere words; it includes the things that it speaks about, the legomena. From the philosophical perspective, we can say that the human conversation encompasses noematically its objective correlatives: the speakable and the spoken (as well as the unspeakable and the unspoken). It includes Dwight Eisenhower (and also trees and turtles), but as spoken about, actually or potentially. It includes the intelligibility of Dwight Eisenhower (as well as that of trees and turtles). I cannot speak philosophically about the intelligibility of Eisenhower "in" me without speaking about it "in" Max Hastings as well as "in" you, the reader. One mind all by itself is, effectively, no mind. One mind cannot be actualized as a mind without the stimulus of speech with others. Human reason is essentially distributed. The intelligibility of Dwight Eisenhower dwells in the "third realm" that Frege says we must recognize, a realm different from both the things we know and our psychological activities of thinking, knowing, perceiving, and imagining.[10] The human conversation within which the intelligibility of Eisenhower and all other intelligibilities are actualized and located is not a formal, structuralist system. It subsists only in the people who carry it along and who are actual or potential conversants in it. The intelligibility of Eisenhower exists in Eisenhower and in the minds of those who, in principle, can speak and think with one another about him and what he is.

Have I gone too far with this? Why not say that each person walking around has his own understanding of Dwight Eisenhower, just as each person has his own private memories or imaginations of him? But language cannot be private, even though memories can be and phantasies are. If we use a name, we know that other people can use that name as well, and it is not just because we as speakers all use the same name, but also

---

[10] Gottlob Frege, "Thoughts," trans. Peter Geach and R. H. Stoothoff, in *Collected Papers on Mathematics, Logic, and Philosophy*, ed. Brian McGuinness (New York: Blackwell, 1984), 363: "A third realm must be recognized."

because the thing in question is nameable by that name. That name clothes his intelligibility (not just him) "like a garment," as Husserl puts it.[11] The person's name, because it enlists him and his intelligibility into syntax, is different from a mere signal, such as an affectionate "name" used by people who are infatuated with one another. If two lovebirds use the "word" *Schmoopy* for each other, they are not designating each other's intelligibility; *Schmoopy* could not be used by them in a real sentence. It's part of billing and cooing, not naming. Other people would not use that sound to name the persons in question. Names lock the object into syntax and subject it to the rigor of logic and the control of experience. They publicize the thing named. We have to be able to verify and confirm what we say, but we are not so constrained when we use a sound like *Schmoopy*. A sound like this pulls its users into mutual privacy, not into public reason.

Because a name works in the human conversation, anytime I use it I am aware that my understanding may be greater or less than that of others. Using the name of something to designate it does not present the full and adequate intelligibility of the thing. It designates the intelligibility but does not yet unpack it. It presents the intelligibility as to be unfolded through predication. In one sense, it does present the full intelligibility, but only as potential, not as already achieved. Suppose that Oliver does not know much history and hears the name *Dwight Eisenhower* in a conversation; he might say, "Oh yes, the general in the war." He does identify Eisenhower, and he is caught up in the question of Eisenhower's intelligibility, even though he knows practically nothing more about him. He is engaged in the syntactic game, in which something has been brought to mind, something that can be expanded. Oliver is engaged in the full intelligibility of Eisenhower, and if Max Hastings were to appear on the scene and begin talking about Eisenhower, both he and Oliver would be talking about the same thing and unfolding its intelligibility. By virtue of the name, that particular intelligibility, that and none other, has been present to both speakers from the start. This is how names work; they work paradigmatically in public, not in solitude.

It is easy to see why thinkers like Alfarabi, Avicenna, Averroes, and the Averroists might conclude that there is a separate "active intellect" for all human beings.[12] The identities we achieve in language seem to transcend

---

[11] Husserl, *Logical Investigations*, Investigation VI, §6, p. 202, and §12, p. 213.

[12] See Herbert A. Davidson, *Alfarabi, Avicenna, and Averroes, on Intellect: Their Cosmologies, Theories of the Active Intellect, and Theories of Human Intellect* (New York: Oxford University Press, 1992). The general problem is: how can the human being and the human mind, which are "generated-destructible," become identified with forms or powers that are incorporeal and eternal? See p. 331. (Averroes differed from Alfarabi and Avicenna; in his later work he claimed that even the passive or material intellect, and not just the active intellect, transcends the human being.) Much of the motivation for this doctrine in these thinkers arose from their reading of the texts of Aristotle, but they must also have been

us as individuals, and so we might well suspect that something beyond us is at work in us when we manage to touch the intelligibility of things. These thinkers believed that we each have our own imaginations and that we supply the phantasms for the cosmic mind, but that it is the separate intellect that does the thinking in us, not we ourselves. There are analogies to this doctrine in more recent writers, who have located human thinking in the structuralism of language or in intertextuality. The response that I would offer to this proposal is that thinking does not occur in structures or texts but in their use, and in order for the use to occur there must be a user of language or a dative of manifestation, an agent of truth. It is true, however, that we are often carried along by what everyone says, by the formularies of the language we belong to and the opinions and appearances that float around in it; we often just say what "they" say; but in such a condition we speak only vaguely and inauthentically. We are always able, however, in principle if not in fact, to bring our vague speech to authentic distinctness, and to become responsible for what we say.

Each of us has his own understanding, or at least we are in principle capable of having it; but it is an understanding that is curiously public, and it calls for its own philosophical description, which we can achieve by exploring the kind of identities that language brings to light. We each have our own rationality, but it is not segregated from that of others with whom we can converse. If we individually succeed in having a thought, the human race has succeeded as well. Things are displayed for us in common, but to each of us in a greater or a lesser degree.

Proper and Common Names

We have used the name of Dwight Eisenhower to work out the intentionality and presence proper to intelligibility. *Dwight Eisenhower* is a proper name, but in using it we also connote features that can belong to other entities as well as to the person the name designates. When speaking of Eisenhower, we might speak about him as a general, for example, and the word *general* is a common noun. It designates an intelligibility, but one that can belong to other individuals besides Eisenhower, such as Erwin Rommel and Georgi Zhukov, as well as Vassili Danilovitch Sokolovski. A common noun expresses an intelligibility that is universal; it can apply to an unlimited number of cases.

The reason why such an intelligibility can be universal is that it encompasses explicitly only the essence and the properties of the thing it

influenced by their own reflections on human knowledge. This issue is analogous to the modern problem of how human cognition, which is subject to psychological laws, can enter into the domain of logic. It is the problem of psychologism, but projected by these thinkers onto the cosmic scale.

names. It sheds the particular accidentals. Its "content" contains only the essentials and leaves the accidentals indeterminate. The intelligibility of a general, for example, implies that the general will be involved with an army; this is one of the properties of being a general; but the army could be American or Russian, twentieth- or nineteenth-century, large or small, victorious or defeated. All these features are accidental, even though each general will have the properties of belonging to some community, being located at some period in history, and being involved with an army of some particular size. A proper name designates an intelligibility that includes these accidentals, but the intelligibility designated by a common name does not.[13]

As we have noted at the end of Chapter 8, any name can fluctuate between being used as a proper name and being used as a common noun. We can speak about "the general" and signify either Eisenhower or the general as such, as in "The general must command respect from his men."[14] In the second case, the term is used to implicitly designate all generals and not just this one, but more directly it is used to explicitly designate the intelligibility of being a general. This oscillation in usage is not just a matter of linguistic practice. It reflects what is designated by the use of words. If we designate individuals, they are always designated as being individuals of a certain kind. Even a proper name connotes a kind; *Dwight Eisenhower* is typically a name for a man, and *Rover* is typically a name for a dog. Furthermore, even the proper name *Eisenhower* can become a common name if generalized, as in the phrase "He is a real Eisenhower." If we directly designate individuals, we connote the intelligibility behind them, and if we directly designate the intelligibility, we connote the individuals that embody it. There is no individual without intelligibility, and no intelligibility without at least the possibility of instantiation or embodiment. Any use of names has these two dimensions in its reference. Names inherently lend themselves to dual use, and they can do so because they capture the intelligibility of things.[15]

---

[13] I hope that this way of speaking about "concepts" can help clarify the fact that they are universals. In the classical mode, we are told that concepts are particular, accidental entities existing in the mind or soul of the knower; but although particular as entities, they are universal in content. They seem to have contradictory properties. By speaking about intelligibility I hope to escape this paradox.

[14] Other verbal forms can be used in the same dual manner. We can say, "A general ..." and signify either that there is a general who did this or that, or that generals as such must do this or that ("A general must be decisive"). Plural forms have the same range of meaning: "Generals died in the battle," and "Generals look for weaknesses in the enemy's line."

[15] Kurt Pritzl claims that in Aristotle's description of truth, the initial, pre-predicative reception of form by the mind puts us in touch with an intelligibility that is neither universal nor individual. He made this point in a lecture entitled "Aristotle's Door" given at the Catholic University of America on September 6, 2002. The lecture will appear in a collection of essays edited by Pritzl to be published by the Catholic University of America

The intelligibility of a thing does not just function in regard to our cognition. The intelligibility of a thing belongs to that thing and makes it to be what it is. Our reference to the thing connotes a sense, that is, a meaning or an intelligibility that determines that thing and makes it capable of being a "one" in its kind. Our speech and the understanding it expresses does not just show what we have in our minds; it shows what the thing is, its entity. A thing is nameable as one and as an instance of a kind because it *is* one and an instance of a kind, and its intelligibility makes it to be so.

Are Concepts in the Head?

What, then, shall we say about mental representations? There is an intelligibility in Eisenhower; is there another intelligibility "in our minds" that is a kind of copy or similitude of that which is in Eisenhower? Or is it the same intelligibility? Is it somehow in two or more places, in Eisenhower on the one hand and in Max Hastings, Oliver, and me on the other? Do we each have a different intelligibility, a different mental representation?

We state words; what do our words express? Shall we say that they express concepts or meanings that are in our minds? I would rather not put it that way. This way of saying it makes the concepts or meanings too much like mental images, and it traps us into the "way of ideas" of the British Empiricists. I would rather say, with Husserl, that the words we speak express the things we talk about.[16] If I say that Eisenhower was an excellent coordinator of the Anglo-American military alliance, I am expressing Eisenhower, not a concept that I have of Eisenhower. If I say that leopards pose a threat to a village, I am expressing leopards and not a concept of mine.

We recall the typographic conventions we wish to follow.[17] I use a term in italics (*leopard*) to designate the word, the term enclosed in single quotation marks ('leopard') to designate the concept or meaning, and the term without any modification (leopard) to designate the thing. To repeat our earlier example: "Simon used the word *leopard* to warn everyone that a leopard was in the area, and their concept of the beast, their 'leopard,' led them to take the proper precautions." To formulate this in regard to our most recent paradigm: "*Dwight Eisenhower* is used to name Dwight Eisenhower, and Max Hastings' 'Eisenhower' is very rich and detailed, especially when compared with my own 'Eisenhower'."

Press. My analysis in this section would also hold that the intelligibility that we take in can be employed in both ways.

[16] As noted earlier in Chapter 6, Husserl says that words express the content of acts of fulfillment or perception. See *Logical Investigations* I, §14, pp. 199–200.

[17] See Chapter 4 of this volume.

I want to say that *leopard* expresses leopards and *Eisenhower* expresses Eisenhower. But what about 'leopard' and 'Eisenhower'? Where do they fit in? Do we really need them? How are they different from the leopard and Eisenhower? The problem resolves itself into a problem of identity. How are concepts or meanings related to what things are? Are we dealing with two things here? Are we dealing with concepts and meanings "in the head" and with things and their "whatness" or "kinds" and properties out there, "outside the head"?

Instead of speaking about concepts and meanings, I would rather speak about the intelligibility of things. This way of speaking allows us to see more clearly that we are not dealing with two disjunct entities. We are dealing with a subtle and perplexing issue about appearances and the identities that occur within them, not with a problem about how we get from one thing to another. We are dealing, also, with an issue that arises only when words, with their syntax, come into play; we have no visions without syntax. If we did not have names in action, we could leave this problem at the simpler level of imaginations and memories, with their less bewildering forms of identification. But, of course, if we did not have words we would not have a problem about knowledge either, so the whole issue would never have arisen.

The identity that occurs in pictures seems so much easier to handle because we can attach the identity to the picture, which has such a graphic presence. Is there anything like this to which we can fix the intelligibility when we know it with our minds? Is there any analogous "graphic" embodiment for it? There is the mental image, the phantasm, but better by far is the name of the thing. The name can serve as the vehicle that carries the intelligibility of the thing. Even the mental image is not specified enough to yield the understandability of the thing until the word comes into play. The word might be fleeting, metaphorical, internally spoken, or barely pronounced – there might be only the whiff of a word – but it does capture the thing's intelligibility. John Aubrey, in his life of Thomas Hobbes, writes, "He walked much and contemplated, and he had in the head of his staff a pen and ink-horn, carried always a note-book in his pocket, and as soon as a notion darted, he presently entered it into his book, or else he should perhaps have lost it."[18] But it was not just a notion that darted; there was also a word that crystalized the notion, and the thing that Hobbes entered on the paper was the word, which carried the notion. A word is even more suitable than a picture as a holder of the pure intelligibility of a thing because of the very lack of similarity between the word and the thing: there are no accidentals that come with the vehicle to

---

[18] John Aubrey, *Aubrey's Brief Lives*, ed. Oliver Lawson Dick (Ann Arbor: University of Michigan Press, 1957), 151. See also p. 9, where Aubrey describes how Hobbes, as secretary, wrote down "notions" that "darted" in the mind of Francis Bacon.

distract us from what the thing is simply in itself. The name contains *just* what it is for the thing to be, nothing else, whereas the picture will contain many accidentals merely as a graphic and not as a representation. The word is more transparent. For this reason, its compositional syntax is more explicit than that which is embedded in a picture, and what we say about the thing is more discretely identifiable, albeit less suggestive. The word is also more manageable. We can more easily lock it into grammatical combinations as we converse with others and bring out more fully the intelligibility of the thing.

There is only one intelligibility for Eisenhower, and it exists primarily in him. If Max Hastings and I take in that intelligibility when we use the name *Eisenhower,* that one understandability becomes present to both of us, but it remains one and the same. There cannot be many intelligibilities of a given kind, neither for Eisenhower nor for leopards. An intelligibility cannot be duplicated, triplicated, or multiplied in any way, not even in the way that one and the same Eisenhower can be multiplied in the many pictures that are made of him; in each of these images, there is another material object that carries one and the same presence, and the multiplication of carriers introduces a kind of distribution that does not occur in the case of an intelligibility. The understandability is more intensely one, more resistant to any kind of multiplication. 'Understand-ability' is not compatible with 'many.' In this respect, an intelligibility is like a piece of music. Every performance of the *Goldberg Variations* is a presentation of one and the same "thing."

When Hastings, Oliver, and I speak about Eisenhower, there is only one intelligibility in all three of us, but if we each had a picture of him there would be three different presences because of the three different material carriers. Names do not multiply presences the way pictures do. Even our personal remembrances and our private imaginations multiply the presences of Eisenhower in a way that our knowing and naming do not. Because our elevation into language, syntax, and naming allows us to present an intelligibility, it also allows us to get into a kind of identification that is otherwise unavailable. An identity is achievable by intellects that is not achievable by images, whether real or mental. The identity of an intelligibility is what makes it possible for many persons to establish a common reference with their words and to speak about that referent in both its presence and its absence. When we speak philosophically about knowledge and speech, it is better to speak about intelligibility than to speak about the form or the *eidos* of things, because the terms *form* and *eidos* almost inevitably lead us to posit mental copies and similitudes, whereas the term *intelligibility* does not.

The intelligibility that exists in Eisenhower is the source from which his properties flow. His understandability is his essence or definition, and his properties, such as his being involved in victory or defeat, derive from it.

When Eisenhower's intelligibility takes up residence in Max Hastings, Oliver, and me, it also works as a source of properties, now as formulated in speech and perhaps in our actions toward Eisenhower. The degree to which the intelligibility exists in each of us will be reflected in the richness of the properties and accidentals that we are able to recount; Max Hastings can say much more about Eisenhower than Oliver and I can, and so we can see that Eisenhower's intelligibility exists more fully in him than in us. He can express Eisenhower better than we can: not his concept of Eisenhower, but the man and the general himself; he expresses not 'Eisenhower' but Eisenhower when he says *Eisenhower* and continues to talk about him. If Hastings expressed only 'Eisenhower,' his speech would not be public and we could not talk with one another.

The reason why an intelligence allows a more intense identification than do pictures and mental images is that the latter draw on the embodiment of the intelligibility while intelligence draws simply on the intelligibility of the thing. We can have pictures of Eisenhower because his intelligibility resides in him as an individual, bodily entity, and the pictures represent the bodily dimension. A name, by contrast, highlights and focuses on the intelligibility of the thing as it initiates our predications. We know we cannot separate the intelligibility from the thing (the thing would not be what it is without it), but we can talk about and unfold the intelligibility even when the thing is not there. Pictures and mental images, by contrast, make the thing present pictorially, even while leading us to "see" the intelligibility in them, the intelligibility named by our words.

If we wish to clarify, philosophically, what thinking is, all we can do is to speak about the kind of identity that is presented to us in knowledge and distinguish it from the kinds of identities that occur in pictures, mental images, and the direct perception of things. Philosophically, we can say, "This is what happens in knowing and naming: this kind of identity is achieved." The main thing we do *not* want to say is that in knowing we have a copy or a likeness of the intelligibility of the thing. Even the word *similitude* seems problematic and out of place; it is better not to say that in knowledge we acquire a similitude of the thing known or of its intelligibility. It is acceptable to say that we assimilate the intelligibility, but not that we acquire a similitude of it. To say the latter confuses the phenomenon of knowing and naming with that of imaging, with disastrous results.

1 1

What Is a Concept and How Do We Focus on It?

We have been distinguishing among *leopards,* 'leopards,' and leopards, and among *Eisenhower,* 'Eisenhower,' and Eisenhower; among, that is, the word, the concept, and the thing. We need to make one further clarification concerning the concept. We will now clarify how 'leopard' and 'Eisenhower' become part of our philosophical vocabulary as signifying concepts as distinguished from things and names.

The Concept Is an Intelligibility Taken as Present to Someone

We have discussed the interaction between the name and the thing, between *leopard* and leopard. The name targets not just the thing but also its intelligibility. The name does not just call the thing to mind; the name is not just a signal; the name, like a key, unlocks the thing to capture its intelligibility and to enlist the thing and its understandability into syntax. The name presents the thing in its intelligibility.

This intelligibility is disclosed both to the user of the name and to the dative of the name, to the speaker and to the listener (the potential respondent, who can also use the word). Normally, the listener is simply guided by the words of the speaker to focus on the thing in its intelligibility. It is better, incidentally, to say "the thing *in* its intelligibility" than "the thing *and* its intelligibility," because the latter suggests that the intelligibility and the thing are two different "entities," whereas the former makes it clear that the thing subsists only by being intelligible. The thing, so to speak, basks or marinates in its intelligibility. It wouldn't be *what* it is without it, and it wouldn't *be* without it. It would be neither *one* entity nor an *entity.* The intelligibility makes the thing to be what it is.

The listener, under the guidance of the speaker, thinks through the thing. But sometimes the listener can change his focus. Instead of simply being captivated by the entity the speaker is talking about, he can make an adjustment in his attention. He can change the direction of his intending.

He can begin to focus on the target and its intelligibility *as being presented by and to the speaker*, and he can take them as such. The ability to carry out this intellectual deployment is essential to human rationality, and it issues in what we call the concept. A concept or a meaning is an intelligibility, but taken as being possessed by someone, as being present to and in someone, as being expressed by someone. It is not just taken in by the listener; it is taken as being presented by a speaker.

Suppose there is a conversation involving Max Hastings, Oliver, and me. Hastings talks about Eisenhower. Oliver and I simply go along with what he says, fascinated by the stories he tells. Under his guidance, obeying his grammatical signals, we articulate Eisenhower. We are focused by Hastings' words on the entity he is talking about, and we have the intelligibility of that entity unfolded for us, even though Eisenhower is not bodily present while Hastings speaks.[1] But at some point, Oliver interrupts this subservient listening and reflects: "It's amazing how much this man knows about Eisenhower! He has the most thorough understanding of Eisenhower one could imagine. What a rich conception of Eisenhower!" Oliver might also have said, "What an 'Eisenhower' Hastings has!"

Oliver has slightly suspended his forthright listening to Hastings and has reflected on ... – on what? On Hastings' knowledge of Eisenhower. Yes, but more precisely, on Eisenhower's presence to Hastings. And still more precisely, on the presence of Eisenhower's intelligibility *to* Hastings and *in* Hastings. Oliver has ceased thinking simply about Eisenhower and has begun to think about Eisenhower's manner of being presented to Hastings. He has ceased thinking just about Eisenhower and his intelligibility and has begun to think about the concept of Eisenhower, on how Eisenhower has been conceived (cognitively, of course) by this eloquent speaker.

When Oliver expresses his amazement at how rich Hastings' conception of Eisenhower is, he does not turn away from Eisenhower and begin speaking about something in Hastings' mind or head. He does not begin to talk about an entity in Hastings, some sort of mental embryo that looks like Eisenhower. Oliver continues to speak about Eisenhower, but now as present to and understood by Hastings. If we insist on saying that Oliver is talking about an idea in Hastings' mind, we still have to remember that this usage of the preposition *in* is highly metaphorical and does not connote spatial location or spatial difference. The Eisenhower in Hastings' mind is the real Eisenhower in his understandability, not a picture or copy of him. We should also remember that the term *idea* is closely related in its original meaning to the term *look*, and if we were to say that Hastings' concept of Eisenhower is the look of Eisenhower in his mind, we would be

---

[1] The subject the conversationalists are speaking about might well be made present in a picture. That is why history books and biographies are enriched by photographs or depictions.

closer to the mark and less inclined to posit a copy of Eisenhower in him. A look is not a likeness or a copy. Hastings' concept of Eisenhower is not something in Hastings' mind that looks like Eisenhower; it is, rather, the understandable look of Eisenhower in Hastings' mind.

While I have gone on naively following what Hastings says, Oliver has executed a marvelously sophisticated maneuver. He has changed and amplified his intentionality. He has enlarged his thinking. He does continue to follow Hastings' lead; he does continue to articulate Eisenhower; but he also adds a reflective moment in which he thinks about how Hastings is articulating Eisenhower. He now focuses on something in the domain of meaning, sense, concepts, and propositions. The very domain of meaning, concepts, and propositions arises as correlated with such reflection. Oliver does not subtract anything to get to the concept of Eisenhower; he does not subtract real existence to get to a mere idea; rather, he adds a dimension by making a reflective turn.

So now Oliver does not just think about Eisenhower; he thinks about Eisenhower as present to Hastings. *That* is the concept of Eisenhower. That is 'Eisenhower.' The concept of Eisenhower is the intelligibility of Eisenhower taken (by Oliver) as present to Max Hastings, or, in a more general way, the intelligibility of Eisenhower as it might be present to anyone who is up to date on what people now know about Eisenhower. Still more completely, it is the intelligibility of Eisenhower as it could in principle be wholly present to anyone. To spell this out in regard to our other example: 'leopard' (the concept or the meaning) is the intelligibility of leopards, that which makes them to be what they are, but it is the intelligibility being explicitly taken as "possessed" by someone or as present to someone. It is that intelligibility as taken in by someone or even by anyone in general.

Notice how important the intelligibility is here, and how it is correlated with the name. If we were just dealing with bringing Eisenhower to mind, an ordinary sound or smell or associated object would suffice. Such a reminder would present Eisenhower, perhaps in image or in a recollection, but it would not present his intelligibility, nor would it set Eisenhower up for predication, articulation, or display. It would not call up his understandability. Only because human speakers can, by the use of names, bring an intelligibility to mind can they also focus on that intelligibility as present to someone, that is, as conceived.

I have taken and adapted this analysis of the status of concepts from Husserl, who develops it in *Formal and Transcendental Logic*, a work published in 1929, just after the author's retirement from teaching.[2]

---

[2] Edmund Husserl, *Formal and Transcendental Logic*, trans. Dorion Cairns (The Hague: Martinus Nijhoff, 1969). The contrast between focusing on things and focusing reflectively on the judgmental sphere (or the sphere of sense) is worked out in Part 1, Chapter 4.

This interpretation of the domain of concepts or meanings is clearly present in that book, but strangely it is not, to my knowledge, discussed explicitly by Husserl in other works. Perhaps he himself did not see its importance. My interpretation differs from Husserl's in that he develops it in regard to a single mind moving from a focus on things (in the ontological domain) to a focus on things as presented (in the domain of sense), while I develop it in regard to two or more minds. Husserl deals with the single ego, while I deal with Max Hastings, Oliver, and myself. Husserl adds the intersubjective dimension later on, but I prefer to have it there at the start.

The domain opened up by this reflection is not limited to single concepts and intelligibilities, but extends also to entire propositions. In the latter case, the correlation is between a state of affairs (an object and its features) and a proposition or judgment, which is a state of affairs taken as proposed or as presented by and to a speaker. The domain of sense is also the domain of propositions. It is what Husserl calls the apophantic realm, which is reached by what I would like to call propositional reflection. A concept or a sense finds its place here because concepts and senses are meant to become ingredient in propositions, that is, they are meant to be enlisted into syntax.

The Focus on Concepts and Propositions and the Issue of Truth

The constitution of the domain of concepts, the differentiation of 'leopards' from leopards and 'Eisenhower' from Eisenhower, is the opening up of a new dimension in appearances, not the fabrication of a new entity. Things were already appearing because they were being articulated by syntactic intentions; they were being conceptualized in our

In §§37–41, Husserl repeatedly asks whether there is a difference between focusing on judgments and focusing on states of affairs. The title of §42 is "Solution of this Problem," and in it Husserl shows that most natural judging is directed toward objects. In §43 he shows that we can formalize such objects and build up a formal ontology, which still is object-directed. Finally, §44 makes the crucial move that explains how the judgmental or apophantic domain, the domain of sense and concepts, is differentiated from the ontological domain. A state of affairs in the ontological domain is taken "as proposed" by a speaker, and with that reflective move, the whole apophantic domain is differentiated from the ontological. One of the subsections here is entitled "Phenomenological clarification of this change of focus." This conclusion is confirmed in §45, and in §46 Husserl discusses the two concepts of truth, the truth of correctness and the truth of disclosure. Then, Chapter 5, §§47–51, expands the apophantic domain to include all kinds of "senses," even those that are not predicative. I have given a closer exegesis of these sections of *Formal and Transcendental Logic* in *Husserlian Meditations: How Words Present Things* (Evanston, IL: Northwestern University Press, 1974), 271–89. See my *Introduction to Phenomenology* (New York: Cambridge University Press, 2000), 187–99, for a statement of how propositional reflection differs from philosophical reflection.

conversation and the conversation of mankind; but now they can be taken as appearing. None of this could happen if human awareness did not become syntactic. The power of syntax that marks the difference between human speech and protolanguage also makes it possible for people to reflect on what is syntactically articulated in the world and to see it as being presented to or proposed by the speaker.

Such reflection also makes it possible for human beings to ask about the truth of what is being said by a speaker. We are not slaves to our inter-locutors. We might be naively guided by them, but in principle we can always pull back and ask, "Wait a minute, what is he telling me? Is this really the case?" Oliver can ask, "Is Hastings right in saying that Eisenhower managed the Anglo-American alliance well?" When Oliver does this, he performs a zig-zag motion, as Husserl calls it ("ein Urteilen sozusagen im Zickzack"), between focusing on the judgment and focusing on things, and through this movement he can see whether the judgment and the state of affairs can be blended with one another.[3] This oscillation is the origin of the kind of truth we call correspondence. It is a back-and-forth between two attitudes and two ways of taking the state of affairs, not between two things.

I will use the term "propositional or conceptual reflection" to name the kind of focus that differentiates the propositional domain, the domain of sense, from the ontological. This reflection takes place within the natural attitude. It raises the issue of the truth of what a speaker is saying.

The Philosophical Perspective

One final distinction needs to be made in order to pin down the reflection that focuses on concepts and propositions. We have been describing a conversation carried on by Hastings, Oliver, and me. Within that con-versation, a kind of reflection takes place that focuses on concepts and propositions. This reflection allows us to distinguish among *leopards*, 'leopards', and leopards, and to consider a state of affairs only as being proposed by someone. This reflection allows us to test the truth of what others are saying.

But, dear reader, you and I are not part of the conversation we have been talking about. We are speaking from yet another perspective, the philosophical. We are engaged in another kind of reflection, with a special kind of detachment. Philosophical reflection is different from proposi-tional and conceptual reflection. Hastings, Oliver, and I, in our conver-sation in the natural attitude, can recognize and make use of the intelligibility of Eisenhower, but we, the three of us, do so with a kind of naivety. You and I, by contrast, can describe that same intelligibility from another angle, and we can show how it is the central ingredient in the

---

[3] Husserl, *Formal and Transcendental Logic*, §44, p. 125.

conversation being carried on by our three speakers and listeners. We can show how the intelligibility of things is related to names and to the syntax of thinking. We are the ones who say that the intelligibility of a thing is targeted, captured, and carried by the name of the thing. These things remain operative but hidden from people engaged in the natural attitude and its discourse. They speak in natural languages, while you and I speak in transcendentalese.[4]

You and I, from our happy and relaxed philosophical stance, can contemplate the human condition and the conversation that makes it to be what it is. We can watch how people turn to and from one another in speech and how they act as agents of truth, declaring themselves from time to time. To engage in this philosophical analysis is not a terrifying or alienating venture but a special and lucky completion of the rational life carried on in human discourse. After all, I who now speak to you am the same speaker who was engaged with Hastings and Oliver in the conversation we have imagined, and I have also been engaged in real conversations with someone on the telephone an hour ago and with a friend yesterday, and I was not speaking in transcendentalese when I arranged with the plumber to come to fix some pipes. My philosophical reflection does not tear me away from these exchanges, but it does give me a new perspective on them, a perspective that every human being has at least an inkling of.

It is when we speak reflectively as philosophers, in transcendentalese, that we say that concepts are "in" people, or that Dwight Eisenhower or leopards can take up a cognitive existence "in" the minds of those who know them. We are speaking as philosophers, not as lawyers, doctors, psychologists, or biologists, when we say these things. What sort of an *in* are we speaking about? The role of prepositions in transcendentalese is tricky. They are subtly transformed when used in this language, and it is easy to lose our grip on them and to allow them to slip back into the meanings they have in mundanese, the language of the natural attitude. The preposition *to* is less misleading, in this new perspective, than is *in*. If we

---

[4] For the term *transcendentalese* as the name of the language spoken from within the transcendental attitude, see Thomas Prufer, "Quotation and Writing, Egos and Tokenings, Variables and Gaps," in *Recapitulations: Essays in Philosophy* (Washington, DC: Catholic University of America Press, 1993), 61–2. Prufer uses the contrast between use and mention to state the problem of how someone in the transcendental attitude can address someone in the natural attitude: "If the speaker can only mention speeches in the hearer's language, how can he teach users of that language to use his own language (transcendentalese)?" (p. 61). The move from natural languages to transcendentalese is different, of course, from the move from natural to artificial languages, such as those in computer programs or mathematics. Both natural and artificial languages come about within the natural attitude. The philosophical attitude reflects on both of them and shows how the artificial language is generated by the use of the natural language. Artificial language cannot be generated by itself.

say, philosophically, that the understandable look of Eisenhower or that of leopards is present *to* those who know them, we are less inclined to postulate copies of the intelligibility in the knowers, but when we say the intelligibility is *in* them, the danger of positing a copy looms large. The spatial meaning that *in* has in natural speech asserts itself even in philosophical discourse, and we become inclined to postulate a copy "in here" as opposed to the original intelligibility "out there," in the thing itself. Even Plato (if we take him literally) seems to go astray in this regard, postulating forms in a place apart from the things that participate in them. If, however, we are carefully attentive to the transpositions of sense that occur when we start to speak transcendentalese, we could legitimately say that the intelligibility of Eisenhower or that of leopards is, indeed, "in" the mind, or that Eisenhower and leopards exist cognitively in those who know them. We could even say that the concept of Eisenhower or the concept of leopards is "in" the people who conceive these entities. But we have to remember the new sense that the word *in* has taken on in such speech. The word has shed its materially spatial sense, in which one place is differentiated from another, and has moved into that common "space" that is the domain of thought or the space of reasons; this space is entered when we identify things across their presence and absence, and when we make pictures of things and thoughtfully imagine them. It is the strange space we enter when we begin to name things and thereby capture their intelligibility.[5]

Words as the Hinge for the Constitution of Concepts and Propositions

Let us return to the topic of propositional or conceptual reflection. Oliver, listening to Max Hastings, interrupts his focus on Eisenhower and begins to think of the concept 'Eisenhower' possessed by his interlocutor. Oliver's intellectual maneuver, his reflection, could not occur without the presence of words. Spoken words function as the pivot or fulcrum around which such reflection can take place.

Normally, words function as names and signals. When spoken by a speaker they bring things to mind, and their grammar signals how the thing is to be articulated. The names and grammar also signal that the speaker is speaking, and they signal to the listener to think through what the speaker speaks. However, what happens in the kind of reflection that we are describing is that the listener turns his attention away from the thing spoken about to the words and signals being uttered, and he begins to think of the thing spoken about *as being spoken about* by the speaker, that

---

[5] The strange, "intelligible" space we are speaking about is analogous to the strange temporality of intellectual things, which we earlier compared to *aevum* (see Chapter 8).

is, he begins to think of the thing as being displayed by the speaker or as being present to the speaker. To take the thing and its intelligibility in this way is to think of the concept of the thing. The listener uses the spoken words, in their evanescence, as the hinge around which he can make this maneuver.

In this turning around, the listener does not turn away entirely from the thing in question. He does not move away from the thing to something else, to a new entity in the speaker, a mental entity that one could call the meaning or concept. Rather, he stays with the thing and its intelligibility, but he thinks of it as being present to the speaker (or to someone or anyone else). A new dimension is brought into focus, but it is a new dimension that ultimately belongs to the thing in its display.

Do we want to say that there is one intelligibility in the thing and another one in the person who speaks and knows? Or that there is one intelligibility in the thing and a copy or similitude or likeness of it in the person who speaks and knows? I do not think so. A thing's intelligibility is not the kind of entity that can be duplicated in these various ways. There cannot be a copy of the thing's intelligibility. There is just the intelligibility of the thing, and it can be present to many minds, but it is always one and the same as it is present to and "in" them. When we know a thing, we become one with the thing known because its intelligibility is "in" us; we become qualified by it and qualified to deal with it and speak about it; we do not have a likeness of the thing instead of the thing.

Everything in these intendings and shifts of attention revolves around words that are being used. It is because words are there to be taken in different ways that such reflection is possible. Oliver, listening to Max Hastings, normally focuses on Eisenhower as Hastings talks about him, but he can also shift his regard and begin to focus on Hastings' words – his names and grammatical terms, his signals – precisely as signals, and when he does so, he thinks of Eisenhower as being presented by Hastings. He does not just follow the signaling going on in the words; he thematically appreciates the words as signals.[6] Then, Oliver is able to attribute a certain presentation to Hastings, and he becomes able to distinguish between himself (Oliver) as an agent of truth and Hastings as an agent of truth, as someone using language to display something. He can then say something like, "Well, *you* may think so, but *I* really couldn't agree with that." He can name both Hastings and himself as using a sign design at the moment to bring something to light: he can use first- and second-person declaratives.

It would be helpful to use a bodily analogy to describe what occurs when we make a propositional or conceptual reflection, when we turn from

---

[6] On how spoken words allow us to focus on concepts and to perform the propositional reflection, see Robert Sokolowski, *Presence and Absence: A Philosophical Investigation of Language and Being* (Bloomington: Indiana University Press, 1978), 102, 118, 122.

focusing on a thing (under the guidance of someone's speech) to focusing on the speech and the speaker. In our normal attitude, we focus the searchlight of our attention on the thing, with the speaker and his words remaining on the margin. In propositional reflection, we turn the searchlight toward the speech and the speaker, but we do not lose the thing spoken about; it now gets moved to the margin, as that which is being proposed by the speaker. This turnabout of the searchlight of our focus depends on the spoken words, which serve as the tangible (or audible) swivel on which it rests. (Philosophical reflection, however, bootstraps us into still another dimension; we look down from the rafters on the entire scene below us, reflecting on the speakers, the spoken words, the searchlight itself, the things that have become legomena and phenomena, and the shifts of perspective that take place. But this reflection also is made possible by the availability of spoken words.)

Psychologists of language who discuss the development of human speech will often ask at what point a child acquires a "theory of mind," by which the child can attribute beliefs and desires to others.[7] They might also say that animals do not have a "theory of mind" and, therefore, cannot enter into the kinds of exchanges that take place in real speech. I think that this term, "a theory of mind," is awkward as a name for what establishes speakers, and I think my description of how speakers react to words is a more pertinent analysis of the phenomenon in question. A theory of mind is too definite and intellectual a thing. It is too cut-and-dried and too complex. Can children develop something we can call a theory? Something more elementary goes on between speakers; words become taken and followed in new ways: first they serve as signals for categorial, thoughtful, syntactic action, and then they become the pivot that allows us to see something as merely someone's conception, not as the thing pure and simple. The interaction is more rudimentary than the formulation of a theory of mind. It is a matter of shifts in perspective that open up new dimensions.

Spoken words are almost insubstantial, and yet they are immensely powerful. They enable large-scale conversations to occur around them, and can be taken in a great variety of ways. Hastings' speech unfolds Eisenhower for us; it signals to us that Hastings is thinking; it signals to Oliver and me to think Eisenhower through; and it enables Oliver to see Eisenhower as known and presented (conceived) by Hastings. Speech does

---

[7] For a brief history of the concept of a "theory of mind" in psychological research, see Janet Wilde Astington, *The Child's Discovery of the Mind* (Cambridge, MA: Harvard University Press, 1993), 3–6. For an exploration of the "theory-of-mind" theory, see Alan M. Leslie and Tim P. German, "Knowledge and Ability in 'Theory of Mind': One-Eyed Overview of a Debate," in *Mental Simulation*, ed. Martin Davies and Tony Stone (Cambridge, MA: Blackwell, 1995), 123–50.

all this, and it materializes the display of things, even for very large crowds of people, where it can bring about such colossal effects as wars and revolutions, and yet it is the most evanescent kind of being. A picture of Eisenhower has much more substance. It lasts through time and can be placed elsewhere. Eisenhower is more tangibly materialized in a picture or a statue. When he is named he is materialized only in the vibration of air, and yet this tenuous embodiment permits the most precise unfolding of his intelligibility. The spoken articulation of Eisenhower is more complete and exact than the pictured, and the latter could take place only with the help of the former.

Writing changes this situation and gives spoken words some of the substantiality of pictures. Indeed, ideographic writing, which obviously preceded alphabetic script, is only a slight transformation of picturing. Like a comic strip, it simply puts pictures in sequence and installs a minimal syntax; it exploits the hiatus between protolanguage and language. Once writing succeeds in encoding speech and not pictures, however, it separates the grammatical signals from the person who speaks in them (and who is signaled as speaking by them). It embodies the names and grammar on the page or on the computer monitor. You, as reader, can then pick up my syntactic actions and co-perform them, even though I am not bodily present to you and you do not hear the acoustic vibrations I cause. Speaker and listener become separated from one another, and both speaking and listening become much more private. The reader can also become much more suspicious of what he reads; it is easier to adopt a propositional attitude toward what is written than toward what is said. Only because of this transformation into writing and its privacy could Descartes and Husserl have thought of human thinking as done by a solitary ego. But behind writing and its textuality there will always remain speech and the speaker who declares himself in it.

Human Speech and the Ends of Things

Before concluding this chapter on concepts and speech, we must introduce an issue that has not yet been explicitly treated in this book but that will become important in our later chapters. We introduce the end or *telos* of things.

Names target not just things but the intelligibility of things, which they introduce to be unfolded in our predications and in our conduct. But the intelligibility that we grasp in things is not unrelated to the goodness or the perfection of those things. We never work with things simply as they are; we always see and understand them against the background of what they *can* be and what they *should* be.

The intelligibility that a name captures in a thing is not static. The intelligibility is the essence of the thing: it is the source from which the properties of the thing flow. The properties of a thing are activated over time in the thing's accidents, in what "happens" in it. In the natural order of things, in the world that we know and in which we act, the world in which things change, things *become* more amply what they are as time goes on, and if they are fortunate, they become more perfectly what they are. They ripen, and their ripeness is their *telos*. We understand things in the light of their best way of being. A thing that is adolescent is profiled against its mature condition, and a thing that is declining is experienced against what it was for it to be. The best of an entity is always present to us in any experience we have of it, provided that our experiencing is intelligent. The thing is not just what it is at the given moment in which we come to name it. It is also what it is capable of being, and it is experienced as such. The intelligibility of the thing, therefore, includes the thing at its best. Only from that perspective is the thing understandable, and only from that perspective does its name have meaning.

We can get a clearer sense of the natural ends of things by distinguishing them from human purposes.[8] Purposes are the intentions that we have when we act. They derive from our wishes. They move us to act, and without human beings there would be no purposes. Ends, by contrast, belong to things apart from human desires and projections. They are the perfections of things, the way things are when they are working at their best. There are, obviously, ends to nonhuman things, such as leopards, spiders, and trees, but there also are ends to human beings and to things involved with human beings, such as practices and institutions. Thus, there are ends to the arts and sciences of medicine, engineering, and law; there are ends to human health, sexuality, and nourishment; and there is a *telos* to the human life of thinking. There is even an end, or there are ends, to human beings as such. The ends related to human beings appear to us most vividly in contrast with the purposes or intentions we have when we act. Ends and purposes come to light by being differentiated from one another.

There is relatively little controversy about the ends of leopards, spiders, and trees. We rather easily know when they are acting well according to their kind. We would all agree that a spider that constructs a disheveled web and does not know what to do when an insect is caught in it is not what a spider should be. It is sick as a spider. There is much more controversy, however, when we try to speak about the various ends associated with human beings, because such ends bring obligations with them, and such obligations may run counter to our purposes. We cannot do anything we wish in regard to human nourishment, for example; some ways of eating and drinking destroy the very thing they are supposed to perfect. Our purposes can conflict with the way we should be. The greatest controversy

---

[8] The distinction is made by Francis Slade, as noted earlier in Chapter 7.

arises concerning human happiness as such. We might, as Aristotle observes, generally agree on *eudaimonia* as the name of this end (and this minimal, nominal agreement is no small matter), but the question of what the name concretely signifies is bound to cause disagreements.[9] It even leads to differing political arrangements, with their diverse ways of life. The meaning of human success will differ, for example, in oligarchies and democracies, and this will lead to different kinds of laws.[10]

Only ends bring out the full intelligibility of things. When we name things and thus bring them into language, syntax, and human conversation, we do not introduce them as inert items; they enter into language as intelligible, and their intelligibility involves more than just a mathematical presence, which would be indifferent to the good implied in the thing.[11] When they are named, they are profiled against their best, and their best is not just what is good but also what is beautiful or admirable in them, their *kalon*. The Greek *eidos* and the Latin *species*, as well as *forma*, mean not just looks but good looks. Casual speech may not pay attention to this, but elevated, poetic speech does more than just identify things; it allows us to admire them for what they are.

As we learn our native language, we learn the names for things, and in doing so we are introduced to those things as they can and should be. A sense for ends is built into human words, but it is not inserted into them by our speech – we and our language do not project the thing into its optimal condition. Rather, the thing itself, insofar as it and its intelligibility are captured into speech by being named, shows what it can be: *res ipsa loquitur*. We might project our *purposes* into the things we name, but we do not project the ends that the things have; things come with their own ends, and we glimpse them if we have gotten some idea of what the thing is. If we capture the thoughtful look of a thing, we have it profiled against what the thing can be when it is at its best. If we get the point of a thing, we have grasped its *telos*.

We can make this claim about language and *telos* because we have come to know that names and language express not a mental copy of the thing, not a representation of the thing, but the thing itself with its potentialities as well as its present actuality, with its full actuality or *telos* as well as the snapshot we might have of it at any given moment. Our words capture the same intelligibility that is embodied in the thing itself and encompasses

---

[9] On our agreement on the name for happiness but our disagreement concerning its significance, see Aristotle, *Nicomachean Ethics*, I 4, 1095a17–22.

[10] In the *Politics*, Aristotle says that each of the political forms, good or bad, has a different understanding of justice and human virtue. See *Politics*, III 9, 1280a7–1281a10, and III 11–13, 1282a39–1284a3. Aristotle says that the "science or ability" that looks to the human good overall is political. See *Nicomachean Ethics*, I 2, 1094a27–8, b11.

[11] Aristotle, *Metaphysics*, III 2, 996a29–30: "In mathematics nothing is proved through this cause [the good], and no proof is given 'because something is better or worse'."

the thing as it could be at its best. This is what names and speech do: they let things come to light in their completion as well as what they at the moment manifest to us. In fact, a present snapshot of a thing, shorn of the thing's dynamics, would not present the intelligibility of the thing at all. It would only present its shape. There is a natural evidencing of things, and it presents the *telos* of the thing in contrast to the purposes we may have when we enlist the thing into our service. We do not add a sense of the good to the things we name; the things come with their own perfectibility. If, by contrast, we were to claim that our words expressed only our mental representation of the thing, a kind of mental copy of it, then we would have to add the *telos* of the thing to this copy. We would, with Hume and Kant, be forced to separate values from facts. Facts would involve only our mental representations, and values would have to come from elsewhere, whether from our desires, from our categorical imperatives, or from our aesthetic sense of how things ought to be.

We do not get the point of a thing except within syntactic articulation; there is no vision without syntax. But syntax without vision is also undesirable. If we are syntactically nimble but substantially thoughtless, we will have no appreciation of what we are dealing with. We will be rational but not reasonable.[12]

We will return to the issue of the ends of things when we discuss human wishes. Before that discussion, we conclude our treatment of human understanding by examining the relation of the body to the activity of thinking in the medium of words.

---

[12] In moral matters, some people may be clever but wicked, hence rational but not reasonable. Aristotle calls this quality *panourgia*, villainy or knavery: being quick-witted but up to no good, or, as *Liddell and Scott* puts it, "ready to do anything." The aim (*skopos*) of such agents is base (*phaulos*). See *Nicomachean Ethics*, VI 12, 1144a26–7.

PART III

THE BODY AND HUMAN ACTION

12

The Body and the Brain

If we are to explore what human conversation and thinking are, we must say something about the neurophysiology that underlies them. The brain, obviously, is involved in human experience and thought, and some people claim that thinking and consciousness can be completely explained as activities of the brain and nervous system. How shall we address this topic?

There are two ways of exploring the physiology associated with thinking. One is to pursue scientific research into the nervous system, to determine its structure and function, its chemical and electrical components and activities, and so on. Immense progress has been made in this project, and still greater advances are anticipated. The second way of exploring this issue is scientifically much more modest, but it has its own importance. It is to discuss how we speak about the brain and nervous system, and how our scientific speech about it can be integrated with our speech about ourselves as responsible speakers and agents. We can easily fall into confusion in this area; we might say, for example, that the brain feels pain, or that my brain recognizes my grandmother, or that the brain causes my thoughts. These statements are confused because it is not my brain but I myself who feel pain, recognize people, and think, just as it is I and not my brain that votes in an election or salutes an officer. It is not my brain but I myself who use pronouns in a declarative way and thus take responsibility for my thoughtful speech. The brain does not function as an agent but as part of me; I am the one who does these things. The terminology used here is often slippery and misleading. Sometimes the troublesome expressions are only shorthand for more respectable claims, but some thought should be given to how the vocabulary and syntax used in brain science can fit coherently with the vocabulary and syntax we use when we speak with one another and when we speak about ourselves as thinking, knowing, conversing, and acting, that is, when we speak about ourselves as responsible agents. This chapter and the next two will explore this topic.

Bodily Presence and Absence

To discuss the way human thinking is related to the brain, we must first speak more generally about the human body, of which the brain is one of the governing parts.

Our body is one among many bodies in the world, but it is experienced in a way different from any other, and a number of authors have examined how our own corporeality is given to us.[1] Other bodies can be placed over against ourselves, and we can even remove them entirely from our presence, but my own body always remains the "zero point," the *Nullpunkt*, as Husserl calls it, from which my experiencing takes place and around which the world is spatially and temporally centered for me.[2] My own body is always an inescapable "here" for perception, action, and speech. Even when we speak over a cell phone, when I and my interlocutor are far removed from one another, I highlight the point where I am located and from which I intervene in the world, whether by motion, action, or speech. I might be having an effect a thousand miles from where I speak, but that effect is defined as being a thousand miles from *here*.

My own body has distinctive patterns of presence and absence. Any body that is facing me can be gone around, turned around, or disassembled, so that all its parts can be laid open to my experiencing, but my own body, as a center of experiencing, essentially involves special kinds of absence, which Drew Leder, in his book *The Absent Body*, has called forms of disappearance.[3] Even though my body is with me always, it has distinctive forms of inaccessibility. Leder distinguishes three "modes of disappearance" in human corporeality.

The first is what he calls "focal disappearance," which occurs in the senses and other parts of the body that are engaged in our perceiving. As we focus on the thing that we are experiencing, our organs of perception become transparent to us. When I grip a baseball or move it around in my hand, for example, I do not feel my own hand; I feel the stitches and the surface of the baseball, and my hand focally "disappears." True, I can turn my attention to my hand, but then I marginalize my perception of the ball.

---

[1] Among the authors who explore the special experience of human corporeality, one can mention Edmund Husserl, Maurice Merleau-Ponty, Jean-Paul Sartre, Erwin Straus, Hans Jonas, Leon R. Kass, and Drew Leder.

[2] For an elegant formulation of the body as the zero point, see Edmund Husserl, *Analysen zur passiven Synthesis (1918–1926)*, ed. Margot Fleischer, Husserliana XI (The Hague: Martinus Nijhoff, 1966), 297–8. On p. 298, Husserl says that the body is a special object in that "it always 'bears in itself' the *Nullpunkt*, the absolute 'here,' in relation to which every other object is a 'there'." In a footnote he observes that the zero point is also the center of orientation for the above and below, the right and left, the front and back of our own bodies.

[3] Drew Leder, *The Absent Body* (Chicago: University of Chicago Press, 1990), 25–7, 53–6.

I stop exploring it. When I look at a soiled carpet or listen to someone sing, my eye and my seeing and my ear and my hearing give way to what I am perceiving. They disappear; I am focused away from the participating parts of my body.

A second form of bodily absence is what Leder calls "background disappearance." As I concentrate on seeing or touching something, there are parts of my body – my legs, for example, or my back or the arm that hangs by my side – that are not involved in the perceiving. They also recede from my awareness, but in a different way than the parts presenting the thing in question do so. The background parts are not transparent but disregarded. They might attract my attention, but if I were to turn to them I would turn away from the object I was experiencing and would make them my focus; until then, however, they fall into background disappearance. At any moment, some parts of my body are involved in focal disappearance and others in background disappearance. The latter provide a context for the former.

A third kind of bodily absence is "depth disappearance," and it deals with the dimensions of my body that are not available at all to my immediate perceiving, such as the viscera, heart, lungs, and veins. When I chew a morsel of food, for example, I touch, taste, and smell it, but swallowing makes it vanish as an object of perception. It goes into my insides and disappears in a way different from the way my eyes and hand disappear when I see and touch things, and different also from the way my back and legs disappear when I am reading a book. The motions of these "deep" parts of my body, furthermore, are not subject to my direct control, as are my back, legs, and arms, and I could not perceive them from within even if I wanted to. They function anonymously. I can sometimes feel them when there is some dysfunction, but the feeling is generalized, not easy to locate, and does not present the organ as such. Cramps are not a way of perceiving the stomach. Digestion, the circulation of the lymph and blood, chemical activity in cells, and even respiration occur in such deep bodily hiddenness; I can affect my breathing to a slight degree, but I cannot affect the chemical absorption that occurs in the lungs. Being a dative of ingestion is very different from being a dative of manifestation.

The three forms of absence are proper to our own body, the only one we have. They are not like the absences that occur when a tree or a dog is presented to us; they occur only in the way we are bodily present and absent to ourselves. We are, therefore, inevitably engaged in two fields of experiencing, and they complement and interact with one another. Whenever we experience something in the world, we also experience our own body. Each of these domains is open to our intervention to some degree; each is, in its own way, what Leder calls an "actional field." The world we experience is a world in which we act, and the things in the world invite our intervention. To use a term of James J. Gibson, the things we see are not just neutral objects that we contemplate, but "affordances": the surface that we see presents itself as something that can or cannot be walked on (it "affords" walking); the box can or cannot be lifted; the water affords swimming.[4] Affordances are not added to objects but pervade the things we experience. They show up as relational properties of things. Our own bodies, furthermore, are also actional to some degree, like any other thing we experience; I can treat a wound in my own leg just as well as I could treat one in someone else's. In addition, some parts of our own bodies are more immediately actional in that we can raise an arm or turn our eyes to the left or the right without doing anything else to bring this about.

To distinguish the three kinds of disappearance – focal, background, and deep – is philosophically illuminating, and it shows how making distinctions can articulate and hence disclose a domain of experience. By showing the various ways in which our own body is absent to us, this analysis brings out by contrast the various ways in which we are present to ourselves: the felt distance between my chest and my arm, the kinaesthetic sense of my legs in running, my sensations of relaxation, discomfort, and irritation, are all forms of presence that are proper to my own body and are not found in my experience of other things.

Any absence involves a contrasting presentation, with a particular kind of identity constituted between the presence and absence. Thus, I can overcome the depth disappearance of my body by looking at my liver or stomach in a CT scan, but this is a different kind of presentation from turning my attention to my hand or my ear (thereby overcoming a focal disappearance), or to my legs or back (thereby overcoming a background disappearance), and it is also different from, say, looking at the back of my head by using a mirror. Different kinds of absence are overcome in different kinds of ways, and the manner of overcoming our own corporeal absence is different from the way we overcome absence in regard to things outside our own bodies.

An interesting variation on focal disappearance, incidentally, can be found in the use of tools, walking sticks, and prosthetics, in which a bodily object becomes incorporated into my own body and serves as its extension. A hammer, crutch, or golf club is at first tangibly present to me, but as I get used to it, it becomes focally transparent almost like my own hand, arms, and legs. I become somewhat able to "feel" things at the end of my cane. Such attachments, of course, have to be shaped to fit neatly onto my body in order to be continuous with it. Some tools fit the hand much more comfortably than others and quickly become unnoticed, while the

---

[4] James J. Gibson, *The Ecological Approach to Visual Perception* (Hillsdale, NJ: Erlbaum, 1986), Chapter 8, "The Theory of Affordances." The term *affordance* is used throughout the book.

uncomfortable ones continue to draw attention to themselves instead of the task at hand. They resist focal disappearance.

Presence and Absence of the Brain

What about the brain and nervous system? What mixtures of presence and absence do they offer to us? I have said that the brain is one of the governing parts of our bodily organism. Another governing part is found in the DNA molecules in our cells, which hold sway over our embryological development following the fertilization of the egg, and also guide cellular metabolism throughout life. The brain and the DNA influence each other reciprocally: the brain is generated as a part of the organism, and to that extent it is ruled by the body's DNA, but once established it can affect the chemical activities that the DNA molecules carry out in the cell. Strictly speaking, however, one cannot say that only the brain and the DNA govern the body; there are other irreducible governing powers, such as the heart, and in the end one should say that the ultimate governing agency is neither the brain nor the DNA nor any other part, but the entire organism. The brain, the DNA molecules, and the heart are only parts of the whole, and the organism is there before it has a brain.[5]

Leder makes the point that the brain enjoys two of the three kinds of disappearance: it enters into both focal and deep disappearance. My eyes disappear when I see a waterfall, and my fingers disappear when I feel a piece of fabric, but my brain and nervous system disappear even more radically as I perceive things in the world; they are even more remotely "behind" my perceiving, even though they are involved in it. They disappear so thoroughly that I could not turn to them in any way at all, as I might turn to my eyes or to my hand. And even if someone were to have access to my brain, I would not feel anything if he did anything to it, because the brain itself does not have any sensation, despite its being the coordinator of all other perceptions and feelings. Leder speaks of the "almost complete disappearance of the brain" and says that it has a "focal disappearance surpassing that of other surface organs."[6] Since the brain lies behind all my perceptions and actions, it recedes into focal absence even more than other organs. In addition, the brain undergoes extreme depth disappearance, because it is buried more profoundly in the body than other organs, protected as it is by the bony encasement of the

---

[5] Some recent authors have emphasized the fact that DNA is only a part of the cell and the organism, not a single governing part; the cell itself exercises control over the DNA. See Evelyn Fox Keller, *Refiguring Life: Metaphors of Twentieth-Century Biology* (New York: Columbia University Press, 1995), and *The Century of the Gene* (Cambridge, MA: Harvard University Press, 2000).

[6] Leder, *The Absent Body,* 111, 114.

cranium. It lies deeper within us than the heart, which is protected by the rib cage and sternum, and the stomach, which has no armor of bone at all but is cushioned by muscle and fat.

We have explored some of the special features of the brain, but before pursuing this topic we need to say more about the entire human body and its place in the world.

Ambient Energy and the Five Senses

As James J. Gibson points out, it is important in our analysis not to separate the senses from one another.[7] All our external senses form part of a single perceptual system in a single organism supported by its skeletal structure. We recall the classical distinction between the five "external" senses (vision, hearing, touch, taste, and smell) and the four "internal" ones (common sense, memory, imagination, and estimation, the sense for what is harmful or helpful). It would be misleading, in discussing these powers, to begin with the separate external senses and to work our way back to the more synthetic internal sensibility, as though the unification came last. Rather, it is more appropriate to begin with the sensitive organism as a whole, with the "common" sensibility as the root for all the five senses and the source for memory and imagination.

We can distinguish the external senses in terms of the features that they present. Vision presents color, light, and shadow; hearing presents sound and its loudness and softness; touch presents surface and texture, and so forth. But it would also be helpful and perhaps more fundamental to think of the senses in terms of the ambient energy they are each involved with.

The world in which the human organism is embedded is pervaded by many kinds of energy, such as the gravitational, mechanical, fluid, thermal, chemical, electromagnetic, and nuclear. Once the earth had become hospitable enough, living things developed on it, and they did so by both taking advantage of and responding to the various kinds of surrounding energy. The earth provided a niche for life, and the differentiations of energy provided more specific niches for the various kinds of living things, which responded not only to the accessible energy but also to the other kinds of living things that were present. Living things need to ingest energy as well as chemical elements in order to carry on the processes of life, and they also have to respond, even genetically, to what else is out there. Without the widespread presence of bacteria, for example, none of the higher forms of life could have developed.

As living things became complex enough to develop awareness and to have wants, their sensibility became differentiated in response to some of

---

[7] James J. Gibson, *The Senses Considered as Perceptual Systems* (Boston: Houghton Mifflin, 1966).

the forms of energy that surrounded them. Since we are immersed in energy, it is not surprising that we became able to react perceptually to it in its various kinds. Thus, vision developed in the medium of electromagnetic energy; hearing developed in the fluid media of water and air; touch developed in the medium of mechanical energy, with its pressure and motion; and taste and smell developed in response to chemical energy. A sensibility for heat and cold responded to thermal energy, and kinesthesia responded to forms of kinetic energy associated with the force of gravitation. We might think of living organisms as unfolding and becoming more complex in order to take advantage of the resources these forms of energy afford. Organisms evolved not only to survive but also to explore and exploit. We developed vision, for example, not just because things can appear shaded and colored, but because electromagnetic energy surrounds us. Some forms of sensibility, furthermore, may be hard to classify. What kind of sensibility is at work when an animal feels vibrations in the ground produced by a stampeding herd or a low-flying jet airplane? It is not just touch, because it goes deeper than the surface of the skin; it is felt throughout the body. It is still, however, a response to something presented through the medium of mechanical energy. This feeling might be taken as just the trembling of my own body, and in that case it would not be part of a perception of anything outside me; but it can also focally disappear and manifest to me an event that is happening beyond my own body. And finally, one might raise the question whether there are still other, hitherto unidentified kinds of energy that permit forms of experiencing and communication that we have never clearly classified but that we may have glimpsed in unusual circumstances.

When I speak of ambient energy, I take the meaning of the term *ambient* from James J. Gibson, who, in his study of vision, applies it specifically to light.[8] He speaks about "ambient light" and "the ambient optic array." In its standard usage, the word is an adjective that simply means "surrounding," as in "ambient air" or "ambient noise." It is the air or the noise that "goes on about" a subject (from the Latin *eo, ire,* "to go," with the prefix *ambi-,* "around"). The term has been used recently in a technical sense to refer to energy freely available around us, in the earth, water, air, and sun, which can be used to obtain heat and light without the burning of fuel; such uses are called "ambient energy exchanges." But Gibson adds something special to the standard meaning of the term. When he speaks of ambient light, he means not just the light that surrounds an organism, but light that has been reflected off a surface. Because it has been reflected, it is modified or configured, and hence it is able to transmit the color and shade of the surface to a perceiver. The light becomes a medium and not

---

[8] Gibson, *The Ecological Approach to Visual Perception,* 47–58. Chapter 5 of the book is entitled "The Ambient Optic Array."

just a field. Ambient light is different from light that comes directly from
a source, such as the light from a star, a lamp, or a fire, which Gibson calls
radiant light. Strictly speaking, light from a source does not transmit color;
it only illuminates. It is light pure and simple. The source itself may modify
the light and give it something like color, but such a modification does not
arise through reflection. When the light hits a surface and is reflected,
however, its waves or particles become absorbed and configured in such
a way that they carry the appearance of the thing whose surface it is. The
light now contains what Gibson calls a structured "ambient optic array."

Analogies and Contrasts among the Senses

We can get an intuitive idea of a medium transmitting appearances by
thinking about radio waves. Suppose I have a battery-powered radio in
my hand. As I move the dial, different programs are heard, one after
another, some presenting voices, others music. Where do these programs
come from? The electromagnetic field surrounding me "contains" and
"transmits" them. The programs "are" somehow there in the field, which
because of this modification is now a medium and not just a field. (Fortunately, the programs are in the electromagnetic field and not in the fluid
field of air, which would produce an intolerable cacophony.) The programs normally do not get tangled up because each occupies a distinctive
wavelength, but one of them can drown out another if the wavelengths are
close together. If I travel a long distance, some of the programs will fade
out and others will fade in; if I am in a certain part of a building, I may not
be able to get one program or another because the ambient field is
occluded. My ambient field contains many transmissions that my pocket
radio cannot pick up, such as short-wave and television broadcasts. I need
an appropriate receiver, such as a short-wave radio, a scanner, or a television set with an antenna, to bring in each of these.

When I tune my radio to one of these programs, the electromagnetic
signal becomes transformed into an acoustic pattern. It is turned into
sound that radiates from the radio into the environment. It projects
a different kind of configured wave of energy; it makes use of a pressure
wave, embodied not in the electromagnetic field but in the fluid air, and
when it strikes my eardrums, I hear the voice that had earlier been carried
by the radio waves. Thus, the appearance that had been carried by the
electromagnetic medium has been transferred to the medium of air and
now registers with me.

When I hear one of these programs, I do not perceive the intervening
electromagnetic or acoustic waves. The ambient energy, whether electromagnetic or acoustic, is transparent to me. Instead, I hear the voice of Paul
Harvey, who is telling me about something happening, some intelligibility
taking place, in Boise, Idaho. This is a mixture of presences and absences

that is very interesting philosophically, no matter how trivial the event being reported.

We can draw out the analogy between radio waves and vision. In the case of vision, I am surrounded by ambient light rebounding off surfaces. The light is configured in countless ways, transmitting the colors, shades, and shapes of the things around me, and it depends on the direction of the reflection. As I move around, different colors and different things come into view and others go out of sight. The field is there, and I fill a niche within it. Fortunately, I have the appropriate receiver, which my ancestors and I have developed for situations just like this. In fact, I would not even *be* in this situation, nor would this *situation* as such exist, had we not developed our receiver. I can subsist as what I am because I enjoy the power of vision, along with other powers related to it. When I see things in their colors and shades, I do not see the configurations in the ambient light that mediate them to me. Something nonvisible has to intervene between me and what I see, just as something nonaudible has to intervene between me and what I hear. If the visible and audible things merely slammed into my eyes and ears, if they became reduced to mechanical energy, they would not be seen or heard; in fact, they would not even be touched, any more than a club being used to strike my hand can be said to be touched. Distance and a medium are required for perception, as well as active intervention on the part of the perceiver. We do not just receive when we perceive.[9]

I would like to extend Gibson's sense of ambience to all the forms of energy that can be involved in perception. All of them transmit by being modified. They are structured in a manner that is appropriate to them as the carrier of the structure. We have already discussed vision. Hearing, of course, is related to sound, which involves a modification of the air (or water) surrounding the perceiver.[10] The fluid pressure waves in the air are so configured that they mediate and transmit something to be heard. It is interesting to note, however, that sound waves are not configured by being reflected from the object they manifest, as light rays are. Sound waves are generated by the object that is heard as it speaks, chirps, howls, groans, or rushes down a cavern. Sound *starts* from the thing being heard, but light is just reflected off the thing being seen; it doesn't start from the thing. When soundwaves bounce off a surface, they transmit an echo, which discloses not the surface but the original source of the sound. An echo in

---

[9] It is sometimes said that mechanical philosophers like Hobbes reduce all perception to the tactile, but this is not true; they reduce it to mere impulse and striking, and then they cannot explain how the impact can become an appearance. They have to say that the brain constructs the seeming. The problem would be less intractable if they did reduce the other senses to touch, because touch does involve appearances.

[10] There is an interesting difference between air and water as mediums for sound; water allows the transmission of something like vowels but not consonants, whereas air permits both.

a cavern informs me not about the canyon walls but about the yodeler, but light bouncing off a tapestry informs me about the tapestry. If colors worked as sound does, the surfaces of things would merely reflect the sun or the lamp that illuminated them.

Touch involves a direct contact between the thing and the dative, but if it is to rise to the level of perception it must also involve exploration by the perceiver. I perceive and identify a piece of cloth (cotton or linen?) by moving my hand over it and getting a feel of what it is. I feel the texture and resistance but not its being cotton, which is a matter for my understanding. The kinetic and mechanical energy involved in my touching is thus modified by what the thing is, and it carries the appearance of the thing to me. Taste and smell, finally, involve some contact between object and perceiver, but they are not reduced to touch. We touch the spoon with our mouth, but we do not taste it; we taste only the soup in the spoon. Forks, spoons, chopsticks, and cups that reacted chemically with the tongue would not be transparent to taste and would overwhelm the food being eaten or drunk. In contrast with the mechanical energy involved in touch, taste and smell involve chemical reactions, which are provoked by enzymes (biological catalysts) in the saliva and olfactory mucus. The chemicals and their reactions differ according to what is being tasted or smelled, and the chemical energy being released in each case becomes configured and transmits the qualities of the object perceived: steak and eggs, roses and seaweed. Taste and smell are both closely related to nourishment, but there is an interesting difference between them. Taste is reduced to very close proximity, while smell can range from near to relatively far. Taste is related to immediate intake, smell to exploration and flight as well as ingestion.

Ambient energy is involved in all the external senses, and the various senses engage different forms of energy. In each case, however, the energy has to be configured in a certain way. There is in each case something analogous to what Gibson calls the ambient optic array. There is a special kind of array in the sound waves that enable us to hear and another kind in the chemical reactions that enable us to taste and smell. The mechanical energy that enables us to touch things also enjoys its own kind of array or arrangement. Perhaps the word *ambient* is most appropriate for the senses of vision, hearing, and smell, because they extend through the space that surrounds us; it may be less appropriate for touch and taste. Even in these cases, however, there is more than mere contact; there is a release of patterned energy in the environment.

How Ambient Energy Gets into the Brain

The external senses respond to many different kinds of ambient energy, but the assorted forms of configured energy become reduced to one kind when the process leaves the medium and enters the nervous system. Everything becomes translated into electrical impulses moving along and among neurons, but these impulses are not just electrical; they are based on chemical changes in the neurons. Even these impulses, however, are appropriately configured. We still are dealing with energy and the transmission of its configuration, but this energy is no longer ambient, and it is no longer diverse in kind. It and its motions are located within the human body, specifically in the neuronal structures. All the various forms of energy – electromagnetic, fluid, chemical, mechanical – become transformed into one form within the body, the kind that takes place in the nervous system and brain.

The nerve cells and brain involve an electrical impulse that travels down the axon of a nerve cell and is picked up by the dendrites, body, or axon of the next cell. This electrical impulse, however, is not like the kind that occurs in copper wires, in which free electrons simply move through a conductor (the copper wire is a "dry" conductor, while the neuron is a "fluid" one). In the neuron, the charge, the "action potential," occurs not by the simple movement of electrons but through a complicated chemical and electrical dance. Ions in the cell and in the fluid surrounding it are moved about in such a way that the electrical charge (the "potential") between the cell and its extracellular fluid changes; this chemical adjustment and its associated electrical "spike" flow down the axon in the form of a wave. The impulse occurs, of course, not just in single cells but in bundles of them, and the frequency, pattern, and location of the transmission through the nervous system and brain make up the material substrate for the experiences and responses of the living body. Also, while copper wires must be plugged into one another in order to transmit a charge, the neurons are not directly connected to one another; they are separated by an interval called the synapse, which is bridged not by electrical but by chemical energy. The electrochemical signal, therefore, becomes simply a chemical signal as it moves between neurons, but then it become electrochemical again as it moves through the next neuron.

All this happens inside the nervous system and the brain. There is, however, an intermediate stage between the diverse forms of ambient energy outside the organism and the univocal electrochemical impulses within the nervous system. Between the energy in the external medium and the chemical-electrical energy in the neurons, we find the sense organs and their activations. The skin, the retina, the eardrum, and the taste and olfactory buds come between the ambient energy and the activities of the nervous system. The sense organs are different from one another in the ways they process energy (the inner ear, for example, involves an ingenious sequence of drums, hammers, anvils, and stirrups, with mechanical energy transmitted through them), but all the senses turn their respective incoming energy patterns into one kind of energy and one kind of patterning as they funnel everything into the nervous system and the brain. The nervous system itself, whether the central nervous system (brain, spinal cord, and optic and olfactory nerves) or the peripheral nervous system (everything else), involves only one kind of medium, the neurons and their synapses, and one complex kind of energy. The sense organs, thus, are the translators or transducers between the variety of energy that lies outside the body and the unity that lies within.

Furthermore, we are not passive in perception. Touch requires that we move our fingers in order to perceive the thing we are touching, and similar active participations are required by all the senses. The brain and nervous system involve not just afferent impulses from the outside to the brain, but efferent ones as well; perception requires a back-and-forth motion between the brain and the organs of sense, a topic that we will explore in the next chapter. We do not start off being passive, waiting for a stimulus before we take any initiative; from the beginning, we investigate and then respond to what we discover, even on the level of sensibility. Sheer animal perception requires that the animal take steps (literally and figuratively) to provide further experience. This reciprocity between being active and passive and again active continues all the way up the cognitional scale to the level of reasoning, where it becomes conversation, in which we reciprocally address others and hear what they have to say about things in the world in which we live. This conversation also has an effect on our perceptions; what we look for and what we expect to hear and feel depend not only on the neural networks that have been determined by previous experience but also on what other people tell us and what they lead us to experience. Thus, our syntactic structures exercise pressure on what we perceive, and our declaratives do not extend just to our categorial articulations. They also reach into our bodily experiencing; we can also report on what we see, hear, taste, and touch, and on how we feel.

13

Active Perception and Declaratives

One way to study thinking is to begin with perception and work up to rational activity. In this book, we have proceeded in the opposite direction. We began, not just with thoughtful speech, but with something even higher, with the declarative appropriation of our thoughtful speech. We then analyzed the syntactic articulation that constitutes thinking and spoke about the linguistic signaling of categorial activities. We went on to treat imagination as more elementary than speech, but so far we have spoken only occasionally about perception. Now that we have introduced the topic of the body and the brain, it is appropriate to say more about perception, which is the most original mode of human experiencing, more fundamental than imagination, memory, and thinking.

The Enactive Theory of Perception

As Husserl's phenomenology shows, perception is not the mere taking in of impressions; rather, it involves an activity in which a thing is experienced as an identity within a manifold of appearances.[1] To perceive a tree is not simply to receive a series of sensory impacts and to construct a mental model of the thing that is behind them; to perceive a tree is to move around it and to see it from many angles and in many illuminations, to touch it, to hear it rustle in the wind, to smell its scent, and so on. In all these presentations, one and the same tree is being experienced, and all the presentations are experienced as belonging to the one thing. A manifold of sides, aspects, and profiles of the object allows the tree to be continuously identified as one and the same throughout. The identity of the tree, furthermore, does not show up as one of the sides, aspects, or

---

[1] On the theme of identity in manifolds as central to Husserl's philosophy, see Robert Sokolowski, *Husserlian Meditations: How Words Present Things* (Evanston, IL: Northwestern University Press, 1974), Chapter 4, pp. 86–110.

profiles; it manifests itself precisely as the identity within them all, not as one more in their series, and this identity is what we refer to when we use the word *tree*. Perception, therefore, is not just passive; it involves active motion and probing on the part of the perceiver. It does, however, also have a passive element, the reception of the looks and the identity of the thing. Such perceiving is different from syntactic thinking, because it is continuous, immediate, and engaged in its environment, while the thinking marked by syntax is discrete, complex, and detachable from its surroundings.

A number of writers in cognitive science have made use of resources in phenomenology to explore perception and to relate it to discoveries in neuroscience. They employ the philosophical writings of Husserl and Merleau-Ponty, and have been much inspired by the work of Francisco Varela. They also make use of the ideas of James J. Gibson. They develop what is called the "enactive" theory of perception. They insist that perception should not be described as the formation of internal mental representations; it does not involve the construction of models of things or of the world; it is not a matter of self-standing, internal experiences. Alva Noë, for example, asks the eminently sensible question, "Why should the brain go to the trouble of producing a model of the bottle when the bottle is right there to serve as a repository of information about itself?"[2] These writers develop their enactive theory of perception in contrast with what they call the "orthodoxy" – or even worse, the "traditional orthodoxy"– of the establishment theory, which does posit the formation of some sort of mental representation. As Alva Noë states, "Traditional orthodoxy addresses the problem of perceptual presence by supposing that we build up an internal model corresponding to, say, experienced detail."[3] The standard theory expects to be able to match internal representations with specific "neural correlates of consciousness."[4] Thus, in the hopes of advocates of the established, traditional theory, states of consciousness will be mapped onto brain states, and perception will be described and explained as a matter of internal bodily conditions.

The enactive theory has a more external and public focus. It holds that perception should be described as an interaction between the perceiver and the world, not as an internal state of the organism. Perception is active; it involves proficient, learned conduct carried out by the perceiver, who has to know how to move about appropriately. He must walk around the thing he is experiencing, move his head, glance this way and that, turn his

---

[2] Alva Noë, *Action in Perception* (Cambridge, MA: MIT Press, 2004), 62.

[3] Ibid. On p. 58, Noë speaks of "the ideology of the snapshot convention." Stating his own view, he says, on p. 178, "Perception is not a process of constructing an internal representation."

[4] See Alva Noë and Evan Thompson, "Are There Neural Correlates of Consciousness?," *Journal of Consciousness Studies* 11 (2004): 3–28.

ears in the right direction, sniff and squint, and so on: perception is "a dynamic activity of skillful interaction with things around us. Perceiving isn't representing, or even presenting; it is *enacting* perceptual content – that is to say, making contact with the world through skillful exercise."[5] For perception to occur, the perceiver must also focus his attention appropriately: "If a change takes place when attention is directed elsewhere, the change will tend to go unnoticed. In general, you only see that to which you attend."[6] Because the perceiver must position himself and continually respond to the thing perceived, experience involves the whole animal or human being, not just the brain and nervous system. It is built on the efferent as well as the afferent components of the nervous system, both working together: "It is not the brain, it is the animal (or person) who sees. It's the person, not the brain that has semantic powers."[7] Perception involves probing as well as receiving. As Noë puts it, we might "think of the eye/brain as a sort of visual hand."[8]

The thing perceived, furthermore, is never perceived in its totality and all its detail. There are always gaps in what we directly experience, and the gaps are of varied kinds. Not only are there "other sides" of the thing to be explored, but even the sides facing us are occluded or indistinct, and these absences invite further exploration and closer scrutiny: "This sense of the presence of what is out of view is an experience of it as accessible."[9] The availability of absent sides and aspects is correlated with the perceiver's sensorimotor abilities. The thing is given as a whole, but as a whole that involves many absences of different kinds. The "other side" of the thing, for example, is given as a specifically visual kind of absence, different from auditory or tactile absences.[10] Things and aspects that were absent can become given through appropriate activity by the perceiver: "They are present as absent, but as available to perception through appropriate movement."[11] The phrase "present as absent" and its variants recur as a refrain in Noë's work.

It is not just the thing as a whole that is perceived as an identity in multiple presentations; each one of its features is also given in a mixture of

---

[5] Noë, "Real Presence," to appear in *Philosophical Topics*, draft of January 9, 2006, p. 27, as available at http://socrates.berkeley.edu/~noe.

[6] Noë, *Action in Perception*, 52.

[7] Ibid., 29.

[8] Ibid., 130. Analogously, taste can be considered as intensified touch. See John Milbank and Catherine Pickstock, *Truth in Aquinas* (New York: Routledge, 2001), 97.

[9] Noë, "Real Presence," 24–5.

[10] The "other side" of the thing is not a tactile absence, because in touch the perceiver does not take in a whole side of a thing; he is in contact with only a small region. For touch, taken by itself, there is the "rest of the thing" but not other sides. There are tactile absences, but they are different from the visual.

[11] Noë, "Real Presence," 16.

presences, absences, gaps, highlights, and vagueness. Colors, for example, are given through many shades, changes, and irregularities; as Noë says, "Colors have hidden sides to them, just as shapes do."[12] He also says, "We are able to experience the actual color of the object as, so to speak, that condition which governs or regulates the way these changes unfold."[13] This remark calls to mind Husserl's observation that the perceived thing is grasped as the rule for the changing manifold of sides, aspects, and profiles that it offers to the perceiver. In fact, Husserl claims that each basic region of entities (material objects, plants, animals, human beings, cultural objects, etc.) involves a "rule," "guiding thread (*Leitfaden*)," "index," or "frame" for the multiplicity of experiences, presences, and absences that are proper to that region.[14]

The Dual Character of Perception

One of the most valuable ideas developed in the enactive theory of perception is the claim that perception has a dual, "two-step" structure.[15] Whenever we perceive something, we are aware of the thing we perceive, but we are also aware of how the thing appears *to us* in the present circumstances, and both dimensions are perceptually given to us. Consider the experience we have of a dinner plate. The plate is circular, but when we view it from an angle, it looks elliptical. The elliptical look is one of the aspects in the manifold through which the shape of the plate is perceived, and, as Noë puts it, "We see its circularity *in* the fact that it looks elliptical from here."[16] As we perceive the plate, we distinguish between the way it is and the way it looks to us here and now, from this angle and in this environment. According to the enactive theory, all perception has this

---

[12] Ibid., 14n. One might refer again to Andrew Parker's *Seven Deadly Colours*, which discusses the colors of animals; see Chapter 4 of this volume.

[13] Noë, *Action in Perception*, 128.

[14] See Edmund Husserl, *Ideen zu einer reinen Phänomenologie und phänomenologischen Philosophie, Drittes Buch*, ed. Marly Biemel, Husserliana V (The Hague: Martinus Nijhoff, 1952), §7, pp. 25–37. Other passages on the identity of an object as a rule or index that guides our experiencing can be found in Husserl, *Ideas: General Introduction to Pure Phenomenology*, trans. W. R. Boyce Gibson (New York: Macmillan, 1931), §§149–50, and *The Crisis of European Sciences and Transcendental Phenomenology*, trans. David Carr (Evanston, IL: Northwestern University Press, 1970), §50. I cannot forbear quoting the passage on p. 35 of *Ideen III* that concludes with a musical note, certainly unintentional, that is uncharacteristic of Husserl: "Aber wie immer es sich ändern mag, solange überhaupt erfahren ist, solange überhaupt die Wahrnehmung, die den Gegenstand setzt, ein Recht hat, ist Ding Ding."

[15] Noë, *Action in Perception*, 164.

[16] Ibid., 84. The perceptual appreciation of the difference between the thing and how the thing looks to me from here is a kind of proto-distinction, analogous to what occurs in protolanguage.

duality; all perception is "folded" in this way.[17] If we perceive a certain color, we distinguish between the color as it is and the color as it looks to us at this moment and in this light. We distinguish between what a sound is and how it sounds to us here and now.

An artist who paints a scene or a person will capture this duality; he will show not only the thing but also the thing as seen from a given angle and in a particular illumination. A child, however, will not make this distinction when he draws a picture; he will just shape and color the thing as it is in itself, without regard to the way it would look from the viewer's angle or in the current environment: "The child makes grass green, even if he or she is depicting it in a situation in which it would look golden brown, and the car is made larger than a man, even though the man is in the foreground and the car is a good distance away."[18] A successful painting, by contrast, will imitate a perception in having the dual structure of both the thing itself and the thing as appearing here and now, but "the child ... draws what is there without regard to how it appears, and thus fails, in a sense, to make a picture."[19]

This difference between childlike and sophisticated picturing holds even when the style of depiction does not follow the laws of perspective or literal representation. Images might, for example, depict important figures as larger than others (the king and queen are depicted as larger in size than their courtiers and larger still than their common subjects), but such depiction also expresses the dual, folded character of perception; it also distinguishes between the figures and how the figures look to the viewer. In this case, the major figures are bigger than the minor ones because they are more imposing, not simply because they take up more visual space in the perspective of the picture. The viewer is being instructed by the picture that he *should* see them in this proportion. A depiction will teach us how to see and to understand, how to "take," the object it depicts. It bestows a sense, a mode of presentation, on the referent.[20]

---

[17] Ibid., 246, n. 11.

[18] Ibid., 176.

[19] Ibid.

[20] A child depicts just an object, but a mature painter depicts both the object and the way it looks from "here." This contrast is intuitively obvious in depiction, and so we can use it to clarify the other ways we distinguish between things and their manifestations. (1) On the level of simple perception, we can sense the difference between what we are seeing and how it looks to us from here; we can move around to get a better view; and we can see the round surface in the elliptical slant. (2) When we depict something, we distinguish, if we are mature, between the object and how it looks or should look to us. (3) When we predicate, we distinguish between the thing and the feature that we wish to highlight in it; we want to specify how the thing shows up. (4) In propositional reflection, we make a sharp distinction between the way something is and the way a speaker is presenting it to us. (5) Finally, in phenomenological reflection, in philosophy, we make a systematic distinction between the world and the manifestation of the world, in presence and absence, to the dative of manifestation. Each of these kinds of reflection is distinctive, and

Perception, therefore, has a dual structure. This structure is not to be explained by saying that the thing itself is "out there," existing apart from the perceiver, while the way the thing looks from this angle is "in here," somehow inside the perceiver: "The variations in how the object looks are not a matter of 'mere sensation'."[21] The traditional theory will tend to claim that the appearances of things are really properties of our sensing, not of the thing itself: "Color, according to these theories, is *in us*, not *in the world*."[22] It will spatially separate the thing and its appearance. Thomas Hobbes forcefully and unmistakably expresses this standard, traditional theory, in which the looks of things are made subjective, internal, and separated from the things of which they are the looks. In the *Elements of Law* he says that an image or a color "is but an apparition unto us of that motion, agitation, or alteration, which the object worketh in the brain or spirits, or some internal substance of the head."[23] He goes on to generalize the point: "That as in conception by vision, so also in the conceptions that arise from other senses, the subject of their inherence is not the object, but the sentient." He also says, "So neither is sound in the thing we hear, but in ourselves,"[24] and smell and taste are "not in the thing smelt or tasted, but in the men."[25] Hobbes says that we are persistently misled by perception into thinking that the appearances of things belong to the things themselves and not to us; he calls this "the great deception of sense."[26] He develops the same idea at the beginning of *Leviathan*, where he says, "And though, at some certain distance, the real, and very object seem invested with the fancy it begets in us; yet still the object is one thing, the image or fancy is another."[27]

To reinforce his argument, Hobbes appeals to natural reflections, such as a tree's being reflected in water or a face's being reflected in a mirror. These phenomena, he says, show that an appearance can be detached, even spatially, from the thing – the thing can be *there* while the mirrored appearance is *here*. Such reflections show that "color and image may be there where the thing seen is not,"[28] and that "we know the thing we see, is in one place; the apparence, in another."[29] Hobbes says that the image is

we must take care not to reduce one to another. It is especially important to avoid collapsing the philosophical distinction to one of the others, such as (4) or (1).

[21] Noë, "Real Presence," 19.

[22] Noë, *Action in Perception*, 150.

[23] Thomas Hobbes, *The Elements of Law, Natural and Politic*, ed. Ferdinand Tönnies (London: Frank Cass, 1969), Part I, Chapter 2, p. 4.

[24] Ibid., 6.

[25] Ibid., 7.

[26] Ibid.

[27] Thomas Hobbes, *Leviathan*, ed. Richard Tuck (New York: Cambridge University Press, 1996), Part I, Chapter 1, p. 14.

[28] Hobbes, *Elements of Law*, 4.

[29] Hobbes, *Leviathan*, 14.

"a thing merely phantastical,"[30] and that the "apparition of light without, is really nothing but motion within."[31] Hobbes claims that a similar detachment occurs in perception. To perceive something is, in his view, like seeing it in a mirror, with the appearance being located in a place different from that of the thing itself. Hobbes repeats his doctrine about the subjectivity of appearances toward the end of *Leviathan* ("which imagination is called sight; and seemeth not to be a mere imagination, but the body it selfe without us").[32] He claims that taking something we imagine as a real thing is the source of pagan demonology, and he lists it as one of the four works of darkness in the "kingdom of darkness." I note in passing that Hobbes's use of the preposition *in*, in many of the passages I have cited, clearly reverts to the "natural language" sense of the word, even though he is speaking from a philosophical perspective. Hobbes spatially removes the perceptual image from the thing perceived.

Separating Appearances from Things

This image theory of perception, furthermore, is often casually restated as though it could be taken for granted. We have, in Chapter 5, already quoted Bickerton referring to "the picture of reality you carry about with you in your brain,"[33] and we can also cite Paul Churchland, who says that "the overall pattern of neuronal activation levels at any given instant constitutes the brain's portrait of its local situation here and now."[34] Churchland mentions "the brain's ongoing portrait of an ever-changing world." In another passage he goes so far as to refer to the "common movie screen at the rear of the brain," which he says "is 'illuminated' simultaneously by two projectors [the eyes] instead of one."[35] Realizing how bold this expression is, he continues, "The metaphor of the preceding sentence is not entirely idle. The visual cortex is a thin, two-dimensional sheet of neurons, and the neuronal activity across its surface is a fairly faithful projection of the neuronal activity across the retina." Churchland says that the "literal image at the one place [on the retina] reappears as a neuronal 'image' at the other." We have, therefore, a retinal image giving rise to a cortical image, and we might ask whether the cortical image is an image of the retinal image or of the thing pictured by it. Do we have a picture of another picture, or a copy of a picture, or are both pictures

[30] Hobbes, *Elements of Law*, 4.

[31] Ibid., 5.

[32] Hobbes, *Leviathan*, Part IV, Chapter 45, p. 440.

[33] William H. Calvin and Derek Bickerton, *Lingua ex Machina: Reconciling Darwin and Chomsky with the Human Brain* (Cambridge, MA: MIT Press, 2000), 15.

[34] Paul M. Churchland, *The Engine of Reason, the Seat of the Soul: A Philosophical Journey into the Brain* (Cambridge, MA: MIT Press, 1995), 6.

[35] Ibid., 60.

simply images of the original object? The logic of picturing runs into quicksand in this analysis.

It gets even worse if we suppose that the brain is that of a person who is looking at an image in the world. Suppose he is looking at a picture of a tree. There is the picture on the wall, the image on the retina, and the image in the visual cortex. Are the retinal and cortical images pictures of the worldly picture or of the tree that it depicts? Churchland does have something to say about this; he observes that if radioactively marked glucose is injected into a monkey and the animal is made to look at some external image, that is, if the animal looks at a simple pattern in the external world, "an internal copy of that image, painted in radioactive glucose, will build up at the monkey's visual cortex." Of course, the internal copy in question would be seen as a copy by the observers who look at the animal's visual cortex, but not by the animal, and the question also arises whether the copy is itself a picture. At any rate, after showing the similarity between the retinal and the cortical representation, Churchland concludes, "So your cortical surface is indeed a sort of projection screen, and your two eyes are the projectors."

Churchland even says that "with appropriate socialization" we – all of us – might become able to speak about ourselves and our experiences entirely in the terms of scientific discourse: "What was the exclusive possession of a scientific elite during one age can become the working possession of Everyman in another."[36] He speculates, "The new framework, like any other, will gradually work its way into the general population. In time, it will become the common property of folks generally. It will contribute to, or even constitute, a *new* folk psychology – one firmly rooted, this time, in an adequate theory of the brain."[37] If this transformation were to occur, it would follow, presumably, that anything that seems to be a declarative use of the first person pronoun will give way to strictly scientific, informational discourse.

Against the view that separates the appearances of things from the things themselves, Noë says, "There is no reason to think that appearances – how things look, sound, or feel – are sensations or mental items. How things look ... is precisely a feature of the way things are."[38] In another formulation he says, "To discover appearances is not to turn one's gaze inward, as it were, to sensation and subjectivity,"[39] and again, "Looks are not mental entities. Looks are objective, environmental properties."[40] We might note that his use of the word *looks* in this passage is similar to that of

---

[36] Ibid., 277–8.
[37] Ibid., 323.
[38] Noë, *Action in Perception*, 164.
[39] Ibid., 179.
[40] Ibid., 85.

Jacob Klein, which we discussed earlier in Chapter 7, except that Klein would apply it to the thing's intelligibilities and not just to its visual appearance. Noë also says, "Visual appearances fall squarely on the world side of the mind/world divide,"[41] and again, "Experience presents us with how things are – for example, with deer grazing on the meadow – *and* it presents us with the world *as it appears from here.*"[42] He says, "we move about in a sea of perspectival properties and are aware of them ... whenever we are perceptually conscious."[43] To be able to navigate through the world in this dual, folded manner is part of what makes us human: "We are smart enough to balance these two different interpretations of how things look at once."[44]

It is clear that the "traditional" theory of perception and the "enactive" theory would have different expectations regarding the possibility of finding neural correlates for our conscious experience. If the looks or representations of things are really internal to us, it would be plausible to try to map them onto the brain and to look for some sort of isomorphism between mental states and brain states. If, on the other hand, the looks of things belong to the things in their interaction with us and the environment, one would not expect to find such an isomorphic correlation between experiencing and the brain. In fact, the issue of whether or not there are neural correlates of consciousness has been a point of controversy between advocates of the two theories.[45] The two approaches even lead to two different conceptions of brain science; the enactive approach will look for "a neuroscience of embodied activity, rather than a neuroscience of brain activity."[46] The enactive approach to perception and neuroscience would not expect to find definite correlations between various conscious experiences and neuronal activity. It would claim that the neuronal activity is more flexibly and generally distributed throughout the brain and nervous system.

The Impact of Syntax on Perception

It is philosophically illuminating to think of perception as "dual" and "folded." This structure implies that there is a whiff of reflection even in perception. We are aware of the thing we are perceiving, but we also have a sense of it as present to us, and we make a distinction, however primitive and precategorial, between the way the thing is and the way it looks to us.

---

[41] Ibid., 105.
[42] Ibid., 205.
[43] Ibid., 167.
[44] Ibid., 140.
[45] See Noë and Thompson, "Are There Neural Correlates of Consciousness?", 3–7, 25–6.
[46] Noë, *Action in Perception*, 227.

The difference becomes more vividly expressed when we make a picture of the thing; in picturing, we sharply and deliberately contrast the way the thing is and the way it looks (or should look) to the viewer. We more explicitly contrast reference and sense.

Do animals also distinguish between the thing and the way the thing appears to them? Is this distinction the result of an overflow of reason into perception, and is it, therefore, limited to human beings? Certainly, the distinction is much more vivid for us than for animals, and it seems an obvious fact that animals do not make pictures of things. They do seem to recognize some difference between the thing perceived and its perspective, but I would like to suggest that the folded nature of perception, as *we* experience it, is a result of the downward pressure of reason and syntax on perception.

Language and syntax make it possible for us to carry out full-fledged reflection. In Chapter 3, we discussed the syntactic articulation of things, in which we go beyond the continuity of perception and constitute states of affairs. We then introduced, in Chapter 11, the distinction between the straightforward constitution of a categorial object and the propositional reflection in which we take the state of affairs as being merely proposed or presented by the speaker. This distinction takes place within the natural attitude, and it permits us to investigate critically the truth of what our interlocutor is telling us. The proposition, as we said, is a state of affairs taken as proposed, and because we can take it as proposed we can verify whether it "matches" the states of affairs that we can articulate on the basis of our own perceptions. Propositional reflection makes it possible for us to quote other speakers; we can take a distance to what they say about something and see it as being said by them, and in some cases we may want to verify whether what they say is true or not. We can test what they say for the truth of correctness.

I would suggest that the dual, folded character of perception occurs as it does in human beings because the power of propositional reflection penetrates downward into our perceptions. It enables us to distinguish rather explicitly between the thing we see and how we see it. Once we have exercised reflection on a propositional level, it seeps into our perceptions, where we can also look for something analogous to a "truth of correctness": we can try, deliberately, to get a better view of the thing, or we can make sure that we really are seeing what we think we are looking at. The distinction between the thing and its look comes into play in perception, even before we move into categorial articulation. On this perceptual level, the distinction between the thing and the thing as presented is not as sharp as it is on the propositional level, because we do not, on the level of perception, have the instrumentality of words to break up our perception and make it more discrete, and to swing our attention from the thing being disclosed to the speaker who is articulating it for us.

On the level of sensibility, the play of our imagination reinforces the distinction between the thing and how it is given. We visually remember or daydream and find that we can "have" the perception again and again, and we also find that we can manipulate the way the thing looks even while holding on to its identity. Finally, we can go a step beyond imagination and make a real picture of the thing, in which we sharply distinguish between the thing and the way it looks, and we do so not only for ourselves – as we do in phantasy – but for others as well. We will show others, publicly, how the thing can be seen, and we will thereby bring out more of its meaning, not only in words but also in the way it looks. Indeed, the very speechlessness of picturing, the fact that picturing does not articulate things verbally and grammatically, gives it an expressive force of its own. It can express things that cannot be expressed in words. It can declare in its own way, with its own forms of composition, rhythm, and rhyme, and with its own rhetorical effect.

It seems to me that the writers who develop the enactive theory of perception do not get very far into categoriality and syntax. They are more like Merleau-Ponty than like Husserl. They tend to remain with perception and corporeality. They make a considerable contribution to philosophy in their analysis of this domain, but I think their work can be enhanced by being related to the domain of reason and categorial articulation.

Speaking Scientifically and Philosophically about Ourselves

One of the more striking claims made by Paul Churchland is that it would be possible for human beings to speak in the language of neuroscience when speaking about themselves and their experiences. Scientific language, he says, could become a new "folk" psychology, and it would have the advantage of being based on an adequate science of the brain. Churchland's thought experiment is not meant as sheer phantasy; he claims that this replacement of our current commonsense notions could come to pass and that we would be the better for it. I find it hard to imagine this change, especially when I try to project it into a wider context. Imagine a vast crowd of people being stirred up by a demagogue; could he and they also speak about themselves and others in terms of "thermal gradients, voltage drops, ... and hyperactive amygdalas"?[47] Could they describe what was going on in the terms we use to describe tornadoes or electrical storms? I think it is unimaginable. And what would happen in regard to the distinction between informative and declarative uses of the first-person pronoun? Would it be possible for a speaker to appropriate his own assertions by saying, "I know ..." or "I suspect ..."? If all speech were to be translated into scientific discourse, which would have to be spoken in

[47] Churchland, *The Engine of Reason, the Seat of the Soul,* 278.

the third person, would not the speaker be rendered incapable of declaring himself as one speaker among others? It seems to me that the whole dimension of human responsibility and veracity would have been dissolved; it would have been reduced to a natural process, and yet people would still be there, speaking to one another and making claims. There would be science but no one to own and appropriate it. It would simply be attached to certain bodies.

To expand our scope a bit, it is hard to see how Thomas Hobbes himself does not fall prey to this reduction of truth to a merely natural operation. In Chapter 9 of *Leviathan* he gives an outline of the various sciences, and he includes ethics, poetry, rhetoric, logic, and the science of the just and unjust all under "natural history," the science of the consequences that follow from the accidents of natural bodies; he thus groups these "human" sciences under the same general heading as geometry, geography, and meteorology.[48] The central question for Hobbes, Churchland, and the philosophical viewpoint they represent is whether modern scientific discourse can account for the person who is engaged in the scientific investigation of the truth of things, as well as all the other forms of being truthful, including dialectics, rhetorical persuasion, and picturing.

Certainly, most people would hesitate to say that we could speak about ourselves and everything else in scientific terms only, but the great theoretic and practical successes of science might make us wonder at times, and there are some writers, like Francis Crick, who think that we really are only what natural science says we are. The issue should be explored, and to that end I would like to distinguish a number of different ways in which we speak about the world and about ourselves. We have already distinguished between the language of the natural attitude, "mundanese," and the language spoken from the philosophical, reflective viewpoint, "transcendentalese." We need to introduce one more kind of language, the kind that is spoken within science, which takes its objects simply as impersonal things in the world governed by the laws of nature. More specifically, we will discuss not science generally but brain science or neurophysiology. If we can distinguish and define these various ways of speaking, if we can demarcate these various languages and the dimensions or perspectives behind them, we may be able to clarify some of the problems that arise in the analysis of human experiencing and truth, and we may also be able to clarify how we relate human consciousness to the activities of the brain and nervous system. When writers discuss the mind-body problem, they usually just ask how the bodily neurons can "cause" our experiences and our thoughts. I would like to address this problem in another way. Instead of talking directly about the brain and human thinking, I will examine how a neuroscientist speaks about the brain and

[48] Hobbes, *Leviathan*, Part I, Chapter 9, pp. 60–1.

nervous system and will try to compare his way of speaking to other ways of doing so.

A. *Conversation*

We begin with the speech proper to ordinary conversation in the natural attitude. We recall some of its features and some of the changes in focus that are available within it. When people talk with one another about things and situations in the world, they obviously take each other as speakers and listeners. They see each other as responsible speakers who can make claims and who can be truthful or deceitful, clever or witless. They also take each other as entities that cannot only hear but also listen: they direct arguments to each other and try to persuade or teach one another. Even more fundamentally, they bring each other into conversation by trying to make their interlocutors willing to listen and to take them seriously. The persons recognized as speakers and listeners may be deemed more or less successful in their speaking and listening, but they are engaged in the activity in a way that animals and plants are not. Some entities in the world stand out as capable of being partners in conversation. It is philosophically noteworthy that not all entities in the world can be taken as interlocutors. Some but not all are admissible into this status. Only those who are admissible are characterized as persons, and only they become able to deploy personal pronouns in a declarative manner.

This engagement with others, furthermore, is not something secondary for human beings. It is not the case that we are first of all "impersonally" related to things and human beings and that we then, derivatively, adopt an "intentional stance" toward them. The intentional stance, in which we take others not only as conscious of things but also as agents of truth, is the default condition for human beings. It is in this attitude that we learn to speak and thus begin to think on our own. We would not have an impersonal view of things if we did not have a personal one beforehand.

Within this conversational attitude, we can focus on the body of the other person. As we converse, our attention may turn away from what we are talking about and may turn to the body of our interlocutor. We might notice the curl of the lip, the repetitive gestures of the hand, the quick and sinister shift of the eyes, the slouching posture. Some of the things we notice may be related to the conversation (a nervous tic might signal that he is lying), but others, like the scar on his arm, may have no relevance to it at all. Such a change of focus does not cancel the basic attitude in which we take the person as a speaker and addressee. It complements the original way of taking him and is one of the possibilities within it, because our speaker-listener is always also a bodily entity among others in the world.

We can focus on the interlocutor's body, but we can also stand back a little and carry out another kind of reflection; we can focus on what he is saying. We can exercise propositional reflection. When we do this, we do not just follow the other person's words and allow ourselves to be led by him as we articulate things; we adopt a new stance in which we take what he says simply as being said by him, not as just the way things are. We might discover that some of the things he says are *not* the way things are (the speaker is lying or mistaken), and so we would take what he says as *only* his statement or his opinion. It would, incidentally, be an interesting project to contrast propositional reflection with reflection on the interlocutor's body, and to play them off against one another; both are reflections, and "interruptions" of our normal course, but they are different in kind.

While in the conversational attitude we can also engage in quotation, which can be done with or without agreeing with what the other person has said: we can quote others either to reinforce what we are saying or to distance ourselves from what they have said. Quotation is similar to propositional reflection but slightly different from it. Still in the conversational attitude, we can take some things as depictions made by other speakers (perhaps we should call them depictors rather than speakers). We can take some objects as images; we can take some bodily conduct of other people as dramatic presentations; and we can take some gestures as imitations of what someone else has done. Here again we can evaluate the truthfulness of what is being depicted, and we can take some depictions as being only the "opinion" of the ones who do the depicting; we can deny the truth of the imaging. There is an analogue to propositional reflection in the domain of pictures, and there is a possibility of pictorial quotation as well.

In all these changes within the conversational attitude, we continue to take others and ourselves as agents of truth. As we move in and out of quotation and propositional reflection, we occasionally use pronouns declaratively and thus appropriate what we ourselves have said. The propositional stance, which interrupts our straightforward focus on the things we are talking about, does not interrupt or cancel our conversational attitude, nor does it cancel the natural, pre-philosophical attitude that we maintain so long as we remain engaged with things. Nor does the focus on the interlocutor's body interrupt or cancel our conversational attitude.

B. Scientific Discourse

Consider now the stance of the scientist. Suppose he is exploring neurons in an organism. He might be examining the nervous system of a snail. He treats the organism and the cells in it as simple objects in the world. He measures, for example, the length of the neurons and the action potentials that take place in them. He does not converse with the organism or the cells that he examines. He does not quote them, nor does he exercise a propositional reflection toward what they do. He treats them simply as objects, albeit living objects. Furthermore, he can carry out the same kind of behavior in regard to a human being. He can treat the human being as simply another object in the world and use only such categories as are fitting for bodies. Sometimes, in fact, people do treat one another in this way. Consider a neurosurgeon brought in to operate on a patient, who is anesthetized upon a table. The surgeon arrives just in time for the operation, enters the operating room, does the job, and leaves. He never converses with the patient and does not explicitly deal with him as an agent of truth. He does not quote the patient. In what he explicitly does, he treats the patient no differently than he would have treated an impersonal object.

If such a "scientific" attitude were pushed to an extreme, it would continue but also a radicalize the bodily reflection we mentioned earlier when we were discussing the conversational attitude. While treating others as conversants, we *can* focus on their bodily features without interrupting or suspending our conversational stance. Presumably, the neurosurgeon who operates on the anonymous patient is acting in this way. He doesn't speak with the patient, but in principle he knows that he could do so; he knows the patient is a responsible agent of truth. But can we project this possibility, of reflecting on the body of another person, into a much more extreme possibility, in which we exclude the entire personal dimension and try to treat the other human being as an entity subject only to the laws of nature? Can we explain the person away into being a prepersonal, natural system? Can a community of scientists speak of him – and of themselves – only in terms of thermal gradients, voltage drops, and hyperactive amygdalas? To claim that they could do so would be to expand a partial view of things, a maneuver within the conversational attitude, into being a view of the whole.

If a person "reduces" his discourse in this way, he will not make use of any of the categories that deal with truth. He will not be able to speak about pictures, about propositions, or about correctness or falsity. Such phenomena will no longer show up on his radar screen. He could not even blame someone else for lying to him or for being careless in collecting information. But, in fact, no one can restrict his discourse in this way. Once we have entered into the activity of speaking with others, we necessarily engage the dimensions of syntax, grammatical signaling, propositional reflection, confirmation and refutation, correctness, picturing, and other issues in truthfulness, including responsibility. There cannot be science without the presence of such aspects of experience. If a scientist is working on the human nervous system, he will also have to ask the subject what he sees at this moment, what he feels, whether the colors look different, or whether the face in this picture is male or female; he will have to make sure his subject understands his questions; and he will have to determine whether his subject has paid attention and whether he has told him the truth. We cannot function in the scientific attitude without also engaging the conversational attitude that is the original, default way in which we are related to things and to one another as agents of truth. The proposal that we could restrict ourselves to the discourse of science amounts to the claim that we could deal with others without the language appropriate to conversation, which we could not do. To spell this out in more detail, we must introduce one more dimension of speech.

C. Philosophical Speech

We can also speak from a philosophical perspective, in which we use philosophical language. It is different from both of the perspectives and languages we have discussed so far. The philosophical perspective is the one that reflects on the very dimension of the human conversation. It is comprehensive; it reflects on the whole of things, but on that whole insofar as it is manifested to human experience and speech. It reflects on all things, insofar as they become phenomena and legomena. Philosophy also discusses the first principles of the whole of things, that which is the best and the highest in the whole, but these principles and excellences are themselves present in their own way to the human conversation, and philosophy tries to show how they are both present and absent and how they are distinguished from that which is governed by them.

Philosophy differentiates and clarifies such things as the moral, the political, and the economic. It distinguishes between doing (*praxis*) and making (*poiēsis*), between friendship and justice, between the living and the nonliving, between the logical and the psychological, and between the genuine and the merely apparent. All these things are already operative within the human conversation and displayed to it, but philosophy turns around and focuses on them in a reflective manner that is different from any approach that is made toward them within the human conversation itself. Philosophy can have this distinctive perspective precisely because it considers the human conversation as a whole, as well as the whole of things as presented to the human conversation. In this respect, philosophy is different from any one of the other voices within the human conversation, because each of them has cut off one part of the whole and focuses its attention on that part. Philosophy looks to the whole, and it also examines how these parts are segregated within the whole. That is why philosophy is said to deal with the "foundations" of each of the arts and sciences: it examines how each art and science, along with the voice associated with it, determines itself as a partial enterprise. If any one of the partial voices tried to examine the whole of things (and the human conversation as a whole), it would, by definition, make a claim to being philosophy. As Oakeshott puts it, "Each voice is prone to *superbia*, that is, an exclusive concern with its own utterance, which may result in its identifying the conversation with itself and its speaking as if it were speaking only to itself."[49]

---

[49] Michael Oakeshott, "The Voice of Poetry in the Conversation of Mankind," in his *Rationalism in Politics and Other Essays*, new and expanded edition (Indianapolis, IN: Liberty Press, 1991), 492.

Philosophy is analytical and descriptive. Because it looks at the whole, it is not a partial venture in competition with other partial projects. It does not have a special access that reveals new things; it does not know some special kinds of objects of which the human conversation is not aware. Philosophy does not come up with new information about hidden objects. It merely reflects on what has been there all along, but it knows the familiar in a new way, in its relation to the whole. Philosophy just lets things be. This might sound like an innocuous and unproductive occupation, but it is not without its own importance, because we do have a tendency, in the human conversation, to let one voice drown out the others and to make the part equivalent to the whole. We have a tendency *not* to let things be, and the result of our doing so is confusion or intellectual imperialism. Philosophy at its best achieves a kind of justice in the domain of truth, with each thing being given what is due to it. Also, philosophy is essentially contemplative. It brings out things of such a kind that nothing can be done about them. What it brings out cannot be changed by human intervention. It brings out the way things are and "the way they have to be," in the double sense of the term: the way they must be, and the way they have their being. The impracticality of philosophy is not due to human weakness but rather to the nature of what philosophy brings to light. People who are in a hurry or who want to get things done are impatient with philosophy, which seems merely to state the obvious, but to state the obvious and the trivial is often necessary, because it can easily become concealed from us. The trivial is not necessarily insignificant.

The Status of Philosophy

The human conversation is a whole; it is the human, subjective correlate to the whole of things. Philosophy reflects on the conversation and its objective correlatives. Is philosophy itself not just one voice within the human conversation? It reflects on the whole, but does not this reflection put it somehow outside the whole? Or does it become just one part within the whole? This conundrum cannot be avoided. It is the perpetual burden (or amusement) of philosophers, and it explains why philosophy will inevitably be misunderstood as being psychology, ideology, rhetoric, poetry, or science. It must simply be recognized and maintained as a special issue within human understanding. It cannot be resolved by somehow detaching philosophy from the whole of things, or by reducing it to a partial science that would refuse to consider the whole. The human theoretic life comes to its completion with this perplexity, which really does not remain disturbing once it is recognized as inevitable. There is no point in fighting against it or worrying about it, nor in trying to deny it or to scrub it. It is simply one more thing to be formulated as best we can.

This dilemma surfaces in the vocabulary used by philosophy. Philosophy has to make use of words that have their natural place within the human conversation. It has to trope the meaning of those words and to make them work within the language of the philosophical attitude. As Thomas Prufer says, philosophy must use the terminology of the sciences and the human conversation "by using it to say something strictly beyond its means."[50] It also has to use these words with their transposed meanings when it addresses people engaged in the natural human conversation. When it does so, it will seem, to those hearers, to be saying things within the conversation, that is, it will seem to them to be a partial voice, one among others. Its distinctive character will tend to go unrecognized. There is no way to avoid this predicament, and it is up to the rhetorical prudence of the philosopher to find a way to distinguish both his own voice and what he uses it to say.

To illustrate the dilemma that arises in this situation, consider the remark I made earlier in Chapter 10, when I said that we could locate the intelligibility of an entity not just "in" the entity itself or "in" any particular speaker or speakers as concepts "in" their minds, but "in" the human conversation, which includes not only words but also their noematic correlatives, the "contents" that the words "contain," that is, the things that they designate. These remarks might have sounded odd, but only if the listener took them with the meanings they have in the language of the natural attitude. It would be strange to say in ordinary discourse that things and intelligibilities are somehow contained in a conversation or in words. But I was speaking in transcendentalese, and terms such as *in*, *contents*, and *contain* take on an adjusted meaning when they are used in that language. The preposition *in*, when used in the phrase "in the human conversation," does not mean in *this* place as opposed to *that* place, any more than Aristotle's description of the soul as the "place of forms, *topos eidōn*," means that it is a particular location near or far.[51] The listener just has to get the point that the normal spatial exclusions no longer apply. What is spoken can be found in the conversation without losing its place in things, and without needing to migrate from things to minds. I also think that the elegant statements made by Alva Noë can be even better understood if one realizes that they are being stated from a philosophical viewpoint and not from a psychological or sociological one. When he says that we see the circularity of a plate *in* the elliptical look that it presents, he is speaking about the

---

[50] Thomas Prufer, "Husserl, Heidegger, Early and Late, and Aquinas," in his *Recapitulations: Essays in Philosophy* (Washington, DC: Catholic University of America Press, 1993), 75. Prufer discusses the difference between the natural and the philosophical attitude in "Husserlian Distinctions and Strategies in *The Crisis*," ibid., 48–57.

[51] Aristotle, *De Anima*, III 4, 429a27–8.

way things appear in human experience and conversation. He is not reporting on a psychological quirk or a custom that an anthropologist might describe.

What then about the scientific attitude and its discourse? Philosophy will consider it to be a special voice in the human conversation, one that engages all the other aspects of human discourse, such as responsibility, accuracy, and honesty, as well as articulation and quotation, and that uses the intense forms of identification that are achieved in mathematics. But some people who write about science, such as Churchland and Crick, claim that science can do more than this, that it can become the knowledge of the whole. It can become philosophy. In order to do so, however, it must disqualify other forms of speaking, or at least translate them into scientific language. It is not tolerant, as philosophy is; it is imperialistic. Real philosophy looks at the whole while respecting all the partial views that it surveys, but science, being one of the contending partial views, the one that considers bodily entities and the laws that govern them, can rule over everything only by laying waste to what the other approaches bring to light.

In particular, the scientific attitude that tries to be the final and only voice will delete the dimensions that make up the human conversation as such. You and I will be boiled down or "reduced" to this body and that body, and yet despite this deletion the ideological scientist will still have to address others if he wishes to carry on his science, and he will have to treat them as responsible speakers. This dilemma is brought out in a wonderful sentence in Francis Crick's book *The Astonishing Hypothesis*. Crick wishes to show that human consciousness is reducible to neural activities and that human life does not need what he understands as soul. At the start of the chapter in which he describes the neuron, he addresses the reader and says, "Since the Astonishing Hypothesis stresses that 'You' are largely the behavior of a vast population of neurons, it is important for you to have at least a rough idea of what neurons are like and what they do."[52] There are two instances of the pronoun *you* in this sentence. The first is put in scare quotes and capitalized, to indicate that "You," the reader, are not what you think you are; you are largely neurons in action. The second instance, however, "it is important for *you* to have at least a rough idea," is not in scare quotes or capitalized (and the italics are mine), because Crick has to take you seriously as an interlocutor. He cannot reduce you if he wishes to talk to you. Furthermore, he wants to make you well disposed, teachable, and attentive to what he himself has to say as he addresses you, and yet in the very same sentence he tells you that you are not there in the way you

---

[52] Francis Crick, *The Astonishing Hypothesis: The Scientific Search for the Soul* (New York: Charles Scribner's Sons, 1994), 91.

think you are to be persuaded or taught by what he says.[53] Crick is a rollicking reductionist whose materialism is refreshingly confident and unselfconscious, so the problem in the viewpoint he adopts shows up vividly in what he says.

Philosophical speech also has a problem in entering into human conversation, as we have noted, but it is aware of the problem and tries to think about the way it tropes natural language as it develops its own voice. Most importantly, philosophy does not disqualify other voices and other languages, least of all the voice and intricate language of science. It confirms the other voices by showing how they differ from one another, and it also tries to prevent any one of them from overwhelming the others. It tries to quiet them down when they get too loud.

---

[53] Thomas Aquinas presents this triad of dispositions – being well disposed, teachable, and attentive – as needed in the introduction or prologue to any written work. See Kevin White, "St. Thomas Aquinas on Prologues," *Archivum Franciscanum Historicum* 98 (2005): 803. Crick's sentence is in a "prologue" to the part of his book that deals with neurons.

14

Mental Images and Lenses

Mental images require more discussion. In Chapters 9 and 11 we tried to show that perception is better described without the involvement of mental pictures that mediate between us and what we experience. Still, there clearly is something that can be called mental imagery; we do experience "images" of some sort when we dream or daydream, whether in memory or imagination. We have tried earlier, in Chapter 9, to clarify such phenomena by saying that they involve not the viewing of an internal image but the reliving of an earlier perception. If I remember a home run in a baseball game that I saw yesterday, what I bring back is not a picture of the event, but myself perceiving the event. I reenact myself seeing the batter hitting the ball. But even in that reenactment, there is something like an image at work, not only an image of the ball being hit but also an image of myself seeing it. Or rather, there is one complex internal image involving both myself and the event. What sort of imagery can this be? How can it be related to our physiology without being taken as the viewing of pictures? How is this imagery materialized?

The Problem of Mental Images

The problem of mental images is not just a local or temporary philosophical problem. It is chronic; it has persisted throughout the history of philosophy, in regard to perception as well as imagination. Descartes is notorious for introducing mental pictures into the process of perceiving. In *The Passions of the Soul*, he writes, "There must necessarily be some place where the two images coming through the two eyes, or the two impressions coming from a single object through the double organs of any other sense, can come together in a single image or impression before reaching the soul, so that they do not present to it two objects instead of one. We can easily understand that these images or other impressions are unified in

this [pineal] gland."[1] He goes on to say, "If we see some animal
approaching us, the light reflected from its body forms two images, one
in each of our eyes; and these images form two others, by means of the
optic nerves, on the internal surface of the brain facing its cavities. Then,
by means of the spirits that fill these cavities, the images radiate toward the
little gland which the spirits surround."[2] Further, "In this way, the two
images in the brain form only one image on the gland, which acts directly
upon the soul and makes it see the shape of the animal."[3]

Descartes speaks about retinal and brain images in the *Optics*: "The
objects we look at do imprint quite perfect images of themselves on the back
of our eyes."[4] He says that if you take an eye from an animal, make light pass
through it, and look at the back of the eye, "you will see there, not perhaps
without wonder and pleasure, a picture representing in natural perspective
all the objects outside." He continues, "When you have seen this picture in
the eye of a dead animal, and considered its causes, you cannot doubt that
a quite similar picture is formed in the eye of a living person.... The
images of object are not only formed in this way at the back of the eye but
also pass beyond into the brain." And finally, "When this picture thus passes
to the inside of the head, it still bears some resemblance to the objects from
which it proceeds."[5] He even says that we judge distances by comparing what
we remember of the size of the object to the size of the image it imprints on
us: "We judge their size by the knowledge or opinion we have of their
distance, compared with the size of the images they imprint on the back of
the eye – and not simply by the size of these images."[6] These remarks of

[1] René Descartes, *The Passions of the Soul*, trans. Robert Stoothoff, in *The Philosophical Writings of Descartes* (New York: Cambridge University Press, 1985), volume 1, p. 340.
[2] Ibid., 341.
[3] Ibid., 342.
[4] René Descartes, *Optics*, trans. Robert Stoothoff, in *The Philosophical Writings of Descartes*, volume 1, p. 166.
[5] Ibid., 167. Descartes goes on to say that it is not by virtue of resemblance that these images allow us to know things; see John Hyman, *The Objective Eye: Color, Form, and Reality in the Theory of Art* (Chicago: University of Chicago Press, 2006), 113–26.
[6] Ibid., 172. On pp. 153–4 of the *Optics*, Descartes gets rid of any sort of images (intentional forms) flitting through the air. For Descartes, the external medium is purely mechanical. Imagery begins only when the mechanical impulses strike the body. My concept of lensing allows more continuity of transmission between the surrounding medium and the nervous system. There is a long and important passage in the *Treatise on Man*, translated by Robert Stoothoff, in *The Philosophical Writings of Descartes*, volume 1, pp. 105–6, in which Descartes describes the "figures" or "forms" that go through the nerves and brain and finally reach the gland, where they are inspected by the rational soul. He says that only when they arrive at the gland can they be called "ideas." See also Gottlob Frege, "On Sense and Reference," in *Collected Papers on Mathematics, Logic, and Philosophy*, ed. Brian McGuinness (New York: Basil Blackwell, 1984), 160–1, where Frege contrasts "the real image projected by the object glass in the interior of the telescope," and "the retinal image of the observer." He says that each person has "his own retinal image."

Descartes remind us of what Bickerton and Churchland say about images in the brain.

The problem of mental images existed in premodern thought as well. It was radicalized by the epistemology of modern thinking, but it did not begin there. Aristotle rarely speaks about mental imagery, but when he does so, he seems to fall back on the theory of mental pictures. The issue arises in connection with what he calls the phantasm, a term that very likely means an internal image. Two passages in *On Memory and Recollection* show this. In the one, Aristotle says that in memory we "undergo something like a picture, *hoion zōgraphēma ti to pathos.*"[7] The word *zōgraphēma* signifies "something painted from life," the result of the activity signified by the verb *zōgrapheō*, "to paint from life." One cannot get a more "graphic" expression than this, even though Aristotle does insert a qualifier, "something like, *hoion.*" In the other passage he says, "there is something like an impression or a picture in us, *estin homoion hōsper tupos ē graphē en hēmin.*"[8] The Greek word *hē graphē* clearly signifies a drawing, a sketch, or a painting, something "scratched" (the original meaning of *graphō*), and while Aristotle again qualifies his use of the term, saying not that there *is* an impression or a picture but that there is something like one, he still uses the model of a picture to talk about our internal sensibility. In medieval thought, the phantasm, the product of the imagination, one of the internal senses, has many of the properties of a picture. The phantasm played an extremely important role in the medieval discussion of perception and thinking. Descartes continued this tradition and pushed it to an extreme.

By mental images I mean the kind of thing that we experience when we dream or when we recall someone's face or visually call to mind what happened yesterday when we saw two cars collide near the street corner. Mental images certainly occur in us, but they are not like ordinary pictures, even though they are usually taken as such. We all know that mental pictures cannot be just like the pictures we see in a book. Who or what would be the viewer? Who would be there inside the brain "looking" at such images, and how would this viewer even know they are pictures? What is the internal screen on which they are projected? It is easy to reject the simplistic notion that brain images are ordinary pictures, but it is very hard to avoid talking about them as if they were, and it is even harder to state positively what sort of representations they are. We know we have imaginary presentations, and we know they are not like ordinary pictures, but how are we to speak about them so as to bring out their proper character? This is one of the major philosophical challenges associated with the

---

[7] Aristotle, *On Memory and Recollection*, 1, 450a30. For Plato's use of the term *zōgraphēma*, see *Philebus* 39a–40a and 51c.

[8] Aristotle, *On Memory and Recollection*, 1, 450b18.

scientific, neurological project of mapping the brain. It is also a perplexity for anyone who tries to think about cognition.

A New Paradigm: Lensing

I would like to offer an alternative way of thinking about mental images and the physiology that underlies them. My suggestion concerns our philosophical vocabulary. When we speak about mental imaging, we are speaking in transcendentalese, and so I am recommending an adjustment in our philosophical discourse. I propose that we use the phenomenon of a lens as a model for mental imaging instead of the phenomenon of a picture. I offer the following thought experiment as an introduction to this issue.

Suppose I am facing a white wall with a blue square painted on it. I perceive the square on the wall. Suppose also that I have in my hand a colored photograph of the same wall and its square. When I turn from the wall and look at the photograph, I see a picture of the square on the wall. Seeing a picture of the square is different from perceiving the square. Picturing is a kind of intending that has its own presentational structure, different from that of perception. When I look at a picture, I directly perceive an object (a piece of paper with lines and colors on it), which in turn represents another object that could be nonpictorially perceived somewhere else.

Suppose now that I turn again toward the wall. I hold a plate of glass between myself and the square. As I look through the glass, I still see the square and the wall as before. Next, suppose that I hold a large lens between myself and the square. I look at the square through the lens. I still see the square, but now it may be modified by the lens: let's say it converges at the top and bottom and spreads out in the middle. When I see the distorted square through the lens, however, I still *see* the square and the wall behind it; I have not begun to look at a picture of them. I continue to perceive. I have not shifted into a pictorial mode of presentation, as I did when I turned away from the wall and looked at the photograph. The lens does not give me a picture of the square (nor do I have pictures of the square in each of the lenses of my eyeglasses). I see the thing itself, distorted as it might be, through the lens. Also, I see the square *through* the lens, not *in* the lens (whereas, as we said earlier, I see Churchill *in* his photograph, and I see the square *in* the elliptical aspect that it presents to me from this or that angle). The lens is a medium for the thing we see through it. Also, although some lenses distort what we see through them, others may not do so; they may, in fact, allow me to see it more sharply.

We now turn to "mental" experiencing. Suppose I walk out of the room and then remember or imagine seeing the square. I visualize the square. When I do so, *I am doing something that is more like seeing the square and the wall through a lens than like seeing a picture of the square and the wall.* When we visually remember or imagine, we may think we are viewing an inner picture, but in fact what we are doing is more like seeing the object itself again (not a picture of the object), but seeing it through a new medium. When I remember or imagine, I do not perceive something that is a picture of the object; I seem to see the object itself. This is the presentational logic, the intentional structure, of remembering and imagining. And what is the new medium through which I seem to see the object? It is the brain and nervous system, with their electrochemical activity, which are able to replay some of the neural processes that occurred when I actually experienced the square.

To bring out this difference more fully and to tighten my analogy, imagine that we go back into the room and look again at the wall and the square. Then, we put the glass lens between us and the wall and look at the wall and the square though the lens. Now, imagine that it is possible for the square and the wall to be destroyed while the light waves are still passing through the lens. If this were to happen, I would still be seeing the square and the wall, even though at that instant they had ceased to exist. I would still be seeing, not picturing, them even though they were no longer there to be seen. The annihilation of the square does not turn the lens into a picture of the square. Now, let us move ever further into science fiction and say that we have a new kind of magic lens that can store and resuscitate the kind of patterned light waves that the wall and the square gave off when we were looking at them. Suppose we command the lens to revive those waves for us. If this were to happen, and we were able to "see" the blue square again against the white wall, we would not be picturing the square and the wall. We would be *seeming to see* them. These scenarios are purely fictional, of course, because the velocity of light is such as to make the perception cease as soon as the square and the wall vanish, and there is no magic lens that can revive earlier electromagnetic waves, but I propose these thought experiments, these imaginative variations, as devices to help us to become more flexible in speaking philosophically about appearances and to show that we can talk about something other than internal pictures when we discuss mental things.

Visual memories stored in the brain are like captured light waves that can be reactivated later (except that they are electrochemical waves), and when they are reactivated they allow a past perception to occur again, but they do so without establishing a pictorial consciousness. The brain can serve as something like a lens that lets us seem to see something that is no longer there to be visually perceived. Furthermore, it presents not only the thing seen but also myself seeing it, because it also reactivates my background sense of my own body at the time I saw the thing in question. Visualizing something is more like "lensing" it than picturing it. I am working with analogies here, of course, but I wish to claim that the analogy of a lens is a better model to use than that of pictures when we speak philosophically about the presentational and representational activity of the brain. The reason it is better is that it avoids the danger of postulating an internal pictorial entity that is the target of my awareness, an entity that would come between me and the world and conceal the world from me. Like a lens, the nervous system is totally transparent, presenting not itself but that which is given through it (the square on the wall, my own somatic posture and state). Something goes on in the brain that is different from looking at a picture. The more we can emphasize this difference, and the more we can propose alternative models to try to get at what is going on, the better we can avoid the dead ends of thinking of the brain as an internal video screen.

Refining the New Paradigm

I have made the major move in my argument, the claim that when we speak philosophically about mental imagery we can make use of another paradigm, that of a lens, to take the place of the paradigm of pictures, which so grievously misleads us when we speak about the mind. I wish to replace one metaphor, one that tends to misguide us, with another that is less misleading. Many details remain to be elaborated. We must keep in mind that the brain and nervous system carry out their "lensing" not only when we imaginatively visualize or re-present an experience, but also when we directly perceive things.

The "brain-lens" is different from real lenses. A major difference is that I can always make a real lens into an object in its own right. When I am looking through a real lens at a blue square on the wall, I can move my attention from the blue square to the lens itself even while I still see the square, or I can move the lens away and look at it (the lens) directly just by itself. I cannot, however, notice the brain-lens while I visualize someone's face and gestures, nor can I look at it just by itself. I am so embedded in my neural systems that I cannot focus on them while they perform their presentational work. This lens is deep inside me; it undergoes extreme depth disappearance. It is my own nervous system, engaged in its afferent and efferent activities. It is part of my own body, part of me. Someone else can focus on my "lens" and its activity; a neurologist can examine what is going on in my brain when I see or remember something. The networks he sees, however, are not serving as a lens for him. For him they are merely activated neural networks, biological entities at work, not a medium of presentation. He *knows* they are a medium of presentation for me, but he does not experience them as such. His brain and nervous system would have to fuse with mine for him to do so (and even if this fusion took place, how could he experience my somatic states?).

When I actually perceive the blue square (as opposed to visualizing it), a brain-lens, a particular neural loop, is activated, and it is continuously affected by the light waves reflected off the wall and the square. My central nervous system is also continuously being affected by my current bodily condition. My perception is, consequently, steady and well defined. It is stabilized by continuous input. When I visually imagine the blue square, the activity of the brain-lens is more erratic and undetermined, more jumpy and gappy, because it is not under the constant influence of the thing I see and the rest of my body. It is primarily output and not input. The electrochemical energy at work in my nervous system is being activated from within and not being funneled in from all its various sources without. It is not only spatially but also temporally distorted in comparison to what occurs in perception. My imaginings, therefore, are not as steady as my perceptions, and the mental imaging easily becomes degraded.

When we use the lens as an analogy for mental imagery, we should remember that while some lenses distort the thing we see through them, other lenses improve or correct the impression the thing makes, so we should not think that the brain-lens somehow prevents us from ever getting at the way things truly are.[9] It does not interfere; it allows things to be presented to us. It is like the electromagnetic medium surrounding us, which normally does not interfere in our visual perception but allows us to see the colors, shades, and shapes of things.

The lens of the brain and nervous system is comprehensive. An ocular lens, by contrast, is highly partial. It serves only to present a visual object. The brain-lens is not merely visual but engages all the sensory modalities, including my somatic self-perception. The lens that serves as "the mind's eye" also serves as the mind's ear and hand and nose and tongue, and it supports the feeling I have of my entire body. It is essentially manifold and hence much more complicated than the ocular lens. Our nervous system is a very wide-angled lens. All the formed energy funneled through the various senses into the brain and nerves becomes part of one single organic system; it is unthinkable that one could isolate, say, the neurology of vision and experience it functioning all by itself. How could it work without being coordinated with the other senses, with the sense of bodily position, and with the motor activity that is needed to position the eyes to see the thing in question? Perception of an identical thing involves a background awareness of our own bodily identity. For this reason, our remembering or imagining reenacts a full-body activity, not just a picture of an object. I imaginatively experience a second, displaced body within my currently experienced one.

If we were to take picturing as the paradigm for imagining, we would be more inclined to think that imagination isolates the chain of neural activation proper to the sense in question. Seeing a picture is more exclusively a visual action, and to think of imagination as visual picturing would incline us to think that we activate just a single neural loop when we

---

[9] I am grateful to John C. McCarthy for some formulations in this paragraph and the next.

imagine seeing something. Using the lens as the model makes it easier for us to see imagination as more comprehensive. Every sensory modality has its own lens by which the energy array related to it is refracted into our sensibility, but once the patterned energy is funneled into our nervous system, the whole system serves as the internal lens that presents our present situation to us, and when reactivated it is able to bring back our earlier experiencing along with its objects.

My stored imaginings are activated when I dream or daydream, but they are also activated when I experience new things, and when so activated they serve to interpret and modify what I perceive. The neural lens of remembering or imagining blends with the lens of my current perceiving. Many of my remembered experiences carry a strong emotional charge with them, so what happened to me in the past will exercise an influence on how I take what I currently experience, as my past self comes to life in what I am doing now. What sort of neural circuits are at work in such blends of perception and imagination is a matter for empirical study, but thinking about them as lenses and not as pictures is a philosophical achievement.

Lensing and Personal Identity

Our personal identity is our identifiability, by ourselves and others, as agents of truth. It is based on the internal structure of our sensibility, with the possibilities of displacement that such sensibility offers. We can distinguish three dimensions:

1. The first dimension is the direct, perceptual experience we have of our surroundings and our own corporeality. The world and the things in it are present to us, and our own bodily states are also present to us. Even as we know other things, one of the bodies in the world – our own – shows up to us as being different from all the rest. It is where "we" are. We hold sway in it immediately, which is different from how we intervene in the things we experience as "outside" ourselves. Such experiencing, of things and of our own bodies, involves the physiological process by which the energy around us is channeled into the lens of our nervous system and brain.

2. The second dimension is the reenacted experiencing that occurs in our sensibility when earlier perceptual activities of the nervous system are reentered or rerun. These neural activities are also forms of lensing, but they do not present our environment or our current bodily states to us; they present what was given before and elsewhere, and they also present "us" as displaced from our present environment. The reenactment may lose its anchor in any specific place or time and become pure imagination. The imagined or remembered self is located within the currently experiencing self.

3. The third dimension is categorial, syntactic activity, along with the intellection that accompanies it. It is rational activity, made tangible by the use of words or other signs that indicate it as they are used to express the things we experience. The agent carrying out this categorial activity is declared by our use of first-person pronouns. This agent is not displaced within the other two dimensions, as the imagined self is displaced within the perceiver. The categorial agent is not "inside" or "behind" the experienced self, no more than "I" am behind my arms or above my legs. Spatial categories do not apply.

As we reflect philosophically, we cannot neglect any of these dimensions. We cannot isolate, for example, just the third dimension, sheer rationality, and describe it without its roots in sensibility. Also, we cannot isolate any single one of the dimensions of sensibility. We could not speak only of the reenacted, displaced second level, for example, without situating it within the ground-level sensibility and without looking forward to the categoriality that supervenes on it. We also would not want to isolate the first two dimensions, perception and imagination, and treat them just by themselves. They do not function in a human way except as played off against our rational, syntactic agency, which overflows into them. Human experiencing involves an interplay among all these dimensions. "I" am activated as an identity in them. These differentiations among my present self, my past self, and my syntactic self can be blurred by drugs or by intense, rhythmic bodily motions.

Our neural lensing is essentially dual or bifocal. We never have just the actual perception or just the imaginative rerun all by itself. The recreative awareness is always nested within the current, perceptual one, and the imagined body is always nested within the currently experienced body.[10] The two dimensions are always interacting and influencing one another; the reenacted activity pressures our perceptions and inclines us to see things in a certain way. At any given moment one or the other of these dimensions will exercise a stronger draw on our attention. The essentially displaced and dual character of human sensibility is reflected in the word *consciousness*, with its etymology of con-sciousness, from *cum* ("with") and *scire* ("to know, to be aware of"). When we are conscious, we are aware *with* someone, and in this case we are aware with ourselves, with our remembered or imagined selves that always accompany us, whatever is going on at the moment, provided only that we are conscious. One of the levels of sensibility by itself, either level (1) or level (2), would be mere "sciousness," to adapt William James's term, a nondual awareness, an

---

[10] We would push our imaginative variation too far if we were to try to say that my currently experienced body could be nested within my imagined one. That would be an impossibility, and we can see it as such.

awareness without the "with."[11] Perhaps the dreams we experience in deep sleep, the ones we do not remember, when things are undergone without any context or perspective, would be like that, and perhaps simpler forms of animal life enjoy that sort of undifferentiated awareness.

The "I" of our syntactic agency, which is named by our declaratives, is not somehow "behind" the neural lensing or apart from it. The lens is part of me, not something I am "outside" of, and it is I as a whole who say "I." I do not peer at things through the neural lens any more than I look at internal pictures of things. Thanks to the lenses, I live in the immediate presence of things, whether perceived or imagined. I carry out syntactic actions, mainly by using words, and I carry them out on the things themselves as these things appear to me by virtue of the neural lensing. I do not carry out my syntactic actions on replicas of the things in question. I can, furthermore, carry out syntactic articulation concerning my somatic or emotional states, and again I do so directly, without any pictorial intermediary.

Philosophical Discourse about Mental Imaging

When we claim that lensing is a better metaphor than picturing in the analysis of mental imagery, we refer to the use of such terms in transcendentalese, in philosophical discourse, and not in the speech of physiology, psychology, or ordinary discourse. When we talk about mental imagery, we speak from the philosophical perspective, which is the appropriate viewpoint from which to talk about truthfulness. We are speaking about human beings not as biological entities but as agents of truth or datives of manifestation. All the words we use in philosophical discourse need to be adjusted when they are brought in from pre-philosophical language. The terms *mental images* and *mental pictures* have themselves been troped when they are used in philosophy, and they could in principle be safely employed, but we can easily forget that they have a new meaning in this context; we are all too easily misled into thinking they signify an ordinary image or an ordinary picture, a mental thing, and that our discourse is really scientific and not philosophical. In other words, the problem we face is not simply "Are there mental images?" but rather "What sort of language are we using when we speak about mental imagery?" The terms *lens* and *lensing* are new to this philosophical vocabulary, and their very unfamiliarity gives them an advantage.

---

[11] William James, *Principles of Psychology* (New York: Dover, 1950), volume 1, p. 304. By *sciousness* James seems to mean an awareness that knows an object but has no reflective awareness of itself. I take the term in a slightly different meaning, to signify a perceptual awareness without any imaginative accompaniment, or the imaginative awareness without the perceptual accompaniment. For James, consciousness involves an awareness *of* ourselves, but in my usage consciousness involves an awareness *with* ourselves.

One of the advantages is the following. Suppose a neuroscientist detects a retinal image in a subject, and then also detects a geometric pattern or map in the visual cortex that matches the pattern on the retina.[12] He will be inclined to think that the patterns he sees are also experienced in some way by the subject, and that the subject directly knows the images "inside" and not the things "outside." The spatial terms get taken in their natural, scientific, or ordinary-language meaning, not in the troped sense they have as parts of philosophy. Knowing, thinking, and consciousness get boiled down to the physiological. But if the investigator takes the retina and the neural system as a lens, he will be less inclined to think of the patterns he sees as images for the subject. If he had detected patterns in a glass lens placed between an object and a viewer, he would not have thought them to be images that the subject saw in the lens; correspondingly, he will not be inclined to consider the lensing in the neural system to be the target of vision. The category of a lens brings out the sheer transparency of the nervous system, and it allows us to appreciate more intuitively that in our experiencing we directly perceive the things that are acting on us. It also allows us more easily to think of imagination as a reactivated perception or a simulation of perceptual experience, as being perception-like, as Gregory Currie and others say it is, and not as the viewing of a substitute object or an image.

As we have intimated, even spatial terms become troped when they are used in philosophical discourse. The spatial terms *inside* and *outside* can be particularly misleading. Is a concept inside us or outside? If a concept of something is the intelligibility of the thing, how are we to understand "where" that intelligibility is? What kind of question is that, and what sort of answer could be given to it? Clearly, the intelligibility is in the thing, but can it not also be in us? Can it not also somehow be in the word that names it? And where is the linguistic word? To some degree it is outside us, but it can also be inside, as we imagine it, and it really does not exist except as part of a public, historical language. The philosophical problem is not to determine where the word or the concept is, but to determine what *where* means when it is used in philosophy to describe the activities of the agent of truth. Suppose, for example, someone were to ask, "Where is the contract for the house?" One answer might well be, "In the desk drawer." The contract is in the drawer in the sense that the paper on which it is written is there, but the contract enables Harriet to occupy the house and forces Helmut to leave it, so the contract also stands between the two of them, and between them and the house. And where are the words of the contract? They too are in the drawer, but they also are in the minds,

[12] See Paul M. Churchland, *The Engine of Reason, the Seat of the Soul: A Philosophical Journey into the Brain* (Cambridge, MA: MIT Press, 1995), 57–70; and Francis Crick, *The Astonishing Hypothesis: The Scientific Search for the Soul* (New York: Charles Scribner's Sons, 1994), 139–59.

imaginations, and voices of those who are party to it, as well as those who enforce and recognize it; they wouldn't be words if they couldn't somehow also get out of the drawer and be elsewhere. Only in so doing are they words with effective truth, that is, real words with meaning. Concepts or intelligibilities hover around words as much as they reside in the images we entertain about the things they originally belong to. Philosophical language tries to formulate truths about such phenomena, and it has to modify ordinary language and scientific language in order to be able to do so. People often forget about the modification or troping, and tend to think that the mental images and concepts are just like the things they talk about in ordinary speech or scientific discourse. And everybody has to speak about philosophical things from time to time, when, for example, they talk about their memories or their convictions, so it is not as though they had no contact at all with the matters philosophy deals with and the terms it uses.

Another advantage of using lenses as a paradigm for mental imagery is that it allows us to speak with greater precision about the neurological basis for consciousness and the identifications that it permits. Any active perception, as we have seen, involves both neural input and output; it involves a mixture of receptive awareness and mobile positioning. But imagination involves a reenactment of the physiological processes that occur in perception; it involves reentrant or recurrent neural activity. It may not be exactly the same activity as that which occurred during the original experience, but there is considerable overlap.[13] Neural loops are recycled. This recycling takes place against the background of the current input and the experience that it supports. Thus, the neural parallelism can serve as the physiological basis for the displacement of my imagined or remembered self within my current self.

The displacement of ourselves in imagination and memory plays an important role in our sense of personal identity. If my neural activities are reenacted, they bring back an earlier experiencing, including the bodily state I experienced at the time. They bring back an experiencer as well as an experience and a thing experienced. And that experiencer is not just someone or anyone; it is me again, and it could never be anyone else. My *me* or my *I* comes to light in this differentiation and displacement, and

---

[13] See Gregory Currie and Ian Ravenscroft, *Recreative Minds: Imagination in Philosophy and Psychology* (Oxford: The Clarendon Press, 2002), 79–80: "The implementation claim is not the claim that the neural substrates for vision and for imagery are exactly the same, but rather that they substantially overlap. There is good evidence that they do. With the development of precision techniques, the evidence has become more impressive. ... The implementation claim suggests that perception and imagery are related as the two sides of a partly closed zip fastener: the inputs are from distinct sources, but higher-level processing is the same in both." Some reservations about the neural overlap between imagery and perception are expressed on p. 94.

when I take the further initiative to articulate what I experience into a syntactic form, it is still that same *I* that does so. Through my use of syntax I begin to assert myself; I start taking and expressing my positions in my conversational community, and I must integrate that position taking with my own ability to reenact my past self, with its emotional components, and must not allow, for example, my resentments or my affections to flood inappropriately into what I am saying now to someone else. I have to be able to distinguish my present self from my past self in order to declare myself intelligently in my present conversation.

15

Forms of Wishing

We get a glimpse of the human person in the declarative use of the word *I*. For another perspective on the personal, we now turn to the phenomena of human choice and human intentions. To get a good view of these things, let us, like photographers, arrange a background, a context in which the target can be brought into sharper focus. We will not just speak about human beings, but will place them against plants and animals, and will discuss the logic of needing, wanting, and wishing. We will then explore the human person as an agent or an actor.

We will, therefore, highlight the human person by placing him against the background of prepersonal phenomena. Our procedure here will be analogous to what we did when we positioned language, with its syntax, against the background of protolanguage and mere vocalization. In this case, however, we will be dealing not just with cognition but with desire and conduct.

Needs, Wants, and Wishes

Plants *need* certain things: they need light, water, and nourishment. A plant takes in certain things from its environment and makes them part of itself in order to keep itself alive. It could not remain itself without metabolizing other things into itself; it needs these other things. Need is associated with life.

Animals, like plants, also need certain things, but in addition they *want* certain things. Some of the things that they want they also need, such as food and shelter, but other things that they want they simply enjoy, such as playing at this moment with other animals or frolicking in the meadow. Animals go beyond needing into wanting. Plants don't want anything, because they are not conscious, but animals both need and want, because they are aware of some of the things that they need and desire. Wanting is associated with conscious life. Animals might overeat because they enjoy eating, but plants do not overindulge, nor do they stretch their branches because it feels good. They have no motivation to do so.

Human beings go beyond both needing and wanting. Of course, like plants and animals, human beings do need some things – food, shelter, company, assistance – and like animals they also consciously want some things, but their wanting can give rise to new forms of desire. Besides needing and wanting, human beings can *wish* for certain things. Wanting is conscious desire, but wishing is intelligent desire. Aristotle calls it *boulēsis*. Wishing is the kind of wanting that rational animals, human persons, are capable of. It becomes possible when we enter into language and its syntactic structure, with its targeting of the intelligibility of things. Wishing is a kind of wanting that has its own syntax and its own hierarchic embedding. It is associated with rational life.

Needing, wanting, and wishing are each involved with different forms of life. Each is nested within its predecessor, and all three are nested within the nonliving. Is there anything analogous to need, want, and wish in nonliving matter? Do sheer chemical elements and compounds have to "metabolize" other things into themselves in order to remain themselves? Such elements and compounds obviously do not engage in wishing or wanting, but they also do not seem to involve any need; a particular atom or compound does not seem to "feed" on other things in order to remain itself. Atoms and molecules as such do not try to maintain their identities. If one of them changes into another atom or molecule, nothing important seems to have happened: a rearrangement has taken place, but no significant individual has perished and nothing has "died." When an atom emits a particle, nothing has really been lost. Nonliving things are indifferent to such changes. It is true that an atom or a molecule may "need" the gravitational field and the other forces that help compose it, and may "ingest" the wandering electron or neutron or energy from its surround, but these interactions are different from feeding, and a word other than *need* should be used to name the dependence that atoms and compounds have on things outside themselves.

Need, want, and wish can be more precisely understood by being contrasted with the kind of reactions and stabilities that take place in the purely material, nonliving context in which they are found. Our concern, moreover, our primary target, is the human person and the wishing that is specific to him. It would not be appropriate to try to discuss wishing and other forms of human thinking by contrasting them with inanimate matter, as Descartes attempts to do. Needs and wants provide us with the immediate context, the set of proper distinctions, that help us clarify what wishing, or rational wanting, is.

Three Kinds of Wish

Aristotle shows, in *Nicomachean Ethics*, III 2, that our wishes can be directed toward three different kinds of things.

First, we can wish for things that are entirely impossible; Aristotle's example is the wish for immortality. Other examples might be wishing for utopian social arrangements, wishing to learn all of Shakespeare by downloading his works into our brains, wishing to be in two places at the same time, wishing to be in the same place during two lifetimes, such as being in Rome now and at the time of Julius Caesar, wishing that we were young again, or, finally, wishing that the past had not been determined as it has. All these things cannot be, but we can still wish that they could. In order to wish for such things, we must be able to formulate impossibilities, and obviously only a rational creature can do so.

Second, we can wish for things that are a mixture of impossibility and possibility: they are impossible for us, but they can be done by someone else. We might wish, for example, for the New York Yankees to win the World Series, for this or that political candidate to win an election, for this or that person to be appointed chairman of the board of the company I work for, for this relative of mine to get his life in order. Such things are within the realm of possibility, but not within our possibility. I can wish for them, but it is up to someone else to do them. They can be done, but not by me.

Third, we can wish for things that we ourselves can achieve. What we wish for is now within the range of our artillery. Even here, however, there is a distance between what we wish for and what we can directly do. To extend the military analogy, we do not press the muzzle of our howitzer right onto the surface of the thing we wish to hit; we do not immediately achieve the thing we wish for. Things that we wish for can be attained only mediately, through choices that lead to them, and hence we *wish* for them and do not just perform them. Wishing essentially covers a distance. For example, we can wish to be healthy, but we cannot become healthy by an immediate performance, as we might simply drink some water; we must do other things that bring about health; we cannot "do" health itself. We might wish to play the violin well, but we cannot do so immediately; we can achieve our wish only by choosing, over and over again, to practice here and now. I may wish to live in Albuquerque, but I cannot immediately live there the way I can directly raise my arm; I must do a series of other things in order to take up residence in that city. Such wished-for satisfactions are distant to us, but despite their distance we are able to reach them through our choices. By contrast, if I want to get up from my chair, I really cannot be said to wish to do so, unless there are impediments and I have to figure out how to get up. Normally, I do not *wish* to get up; I just get up.

When this third kind of wish becomes truly engaged, when it gets into gear and kicks into action, when it effectively starts directing what we do, it becomes an *intention* or a *purpose*. An intention is a wish that has begun to hold sway over deliberation and choice. An intention is a wish at work. Wishes for impossibilities and wishes for what only others can do cannot become our purposes or intentions.

This threefold range of things we can wish for – the impossible, that which can be done but only by others, and that which can be done by us – sheds light not only on human volition, but on human rationality and human personhood as well. Human rationality allows us to introduce syntax, part-and-whole structure, into our experience, and such articulation can take place not only in regard to what we can say and register, but also in regard to what we can desire. Syntax also allows us to deal with a more radical kind of absence than the kind that animals can cope with, and each of the three forms of wishing is concerned with a distinctive kind of absence: that of sheer impossibilities, that of things that only others can do, and that of things we can do through the mediation of choices. Plants need things, and animals both need and want things, but neither plants nor animals can wish for things because they do not have the articulation and the rational control over the absent that reason gives to human beings. We human beings, we rational animals, by contrast, can do all three: we need, want, and wish for things, and our wishes can take on three different forms.

Wishes Cover a Distance

The three kinds of wishing all deal with things that are distant from us, and hence to some degree absent, and we recognize their absence. The most distant of all is the impossible; it cannot be achieved by anyone. But even though it cannot be achieved, it still, remarkably, can be conceived by us, and even more remarkably, it can be wanted by us, even though we know it cannot be achieved. How odd this is, and how unsettling. It is strange enough that we can conceive of things that cannot exist, but it is supremely curious that we can wish for things even while knowing that they are impossible. The wishing in question might sometimes be a merely idle thing – we might casually think, "Well, it would be nice if that were to happen" – but it can also be a deep and powerful desire, a yearning for what we know cannot be. Such longing for the impossible, furthermore, is not a result of confusion; it is not a matter of being mistaken, of taking something as possible when it really is not. That would not really be wishing for the impossible, because we in our confusion would be taking it as something that could be done, by others if not by ourselves. Rather, we know clearly and certainly that the thing cannot be attained by anyone, and still we can and do wish for it.

We might, for example, wish that we were younger, or that we would never get sick, or that we had not taken some action that we did in fact commit. We can live "somewhere, over the rainbow, way up high." Some of us spend a lot of time thinking about such things and singing about them. Many popular songs propose unattainable things to us: with great fanfare and drama, we are encouraged to "dream the impossible dream." Classical music, lieder and operas, do the same thing in their own way, and fables, legends, movies, musicals, and advertisements all present appealing situations that we know could never be. This sort of wishing has something bittersweet about it, a *Sehnsucht* for things we know cannot be possessed. It exposes us to what can be wanted but never enjoyed.

Why do we waste our time wishing for the impossible? Why don't we limit our rational wanting to things within our power? It seems that we need this sort of wishing to provide the outermost context of our practical world. It is the boundary that serves as the foil for the wished-for satis-factions that can be realized, by others or by ourselves: wishes that can be fulfilled seem to need wishes that cannot be fulfilled for their definition. It seems that our rational appetite – not just our reason, but our appetite also – needs to stretch beyond the range of its own effectiveness, in order to define the region where it *can* be effective. Only a rational being, someone who can intend things in their radical absence, could wish for impossi-bilities. Animals are not subject to that kind of longing; they are more matter-of-fact in what they want. Animals could never want something that is impossible, because they would be unable to conceive it. This kind of wishing, idle as it might seem, does reveal our rationality.

We must note that the zone of wished-for impossibilities is not the absolutely outermost sphere of our world. Beyond it, even more distant from us, is the indifferent cosmos, the world that just is what it is and does not engage our wishes in any way. We can know something of that world, and we can also know that we can only contemplate it. We know that it transcends the practical. It is the target of the understanding mind, not the target of any wish and still less of any intervention. We recognize it as the domain of necessity and chance, the domain of the laws of nature and contingent conjunctions. Our reason does stretch out to it, and so it does become present to us, but we do not wish for anything in it. Our theoretic reason reaches beyond the practical. This domain, before which we are spectators and nothing more, is the most encompassing of all the parts of the world. It marks out the largest whole. The practical domain, the one in which we both wish and intervene, is nested within it, and is rather small by comparison. The zone of wished-for impossibilities marks the transition between the world that can simply be known and the world that can be wished. It is where wishing awakens. It marks the farthest reach of the practical mind, and it is so far out that although we can wish for certain things to be within it, we know that no one can do anything to bring them about, because they are things that could never be. Our knowledge checkmates our desire. Wishing for the impossible is, in fact, something of an overreach, but one that we cannot avoid and would not want to be without.

Let us now consider wishes that extend to a less distant impossibility. We can wish for things that we ourselves cannot attain – they are impossible for us – but that others can bring about. This form of wishing brings us well within the domain of the practical, but it is a part of that domain in which we remain helpless while others can act. We can only sit there while others do things, and we know that we are immobilized while they can perform. This kind of helplessness is different from the wish for impossibilities, and it highlights our dependence on other people. Examples of such wishing abound in sports. Millions of people may passionately wish that the Redskins get to the Super Bowl and win the championship, but only the team and its management and owners can accomplish this wished-for satisfaction. The management may tell the fans that they should support the team and thus enter into the effort, but in fact what I do personally in this matter is of almost no consequence at all. I might wear a red shirt to the game, I might shout a lot, but my choices do not count for much in accomplishing this goal; and yet I and millions like me may earnestly wish for the outcome. The wishing is there.

This second form of wishing vividly brings out the intersubjective character of human volition. I can strongly desire certain things that I know cannot be done by me but can be done by others. Even the first kind of wishing, the one directed toward impossibilities, has an intersubjective dimension. There, I know that the thing I wish for is impossible for everyone and not impossible only for me. If the intersubjective aspect were not part of this first kind of wishing, if all the "impossibles" we wish for were impossible only for me alone, then we would not be able to distinguish the first kind of wishing from the second, since both "wishables" are impossible for me individually. This is not the case, however; we know that there are some things that we eagerly wish for that we know can come to pass, but we know with equal certainty that we ourselves cannot do them while others can. Sports are an obvious example of this sort of wishing, but politics is another, and there are many other kinds of desiring in all areas of life in which we are entirely dependent on others for their fulfillment.

It is not the case that we first begin wishing and doing things that are possible for us, and only subsequently attribute the same kind of wishing and execution to others. We could not start off in solitary action and choice, no more than we could start off with a solitary language. Instead, we begin, as infants and children, with needs and wants and then wishes that must be fulfilled by others, just as we start to use a language under the guidance of other people, who can speak before we can. The first needs, wants, and wishes that we have are satisfied by others and not by ourselves, and we must start off with dependency and trust. We gradually differentiate our agency from that of others: we absorb the possibility of taking our own steps to fulfill our wishes by living with others who, at the beginning of our lives, implement our wishes for us and then awaken our minds into practical rationality. We learn the language of wish fulfillment from those on whom we depend. In the logic of wishing, deliberating, and choosing, we are originally attached to others, and we must wean ourselves from them; wishing is not solipsistic at any point in its development. And later on, all throughout our lives, much of what we wish for can only be done for us by other people.

A particularly interesting question arises in cases when we ask others to deliberate and choose for us, when we entreat or persuade others to be the ones who fulfill our wish. Do we subordinate them to our own deliberation and choice, so that *we* become the initiating agents, the actors, and they become merely one among many of the means that we have chosen? Do they become our instruments? Or do we remain subject to these other persons, these other agents, and must we simply put our trust in them for the fulfillment of our wish? Are they and they alone the effective agents? I would suggest that if we were to command, coerce, or force them to fulfill our wish, then we would indeed be the agents of the fulfillment, but if we were simply to ask them to act on our behalf, we would not take over the agency. We would have a kind of initiating role in the action, but one that respects the irreducibility and rationality of other agents.

How Wishes Become Intentions

We move on to the third case, in which we wish for things that we ourselves can bring about. As I have mentioned earlier, even in this case there is some distance between ourselves and what we wish for, because we cannot immediately accomplish what we desire. If we could achieve it immediately, we would not need to wish for it; we would just do it. For example, if my ear itches, I raise my hand and scratch it. There is no distinction between means and purposes in this performance. It is not normally the case that I first wish to scratch my ear, then deliberate about how to attack this problem, and finally choose to raise my hand and scratch as a means to attain that purpose. The action is not that complicated. The logic of wish, deliberation, and choice does not come into play in such immediate satisfactions. We are dealing here not with wishing, but with the more simple *wanting*, and there is practically no distance between what I want and what I do.

There is practically no distance, but there is some distance, a very small one. It is not the kind that functions between a wish and a choice; rather, it is the kind that is found in sensibility and perception, not in thinking. My ear itches, and it takes a moment for me to raise my hand and rub my ear, but this distance is merely sensory, the kind that occurs in perception, where we move around an object to see its various sides. Itching calls for scratching, and the scratching is done directly; the procedure is seamless. No thoughtful distinctions are called for, no breaking apart of the situation into ends and means. There is no practical syntax. I don't have to think between the itching and the rubbing. This kind of small-scale distance occurs on the level of sensibility, and it does not involve logical articulation.

In the case of a full-scale wish, I have to begin thinking of things that are different from what I wish for, and I have to begin thinking about alternatives. I have to insert something between the purpose and myself. I have to articulate parts and wholes much more explicitly. Suppose I realize that I need shelter (and hence I wish for it): I could cut down some small trees and build a lean-to (but my axe is not sharp, and there isn't much time); or I could pile up some rocks (not very stable); or I could go back to the cave I passed a while ago (but it is pretty far away); or I could take some of these materials I have with me and set up a makeshift tent. This kind of thinking, whether fast or slow, very brief or prolonged over days, weeks, months, or years, is deliberation, and it involves shaking out alternatives, things that could be done, and our shaking them out is done in view of the wished-for purpose. All of this deliberation is being carried out under the urgent pressure of the wish for shelter, which is now holding sway over what I think and do. I must evaluate each of the options that I consider, and if I am mature, experienced, and clever in these matters, I will hit upon the best solution available in this situation and will immediately start carrying it out. But what I am directly doing is something other than what I wish for. If someone were to see me cutting down a tree, it would not be obvious to him that I am arranging for shelter (whereas my hand rising up to my ear is more obviously on the way to scratching). I could be cutting down firewood or making a clearing in the forest. If the spectator asked me what I was doing, I would say that I am cutting-down-a-tree-for-a-shelter, I am not just cutting-down-a-tree. Making a shelter is my *intention*, my wish in its active governance, and my action cannot be described without mention of what I intend. My purpose in cutting down the tree is not just to cut down the tree but to make a shelter, and my action would be incomprehensible without that explanation, without the presence of something else – the wished-for purpose – in what I am doing now.

There is more intelligence in cutting down a tree to make a shelter than there is in raising my hand to rub my itching ear. In making a choice, I must distinguish sharply between the purpose I seek and the action I now perform; I must articulate a whole into discrete and heterogenous parts; I must recognize the parts as parts; and I must concomitantly hold all those parts together in an articulated and synoptic whole, the whole that is governed by the purpose and populated by its intermediary steps. This is the thoughtful whole brought about by practical thinking, and it is all engendered by the wish that I started with. It took shape when the wish morphed into a purpose. This is how practical syntax enters into what I do.

In such practical thinking, I must have the intelligence to see the wished-for purpose in the intermediary steps, in the choices I make: the shelter, different as it may be, is visible, to me as a thoughtful agent, in the cutting down of the tree.[1] On a more complicated scale, suppose I wish to become a lawyer. My purpose, my being a lawyer, is visible to me and to other thoughtful appraisers of human action in the applications I make to law schools, in the summer job I now have, which helps pay for tuition, and in countless other activities, each of which may involve branching trees of choices and actions. I don't have to see the scratching of my ear *in* the raising of my hand; there is not enough "otherness" between the two, and my action does not involve a thoughtful articulation and synthesis of "two in one"; but I do have to be able to see "being sheltered" in cutting down a tree, or unfolding a tarpaulin, or piling up some rocks. There is a practical syntax in shaking out possible ways of attaining something we wish for. The wished-for satisfaction has to be seen as other than the actions that lead to it, and yet it has to be seen "in" the actions we are performing (just as, in predication, the whole or the subject must be both distinguished from the part or the feature and also seen in it). Deliberation is a special form of the nested embedding that language makes possible for us: we are able to see the goal in the means that bring it about.

Wishes, Deliberation, and Choice

When we wish for entirely impossible things, no real deliberation takes place; no ladder of possible choices, no menu of things we might do, drops down for anyone from such wished-for impossibilities. Such wishes cannot become intentions. What we would like remains forever unreachable, and we know it. We expend our energy in wishful thinking, not in practical deliberation. When we wish for things that are impossible for us but possible for other persons, then again no ladders of possible choices drop down for us. We may, however, see some drop down over there, for those other agents, and we may encourage those others to take advantage of them. But when our wishes come in closer, when we target things within our own range, things that we ourselves can achieve, then ladders of possible choices come tumbling down in profusion all over us as we deliberate about our course of action, and they will be all the more numerous and all the more realistic the more inventive and intelligent we are.

 Most of the examples I have used to illustrate the fulfillment of wishes through our own actions, such as seeking shelter, getting into law school, and improving our health, have been somewhat utilitarian and self-interested. But our wishes extend far beyond our own individual benefit; they can also be concerned with the good of others, and they can occur on a very large scale and involve many people. Parents of a handicapped child

---

[1] On seeing the end in the means, see Robert Sokolowski, *Moral Action: A Phenomenological Study* (Bloomington: Indiana University Press, 1985), 30–3.

may have to exercise much deliberation to take care of his needs; the director of a hospital may have to make countless evaluations and choices to keep the institution going; the pastor of a church will have to think practically about a wide variety of instrumentalities and personal relationships to keep the parish working well. For an example of a decision made on a large scale, consider the deliberation behind the Normandy invasion in the Second World War. General Eisenhower and his colleagues and staff wished the termination of the European war. This wished-for satisfaction lay within the scope of their own action because of the authority they had been given, and so they were able to engage themselves in bringing it about. It became their purpose. It required, in their judgment, that there be a second front in western Europe, and this in turn required an invasion of France. The invasion in turn called for an enormous amount of planning, extending over years, to shake out the alternatives that could lead to that event. The beaches at Normandy were selected as the site, the troops were amassed, the material stored, the ships lined up, the deceptions put in place, and finally everything that could be readied was ready. The time for a final decision, for a choice, had arrived, but the only thing that was not in place was the weather, which of course lay outside the range of human disposition. It was part of the indifferent universe. The practical and the cosmic interacted with each other. At that crucial point, however, the contingencies, necessities, and deliberations all came into harmony for the Allies as the weather began to clear, at least for a short time. Eisenhower and his colleagues and staff made the choice to go ahead; they announced their decision, and the action began. This was an example of moving from a wish that the agents could fulfill to the deliberation that articulated the resources and alternatives required for its fulfillment, to the choice of the best means available at that time and place and in those circumstances. Everything was done under the sway of the intention, the wished-for purpose exercising its governing power.

Stalin, by contrast, who had been asking for a second front for years, wished for that outcome but was himself not able to implement it. All he could do was petition, cajole, complain, and harass others into action. It was a wish that could be fulfilled by others but not by him. The stubborn presence of other agents, with their own judgment of the situation, stood between him and what he wished for. All such wishes or intentions, deliberations, and choices are public things – they are never just private, solitary, psychological events, any more than a salute or a discourse is a private event – and sometimes they occur on a colossal scale. The world afterward bears the imprint of the wished-for satisfaction and the deliberation and choices made in view of it.

It is also possible, of course, that despite our best efforts our deliberation does not settle on anything that can be done by us. Our deliberation may run into the sand. The purpose that was governing our deliberation never gains a foothold in events, and it begins to recede as a possibility, after having been entertained as one. If at the time of the Normandy invasion the weather had not cleared, the decision would have been left unmade and postponed – for no one knows how long.[2] There are wishes that become intentions and govern as such for a while, but then withdraw again into mere velleity.

The dictionary gives the word *wish* a strong, active meaning. As a verb, it signifies to want, desire, long for, command, or even to force or impose something on someone: "he wished this task on him." As a noun, *wish* signifies a definite mental inclination toward doing or obtaining something, a felt or expressed desire. It signifies volition, wanting something. Our common usage of the word, however, often connotes passivity: we might say, "I do wish it were so" when we cannot do anything about it. We tend to relegate wishing to the desire for impossibilities, or we think of wishing as the alternative to doing. Wishing seems to be allied with sighing. But in our development in this chapter, we have given the word *wish* the meaning it has always had, and have taken it not as an alternative to action but as the principle and origin of action, that which makes the action intelligible: wishing is intelligent, rational wanting, the kind of wanting that persons are capable of, the kind that, in some cases, can engender enormous accomplishments, such as the establishment of a political community, the development of a fleet of nuclear submarines, or the construction of a university.

To make this meaning of *wish* more precise, we have stipulated a distinction between wishing and wanting. Wishing is a rational activity, in which we articulate wholes and parts – practical ones, in this case, such as ends and means – and recognize them as wholes and parts. Wanting is more purely a sensory activity, and it occurs in both men and animals. There is some articulation in wanting, just as there is in sensory perception, but it does not involve the sharp, discrete distinctions, the analysis and synthesis, and the categoriality proper to rational thinking. But there is a problem in human conduct: sometimes our practical thinking is overcome by plain wanting. The thoughtful articulation dissolves, and the distinction between wished-for purposes and the means leading toward them evaporates. Impulse buying is like this, and advertisers and storekeepers know it: "I know I don't need that extra shirt, but it's on sale, and it's here right by the cashier's counter, and after all . . . ."

---

[2] If the invasion had not occurred in June 1944, it would have had to be put off for a month (because of the tides), but a month later the region suffered terrible storms, which destroyed some of the temporary piers at the invasion site. Would the invasion have had to be put off yet another month? Could the Allied deception have been kept intact? Late summer or autumn would not have been a good time to make the assault. What effect would a prolongation of the war in Europe have had on the use of atomic weapons? The historical timing of events at the end of the war was extraordinary.

Buyer's remorse is often a sign that wishing and its deliberation were smothered by simple wanting. This conquest of sensibility over reason is called *akrasia*, moral weakness or incontinence, by Aristotle. It occurs when our impulses get the better of our resolutions, that is, when our intentions lose their force: "I know that I should avoid sweets, but here are some of those chocolate-covered ice cream bars, and after all . . . ." As Aristotle says, the incontinent man is full of regrets.[3]

The shift from wishing, deliberation, and choice to plain wanting can occur even when we utter words that seem to indicate that we are rationally in control of the situation. Words alone do not guarantee that we are rational; it is possible to utter the words, which seem to articulate the situation, while we are acting contrarily. This is one of the illusionary possibilities of language; it can give the appearance of effective, articulated thinking when none is present. What people truly wish for is revealed much more by what they do than by what they say. Animals, because they lack speech, are not capable of this form of camouflage. If they are hungry or angry, they show it, and their barks or growls are veridical expressions of their state of mind. The problem with us is that we are not just animals but rational animals.

We have seen that human beings are capable of wishing for impossibilities. It is part of their nature as rational beings to do so. Normally, we know when we are wishing for what is impossible, but sometimes some people do not see the difference between the possible and the impossible. They think that the impossible can be achieved, and they take steps to bring it about. In some cases such an error will only waste our time and energy, but in other cases it can be devastating. In Cambodia, Pol Pot and the Khmer Rouge wished to achieve a new kind of society that is impossible in fact but that seemed possible to them, and they destroyed a third of the population in their attempt to bring it about. Even in democracies, much political rhetoric promises people things that they sorely wish for but that could never be; what would remain in political speeches if people did not wish for the impossible and politicians did not articulate it for them? Both the tyrannical and the democratic excesses show how the wish for the impossible can fly out of control.

Of course, it is not always easy to say what is possible and what is not. The distinction can be a matter of controversy, and some people will argue that the apparent impossibility of certain goals is due only to a lack of imagination, or perhaps a lack of courage. The impossibility, they claim, is a prejudice, not an evident necessity. Such issues have to be sorted out by argument and tested by experiment. Modern science and technology have done many things that once seemed impossible – curing some diseases, splitting the atom, exploring outer space, cloning sheep – and these

---

[3] Aristotle, *Nicomachean Ethics*, VII 8, 1150b30–1.

successes have made people think that many other limitations can be overcome, in regard to things like human cognition, familial relationships, societal structures, and human happiness. The limits on such things, it is claimed, are not really part of their definition; they are only prejudicial restrictions, and experiments in living must be carried out to test the borders of what can be done.[4] If such experiments turn out to be like Pol Pot's, they will engender much suffering and sorrow. The modal logic of our wishes works itself out in human affairs.

Wishes as Dispositions

We might think that we should somehow "feel" the wishes we have, that we should be constantly conscious of them, but this is not the case. For us to wish something does not require that we be explicitly aware of the wish at all times. Wishes are, by and large, dispositions, not explicit declarations. If you say that Mildred wishes to practice medicine, you do not imply that she is constantly saying to herself, "I do want to be a doctor, I do want to begin a medical practice." If such an explicit awareness were necessary, we could wish for only one thing at a time, and our wishes would go on and off as our awareness of them started up and shut down. But in fact, we continuously wish many things: Mildred wishes to practice medicine, but she also wishes to stay alive, to understand things, to be friends with certain people, to get a new home, to assist her parents. She also wishes that air pollution be reduced, that the European Union find its footing, that the federal budget be balanced, and that the next Ice Age not come along too soon. She also wishes that she had been born in Arkansas instead of New York, that there were no such thing as cancer or pneumonia, and that people could get along better with one another. Obviously, not all of these wishes can become intentions; not all of them can effectively govern her choices. Some of them are wishes for things that only other people can bring about, and some remain wishes for the impossible.

Some of them do turn into intentions, however, and if Mildred is clever she will see certain situations as opportunities to implement one or other of these enduring wishes. She is disposed, ready to act, because of the wishes she has and the way she understands the world. If a particular situation arises, it will come to light for her not just as a brute fact, but as profiled against one or other of her continuing wishes. Suppose she is walking along some storefronts and sees just the right chair for her parents' home. She sees not just a chair, but the chair that would fit perfectly in her parents' living room and satisfy some need they have. The chair comes into her field of perception, but it brings with it a background, the

---

[4] On experiments in living, see John Stuart Mill, *On Liberty*, ed. John Gray and G. W. Smith (New York: Routledge, 1991), 72.

wished-for satisfaction of her parents' comfort. The fact that the chair is perceived as a means to a purpose does not signify that Mildred had been keeping this purpose, this wish, alive in her mind as she walked through the city. Rather, the presence of the chair triggers the activation of this enduring wish and turns it into an intention, and if Mildred had seen something else, that other object might have triggered the activation of some other wish. Instead of seeing a chair, she might have met someone who spoke to her about some medical opportunities that could assist her ongoing effort to locate a medical practice. Wishes and intentions are dispositional, not continuously active.

Our wishes reflect our character. What looks good to us depends on the kind of person we have come to be. Certain kinds of people wish for certain kinds of things, and these wishes turn into intentions when the opportunity presents itself. The things they wish for do not need to be established as such for them by argument; they appear as such because of the way these people are. It might take time for the dispositions of certain people to manifest themselves. Someone may have a brutal disposition, and we might not know it, but after we have let him into our lives – he marries into the family, he takes a lease on our house, he becomes the head of state – we begin to discover what he wishes. His wishes become intentions as he begins to act in keeping with the kind of person he is, but the disposition behind the wishes and the actions was there all along. It is important to be able to pick up clues about people that reveal the way they are disposed.

It is, therefore, not the case that we are engaged in wishing only while we are implementing a plan. Aristotle's classical description of practical reasoning runs like this: we begin with a wish, that X should come to pass.[5] When this volition becomes effective, it turns into an intention, which becomes the starting point for our deliberation. We then reason backward in the following way: to achieve intention X, we must do A; to get A, we must do B; to do B, we must do C; but C is within our power and so we do it, we make it our choice. If things go according to plan, C brings about B, which brings about A, which in turn brings about X, the thing originally intended, with which we began. This schema accurately represents practical thinking, but it does suffer from a deficiency. It suggests that intentions exist only when we are actually thinking them and deliberating under their guidance. But that is not the case; most of our intentions are virtual, not actual, and each of us embodies many intentions all the time, some of which may be obscure even to ourselves. We always want a multitude of things to happen, and as situations develop around us we respond to events, we deliberate, and we take steps to bring our purposes about. We are always ready for targets of opportunity, of many different

---

[5] Aristotle, *Nicomachean Ethics*, III 3, 1112b11–1113a2.

kinds. If we ran into an opportunity and did not seize it, our failure to act would show that the wish in question was a mere wish and not one that could become an intention. The fact that we did nothing when the chance presented itself would show that our wish was only a velleity, not an effective wish or a real intention, no matter what we might have said about it. In some cases, of course, we do set out with a plan, with a definite purpose in mind, and start shaking out the means that will lead to it, but this is not the only way we wish for things; it is, in fact, the exception rather than the norm.

16

Declaring Our Wishes and Choices

We have examined some of the forms that wishing takes on. It is obvious that we do not possess our wishes in internal solitude, as merely private experiences, nor do we express them only by our bodily conduct; we also *say* that we wish for this or that, and we use the declarative form of the term *I* as we do so. We will now discuss how declaratives function in the expression of our wishes. In some cases, our wishes become intentions, which in turn stimulate and govern our choices. These choices too can be expressed and appropriated by declaratives. In this chapter we will also study how the first-person pronoun is used in the expression of choice. We can declare our wishes and our choices because they both involve syntactic articulation.

How We Declare Ourselves in Our Wishes

In Chapters 1 and 2 we examined cognitive, emotive, promissory, and existential declaratives, and we mentioned the special kind of declaratives that occur in philosophy. First-person declaratives, which express the agent's engagement in what it articulates, can, obviously, be used in stating our wishes. We say, for example, "I do wish the rain would end," or "I so wish to play soccer," or "How I wish I were younger." We formulate our wishes and declare ourselves as the ones wishing them. Wishes are the intelligent form of wanting, and declaratives express us as rational beings involved in such desires: we engage, ratify, and manifest ourselves as rationally wanting the thing in question. Such declarations occur even when we wish for impossibilities.

If the thing that we want is not the object of a rational desire, if it is merely the object of a nonrationalized inclination, the statement that we want it is informative and not declarative. Suppose I am trying to stop smoking but still strongly want a cigarette; if I were to say, "I really crave a smoke," I would be telling you what desires are in me, but not what

I wish. The same thing would occur if I were to say, "I am getting hungry." I would be informing you about my compulsions or my wants, not about my rational desires. I would not be engaging my reason in my desire, and I would not be willing these things; I would not be endorsing or ratifying them when I use the first-person pronoun. My desires would be conscious but not willed, felt but not appropriated, experienced but not made truly my own. I would be expressing "something else" that desires in me: not *someone* else but *something* else. Still, these cravings, these desires, and even these compulsions are indeed *mine* in some sense (hence they can be a problem for me), but they are not mine as rationally appropriated. I have not invested my rational desire in them, and yet they truly are in me. If such desires were the outcome of earlier choices I made, of earlier investments of my reason, then the divergence in me would be not between me and my inborn wants but between me now and my earlier self and the deposit that my earlier self has left in me now. My earlier self has endowed me with inclinations that I now regret having. Sometimes my rational and my nonrational desires exist peacefully side by side, but often enough there is a bitter conflict between them: I have to struggle with myself to do what I wish to do.

If I were to act on my desires, however, I would have made them my own. They would have become my intentions, and they would have become rationally appropriated as mine. I would have made a choice under their guidance. Even if I were just to begin deliberating under their aegis, they would have become more than just a subpersonal part of me; I would have elevated them from being just desires to being wishes and then to being intentions.

The conflict that can occur between what I want in a subpersonal way and what I wish for in a rational and hence personal way has been recognized since the beginning of philosophy as the place where ethics arises, as well as the place where human self-identity is achieved. Plato describes this struggle in the *Republic* (IV 439e–440b), where Leontius becomes angry with himself because he is overpowered by the shameful desire to look at corpses outside the city. Plato uses this example to describe human identity, to show how a human agent is both one and many, one self with many parts, some of which war against the others. Before Plato there was Homer, who, in a passage quoted twice by Plato, describes Odysseus as arguing with his own desires: "[He] struck his chest and spoke unto his heart: 'Endure, my heart, you have suffered more shameful things than this'" (*Odyssey* 20, 17–18; *Republic*, III 390d; IV 441b). Aristotle describes the same discord in Book VII of the *Nicomachean Ethics*, where he discusses *akrasia* and *enkrateia*, incontinence and continence, or moral weakness and self-mastery. Both the weak and the self-mastered agents experience antagonism between their desires and their reason; the weak usually succumb to their emotions, while the self-controlled manage to keep theirs in check. Such self-mastery is, of course, not the same as virtue, which brings about a harmony between passion and reason. In teaching or reading the *Nicomachean Ethics*, it is pedagogically and phenomenologically advisable to begin with the initial ten chapters of Book VII, where Aristotle discusses moral weakness and self-mastery, then to proceed to Book II for the definition of virtue, then to go through Books III to X, and to treat Book I only at the conclusion. The description of moral conflict in Book VII offers the reader the most intuitive presentation of human agency. To read the book in this sequence is to move from what is clearest to us to what is clearest in itself. It is interesting to note that Aristotle's *Eudemian Ethics* introduces continence and incontinence very early on, in Book II, Chapters 7 and 8, where they are used as the immediate foil for the definition of virtue.

The relationship between desire and reason, between what I have called wants and wishes, is discussed in contemporary psychology. Allan N. Schore has written a book entitled *Affect Regulation and the Origin of the Self*. Its subtitle is *The Neurobiology of Emotional Development*.[1] The book, according to a remark in the Foreword, examines how the infant emerges "as a neurobiological-social-emotional self."[2] Schore describes how the interaction between the infant and the mother allows the infant to control his affects or emotions and to raise them into the human register, into a rational and hence personal life. Most of the book is devoted to the neurological basis for such development, but the human definition of what is going on is given by a description of what the infant becomes able to do in the emotive and practical exchanges between himself and the mother. In our terminology, the infant has wants from the beginning, but he develops wishes only gradually, as he learns, through his interaction with others and through the involvement of linguistic syntax, to appropriate those wants and to begin thinking practically (deliberating) in view of them. The child must learn, not only to express his wants through crying or gesturing, but also to declare them, and as he declares them more and more thoughtfully, he begins not only to want but also to wish, and then to deliberate and choose. And learning to manage our emotions is not just a task for us as individuals; the human race has had to do it in stages. When we learned to control fire, for example, we needed to find out how to start a fire, how to keep it alive, and how to limit its spread, but besides these external discoveries we also had to learn how to control our natural fear of fire, which even now is hardly extinguished and never will be.

We certainly have needs before we are born, and we probably have some wants – early conscious needs, with pleasure and pain – while we are still in

---

[1] Allan N. Schore, *Affect Regulation and the Origin of the Self: The Neurobiology of Emotional Development*, Foreword by James S. Grotstein (Hillsdale, NJ: Erlbaum, 1994).
[2] Ibid., xxii.

the womb. We obviously have wants after we are born: Prospero tells Miranda how they came to their island, and how their enemies abducted "me and thy crying self" from their home in Milan (*Tempest*, I ii). This phrase, "thy crying self," could be used to describe any one of us as we express our undifferentiated and as yet unappropriated wanting at the "abduction" that occurs at birth. But as time goes on we turn our wants into wishes, and our wishes into purposes. As we do so and concomitantly absorb and initiate language, we differentiate our uses of the word *I* into the informational and declarative forms. It may be difficult to tell exactly when the distinction occurs, and it may be hard to say whether this or that use of the word *I* is merely informative or fully declarative or something in between, but the difference does emerge as we invest our reason into our desires and make them into acts of willing.

I should also say a word about the contrary of wishes, namely, fears or worries. We may wish that certain things will or will not happen, but we also fear that certain things will or will not happen, and such fears, because they are focused on distant objects and not on proximate things that frighten us, could be called worries. Worries are the inverse of wishes, and they too are proper to intelligent beings. As Thomas Hobbes puts it, man cannot escape being "in a perpetual solicitude of the time to come."[3] The other animals "are not rapacious unless hungry and not cruel unless provoked, whereas man is famished even by future hunger."[4] Hobbes's eloquent, alliterative Latin phrase is "etiam fame futura famelicus."[5]

How We Declare Ourselves in Our Choices

Declaring ourselves in our wishes and worries is not very much different from declaring ourselves in our cognitions, emotions, and promises. So long as we only wish for things, we continue to stand at a distance from them, a distance similar to the kind at work when we simply know or suspect something. Our emotive responses also are not actions or interventions but only attitudes or feelings, and even our promises are made in words and not yet in deeds. In all these cases we may wish, know, or feel, but we do not act. But declaratives can also be used in regard to our actions. We can also declare ourselves in regard to our *choices*, as opposed to our wishes. When we do so, we manifest ourselves in our active practical

---

[3] Thomas Hobbes, *Leviathan*, ed. Richard Tuck (New York: Cambridge University Press, 1996), Chapter 12, p. 76.

[4] Thomas Hobbes, *On Man*, in *Man and Citizen*, ed. Bernard Gert (Garden City, NY: Doubleday, 1972), Chapter 10, §3, p. 40.

[5] Thomas Hobbes, *De Homine*, in *Opera Philosophica quae Latine scripsit*, ed. William Molesworth (Aalen: Scientia Verlag, 1961), volume 2, Chapter 10, §3, p. 91. A little further on (p. 92) one finds a clear expression of Hobbes's denial of the superiority of the theoretic life: "Itaque oratione homo non melior fit, sed potentior."

rationality. Wishing by itself does not make us practical agents; by itself, it is rather passive: we want something to happen, but we cannot or do not do anything about it. Only when a wish becomes an intention, and only when the intention effectively determines actions that we perform and choices that we make, have we become truly active. For a choice *is* an action, a doing of something; it is not just marking a ballot or taking lemon instead of lime, nor is it something we do before we act. It is an intervention, and it creases the world in a way that exhibits rational articulation. A *proairesis* is a *praxis*.

Choices are not necessarily done in language (they can be simply done and not spoken), but they can be crowned in speech by declaratives. We decide and do something, and then we say what we are doing or what we have done: "I am doing this to save someone from drowning," "I'm buying this automobile," or "I've cleaned the snow off the sidewalk, since no one else was willing to do it." We thereby ratify and manifest ourselves not merely as wanting something to occur but as actually determining the way the world is. We have acted and we have spoken, and we thus exhibit ourselves, as agents who have made a difference in the world, in two ways: first in deed and then in words. It is important to note that the choice comes first; we *do* something, we crease the world, we intervene and change the way things are, and often we carry out that performance without saying anything (we jump into the water to save the person who is floundering; we start shoveling the snow off the sidewalk). We have engaged our rationality in a bodily way, and we can be seen as doing so. What makes it a rational action is not that we have been in motion, but that we have acted in a rational manner, in view of a purpose that we have in mind and that we can formulate.[6] The part-whole structure has been articulated and embodied in what we do. Our conduct involves practical syntax, with *this* being done in view of *that*. Then, as we do it or after we have done it, we might declare what we are doing or what we have done, and we thereby give a further rational form to our conduct. We not only swim over to help the person in distress; we also say that we are doing so. This verbal supplement is a further public appropriation of what we have already appropriated by our deliberation and chosen action. We can also, of course, say what we are going to do before we do it, but there is always some risk in this sequence, because we may never get around to

[6] On the need for words to complement deeds, see Hannah Arendt, *The Human Condition* (Chicago: University of Chicago Press, 1958), 176: "Speech and action reveal this unique distinctness.... . A life without speech and without action ... is literally dead to the world; it has ceased to be a human life because it is no longer lived among men." See also p. 179: "No other human performance requires speech to the same extent as action." I would disagree, however, with Arendt's claim that biblical morality involves a disappearance from the world of speech and actions among men. Biblical morality enlarges the context for human performance, it does not constrict it.

performing what we announce in advance. Speech that accompanies or follows what we do articulates things that are already there.[7]

When we declare what we are doing, furthermore, we do not just describe the immediate conduct we are carrying out; we do not just say, "I am swimming." Rather, we must express the purpose that animates the thing we are doing: "I am swimming over there to rescue someone." Our declaration has to include the complex state of affairs made up of an intention and the deed chosen under the sway of the intention.

Suppose we see someone doing something, but do not understand what he is doing. The action we see him performing is unintelligible to us. It needs to be explained. We ask him what he is doing, and he replies by telling us, not just about the action itself but about the purpose governing it. I meet a friend who, to my surprise, is digging a hole in front of a house. I ask him, "Jim, what are you doing here?" It would make no sense for him to say, "I'm digging a hole." He doesn't have to tell me that; I can see it for myself. He needs to say he is doing something else, something more than digging a hole. He *is* digging, but he is also doing something not immediately visible in his digging. He might say, for instance, "The water system in this house has to be replaced. The owner is going to replace the pipes. I'm digging a hole so that the plumbers can get to the outdoor pipes." Jim's digging is not in itself a replacement of the pipes, nor is it a repair of the house's plumbing, but it is a means thereto, and it participates in it. Jim declares himself as doing something in view of something else. He tells me what wish or intention is governing his obvious conduct.

Jim does not declare himself as just saying, knowing, seeing, or thinking something; his declaratives do not express just a cognitive engagement. They express him as engaged in an action, in bodily, perceivable conduct, and as intending something by that conduct: his digging – and not just his idea of digging – is part of renewing the plumbing in a house. Jim has thoughtfully articulated the job he is doing. He, along with the plumbers and the owner, has distinguished between ends and means and has chosen to perform one of the means that has been shaken out by the deliberation of the parties involved (he is digging with a shovel and not, say, using a mechanical ditch digger, or burrowing out from the house). He has already invested himself in his thoughtful bodily action. When he goes on to declare what he is doing, he describes his action and also further appropriates the choice he has made. He not only informs me about what he is doing; he also confirms that *he* is doing it and that he has chosen or at least agreed to do it. He acknowledges himself as already doing what he

---

[7] It is also true that we can do something just by speaking, as when we insult someone or praise him. A choice can be made simply in language. See Robert Sokolowski, *Moral Action: A Phenomenological Study* (Bloomington: Indiana University Press, 1985), 77–95.

announces, so he displays himself as already active as an agent. His acting personhood is not first established by what he says, but it is more completely and more decisively manifested by his words.

Furthermore, Jim would still be personally engaged in the action even if he had been coerced into performing it. If someone had threatened him into doing this work, he would still have chosen to do it, albeit not in itself but only to avoid the harm that was menaced; his report of what he was doing, his declaration, would have been the same, but it would probably be accompanied by expressions of regret or shame: "They are fixing the plumbing and I'm helping them, but I am very unhappy about this job; they forced me into it."

When we discussed cognitive, emotive, promissory, and existential declarations in the first two chapters, I made the point that each declaration presupposes a rational articulation. The articulation, the spreading out of parts and wholes, is confirmed and appropriated by the declaration. We first articulate, "S is p," then we go on to say, "I know that S is p." The articulation may have been a registered fact, or a state of affairs to which we respond emotionally, or something that we promise will come into being. The same sort of prior articulation is also presupposed in the declarations we are now discussing, but here the articulation is found in a deed and not just in words. The articulation involves actually performing "x in view of Y," and x and Y are distinguished and united in the way that is appropriate for practical reasoning, not in the way that is appropriate for predication. The declaration does not just express the agent's articulation in thought; it also expresses his bodily involvement in the action itself. Jim says, "I am *digging* in order to get to the pipes and to repair the plumbing." He does not just declare his knowledge, attitudes, or promises. The agent's practical reasoning was already invested in the bodily activity he chose to perform, and now his declarative use of the pronoun confirms and reveals him as having made that investment, as having made that choice. The declaration appropriates and ratifies, not just an opinion or a promised state of affairs, but physical conduct, something being done. In this case, therefore, the declaration names the speaker not only as an agent of truth but also as a practical agent. But a practical agent is still a rational agent, so the declaration again brings the rational individual to light.

Internal and External Explanations of Our Actions: Ends and Purposes

We can use speech to describe and explain what we are doing. We can do so, however, in two different ways. We can give an explanation that is *internal* to the action we are performing, or one that is *external* to it. Internal descriptions and explanations show how our action is related to the *ends* in which our conduct is involved, while external descriptions and explanations show how our action is related to the *purposes* we have in mind as we act. The distinction between ends and purposes was, we recall, introduced at the close of Chapter 11.

Jim's reply explained the practical thinking that was internal to the action he was performing. He was digging a hole, and the hole was being dug in order to change the pipes in the ground. The pipes drain the water from the plumbing in the house. The water has to circulate in the house and be drained away for washing, consumption, and waste removal. So Jim's digging of the hole participates internally in the water-based activities in that dwelling. Jim could have replied in another way. Instead of giving the practical logic, the network of means and ends, of the bodily action he was performing, he could have given the logic of his own purposes, which, strictly speaking, would be external to the specific thing he was doing. In reply to my question about what he was doing, Jim could have said: "I've got this extra job for the summer. We need more money." I could then ask the next question: "Why do you need more money?" He answers: "For food, car payments, and the mortgage. We're falling behind."

In the explanatory logic internal to the action, Jim is irrelevant or accidental. Any other person could have served in his place to dig the hole. It is the action itself, by whomever performed, that is linked in the chain of means toward ends. This chain has an internal coherence and may even have an internal necessity, if the immediate steps are the only ones that could bring about the end in question. In the explanatory logic external to the action, however, we move off to another practical chain, one determined not by digging as such but by any action that, here and now, could get Jim some extra money. He could have become a bicycle messenger, or a taxi driver, or an office temp. Even if the construction job was the only one he could obtain at the moment, it is not from the "digging as such" that he earns the extra money, but it *is* from the "digging as such" that the plumbing is improved, even though the contractor might have done something else than dig in order to get the same result.

The metaphysics of the *per se* and *per accidens*, the *kath' hauto* and the *kata symbebēkos*, the *in itself* and the *accidental*, is at work here in a particularly tangible way. The digging is linked in itself with the repair of the pipes, but Jim is linked only coincidentally with the digging and the repair. The earning of money is linked accidentally with the digging and repair, but it is linked in itself with Jim, because it is his own determined purpose. In this context, Jim is essentially a wage earner. But even though Jim is only accidentally linked with the digging, he is still truly and actually linked with it; it does remain his own action, and he has invested himself in it. His accidental involvement is not nothing. He has in fact become not only an earner of money but also a digger, even though he is an earner of money and supporter of his family *per se* and a digger of the hole *per accidens*. If Jim had decided to make some money by performing a criminal act, the act would still be his doing even though he did it only for the money and not because he was the sort of agent that normally did such things. He was only accidentally linked to the act, but it *was* his act or him in action, and so he was truly qualified by it. He may not have been a murderer, but he did commit murder. The accidental is not unreal.

We have outlined two chains of practical logic that are at work in Jim's digging: one leads to improved plumbing in the house, the other leads to more money for his family. The first chain leads to the end of the action he is performing, the second fulfills the purpose he has in mind for himself as he performs the action. There might be still other purposes at work in Jim's action: he may also wish to impress his neighbors by his industry; he may wish to placate his wife and parents, who tell him he should work harder; he may wish to give a good example to his children. Each of these reasons can be declared: "I'm doing this for the money, which my family needs; and I also want to show them that I'm not lazy." Jim may be more clearly aware of some of these purposes than of others, and some may be subliminal; he may still be working out a response to some criticisms he suffered as a child. All of these purposes or intentions may have been dispositional wishes in Jim for many years, but they are activated as intentions in what he is doing now. Jim's reason was invested in his action in all these ways, and he endorses them in his declarations.

There is a difference between the two chains of logic, however, because there is only one chain and one end internal to the action, but there can be many chains and many purposes external to it. Jim's digging is just to repair the plumbing; that single achievement is all that it does. But one and the same digging can be done for the sake of money, for the edification of his children, for exercise, for relief of boredom, and for showing people that he can work hard. We can act with many and mixed motives, some of which might be very obscure even to ourselves. However, even in this plethora of purposes, we are able to *do* only one thing in itself. The unity of what is being done is compatible with a multiplicity of "personal" reasons why one is doing it. The simple internal *end* of the action, what Aquinas calls the *object* of the act, must be distinguished from the many *purposes* the agent has in doing it.[8]

It is also important to note that one of Jim's purposes is the natural end of the deed he is performing. Along with his "personal" purposes, he also does in fact intend to repair the plumbing by digging a hole. The internal end of the action is also a purpose he has in mind, but the natural end would be there even apart from his purpose. The achievement is seen as good under two guises: as the object of the act and as wished for by the agent. This point might be made more clearly by using another example. The natural end of the art and science of medicine is the maintenance and

[8] Thomas Aquinas, *Summa theologiae* I II, q. 18, a. 2 and 7.

restoration of the health of the patient; that end is built into the art and science. A doctor might practice medicine for many purposes: to help people, to become famous, to become rich, to support his family, and so on, and some of these intentions may be congruent with his profession and some may not, but one of his purposes should be to maintain or restore the health of his patients. However, even though this is one of his purposes, his wishing it is not what establishes it as the end of the art and science. The art and science has this end apart from anyone's wishing it; the end is natural to medicine. It is not even all the doctors who by their purposes determine the end of medicine. Medicine has its end by virtue of what it is.[9]

The individual agent is not the only one whose purposes are at work in a given action. To return to our example, Jim's purposes in digging are not the only ones governing what he is doing. There are probably many more purposes that belong to the other agents involved in this activity. There are the intentions of the owner of the house, the purposes of the builders, the aims of the parties who are financing the project. There could be dozens of such intentions. These purposes make up a great swarm of purposes flashing by and ricocheting and intersecting and even contradicting one another. They cluster around the single bodily activity, the one real action – Jim's digging a hole to get to the pipes to repair the plumbing – that unifies and concretizes all of them. The one action with its own internal logic is the support for them all. Thanks to the digging, they are no longer mere wishes floating about at random. They have all alighted on this one branch. They would have remained mere wishes if they had not been given substance by their attachment to that substrate, which is a thoughtful procedure and a creasing of the world, a chosen action being done in view of its end. The bodily action crystalizes both the ends and the purposes, just as the verbal sound crystalizes and materializes the intelligibility of what we talk about.

The fact that our bodies as well as our words become involved in syntax leads to the possibility of a discrepancy between what we are doing and what we *say* we are doing. The agent might be using his words *not* to formulate what he is doing, but to divert the listener; he is lying, and this possibility arises because he can speak as well as act. This mismatch is not infrequent; how do we recognize it? We need to be clever enough to see the real syntax in the agent's action. We have to be able to decipher what he is doing and to see that it is not syntactically consistent with what he claims his purpose is. He says he is doing *X*, but everything he does shows that he is doing *Y*, and both *X* and *Y*, being purposes, are not visible to the

[9] See Robert Sokolowski, "What Is Natural Law? Human Purposes and Natural Ends," in *Christian Faith and Human Understanding: Studies on the Eucharist, Trinity, and the Human Person* (Washington, DC: Catholic University of America Press, 2006), 219–20.

bodily eye. They call for understanding and not perception, and we need to be clever enough in practical matters to see that this sort of conduct is not ordered to the purpose the agent claims to have in mind. The speech that can be used to illuminate what we are doing can also be used to conceal.

Consequences and Concomitants of What We Do

We have examined some of the ways in which the metaphysical principles of the *in itself* and *the accidental*, the *per se* and the *per accidens*, play out in human agency. The agent is invested *per se* in his purposes or intentions; they are his, and he is in them in the most intimate manner possible, because he is engaged in action primarily for their sake. He is primarily determined as an agent by them. But besides doing what he intends to do (in this case, to earn some money for his family), he is also engaged in an action that has its own integrity and its own logic. He may be engaged in that action only *per accidens*, because he is doing it only to achieve the intention he has in mind, but he *is* doing it. Jim is truly digging a hole and thus helping to repair the plumbing, even though he is doing it only for the money that he needs for his family. He is only coincidentally engaged (he might have done something else instead), but he *is* engaged and he *does* become qualified by his action from that moment on. To be involved accidentally is still to be involved. We are marked by what we do, even if it is only *per accidens* that we do it. The first interaction of the *per se* and the *per accidens* is thus the criss-cross between what we intend and what we materially do.

The two metaphysical principles of the essential and the accidental also function in another way in regard to human action. Consider the material performance itself (in our current paradigm, the digging of the hole). This action has its internal logic. It is a means toward the repair of the plumbing system of a house. We can conceive of the entire sequence, the means and the end, as a single achievement. Because this achievement is a material, worldly activity, it cannot be isolated from other causal chains. It is embedded in a natural and a social network, and it will bring about other consequences besides those aimed at by the agents. For example, Jim, while digging, might disturb the soil in such a way that the roots of the neighbor's tree are affected and the tree dies. The fact that the plumbing has been repaired might lead to someone's being scalded by hot water. Such concomitant or consequent effects are undesirable, but there will also be indefinitely many others that are either neutral or desirable: some neighbors might be inspired to fix the plumbing in their own houses, or Jim might find a buried treasure. I am not saying that there *might* be consequences besides those envisioned in the digging and repair; there definitely *will* be such consequences, good, bad, and indifferent, some foreseeable and some not, because the action being done is caught up in a web of natural and social causation.

If some particular concomitant or consequent effect were undesirable, I would report it as having been done by me, but my use of the pronoun would be informational and not declarative: "I damaged your tree when I dug that hole; I didn't know the tree would be affected; no one could have foreseen it." One could express it this way: "I damaged your tree; but *I* didn't do it. It happened." Such unforeseen and unforeseeable concomitants and consequences may be involuntary, but we are still somewhat tainted by them; if we were driving carefully and a cyclist cut ahead of us and we hit and injured him, we would feel anguish, even though *we* did not do the act. We did do it in a bodily sense, but not in a moral sense, not in a way that engages our veracity and rational agency. It happened through us because of the anonymous course of things, but we did not want it to happen and could not have foreseen it. It fell outside the scope of our foresight. If, on the other hand, the concomitant or consequent effects were foreseen (or should have been foreseen), then they do fall within the scope of our rational responsibility. If we know something is going to happen or is likely to happen because of what we do, then we do accept it as one of our several outcomes.

The ontology of human agency involves, therefore, a complicated syntactic structure, with some elements that lie within the searchlight of our rational agency and others that lie outside it. We might outline this structure in the following manner. The distinctions we develop here can be seen as a gloss on the first five chapters of Book III of Aristotle's *Nicomachean Ethics*. The major difference is that Aristotle begins with the more comprehensive category of the voluntary and the involuntary, whereas we begin with the narrower category of the chosen and work back to the voluntary and involuntary.

1. At the core of human action is an intervention in the world. We crease the world, and once we do so it can never be uncreased; we do something bodily, whether to dig a hole, pull a trigger, sign a decree, thank someone, or hand over a gift. This is the foundational, material embodiment of human conduct, and everything else, all the categorial activity, rests on it.[10] This action, if it is rational, is always articulated or jointed, with *this* being done in view of *that*. This action has its own nature or end or object, which is *what* is being done.

2. Interwoven with the action itself are the many and varied purposes we have in mind when we act. We might be doing what we do in order to impress someone, to become rich, to placate our sense

---

[10] On the materiality of human conduct, see Sokolowski, *Moral Action*, 48–54.

of guilt, or to lose weight. The pursuit of these purposes is also articulated or jointed; again, we do *this* in view of *that*. There can be many purposes hovering around one action, but one of the purposes that we inevitably have is the purpose of doing the action itself. We may regret that we must do it (to get to our other purposes), but in fact we do perform it, and so it is appropriated by us and can be declared as such. I may regret that I have stolen something because I need the money, but in fact I have stolen it, whether I like it or not. I have committed theft, even though I may not be a thief. If, on the other hand, I begin to steal because I wish to do so, I not only have committed theft but also have become a thief.

3. The first two components of a human action are wished for. The third category contains the concomitants and consequents of what we do, and they may or may not be wished for. They just happen along with what we do. There inevitably will be things that happen along with what we do, because we crease the world with our actions (we do not just make decisions in the secrecy of our hearts), and other things will follow on the creases we have made. Because our action is an embodied part of the world, it shakes and rustles things that lie outside our intentions and the proper ends of what we are doing. As Henry James puts it, "The whole conduct of life consists of things done, which do other things in their turn."[11] We may be indifferent to the unforeseen concomitants and consequences, we may regret them, or we may welcome them. Those we are indifferent to are said by Aristotle to be simply nonvoluntary; those we regret are involuntary.[12]

When we speak philosophically about human action, we tend to limit ourselves to rather local performances by private persons. We ask whether this interaction between Julia and Charles was voluntary or not, whether it was virtuous or vicious, and what sort of unforeseen consequences flowed from it. But the very syntax that makes human conduct rational also makes it possible for actions of immense magnitude to be done. Admiral Alfred von Tirpitz and Kaiser Wilhelm II embark on a project to expand the German fleet. Taxes have to be raised, companies have to be enlisted, raw materials have to be purchased, and technology has to be developed. The three categories we have outlined – ends, purposes, and concomitants and consequences – apply to actions such as these as well. The outbreak of hostilities may have been one of the purposes von Tirpitz and the kaiser had in mind, but the establishment of the Soviet Union, which was a consequence of what they chose and did, was probably not foreseen by

---

[11] Henry James, *The Art of the Novel* (New York: Charles Scriber's Sons, 1934), 347. The remark is in the Preface to *The Golden Bowl.*

[12] Aristotle, *Nicomachean Ethics*, III 1, 1110b18–24.

them (although the later German delivery of Lenin to Petrograd may have intended something of the sort). Ends, purposes, and consequences weave in and out as things are done and events occur, on a scale at which millions of agents are affected.[13]

Actions of such enormous size are made possible by syntax. Animals, having only voice and not speech, and wants but not wishes, are content with more proximate satisfactions. The very financing of large-scale conduct is made possible by the distinctive kind of syntax and identifications that money, the sinews of war and other human ventures, introduces into human affairs; both Andrew Carnegie and Bill Gates are products of syntax. The complex diplomatic syntax of the Triple Entente and the Triple Alliance led to the outbreak of World War I, as one choice to declare war followed inexorably and foolishly after another after the assassination of the Archduke Franz Ferdinand at Sarajevo. Declaratives also appear on this large scale, as people own and own up to what they do: they take credit for what they consider their successes, regret their miscalculations, and exculpate themselves for what they did not intend to happen. Declaratives of this kind carry a lot more weight than those expressed by less conspicuous people. Most of us lead modest, bourgeois lives, and hence we philosophize about small-scale actions (we are more like novelists than epic poets), but if we limit our analysis to quotidian matters, we will have failed to appreciate the grandiose scope of rational syntax. World wars are syntactic structures, so is globalization, as well as weights, measures, and prices, which bind people into commercial communities. The various political regimes are categorial wholes that define countries. So are philosophical and literary works, which have their own way of governing or liberating (as the case may be); they hold sway over minds instead of bodies, and they too can extend their influence over large reaches of space and time. Machiavelli is an author who understands reason to be a power of ruling, not theorizing, and he may even have declared himself as doing so; as Harvey C. Mansfield, Jr., observes in his commentary on Machiavelli's *Discourses on the First Ten Books of Livy*, "*Massimo* is the last word in the *Discourses. Io* ('I') was the first."[14]

---

[13] There are different levels of syntax in historical events. On the basic level, there is the practical syntax of the agents, who understand themselves and their situations in a certain way and carry out their actions. There is next the interpretative syntax of those who record what was done or those who try to evaluate the events historically and provide a narrative that covers them, taking into account the intentions of the agents. Third, there is the kind of philosophical reflection we are now carrying out, which theorizes the events as well as the reflective understanding of those who narrate them, and attempts to bring out the structures of manifestation that are at work in both.

[14] Harvey C. Mansfield, Jr., *Machiavelli's New Modes and Orders: A Study of the 'Discourses on Livy'* (Ithaca, NY: Cornell University Press, 1979), 441. Francis Slade says that Machiavelli initiated the modern idea of reason as rule and not as understanding. See "Rule as

Friendship

There is yet one more dimension in the syntax that is woven into human actions. Let us return to our example of Jim digging a hole. We have spoken about the action itself, with its internal end, and the purposes Jim might have in doing it. The purposes we have described have been somewhat pragmatic, such as earning money to support his family. But there is still another way in which Jim could explain what he is doing. He might say, "I am digging to help repair the plumbing in this house, and I'm doing it because the people who live here are friends of mine." In this case, Jim would be doing the action not to support his family, but to perform an act of friendship. Friendship is reciprocal benevolence that is mutually recognized. Friends wish well to each other, and wishing, as we have insisted, is not mere velleity but the readiness to act. In this case, Jim has acted; he is doing something helpful to his friends, and his friendship syntactically informs his action. His benevolence is being both expressed and effected in the bodily action he is performing.

What is the categorial or syntactic formation of his act of friendship? He is doing this action because it is a good for his friends. Having the plumbing fixed is something they need; it is a good for them. He is doing it precisely as such. That is, it is a good for him precisely and formally as a good for his friends. This is a concentrated and thoughtful practical achievement. To do something as an act of friendship is a highly rational action; it is charged with practical intelligence. Moreover, it is charged with morally good intelligence, not just with mathematical cleverness. To do something as good for ourselves might exhibit rational syntax, since we need to shake out means and ends and purposes, but to do something as good for others expands our rational agency and demands that we be more thoughtful than we are when we serve our own purposes. We are very intelligent when we act benevolently in friendship.

Justice itself is a variation on friendship. It is friendship minus one of its features. To act justly is to give each person what is due to him. There is a kind of benevolence in this, not merely a mathematical calculation, because in it we strive to give each person what he decently deserves, but our "wishing well" is impersonal. We do not tailor the good to this person in particular, but to anyone who would fall under the category in question, and of course the benevolence need not be reciprocal. I want to claim that

Sovereignty: The Universal and Homogeneous State," in John J. Drummond and James G. Hart, eds., *The Truthful and the Good: Essays in Honor of Robert Sokolowski* (Boston: Kluwer, 1996), 180: "*Sovereignty* is not just the assertion of the supremacy of a ruler, but of the absoluteness of rule based on the claim made on its behalf by philosophy, and on this ground asserting its supremacy as that of reason. The State is rule that includes philosophy within itself, but philosophy transformed by the erasure of the distinction between *theoria* and *praxis*. Mind defined by this erasure is mind the defining activity of which is rule."

justice, as well as the other moral virtues, participate in friendship, which is the *telos* of human practical activity and the paradigm for the others. The other virtues are not friendship pure and simple – they only participate in it – but their moral goodness comes from what they have of friendship, whether with others or with ourselves. Friendship stands at the focal point of moral conduct. I cannot explore this topic here, but I have tried to argue it at length in other places.[15]

Friendship provides an especially appropriate setting for declaratives. Friendship is mutual benevolence mutually recognized, whether involving two persons or more. The individual persons, therefore, come to the fore; they are not replaceable by anyone else. The singularity proper to a rational agent is conspicuous in this setting. Both attachment and loss are particularly significant. The force of such declaratives is especially visible in expressions of love, in which each speaker recognizes that he (or she) would not be what he is had the other not "granted" him his status. Recognition includes an element of bestowal in this setting. This highly charged use of declarative pronouns occurs not just in romantic love and its expression, as in love songs, but in the significant moments when the friends face life together. It occurs in words and in actions, as well as in words that give a form to the actions. It can also occur in actions and words of a larger scale, in the kind of friendship that Aristotle calls concord (*homonoia*), which occurs not just among small groups of individuals but in larger, political communities; concord transcends political and tribal affiliations.[16]

The syntax of friendship is detachable from any particular material action. It is highly formal. Friends can express their benevolence in many different kinds of conduct, and in this respect friendship is something like money, which is also quite detachable and formal; it too can be earned or spent on things apart from their internal ends. But in friendship there is also a question of truthfulness. The action the agent or agents perform may in fact, by its own internal logic and its natural end, *not* be benevolent. Getting intoxicated together may seem to some to be an act of friendship, but in all likelihood it will be harmful and not a true good, and so the action is malevolent despite what the agents might wish. Not everything can serve as an expression and embodiment of benevolence. Since the action of friendship involves syntax and composition, it inevitably engages

[15] See Sokolowski, *Moral Action*, and also "Moral Thinking," in *Pictures, Quotations, and Distinctions: Fourteen Essays in Phenomenology* (Notre Dame, IN: University of Notre Dame Press, 1992), 245–60; "What Is Moral Action?," ibid., 261–76; "Friendship and Moral Action in Aristotle," *The Journal of Value Inquiry* 35 (2001): 355–69; and "Phenomenology of Friendship," *The Review of Metaphysics* 55 (2002): 451–70.

[16] Aristotle, *Nicomachean Ethics*, VIII 1, 1155a22–5: "Friendship seems too to hold cities together, and lawgivers to care more for it than for justice; for concord seems to be something like friendship, and this they aim at most of all." (Ross translation modified.)

truth. Friendship, with others and with ourselves, is a practical perfection of our veracity.

Speech and Politics

We have only intermittently touched on politics, but we should at least briefly mention the relationship between the use of language and political life. We might think that politics follows on language, that human beings acquire speech in families and tribes and then, as one of its benefits, gradually develop a political life, with its laws, executive and judicial actions, and rhetoric. But if political life is a crown of speech, it also perfects it and makes it more exact. It provides the setting in which speech is most itself. Pierre Manent writes, "It is not the word that produces community, but community that produces and sustains the word. If there are all sorts of communities and, therefore, all sorts of words, all the words nonetheless find the place for their pronunciation (*le site de leur respiration*) in the political association, the city."[17] Within the city, human speech is used for many purposes besides politics, but the background of the political is always there to stabilize meaning and to validate what we say and promise: "If human life unfolds between prose and poetry, between the prose of the useful and the poetry of the noble and the great, it orders itself through the mediation of the just, which is the proper work of politics." The "mediation of the just" does not signify only taxes and traffic laws; it is the presence of a measure for human actions and relationships, and the force of this measure extends into the structure, content, and impact of speech. The sense of the just, which is itself a syntactic accomplishment, gives a particular shape to human life. Neither Shakespeare nor Dante could have done what they did apart from the *civitas* in which they lived, and they, of course, shaped their communities in turn. Manent continues, "The political community holds together all the registers of the word and permits them to reverberate, and every true communication necessarily rests on this harmonic scale."

Manent claims that we cannot expect the language alone to reshape the community. In an age of worldwide communication, one might think that a common language, such as English, and the means of communication, such as televison and the Internet, might bring us into a world in which the ancient differences between peoples and religions will be eliminated and the rough edges made smooth. Manent says that the differences among peoples are more intractable, and that they rest ultimately not on the medium of communication but on the community that supports the language: "We overestimate ... the power of the instruments of

---

[17] Pierre Manent, *La raison des nations: Réflexions sur la démocratie en Europe* (Paris: Gallimard, 2006), 43–4.

communication, in particular that of a language that is just a common carrier." As we have said in this book, predication itself rests on a foundation that is preverbal; the mind does not just assert facts, and it does not float free of its human context. Predication, as well as definition, occurs within a conversation, and this conversation is nested within a community that is political and religious as well as familial and tribal. It is within that community that the human good and the ends of things are made visible to us.[18] Political friendship or concord is a setting for speech. The syntax of justice is one of the conditions for our being able to declare ourselves as speakers who not only can tell things to one another but who can also claim a standing and moral value by means of our declarations.

---

[18] Aristotle, *Nicomachean Ethics*, I 2, 1094a27–b11.

PART IV

ANCIENTS AND MODERNS

17

Aristotle

The resources provided by phenomenology allow us, I believe, to transcend the difference between ancients and moderns. They offer a way to pursue philosophy as such, without being forced to be contemporary only at the price of turning away from the ancients.[1] They permit us to read classical writings not just as historical phenomena but as material for recapitulation. We have in this book made use of authors from various historical periods, but before concluding, it would be appropriate to spell out more explicitly how my approach to language, meaning, and truth is related to classical philosophy. I will comment briefly on Aristotle and Thomas Aquinas.

Aristotle explicitly presents what can be called an identity theory of truth. He claims that the knower cognitively takes on the *eidos* of what is known, and that the knower and the known are cognitively identified. There are, however, also elements of a representational theory of truth in Aristotle. We will examine both these approaches and the tension between them. I believe that the tension can be resolved by appealing to the special character of philosophical language, transcendentalese, and I will present that resolution in Chapter 19.

---

[1] I concur with a remark made by Leo Strauss in 1940: "La querelle des anciens et des modernes must be renewed – it must be repeated with much greater fairness and greater knowledge than it was done in the 17th and 18th centuries." "The Living Issues of German Postwar Philosophy," in Heinrich Meier, *Leo Strauss and the Theologico-Political Problem*, trans. Marcus Brainard (New York: Cambridge University Press, 2006), 137. Strauss continues, "As regards Husserl's work, I can only say that I believe it surpasses in significance everything I know of that was done in Germany in the last 50 years." Strauss acknowledges Heidegger's new approach to ancient philosophy, but he also says, "Heidegger's interpretation of Aristotle, which is not more than a beginning, would not have been possible without Husserl's phenomenology." I would address the issue of ancients and moderns in a way different from that of Strauss.

Two Kinds of Truth

Aristotle, in *Metaphysics*, IX 10, distinguishes between two kinds of truth: truth as the correctness of speech and thought, and truth as the grasping of indivisibles (*asyntheta, adiaireta*).[2]

The first kind of truth involves complex articulation: it requires that the things in question be "combined and divided." If in our thinking and speaking we combine and divide things as they are themselves combined and divided, our thinking and speaking will be true; if we combine and separate things in ways different from the ways they themselves are composed and divided, our thinking and speaking will be false (*Metaphysics*, IX 10, 1051b2–9). It is important to note that this form of truth has *falsity* as its opposite. If I say, "Snow is white," I have composed a statement. I have put thoughts together. If snow indeed is white, my statement and my opinion will be true; if snow is brown, my statement and my opinion will be false. It is the statement and the opinion that are true or false. In *De Anima*, III 8 (432a11), Aristotle says that being true or false belongs to an "intertwining of things thought, a *symplokē noēmatōn*." In this passage, the term we have translated as "things thought," *noēmata*, needs to be clarified, and we will have more to say about it later. The intertwining of things thought is a syntactic achievement.

The second kind of truth involves not complexity but a simple grasp of simple things (*Metaphysics*, IX 10, 1051b17–33). This kind of truth has *ignorance*, not falsity, as its opposite. Suppose I am engaged in conversation and someone begins using the word *eisteddfods*. If I have never heard that word before, I do not take in anything when I hear it now; and since I do not take anything in, I cannot be mistaken. I do not get anything wrong; I simply do not know. My deficiency consists not in falsity but in ignorance. Or suppose something is happening before me and I am completely bewildered by it. Again, I fail to take anything in, and my thinking is not false; it is simply uninformed, which is different from being misinformed. To be exact, I should say not that my thinking is uninformed, but that I simply am not thinking. I have not gotten there yet. I may be trying to think, but I have not succeeded in having a thought, either simple or complex. In the first kind of truth, by contrast, I do have a thought (that snow is white), but it might be false. In

---

[2] My remarks about *Metaphysics*, IX 10, and Aristotle's concept of truth are much inspired by the lecture given by Kurt Pritzl, O.P., "Aristotle's Door," which is cited earlier in Chapter 10. See also Deborah K. W. Modrak, *Aristotle's Theory of Language and Meaning* (New York: Cambridge University Press, 2001), 5: "Aristotle appears ... to be committed to two notions of truth, namely, truth in the familiar sense, where the truth predicate applies to assertions in speech and thought, and a second sense of truth appropriate to the apprehension of an indivisible object of thought."

the second kind, my mind does not rise to the level at which falsity is even possible. My mind may be groping or probing, but it has not yet grasped or apprehended anything. We might add that the phenomenon of vagueness is something like an intermediate stage between ignorance and knowing. When we think vaguely, we have glimpses and glimmers, with names floating about, but no fixed grasp as yet, and so the syntax that surrounds the names is wobbly.

It is the syntactic complexity involved in the truth of correctness that makes it possible for me to fall into error or falsity. I might compose my thoughts – or, to put it in an equivalent way, I might articulate things, or compose the things that are being thought – in ways that are not the same as the way the things themselves are composed. I compose them one way, but they themselves are composed in another way, and they will show up as such to more careful scrutiny or to a more intelligent inquirer. By contrast, the second form of truth or untruth does not involve complexity or composition, and so it cannot be false. In this case, I do not fail to compose correctly; rather, I fail to acquire the very elements of composition. I fail to achieve any *noēmata*, things being thought. My mind does not become engaged with anything definite. No reference is established, and there is nothing for my thoughts to be about, and so I do not have any thoughts. I simply have not taken in the thing in question.

Aristotle's distinction between the two kinds of truth can be made more intuitive for us if we see both kinds of truth as working within a conversation. If we take the two kinds as intellectual mechanisms of some sort in the individual mind, we cannot help but wonder how the mind extracts such simple items and then composes them into larger wholes; it all seems so mysterious. What kind of processor is this intellect? How does it download its contents? But if we take the two kinds of truth first and foremost as steps in conversation, they seem much less enigmatic. Thus, the grasp of indivisibles is simply the introduction of a theme into a conversation, and we either know or do not know what that theme is; we either understand or do not understand the name that has been uttered or the thing that has been presented. In this case, the opposite of knowing and truth is ignorance; the name is unfamiliar, the thing is unrecognized. The truth that involves composition and division occurs when the speaker does something with the theme that has been introduced: he says something about it to the interlocutor. He carries out predications. His predications are true if things are as he says, and false if things are not as he says. We discover whether the statements are true or false by leaving the conversation and experiencing the thing. The opposite of such truth is falsity. Of course, we have to think when we speak, and the two kinds of truth Aristotle distinguishes are two ways in which we think; and, of course, we sometimes carry on this conversation within ourselves, in our imagination, but such silent conversing is parasitic on the public form. The two kinds of truth occur primarily with others in speech, not in sheer mental processing.

Identity of the Knower and the Thing Known

Aristotle repeats his distinction between the two kinds of truth in *De Anima*, III 6. In passages before and after Chapter 6, he makes another point. He repeatedly says that the mind that succeeds in thinking is identical to the things that it thinks. He says, for example, "For the mind somehow is potentially what it thinks (*ta noēta*)" (III 4, 429b30–1). He also says, "Knowledge that is activated is thus the same as the thing" (III 5, 430a19–20), and again, "Thus, in general, the mind that is active *is* the objects" (III 7, 431b17). Speaking of the thinking power of the human being as a part of the soul, he declares, "We say again, the soul is somehow all things" (III 8, 431b21). In these and other passages he expresses what we could call an identity theory of knowledge as opposed to a representational one. In this view, the knowing power does not have a copy or a representation of the thing known; rather, it becomes cognitively identified with the thing that is known.

Aristotle explains how this happens by saying that the form or the "look" (*eidos*) of the thing known comes to exist in the knower, but without the matter in which the form or the look is embodied in the thing itself. Cognitive powers are able to take on and take in the forms of things. Aristotle agrees with the description of the human soul as the "place of forms, *topos eidōn*" (III 4, 429a27–8), but he adds that this feature applies to the soul not as a whole but only in regard to its noetic power.

In the case of intellectual cognition, the achievement of taking in the forms of things requires more than just the presence of the thing and the activity of the intellect as receptive; it also requires the activity of the cognitive power that Aristotle calls the "active intellect" or "agent mind," which he describes in cryptic and mysterious terms in a brief chapter, *De Anima*, III 5. "This alone," he says, "is immortal and eternal ... and without this nothing thinks" (III 5, 430a23–5). Aristotle also emphasizes the role of imagination in enabling us to know. The active intellect does not work on the thing itself, but only on the thing as represented in the *phantasmata* that arise in our internal senses as we take in the sensible appearances of things. The active mind allows the intelligibility of the thing to show up to us in and through the phantasms. Aristotle also says that the identity between knower and known occurs not only in intellectual cognition but in sensible perception as well, both in the external senses and in the imagination: "the knowledge *is* somehow the known, and perception the perceived" (III 8, 431b22–3); "for the phantasmata are like (*hōsper*) the things perceived, but without matter"

(III 8, 432a9–10). The term *eidos* is used in regard to both intellectual and sensory cognition.

A Danger of Representationalism: Likenesses in the Soul

Once Aristotle starts talking about the forms or *eidē* of things as coming to exist in cognitive powers, the danger arises that these forms will be interpreted as representations of the things they come from. The identity theory of knowledge that we found in Aristotle threatens to be turned into a representational theory, with all the difficulties that such a theory entails. There is, furthermore, an important and influential passage in Aristotle's *De Interpretatione* (I, 16a3–8) that increases the danger of representationalism.[3] At the beginning of this work, Aristotle describes the relationships among four items: written words, spoken words, thoughts, and things. It is interesting that Aristotle uses not just spoken but also written words, which are even more external and tangible than spoken ones. Writing gives him both a lever and a contrast for his argument.

The passage is elegant, brief, and highly compressed, and it has been called "the most influential text in the history of semantics."[4] Aristotle says that spoken words are symbols (*symbola*) of "affections" (*pathēmata*) in the soul, and that written words are symbols of spoken words. There is no problem with saying that written words symbolize spoken ones; we have the written marks here and the spoken sounds there, and the former are symbols of the latter. But a problem does arise when he says that spoken words symbolize the *pathēmata*, the "affections" in the soul; what can these *pathēmata* be? He then says that neither written nor spoken words are the same everywhere (they are conventional and differ in different languages). The "affections" of the soul, however, are the same for everyone, as are the things (*pragmata*) – and here is another disturbing term – of which they are "likenesses" (*homoiōmata*). The "affections" in the soul are said to be "likenesses" of things. These two terms, "affections" and "likenesses," make up the heart of the passage, and they also make up the heart of the

---

[3] For a comprehensive commentary on this work, see C. W. A. Whitaker, *Aristotle's 'De Interpretatione': Contradiction and Dialectic* (Oxford: The Clarendon Press, 1996). Whitaker claims that in *De Interpretatione* Aristotle is not simply giving a "theory of judgment" but explaining the prerequisites for dialectical argument. Some very insightful remarks concerning this passage in *De Interpretatione* can be found in Martin Heidegger, *Logik: Die Frage nach der Wahrheit* (Frankfurt am Main: Vittorio Klostermann, 1976), 166–70. Heidegger also comments on *Metaphysics*, IX 10; see pp. 170–82.

[4] The remark is made by Norman Kretzmann, "Aristotle on Spoken Sound Significant by Convention," in *Ancient Logic and Its Modern Interpretations*, ed. J. Corcoran (Dordrecht: Reidel, 1974), 3. Kretzmann's remark is often quoted; see John P. O'Callaghan, *Thomist Realism and the Linguistic Turn: Toward a More Perfect Form of Existence* (Notre Dame, IN: University of Notre Dame Press, 2003), 5; and Modrak, *Aristotle's Theory of Language and Meaning*, 1.

problem. What are the affections of the soul, and in what sense are they likenesses of things?[5]

It is not easy to determine what the "affections" of the soul are. If Aristotle wanted to refer to psychological states, he probably would have used the word *pathē*, the plural of *pathos*. But the word is *pathēmata*, which designates not the state of the soul or the experiencing that occurs in the soul, but rather those things that have been received into the soul, the targets of the reception or experiencing.[6] In Latin, the translation should not be *passiones animae* but something like *passa animae* or *recepta animae*, the things that have been taken in or undergone. In standard philosophical English, the *pathēmata* would be the cognitive contents of the states of the soul, that is, meanings or concepts or thoughts of some sort.[7] But, we may ask, what are these contents or thoughts that our spoken words signify? Are they something other than the things we know, are they some sort of replicas in the soul? Or could they somehow be the things themselves, but considered as present to the person who knows them? I would like to take the latter option, which would reinforce the identity theory of knowledge, but Aristotle does seem to veer toward the former.

The issue of the affections in the soul is difficult enough, but even more problematic is the term *likenesses, homoiōmata*. As Deborah Modrak says, "the notion of likeness is troubling."[8] Does Aristotle wish to say that there are things in the soul that *resemble* the things in the world? How can a meaning or a thought or a concept be called a likeness? How can it resemble a thing? Pictures or statues are likenesses and present no problem, and even mental images could be called likenesses in some extended sense, but what kind of likeness could a meaning or a thought or a concept be? The very meaning of "likeness" in this context is extremely unclear.[9] Aristotle would seem to be saying that the soul contains replicas of things, and that these replicas are likenesses of the things. The identity theory of knowledge seems to give way to a representationalism.

---

[5] Aristotle goes on in *De Interpretatione* to speak about the fact that only compositions of words or thoughts can be true or false, not single words or thoughts by themselves, and he refers to what he says about this in the *De Anima*.

[6] Heidegger draws our attention to this point; see *Logik*, 167: "Aber im Text steht nicht *pathē*, was allenfalls Zustände bedeuten könnte, sondern *pathēmata*, das, was begegnet und als Begegnendes hingennomen wird, Affektion in einem weiten Sinne. Und *homoiōmata* besagt das Angeglichene, was *homoiōs echei*, was als Begegnendes so ist wie das Seiende selbst."

[7] See Whitaker, *Aristotle's 'De Interpretatione'*, 15.

[8] Modrak, *Aristotle's Theory of Language and Meaning*, 21.

[9] In commenting on these terms, Whitaker says that the affections of the soul are thoughts, and he insists that they are not pictures, but he does not spell out more positively what they are. See Whitaker, *Aristotle's 'De Interpretatione'*, 15.

According to another possible interpretation, Aristotle might be saying that the soul or the mind, or a state or act of the soul or mind, just becomes similar to the thing it knows, because it has taken on the form of the thing in question (without its matter) and hence achieved a cognitive "similitude" with the thing. In other words, the soul would become cognitively similar to the thing, but it would not contain an entity that is a likeness. Such an interpretation would dampen the representationalism, but of course what it means would need to be explained. There is a passage in the *De Anima*, II 5, 418a3–6, that might support this reading. Aristotle is describing sense perception. He says that the sensory power is potentially "like" (*hoion*) the object. The subject undergoes an experience (*paschei*), and while undergoing this process it is still unlike its object (*ouk homoion on*). But once it has gone through the experience (*peponthos*) it "has become like" (*hōmoiōtai*), and now "it is like it" (*kai esti hoion ekeino*). The verb *hōmoiōtai*, "it has become like," is interesting here. Aristotle says that the sensory power (*to aisthētikon*) has become like the object. He does not say that it has received a copy or replica of the object; rather, "it has been made like." To adapt a Latinate word, it "has become similar to" or "has been assimilated to," and *assimilation* here does not mean to have taken in a copy. It involves a more flexible sense of *sembling* or *resembling*.

There is another passage in the *De Anima* that is analogous to the one we have been discussing. At the beginning of his discussion of thinking (*noein*), Aristotle says that the part of the soul by which we think must be "receptive of the form" of things, and it must be "potentially such [as the thing], but not it" (III 4, 429a15–16). This last phrase is difficult to translate, but its syntax is revealing. In Greek it reads, "*dunamei toiouton alla mē touto.*" Perhaps a good English paraphrase would be that the mind is "potentially such as this, but not this." A more stilted rendition might be, "potentially this-like, but not this." In Latin one might say, "tale, sed non hoc." The knowing mind must be able to become qualified as the thing, but it does not become the thing. The interplay between the two demonstrative terms in the Greek is suggestive and elegant, and the *toiouton*, "such as this," enjoys an appropriate imprecision. One might say that a man who knows a lot about trees is "arboreal but not a tree," and the way he is arboreal is by having taken in "the tree" and many of its necessities, without having become a tree. He is like *the* tree, but he is not *a* tree. As another example, one might say that a civilian who is a military historian is military-minded but not a soldier; the intelligibility of military things informs his mind but not his substance. To return to our earlier example, we could say that Max Hastings is "Eisenhower-ish but not Eisenhower." To think about knowledge along these lines would prevent us from postulating an entity in the mind that resembles things "outside" the mind. It loosens up our speech about knowledge. It helps us see that the "likenesses" that Aristotle mentions in the *De Interpretatione* need not be replicas, and it helps us see that an appeal to a likeness or an assimilation does not exclude the possibility of a cognitive identification, but of course it still leaves us with the need to clarify what these likenesses and identities are.

This single use of the term *likenesses* (*homoiōmata*) in Aristotle's *De Interpretatione* had an enormous influence on the terminology used in the Middle Ages. It was echoed repeatedly in the Latin term *similitudo*, which occurs over and over again in the description of human knowledge given by Thomas Aquinas and others. As the word *similitudo* becomes more and more common, one becomes ever more inclined to think of ideas as mental copies or representations of things that resemble the things they represent. The identity theory of knowledge seems to yield to a thoroughgoing representationalism, with meanings or senses or concepts being postulated as mediating entities between us and the things that we know, mediators that are only similar to the things we know and not identical to them. Once such mediators, such "shadows" of things, become postulated, the danger arises that we will think that we know just these mediators and ideas, not the things themselves.[10] They become problematic entities between us and things. Aristotle, clearly, does not want to draw this conclusion; his frequent assertions of the identity between knower and known preclude it. But how does he avoid being forced into it? To repeat Modrak's remark, "the notion of likeness is troubling." Also, the identity theory needs further explanation. We might confidently say that the form in the thing and the form in the cognitive soul are one and the same form, but we can't just leave it at that. How is it that one and the same form can exist in these two modes? What are forms, that they can exist in these two ways? We must savor the problem and not rush into one or another quick solution.

Another Danger of Representationalism: The Noema

There is one more term I wish to examine in Aristotle, *noēma* (plural, *noēmata*). One reason I wish to discuss it is that Husserl adopts it as a technical term in his phenomenology. He also adopts the Aristotelian term *noēsis*, and he takes the two terms in parallel: noetic activities, for Husserl, have noematic correlatives, and the noetic-noematic correlation is what phenomenology is supposed to describe. The meaning of the term *noema* in Husserl is extremely controversial. The way we interpret the word will exercise a great influence on how we interpret phenomenology as a whole. It determines whether we take Husserl to be a rather direct realist

---

[10] The image of thoughts as the shadows of things is from Wittgenstein, and it has been skillfully developed by Charles Travis in *Unshadowed Thought: Representation in Thought and Language* (Cambridge, MA: Harvard University Press, 2000).

or a representationalist in his theory of knowledge. The term also plays a strategic role in defining the special character of philosophical language or transcendentalese. The term *noema* is pivotal; a major philosophical controversy is condensed into this one word. The chapter we are presently engaged in concerns Aristotle, so for the moment I will simply comment on Aristotle's use of *noēma*, but I will return to Husserl's usage in my final chapter, when I discuss the nature of philosophical discourse.

The most obvious translations of *noēma* and *noēmata* are *thought* and *thoughts*. There is practically no linguistic controversy about the translation, but the persistent philosophical controversy remains: what are thoughts; how do they exist in us; how are they related to the things of which they are the thoughts?

The word is used only a few times in Aristotle. We have already seen one usage, the *symplokē noēmatōn* of *De Anima*, III 8, where Aristotle says that the true and false belong to an intertwining of thoughts. A similar passage is found in *De Anima*, III 6, 430a27–8, where he says that when you have the false or the true, you have "a certain synthesis (*synthesis tis*) of thoughts being taken as one (*noēmatōn hōsper hen ontōn*)." This passage has the term *synthesis* instead of *symplokē*, but more important is Aristotle's claim that in a proposition the various thoughts have to be taken together as one. If we are to rise to the level of truth and falsity, our thoughts cannot be just a heap and cannot be just concatenated, but must be brought together syntactically into "a one," which then can be either true or false. Thinking is not just a succession of ideas. In this passage and in others, incidentally, the *noēmata* are quite clearly identified with the simples or indivisibles (*asyntheta, adiaireta*) that Aristotle says are at play in the other sense of truth, the kind that has ignorance as its foil. In a passage in *De Interpretatione*, 1, 16a9–10, the *noēma* is said to be "in the soul (*en tēi psychēi*)," and it can be there even "without 'truthing' or 'falsing' (*aneu tou alētheuein ē pseudesthai*)." This remark about the *noēmata* as being in the soul sounds very representationalist, but we should also remember that in the passages where Aristotle expresses the identity theory of knowledge, he says that the cognitive soul can become all things and that the thinking part of the soul can be what it knows. Aristotle also observes, in *De Anima*, III 8, 432a12–13, that a simple *noēma* must not be identified with a phantasm.[11]

---

[11] The term *noēma* is used in a few other passages. In two places in the *Metaphysics*, Aristotle says that there can be a *noēma* not only for full-fledged substances but also for other kinds of beings; see *Metaphysics*, I 9, 990b25, and XIII 4, 1079a21. The two passages are almost the same. They express a position of Aristotle's in the context of an argument against Plato. There is a particularly interesting use of *noēmata* in *De Anima*, I 3, 407a7–8. Aristotle is arguing against Plato's concepts of the soul and thinking in the *Timaeus*, where Plato attributes spatial magnitude to the soul. Aristotle says that the soul does not have spatial magnitude, that its thinking activities are sequential, like the number series, and not

How are we to understand *noēmata*? We could take the easy way out and just say that they are thoughts, that is, simple thoughts that can be interwoven into propositions that can be true or false. Linguistically, there would be nothing wrong in saying this, but what does it mean? If we use the English word *thought*, we run the risk of losing the adherence to the thing known. The thought is just an idea in the mind. The Greek word has an overtone of "the thing being thought." The verb *noein*, "to think," lies behind the noun *noēma*, but the suffix *-ma* signifies the concrete result of the verb's action, and it is here that the problem arises. We seem to be faced with an alternative. (1) Is the concrete effect of the verb's action the production of an internal entity, something that stands in as a representation of the thing? (2) Or is the concrete effect of the verb's action to make the thing known, to make the thing present in its intelligibility? Is there something between us that makes the thing known, or is the thing known directly?

It might seem obvious that Aristotle's use of *noēma* chooses the first, the representationalist option, but we should not rush to this conclusion. The word *noēma* could also be the thing as known, the thing as thought, and when taken this way it could lead us to the identity theory instead.

I believe that the alternative itself is a false or bad dilemma, and that it can be resolved if we pay greater attention to the perspective from which we are speaking and the language we are using. We are making these claims about cognitive representations and identity while we are speaking from a philosophical perspective and while we are speaking in transcendentalese. The problem arises when we confuse this perspective and this language with the pre-philosophical perspective (the natural attitude) and its language. The issue, as promised, will be discussed at the end of Chapter 19.

Predication and Essences

We can draw on some materials in Aristotle's *Metaphysics* and his *Posterior Analytics* to further develop the issue of the significance of things and the meaning of words. Let us consider *Metaphysics*, VII 17, the final chapter in the book in which Aristotle discusses what he means by "substance" or "entity" (*ousia*), which in turn is a response to the question of what we mean by "being" (*ti to on*). In the previous sixteen chapters, Aristotle has introduced the problem of entity; he has considered various ways in which

---

spatial. He argues that the mind (*nous*) is like this because thinking (*noēsis*) is unified by sequence, and that thinking is like this because thoughts (*noēmata*) are unified by sequence. The analogy between the ordering of numbers and the syntax of thoughts deserves philosophical study. Husserl began his work with the philosophy of arithmetic and moved on to logical and categorial investigations.

entity can be said, and he has explored many of the difficulties associated with it. In Chapter 17, he says he wishes to make a new beginning. The ideas he develops in this chapter serve as the basis for his further discussion in Books VIII and IX, where he presents his own understanding of substance and being. This final chapter of Book VII, therefore, can be considered the beginning of his own teaching concerning *ousia.*

If we wish to get at what a thing is, we must, says Aristotle, begin with the right kind of question. The right kind of question must be formulated as, "Why does p belong to S?" We have a subject, S, and we discover that a certain feature, p, belongs to it, and we wonder why this feature is found in this subject. To succeed in discovering the *why* is to succeed in grasping the substance or entity of the thing. It is to grasp the *eidos* of the thing in question and hence to explain its properties, to grasp that from which the properties flow. Aristotle gives two examples in the *Posterior Analytics*, the lunar eclipse and thunder.[12] We experience the eclipse as the darkening of the moon: 'darkness' is said of 'the moon.' This is the phenomenon, the p being said of S. But what is this? Why is this happening? Why is p being experienced and said of S? After diligent inquiry, we find the answer: the moon is darkened by the interposition of the earth between the moon and the sun. This formula is the definition of eclipse; it tells us what it is and expresses its essence or its *eidos.* A similar sequence occurs in regard to thunder, in which the phenomenon of a cracking or rumbling noise in the clouds is discovered to flow from a discharge of fire (electricity) in the clouds, which is the definition of the "substance" of thunder.

We get at the *eidos* of thunder, therefore, not by direct access but in a roundabout way. We do not get the *eidos* by just plucking (grasping) it from the clouds. We must first experience and register a phenomenon, a p being said of S. To know that p is said of S is already to have a bit of knowledge, but it is imperfect and in need of further knowing, and this further knowing is of another kind. What we have so far is, in Michael Oakeshott's elegant phrase, an understanding waiting to be understood.[13] The p is said of S in such a way that we still need to know more; we need to know why it is said of it. Many other examples come to mind: Peter is acerbic toward Agnes; why is this so? What is going on? Why is this p showing up and being said of that S? We find the answer: Agnes revealed the fact that Peter was embezzling funds. His conduct, therefore, *is* revenge. His way of speaking and acting toward Agnes is a property of the *eidos* revenge, and we get at revenge through the properties. Sometimes, of course, the *eidos* behind the phenomenon is not easy to categorize or name. We may be dealing with properties of some mysterious and elusive

---

[12] Aristotle, *Posterior Analytics*, II 8, 93a29–b14 and II 10, 94a3–10, and *Metaphysics*, VII 17, 1041a23–30.

[13] Michael Oakeshott, *On Human Conduct* (Oxford: The Clarendon Press, 1975), 2.

human trait or some hidden natural power. What makes people act this way? Why do they do such things? Why does this chemical element behave in this manner in these circumstances? What forms of energy are at work here? The answers may be hard to find, but the form of the question is clearly visible, and that is the issue with which *we* as philosophers are concerned. We are concerned with it not just as a curious fact about the way people look into things, and not just as a psychological datum, but as a metaphysical issue, as the formal way in which things show up to us. What things are comes to light behind the registered differentiation of a property and its base. The essence of things comes forth through the network of syntactic unfolding.

How is the *eidos* of the thing to be connected with the meaning of words? Step one: we look to the thing we have experienced. There is a rumbling noise in the clouds. We discover that it is caused by an electrical discharge. The intelligibility of thunder is: a noise in the clouds caused by an electrical discharge. This is the sense, nature, or essence of thunder; it is its substance, entity, *ousia*, or *eidos*. Step two: we now turn toward the word *thunder*. This word has a meaning, namely, "the sound produced in clouds by an electrical discharge." This concept is the intelligibility captured by the word *thunder*. It is the meaning behind the name. It is the *pathēma*, that which is received, in the soul.

What is the relationship between the mental concept of thunder, which is signified by our words, and the essence of thunder? Is the mental concept of thunder somehow a likeness of the essence of thunder? Or is it in some way simply the same as the nature of thunder? To return to an example we used earlier: what is the relationship between Simon's concept of the leopard, Simon's 'leopard,' which lies behind the word *leopard* that he and others use, and the nature of the leopards that prowl around the village? Is Simon's 'leopard' merely a likeness of what makes leopards to be what they are?

To say that it is a likeness seems to be very misleading. It suggests that we have an entity in our minds that is merely like or similar to the *eidos* of the thing in question. It seems more plausible to say that the mind that knows thunder is somehow identifiable with thunder, that the intelligibility in thunder is also somehow "in" the mind, and that it is one and the same intelligibility, in both the mind and the thing, even though my 'thunder' may be far less exact than yours, and both of ours are still less exact than that possessed by a meteorologist. All of our 'thunders,' however, are measured by the thunder in the clouds and derive from it. The differences and identities here are analogous to better and worse performances of the Kreutzer Sonata (they are different in quality but always the same sonata, the same intelligibility), except that there is no "real" sonata apart from its performances or conceptions. The sonata lives in its performances, whereas thunder lives in the clouds and not necessarily in its names, although the names do highlight the thunder in the clouds. To say that the intelligibility in our minds is the same as that in the things seems preferable to saying that the concepts in our minds are only likenesses of the nature of the things we know, unless we get used to a much more flexible sense of the term *likeness.*

We can formulate this problem once again, in terms of another example that we have employed earlier in this book. Let us discuss the difference between the significance of Eisenhower (the man) and the significance of *Eisenhower* (the name). The significance of Eisenhower and the meaning of the word *Eisenhower* are the same. There is not one 'Eisenhower' behind the word *Eisenhower* and another 'Eisenhower' as the significance or the nature of the man Eisenhower. It makes no sense to try to multiply 'Eisenhower.' As an intelligibility, it is not the kind of thing that permits multiplicity. Most of all, it seems highly misleading to say that the 'Eisenhower' in someone's mind is merely a likeness of an 'Eisenhower' in the man.

Textually, the difficulty arises especially in regard to the passage in *De Interpretatione*, where Aristotle speaks of the affections in our souls as likenesses of the things we speak and think about. Most of the other passages that discuss this problem in his writings speak of an identity between knower and known, not a likeness. Perhaps the likeness referred to in *De Interpretatione* simply has to be understood as a distinctive kind, one quite different from what is found in pictures and phantasms. It is the kind that can be captured and carried in names – and the role played by names should not be overlooked. If we try to think just about the mind and the "likenesses" that are supposed to be in it, we are left with an obscure, gauzy formulation of the philosophical problem, but if we add the spoken name, whether voiced or imagined, to our consideration, the intelligibility has something tangible on which to rest. The 'Eisenhower' or the 'leopard' is more palpably present because of *Eisenhower* and *leopard.*

In the *Posterior Analytics* and in *Metaphysics*, VII 17, Aristotle shows that we come to the *eidos* of a thing not by viewing the *eidos* directly but by going through the phenomenon in which a p is said of an S. To use the terms we have been developing in this book, this claim can be paraphrased as saying that we get to the intelligibility of a thing only through syntactically articulated states of affairs. Syntax permits us to lay out, in complicated, boxed structures, many displays of things and features, but it also allows us to get to the contents of things, to what they are and how they can be defined. Syntax enables us to get to the essence of things.

18

Thomas Aquinas

The description of knowledge given by Thomas Aquinas is largely a continuation of Aristotle's, but it is more complicated and greatly influenced by the work of St. Augustine.[1] It was also influenced by some Muslim thinkers. Aquinas generally follows Aristotle in describing the external and internal senses, and he stresses the importance of the phantasm in human knowledge. He distinguishes between the passive and the active intellect, and he insists, in opposition to some other interpreters of Aristotle, that the agent intellect is a power within each human being; it is not separate and common to all humanity. Aristotle's own text, the short chapter *De Anima* III 5, is ambiguous on the separateness of the agent intellect, but it could be taken in the way Aquinas and other commentators

---

[1] Translations from Aquinas are my own. Some helpful works concerning Aquinas's theory of knowledge are: Gaston Rabeau, *Species. Verbum. L'activité intellectuelle élémentaire selon S. Thomas d'Aquin* (Paris: Librairie philosophique J.Vrin, 1938); Hyacinthe Paissac, *Théologie du Verbe: Saint Augustin et saint Thomas* (Paris: Cerf, 1951); John Frederick Peifer, *The Mystery of Knowledge* (Albany, NY: Magi Books, 1964); Robert W. Schmidt, S.J., *The Domain of Logic according to Saint Thomas Aquinas* (The Hague: Martinus Nijhoff, 1966); Bernard Lonergan, S.J., *Verbum: Word and Idea in Aquinas*, Collected Works of Bernard Lonergan, volume 2 (Toronto: University of Toronto Press, 1997 [1967]); Benoît Garceau, O.M.I., *Judicium: Vocabulaire, sources, doctrine de saint Thomas d'Aquin* (Paris: Librairie philosophique J. Vrin, 1968); Joseph Owens, C.Ss.R., *Cognition: An Epistemological Inquiry* (Houston, TX: Center for Thomistic Studies, 1992); Leen Spruit, *Species Intelligibilis: From Perception to Knowledge*, volume 1, *Classical Roots and Medieval Discussions*, volume 2, *Renaissance Controversies, Later Scholasticism, and the Elimination of the Intelligible Species in Modern Philosophy* (Leiden: E. J. Brill, 1994 and 1995); Yves Floucat, *L'intime fécondité de l'intelligence: Le verbe mental selon saint Thomas d'Aquin* (Paris: Pierre Téqui, 2001); John Deely, *Four Ages of Understanding: The First Postmodern Survey of Philosophy from Ancient Times to the Turn of the Twenty-First Century* (Toronto: University of Toronto Press, 2001); John Milbank and Catherine Pickstock, *Truth in Aquinas* (New York: Routledge, 2001); Dominik Perler, ed., *Ancient and Medieval Theories of Intentionality* (Leiden: E. J. Brill, 2001); and John P. O'Callaghan, *Thomist Realism and the Linguistic Turn: Toward a More Perfect Form of Existence* (Notre Dame, IN: University of Notre Dame Press, 2003).

take it.[2] On all these points, therefore, Aquinas is in close harmony with Aristotle.

Thomas Aquinas on the "Internal Word"

Aquinas differs most clearly from Aristotle in the description of what the intellect does. In his mature works, he distinguishes two intellectual events that occur when we come to know things. In the first, the receptive intellect takes in the universal form that is freed or abstracted from the phantasm under the light of the agent intellect. Aquinas calls this received form the "intelligible species," *species intelligibilis,* which is a very interesting term. It could be paraphrased in English as the "thinkable look." The active intellect illuminates the phantasm and causes the thinkable looks of things to be received into the receptive intellect. Through this reception, the intellect becomes formed by the species; the mind cognitively takes in the essence of the thing in question.[3] Because it is so informed or actuated, the intellect acquires a new capacity. It becomes enabled to express internally the essence that it knows. This internal "speaking" of what it knows is the second stage in the activity of the intellect. As Aquinas concisely puts it, "having been formed, it forms, *formatus format.*"[4] The mind expresses what it knows by generating what Aquinas calls an "internal word" (*verbum interius*), which in various texts and contexts is also called the "word of the heart" (*verbum cordis*), the "word of the mind" (*verbum mentis*), the "concept" (*conceptus, conceptio*), or the "intention" (*intentio*). It

---

[2] Aquinas does not just argue about the issue of a separate and common intellect for all human beings; he also argues about the textual interpretation of Aristotle, claiming that those who posit a separate intellect are wrong in their reading of his works. See, for example, *Summa contra Gentiles* II, c. 78, which deals with the agent intellect, and *De unitate intellectus contra Averroistas,* which deals with the possible intellect. Averroes and the Averroists claimed that both the agent and the possible intellect were separate and common, while other thinkers, such as Avicenna, said that only the agent intellect was. See also *Quaestiones disputatae de anima,* a. 5, and *In Aristotelis librum De Anima commentarium* III, lect. 7 and 10.

[3] The Latin term *species* may have been misleading and may have caused complications. As far back as Cicero, two Latin words, *species* and *forma,* were used to translate Plato's term *idea.* Medieval translators also used both words to translate *eidos* in Aristotle's works. However, *species* began to be used primarily for the *eidos* as present in human cognition (both sensory and intellectual), and *forma* was used for its presence in the thing. The *forma* was in the thing, and the *species* was in the mind. The thing and its representation tended to drift apart because of this difference in terminology. See Spruit, *Species Intelligibilis,* volume 1, pp. 96–106.

[4] *Summa theologiae* I, q. 85 a. 2, ad 3: "Qua quidem formatus format secundo vel definitionem vel divisionem vel compositionem, quae per vocem significatur." See also *Summa contra Gentiles* I, c. 53: "Intellectus, per speciem rei formatus, intelligendo format in seipso quandam intentionem rei intellectae, quae est ratio ipsius, quam significat definitio."

is even called the "internal word of the heart" (*verbum cordis interius*) and the "concept of the heart" (*conceptus cordis*).[5]

Aquinas thus distinguishes between two stages in knowledge. In the first, receptive stage, the intellect becomes formed or shaped by the intelligible species. It is put into a "first actuality." It takes in the essence of the thing it knows. It is brought into a preliminary state of knowledge, but it does not yet activate or use or express its knowledge. To use an Aristotelian analogy, this stage is like that of a mathematician who has learned his science but is not exercising it. The person at this point does not actually think about what he knows, but he has become *able* to think about it. The thinking occurs in the second stage, in which the intellect internally "speaks" what it knows and thus moves into a "second actuality." It now forms its internal word or concept. The *species*, which is at root visual, is played off against the *verbum*, which is at root auditory. The intellect takes in the look of the thing and speaks to itself the word that presents the thing.

When the *verbum cordis* is constituted the intellect actively thinks what it knows; the internal word is knowledge come to life in the mind. A still further dimension is reached in external speech, the audible use of language, whose function is to express publicly the *verbum cordis*. It is important to note that our public speech does not express the intelligible species, the thinkable look; it expresses the internal word, which is the meaning behind the words we speak. In one of his quodlibetal questions (*Quodlibet* V, q. 5 a. 2, sed contra), Aquinas explicitly says, "The internal word of the heart is what is signified by the exterior word. But the exterior word does not signify the intelligible species." We will make further use of this quodlibet, which was written in 1271, late in Thomas's life.[6]

Because the activity of knowing involves the constitution of this internal word, knowing is not just passive reception but also expression. To know is also to express or to speak, at least internally.[7] We are agents of a sort in

---

[5] For the "internal word of the heart," see *Quodlibet* V, q. 5, a. 2, sed contra, and *De malo*, q. 16, a. 8, arg. 11. For the "concept of the heart," see, among others, *Summa theologiae* I, q. 34, a 1.

[6] For the dating of this quodlibetal question, see Jean-Pierre Torrell, *Saint Thomas Aquinas*, volume 1, *The Person and His Work*, second edition, trans. Robert Royal (Washington, DC: Catholic University of America Press, 2005), 211. See also *Summa theologiae* I, q. 34, a 1: "Vox enim significat intellectus conceptum, secundum philosophum, in libro I Periherm.... Vox autem quae non est significativa, verbum dici non potest. Ex hoc ergo dicitur verbum vox exterior, quia significat interiorem mentis conceptum." See ibid., q. 27, a 1: "Quam quidem conceptionem vox significat, et dicitur *verbum cordis*, significatum verbo vocis."

[7] This active dimension of knowledge is described by Floucat, who shows that Thomas considers knowing to be an intense form of interior life, which involves not just hearing but also speaking. See *L'intime fécondité de l'intelligence*, p. 86. For *constitutum* as a modifier for the internal word formed by the mind, see *De potentia*, q. 8, a. 1: "Praedicta conceptio

knowledge, even if the knowledge is theoretic and not practical. This constituting activity, however, is entirely "immanent," that is, it is completed within the mind itself. It is not a "transitive" action, which would find its completion in something outside the mind or the person. For example, making a table and cooking food are transitive performances, because they are completed in things outside the agent. Teaching someone mathematics would also be a transitive action, since the teacher has not taught until the student has learned. The activity terminates in the student. An immanent action, by contrast, is completed within the agent himself. The internal word is the term (*terminus*) or completion of the action; the action of knowing or thinking is terminated not beyond the knower but within him.[8] The person does not need to speak aloud in order to think, however much the spoken word may help us to think; the internal word is sufficient.

This internal word is interesting philosophically. It is not obviously found in Aristotle's description of knowledge. Aquinas did not develop his doctrine of the internal word just by reflecting on human cognition or by reading Aristotle; his treatment of the topic is strongly influenced by St. Augustine's theological doctrine of the Trinity. The Gospel of St. John calls Christ the "Word," the *logos*, and in its very first lines the gospel says that the Word was in the beginning, that the Word was "with" (*pros*) God, and that the Word was God. St. Augustine, in the *De Trinitate*, makes use of human cognition to shed light on and defend this biblical and theological doctrine, and Aquinas follows Augustine and uses him as an authority.[9] Thus, the doctrine of the internal word is developed at least in part in a theological context. It is used to clarify the sense in which the second person of the Holy Trinity, the Son, is different as a person from the Father, without being different in regard to the divine nature or substance. There is only one God, but the Father and Son (and the Holy Spirit) are different persons in God, and according to the Gospel of St. John, the

---

consideratur ut terminus actionis, et quasi quoddam per ipsam constitutum." See also *Quodlibet* V, q. 5, a. 2, and *De spiritualibus creaturis*, a. 9, ad 6: "Intellectum autem, sive res intellecta, se habet ut constitutum vel formatum per operationem intellectus; sive hoc sit quidditas simplex, sive sit compositio et divisio propositionis." It is interesting that Aquinas uses the adjective or passive participle *constitutum* to describe the internal word, but does not use the noun *constitutio* to name the activity of engendering this word. The term *constitution* is central to Husserl's phenomenology, but he probably took it from Kant and neo-Kantian philosophy. See Robert Sokolowski, *The Formation of Husserl's Concept of Constitution* (The Hague: Martinus Nijhoff, 1964).

[8] *Summa theologiae* I, q. 85, a. 2: "Cum enim sit duplex actio, sicut dicitur in IX Metaphysicorum, una quae manet in agente, ut videre et intelligere, altera quae transit in rem exteriorem, ut calefacere et secare."

[9] Paissac points out the paradox that the "Augustinians" of Thomas's time did not continue the Trinitarian doctrine of St. Augustine, while Thomas, who was more of an Aristotelian, succeeded in doing so. See *Théologie du Verbe*, 116.

Son can also be called the Word of the Father. The Father could be understood, theologically, as "speaking" this Word. Within the Trinity, Aquinas says, the Father is differentiated as a person by being the only one who is *dicens*.[10]

Thomas, in his commentary on St. John's Gospel, distinguishes between the way the divine Word is present among men and the way it is spoken by God. The Word perfects us: "For the Word is with man (*apud hominem*) as perfecting him, because through it man is made wise and good." It does not, however, perfect God: "But the Word is not said to be with God (*apud Deum*) as though the Father were perfected by the Word and enlightened by it. Rather, [the Word] is with God in such a way that it [he] receives the divine nature from the one who speaks the Word, from whom he has it that he is one and the same God with him (*a quo habet quod sit idem Deus cum eo*)."[11] This speaking in God is not transitory or accidental, like our use of language or our internal thinking; it is an eternal and necessary state that, along with the procession of the Holy Spirit, makes up the life of the Trinity. It would also have to be an "internal" speech, prior to and independent of any external action or discourse of God, such as creation or revelation.[12]

One can easily see that this theological doctrine would make Aquinas inclined to stress the reality of an internal word when he uses the model of human knowing to speak about procession within the Trinity. Aquinas discovers this internal word not just by analyzing human cognition, but also by seeing human cognition as analogous to what Christian faith teaches about the life of God. But the fact that the doctrine of the internal word was developed partly in a theological setting need not exclude the possibility that it may shed light on human knowledge. It may still tell us something about what it is for us to know.

Thomas Aquinas, therefore, makes use of the internal word in order to clarify Christian belief in the Trinity, but he also makes use of it in his analysis of human knowing. He distinguishes between the intelligible species, which is received from the phantasm under the light of the agent

---

[10] *De veritate*, q. 4, a. 2, ad 4; *De potentia*, q. 9, a. 9, ad 8.

[11] *Super evangelium Joannis*, Chapter 1, lectio l: "Nam apud hominem est ut perficiens ipsum, quia per illud homo efficitur sapiens et bonus... . Apud Deum vero non ita dicitur esse verbum, quasi pater perficiatur per verbum et illustretur ab ipso; sed sic est apud Deum, quod accipiat naturalem divinitatem ab ipso, qui verbum loquitur, a quo habet ut sit idem Deus cum eo." The *apud* in Aquinas expresses the *pros* in St. John's Gospel.

[12] The changes of context and adjustments in meaning behind Thomas's doctrine of *verbum* are considerable. (1) In the Bible, the Book of Genesis describes God's creative action on the model of human speaking, presenting it as an effortless making of the world and not a struggle with opposing forces. (2) The Prologue of St. John's Gospel recapitulates Genesis but describes the Word as internal to God, in contrast with creation. (3) St. Augustine reflects on speech, creation, and trinitarian procession, with the help of Neoplatonic and Stoic categories. (4) Aquinas integrates all this with Aristotle.

intellect, and the word of the heart, which is expressed within the mind and signified by our speech. In the sixteenth and seventeenth centuries, commentators such as Cajetan and John of St. Thomas further developed this doctrine and introduced some new terminology. They gave the name "impressed species" (*species impressa*) to the intelligible species, and they called the internal word by the name "expressed species" (*species expressa*). These terms became part of the scholastic tradition into the twentieth century, but they are not used in this sense by Aquinas.

The Three Acts of Intellect

Aquinas, with Aristotle, distinguishes between the agent intellect and the "possible" intellect (*intellectus possibilis*). The use of the English word *possible* to modify *intellect* is somewhat strained and perhaps misleading. I find the word rather "leaden" in this context; it does not, I think, carry an intuitive meaning. It seems to me that what Aquinas is getting at would be better expressed by the term "potential intellect." He wants to say that the intellect of a human being does not have any determinations before we begin to know things; it is fully potential or fully open, fully receptive to any and all kinds of being; its range is unlimited. It does not have a structure or a content of its own (if it did, the structure or content would get in the way of what we know). And besides being potential as receptive, the intellect is also potential in the sense of being capable of acting, that is, it can generate an internal word. It needs, however, to be enabled to do so by being informed by an intelligible species, the universal essence that has been freed from its material conditions by the light of the agent intellect acting on the phantasm. Once it has been so formed, the intellect can form its own conception or word: *formatus format*. The intellect, therefore, is potential in being both receptive and active. It is not only a *tabula rasa*, a clean blackboard, but also a *tabula dynamica*, a generative one, a blackboard that can talk.

Aquinas's concept of intellectual memory is interesting. The received intelligible species are stored in the memory. Memory is a kind of reservoir of the intelligible species that have been taken into the mind. Aquinas calls it the "treasury of intelligible species" (*thesaurum intelligibilium specierum*), a phrase he takes from Avicenna (*ut verbis Avicennae utamur*); he considers the term a paraphrase of Aristotle's "place of forms, *topos eidōn*," which in Latin becomes the *locus specierum*.[13] The intelligible species in memory enjoy a continuous but merely habitual mode of being. It is noteworthy

---

[13] *Summa contra Gentiles* II, c. 74. "Patet etiam quod haec opinio est contra sententiam Aristotelis, qui dicit, in III de anima, quod intellectus possibilis est locus specierum: quod nihil aliud est dicere quam ipsum esse thesaurum intelligibilium specierum, ut verbis Avicennae utamur."

that the intellectual memory retains intelligible species, not judgments or opinions, and also not thoughts. The internal word, by contrast, is made up of elements pulled up from memory; the internal word is what we actually think and what we express in speech. *This*, the internal word, is the thought. It exists only while it is being thought. It is at the peak of cognitive activity, but it is intermittent and fleeting, along with the human acts of thinking and speaking that constitute it. The internal words come and go as our thinking turns on and off and as our thoughts and words move from one issue to another. Memory, by contrast, retains the resources that enable such episodic activity.

What sort of mental accomplishment does the intellect achieve when it "speaks" its interior word? Aquinas almost always uses the term in the singular (*verbum*), and so we might be inclined to think that the internal word is just a simple concept, an "indivisible."[14] The intelligible species of things, furthermore, are received into the possible intellect one by one; each of them is a universal essence taken into the mind. One might expect, therefore, that a particular internal word is a sort of mirror image of one of these species, that it is a single, simple, immanent expression of an intelligible species, a simple concept. But this is not the case. In several texts from his mature writings, Aquinas uses the term *internal word* to cover both the indivisibles that we apprehend and the judgments we achieve when the intellect composes and divides. To complicate things even more, he includes under the grasp of indivisibles not only the simple grasp of an essence, but also its definition. This doctrine can be seen in the quodlibetal question we have cited earlier.[15] Aquinas is speaking about the *verbum cordis interius*; he says that it "proceeds" from and remains within the intellect. It is, he says, "constituted, *constitutum*," by the operation of the mind. Then, referring to Aristotle in the *De Anima*, he says that there are two such operations of the mind. The first "is called the understanding of indivisibles, through which the intellect forms in itself the definition or the concept of something simple." Note how the indivisible includes not just the thing's concept but also its definition. Aquinas then describes the second intellectual act: "The other operation is the intellect composing and dividing, according to which it forms an enunciation [judgment]." Then he says, "And either of these (*utrumque istorum*) constituted through the operation of the intellect is called *verbum cordis*." The *verbum cordis*

---

[14] The term is used in the plural, *verba interiora*, in *Summa contra Gentiles* IV, c. 11. This is the only instance reported in the *Index Thomisticus*.

[15] *Quodlibet* V, q. 5, a. 2 c: "Procedit autem aliquid ab intellectu, in quantum est constitutum per operationem ipsius. Est autem duplex operatio intellectus, secundum philosophum in III de anima. Una quidem quae vocatur indivisibilium intelligentia, per quam intellectus format in seipso definitionem, vel conceptum alicuius incomplexi. Alia autem operatio est intellectus componentis et dividentis, secundum quam format enuntiationem. Et utrumque istorum per operationem intellectus constitutorum vocatur verbum cordis."

encompasses, therefore, the simple concept (and the definition) as well as the enunciation. Aquinas adds that the former is expressed in our speech by a simple name (*per terminum incomplexum*) and the latter by a more complex set of words (*per orationem*).

The claim that the interior word covers indivisible concepts (and definitions) as well as judgments is found in other works of Aquinas.[16] In a passage in the *Summa theologiae*, Aquinas may go even further. We might take him to say that not just concepts and judgments but even our reasoning, in which judgments are put together into an argument or proof, can be included under the umbrella of the *verbum interius*. He first makes the point that there is a correlation between acts of thinking and the mental "products" generated by them, between the thinking and the thought: "In the works of reason we must consider the very act of reason (*ipsum actum rationis*), which is to understand and to carry out reasoning (*ratiocinari*), and something constituted (*constitutum*) through an act of this sort." We must distinguish between an intellectual act and the product of the act. He then spells out the kinds of "constituted" products there are, and he lists three: "In speculative reason there is first the definition; second the enunciation; and third the syllogism or argument."[17] Thus, in this passage Aquinas speaks about all three acts of the mind, the grasp of indivisibles, judgment, and reasoning, and their correlative internal products. He does not, in this passage, use the term *verbum* to name the products of these three operations, but since he says they are all "constituted" by the intellect, it would not be unreasonable to infer that the term could be applied to them. Not just a concept and definition, not just a judgment, but even an argument could be called a *verbum cordis*, as an achievement of the mind.[18] And why should it not be included? An

---

[16] Cf. *De potentia*, q. 9, a. 5. *In VI Metaphysicorum*, 4, nn. 1223–4; *De veritate*, q. 4, a. 2; *Summa theologiae* I, q. 85, a. 2, ad 3; *In I Perihermeneias*, lectio 7, n. 5.

[17] *Summa theologiae* I II, q. 90, a. 1, ad 2. "In operibus rationis est considerare ipsum actum rationis, qui est intelligere et ratiocinari, et aliquid per huiusmodi actum constitutum. Quod quidem in speculativa ratione primo quidem est definitio; secundo, enuntiatio; tertio verum syllogismus vel argumentatio."

[18] Schmidt, in *The Domain of Logic according to Saint Thomas Aquinas*, 120–2, says that *intentio*, as well as "intellectual word" and "conception," can encompass the first, second, and third acts of the mind. An important distinction needs to be explicitly made. There are two kinds of "first act" that need to be distinguished in Aquinas's theory of knowledge. First, there is the reception of the intelligible species. This is a purely passive procedure carried out under the light of the agent intellect. It is not yet an intellectual act; it is merely the process by which the intellect becomes enabled to "speak" internally. The intellect is put into a "first actuality" by this event. Second, there are the three acts of the mind: the first act is the grasp of indivisibles, the second is judgment, and the third is reasoning, all three of which can be called the *verbum interius*. It is important not to confuse the reception of the intelligible species with the grasp of indivisibles (the terminology of "grasping" or "apprehending" is misleading here, because it suggests the "taking in" that is proper to the reception of the species). The grasp of indivisibles is called the first act of the mind

argument is merely an ordered bundle of judgments. Thus, the term *interior word* covers the full range of immanent intellectual products. One might observe that Aquinas develops this description with very little reference to the public conversation in which these achievements normally occur.

In Chapter 17 we claimed that Aristotle's distinction between the two kinds of truth can be made more evident if we take it as a distinction between two procedures in conversation, with the grasp of simples being the introduction of a topic into a conversation and composition and division being a predication made about the topic. The same clarification holds for Aquinas and his distinction of the two kinds, and it is even more helpful in regard to the grasp of indivisibles, because Aquinas considers the "first act of the intellect" to include not only the constitution of a concept but also the definition of what is conceived. As we have seen in Chapter 8, the natural place for a definition is also in a conversation. We interrupt the conversational flow of predications because one of the interlocutors does not understand a term that has been introduced. We stop predicating, we back up into a genus that everyone knows, and we make a distinction in order to determine a specific form. If the maneuver of defining succeeds, we return to the conversation and continue our compositions and divisions. Both the concept and the definition belong to the "first act of the intellect," because they precede any further predications or second acts.

Similitudes

Another term that Aquinas uses in his analysis of knowledge is *similitudo.* When we know things, he says, we have, in our cognitive powers, a similitude or likeness of the thing we know. The senses have sensory similitudes, and the intellect has intellectual similitudes. In the intellect, the received intelligible species is called a similitude of the thing known, and the *verbum interius* is also called a similitude of what we know. Thus, in the *Summa contra Gentiles* I, c. 53, Aquinas distinguishes the internal word (which here is called *intentio intellecta*) from the intelligible species. The internal word is the terminus and the species is the principle of the act of thinking: "This intellected intention, as it is the terminus of an operation of understanding, is other than (*aliud a*) the intelligible species that makes the intellect to be in act; it [the species] should be considered the principle of the operation of understanding." Having made this distinction, he says: "But either of the two (*utrumque*) is a similitude of the

(because it is prior to judgment, the second act, and reasoning, the third), but it is different from and posterior to the reception of the intelligible species.

thing that is understood."[19] Both the received species and the internal word are similitudes of what we know.

This multiplication of similitudes is troubling. The internal word is a similitude of the thing known, and the intelligible species is also a similitude of the thing known. Aquinas uses the word *similitudo* very often. It is not an occasional or incidental usage, and it occurs repeatedly in reference to both the internal word and the received intelligible species, as well as in reference to the senses, both external and internal. With so many likenesses between us and things, do we not run the risk of being disconnected from what we know? Won't the likenesses get in the way?

Aquinas's terminology certainly derives from Aristotle's use of the word *homoiōmata*, *likenesses*, at the beginning of the *De Interpretatione*, a passage to which Aquinas often refers. The Latin translation of the word is *similitudines*. As we have seen earlier, most of the time Aristotle seems to hold an identity theory of knowledge, but this passage seems to express more of a representational theory, with some sort of likeness in the mind standing in for the thing that is known and expressed by the words we speak. Aristotle uses the term once, but Aquinas uses it again and again, and thus seems to underscore the representational character of intellectual knowing. One of the reasons Aquinas gives for the need for a likeness in the mind is the fact that we can think of things whether they are present or absent to us. In this respect, the intellect is like the imagination, he says, which also can entertain something whether it is present or absent.[20] Another reason why the mind needs an intellectual likeness is that the likenesses provided by perception and imagination are not sufficient. They present individual, material objects, but the object of the intellect is the quiddity or essence of things, which has to be "freed" from its material conditions. The phantasm prepares the quiddity for this elevation or abstraction, and so it raises it above its status in perception, but it does not go far enough; it does not raise it to the level of intelligence. A higher, intellectual similitude is needed.[21] The similitude seems to stand in for

---

[19] *Summa contra Gentiles* I, c. 53: "Haec autem intentio intellecta, cum sit quasi terminum intelligibilis operationis, est aliud a specie intelligibili quae facit intellectum in actu, quam oportet considerari ut intelligibilis operationis principium: licet utrumque sit rei intellectae similitudo." See *Summa theologiae* I, q. 17, a. 3, where Aquinas says that the intellect is informed by a similitude of the essence or quiddity of the thing known ("intellectus informatur similitudine quidditatis rei").

[20] *Summa contra Gentiles* I, c. 3: "Ulterius autem considerandum est quod intellectus, per speciem rei formatus, intelligendo format in seipso quandam intentionem rei intellectae, quae est ratio ipsius, quam significat definitio. Et hoc quidem necessarium est: eo quod intellectus intelligit indifferenter rem absentem et praesentem, in quo cum intellectu imaginatio convenit."

[21] Ibid.: "Sed intellectus hoc amplius habet, quod etiam intelligit rem ut separatam a conditionibus materialibus, sine quibus in rerum natura non existit; et hoc non posset esse nisi intellectus sibi intentionem praedictam formaret."

the thing that we know, or at least for the intelligibility of the thing that
we know.

Identity and Direct Knowledge

And yet, although Aquinas seems so to emphasize the representational
character of knowing, he also expresses with equal vigor the identity theory
of knowledge. If he understands Aristotle in *De Interpretatione* as positing
a representation in the mind, he also agrees with Aristotle's many statements
that the knower is somehow identical to the thing or essence that is known.
Aquinas often says that the intellect in act *is* the thing intellected. A typical
passage can be found in his commentary on the *Sentences*: "When it [the
mind] knows other things, that which is known in act is made to be one with
the intellect in act (*intellectum in actu fit unum cum intellectu in actu*), insofar
as the form of what is known becomes the form of the intellect, insofar as
the intellect is in act."[22] This phrasing, that what is actually known is one
with the intellect in act, is something like a refrain in Aquinas's writings on
knowledge, a variation, if you will, on a theme in Aristotle.

A passage that expresses this very well can be found in *Summa contra
Gentiles* IV, c. 11, where, in a phrase that is highly compressed and almost
poetic in Latin, Aquinas says, "Intellectum autem in intelligente est
intentio intellecta et verbum." To paraphrase it in English, "The thing
known in the knower is the known intention and word." Let us try to
concretize this by contriving an example from which we can abstract the
point that is being made. Suppose we understand loneliness. Loneliness as
actually known (by us and in us) is the *verbum interius*, 'loneliness.' Going
back to the typographical conventions that we have used to designate the
thing, the concept, and the name, we could write that loneliness as known
(by us and in us) is 'loneliness,' which is immanently spoken as our
internal word, and it is verbally signified by the word *loneliness* when we
utter the sound. The meaning of the word *loneliness* is 'loneliness,' which
is an internal word, the similitude of loneliness. But is it a good idea to
say that 'loneliness' is a similitude, a likeness, of loneliness? It is not a
similitude in the sense of a replica or a picture, nor is it something just *like*
loneliness; it *is* loneliness – but as known by us and hence as "in" us. How
can a likeness *be* that which it is like? To call 'loneliness' a similitude is to
use the word *similitude* in a very unusual sense, and yet Aquinas does say
that "that which is known (*intellectum*) is in the knower (*in intelligente*)
through its similitude."[23]

---

[22] *In quattuor libros Sententiarum*, IV, d. 49 q. 2, a. 1, ad 10. "Secundum autem quod intelligit
res alias, intellectum in actu fit unum cum intellectu in actu, inquantum forma intellecti
fit forma intellectus, inquantum est intellectus in actu."
[23] *Summa theologiae* I, q. 85, a. 2, ad 1.

Despite positing these similitudes in the mind, Aquinas always insists that what we know first and foremost is the thing itself, not any of the intermediary likenesses. We do not infer the thing from what we know in the mind; we know the thing directly. An entire article, *Summa theologiae* I, q. 85, a 2, is explicitly devoted to the question whether the intelligible species is what we know, and Aquinas's answer is clear: "That which is first known (*intelligitur*) is the thing of which the intelligible species is a similitude." In *De veritate*, q. 3 a. 2, Aquinas spells this out even more clearly. He says that the similitudes definitely are not that which we know; rather, they are that "by which" we know the thing directly. Concerning the intelligible species, he says, "We see that the species, by which the intellect is informed in order that it can actually understand, is the first 'by which' (*primum quo*) a thing is known." Then he goes on to speak about the internal word (whether quiddity or judgment): "The quiddity that is formed in the intellect, or even the composition and division, is a certain product of [the intellect], through which the intellect arrives at the cognition of the exterior thing; and thus it is, as it were, a second 'by which' (*secundum quo*) a thing is known."[24] There is a first *quo* and then a second *quo*, and we must traverse both of them. There is a lot of mirroring going on here, even as we directly know the thing in question. Aquinas is saying all the right things; he insists that we directly know the thing and not its likenesses in us; but it still seems that he is courting danger when he says, in this passage, that there are two such likenesses "by which" we know, first the received intelligible species and second the generated internal word. I would also like to draw attention to the term *quondam operatum ipsius*, "a certain product of [the intellect]," which Aquinas uses to designate the internal word; this is a strong term, which clearly makes the internal word rather "thick" as a representation.

Aquinas says, therefore, that what we directly know is the thing, not the likeness by which we know it. He does say that we can "secondarily" know the likeness as well. We do so when we reflect on our minds and our intellectual activities, or rather when the mind reflects on itself. Speaking about the intelligible species, Aquinas says, "But because the intellect reflects on itself, according to that reflection it understands both its own knowing and the species by which it knows. Thus, the intellectual species is

[24] *De veritate*, q. 3, a. 2: "Videmus quod species, qua intellectus informatur ut intelligat actu, est primum quo intelligitur; ex hoc autem quod est effectus in actu, per talem formam operari iam potest formando quidditates rerum et componendo et dividendo; unde ipsa quidditas formata in intellectu, vel etiam compositio et divisio, est quoddam operatum ipsius, per quod tamen intellectus venit in cognitionem rei exterioris; et sic est quasi secundum quo intelligitur." See Floucat, *L'intime fécondité de l'intelligence*, 73.

secondarily that which is known."[25] Aquinas does not spell out this reflective knowledge, but clearly it would not be a perception, since the species is not a perceivable thing, nor would it seem to involve any direct intuition of the species.

Aquinas's insistence that the thing we directly know is the thing itself and not an idea of the thing is reassuring, but the constant use of the term *similitudes* for intelligible species, concepts, judgments, and even arguments does seem to "substantialize" them to an uncomfortable degree. As Bernardo Carlos Bazán says, with this doctrine "Thomas inaugurates a kind of thought through intermediaries whose problems are enormous."[26] Descartes and Locke seem just around the corner.

Reflections on Aristotle and Aquinas

We have been trying to summarize the thought of Aristotle and of Aquinas concerning human knowing, and we have engaged in some commentary as we went along. Let us stand back and comment more explicitly on what these authors say. Some of the things they talk about, such as the agent intellect, the phantasm, the intelligible species, and the word of the heart, may seem strange and perhaps quaint. Can we formulate these things in a less exotic way? What are Aristotle and Aquinas getting at? What phenomena are they describing?

In particular, why do they distinguish between the agent and the receptive intellect? These are not two different intellects but two aspects of one mind. The distinction is their way of accounting for the difference between language and protolanguage. There is a radical break between sensibility and its voiced expression, on the one hand, and intelligence and its linguistic expression on the other; sensibility does not edge gradually into thinking, and the cut-and-dried syntax of language is a symptom of the fact that users of language have moved into an entirely new register. But how do we bootstrap ourselves into this new domain? The agent intellect or active mind is posited as the cause; the agent intellect has to exercise its power on the imagined phantasm in order to allow the intelligibility of the thing to come to light; the intelligibility cannot just bubble up from sensibility. The mind must already be a mind in order to become more thoughtful and to learn new things, and the agent intellect is the mind as already activated. But this seems to be a "just-so" story; the agent intellect seems to be as much a statement of the problem of how we breach

---

[25] *Summa theologiae* I, q. 85, a. 2: "Sed quia intellectus supra seipsum reflectitur, secundum eandem reflexionem intelligit et suum intelligere, et speciem qua intelligit. Et sic species intellectiva secundario est id quod intelligitur."

[26] Bernardo Carlos Bazán, "*Intellectum Speculativum*: Averroes, Thomas Aquinas, and Siger of Brabant on the Intelligible Object," *Journal of the History of Philosophy* 19 (1981): 436.

the great divide as an explanation of how we do it. I offer two considerations that might make the position less disturbing.

First, we should begin our analysis with the phenomenon of syntactic articulation and not with the simple extraction of an intelligibility. In our intellectual life, we do not first collect a lot of ideas and only subsequently conjoin and separate them, weaving them into judgments and arguments. Rather, the power to weave comes first. We become adept at linguistic syntax by learning our mother tongue. We start by picking up the rhythms of the language that our people speak. Gradually they become more than rhythms; they become grammatical compositions, and slowly but surely we become more and more responsible for the ones that we assemble. But these formulations are not just grammatical choreography; there is no such thing as sheer grammar. Grammar is like a net cast into the sea; "looks" are entangled in the grammar; things and their intelligibilities are caught up in it, dimly at first but with more and more differentiation over time. The agent intellect could be understood as a power that does its work through compositional syntax, primarily in language but also in depiction. It provokes (calls forth) intelligibility through grammar, not by silently shining on a phantasm and extracting a single intelligible species. The agent intellect is not reducible to language and its structure; it is a capacity that each of us has; but we have it as speakers of language and makers of pictures, and it cannot be activated except through compositional patterns.

Second, the compositional patterns are achieved first and foremost in public, not in the solitude of our own minds. Judgments are primarily public performances. We learn to predicate by responding to other speakers who bring a subject into view and say something about it; we do not learn to predicate the way we learn to chew. Our teeth grow into our mouths by a gift of nature, but words and grammar and the thinking associated with them come to us by conversation. Our agent intellects could not bring an *eidos* or an intelligible species into our minds if other speakers did not give us the opportunity. If through some great misfortune we miss that window, our minds remain unused and only latent; we live in protolanguage at best and not in language. The agent and potential intellects might seem like antique, picturesque entities, but they are an attempt to deal with a serious problem.

The phantasm is the product of our imagination, an internal sense, and it serves to present a perceived object to the mind. It prepares and elevates the perceived thing for intellection. What this preparation and elevation are can be seen by considering how real pictures can help facilitate an insight. Whenever we depict anything, we slant it so that it will be understood in a certain way. We never just copy; we actively present. A valuable distinction has been made by Catherine Abell and Gregory Currie in regard to photographs and paintings. A photograph, they say, is a *trace* of an object ("nature impresses itself on the photographic plate"), but a painting is a *testimony* of it, and every testimony involves a *testifier*, whose insight and honesty we need to evaluate.[27] A painting is saturated by compositional syntax in theme, color, and line, which is the work of an artist who presents himself as having something to say about the thing in question.[28] The artist can help us to understand the thing depicted: not just to identify, but to understand it, which means to take in the intelligibility or the thinkable look of the thing. The artist or testifier produces a public "phantasm" that will make people think about the thing in a certain way.

Our phantasms are private testimonies we make for ourselves. The thing is viewed and recapitulated in a slanted way, and it comes back in that way insistently, over and over again. We, consequently, are prompted to understand it in a certain way. Since our phantasm is a recapitulation not only of the thing presented but also of ourselves, with our terrors or delights, as we originally had the experience (and were trying to get the meaning), both our way of understanding the thing and the way we will talk about it will be much influenced by the slants our phantasm gives it. Both personal phantasms and public pictures, furthermore, can serve a dual function. They can prompt us to think in a certain way about this depicted individual, or they can use this depicted individual to help us think about the *eidos* embodied and slanted in it; we can think about Churchill, or we can think about "political ruler as such." It all depends on how we tilt the words we use in relation to the image. Imagination is different from depiction, but each can be better understood philosophically by being played off against the other.

The Need for Voiced Words

What about the distinction between the intelligible species and the internal word? Aquinas makes this distinction, but Aristotle does not seem to do so. In Aquinas's view, there seems to be a rather clearly articulated internal parallel to external speech; internal words and compositions track and shadow what we say externally, and the internal can, it would seem, occur quite independently as well. Aristotle does mention the *pathēmata* in

---

[27] See Catherine Abell and Gregory Currie, "Internal and External Pictures," *Philosophical Psychology* 12 (1999): 430: "The terminology we prefer has us say that a photograph is a *trace* of its object, while a painting is *testimony* of its object. One important feature of testimony is that judging the reliability of the information conveyed depends essentially on judging the reliability of the cognitive processes of the testifier, and that is certainly how it is with a painting." There is, of course, some testimony in photography if the photographer does not just point and click but thinks about what he is recording.

[28] On the levels of composition in painting, see Robert Sokolowski, "Visual Intelligence in Painting," *Review of Metaphysics* 59 (2005): 338–43.

the soul that are "likenesses" of things, but the very fact that he calls them *pathēmata* would seem to give them less substantiality and energy than they seem to have in Aquinas, where they are called internal words or words of the heart. They seem more passive in Aristotle, and they are not called words, although there is a long tradition of internal wording in Hellenistic thought, going back to the Stoic *lekton*, the internal "thing that is said."

Clearly, if our spoken words are truly to be words, we must do more than just mouth sounds. We have to think as we speak. A mere rant, an emotional outburst, or associative parroting is not thoughtful speech; it is mock speech. But how much real internal speaking can we perform without speaking publicly? Let us draw an analogy with voting. I obviously cannot perform a vote internally. There is no "vote of the heart." I might be inclined this way or that, but I have not voted until I have cast a ballot. But can I at least make a decision, in my heart, about how I am going to vote? Can I make up my mind internally? Not completely; I would even question whether we should say, philosophically, that I have fully made up my mind until I have actually voted or at least taken some steps (made some choices) in view of voting in the intended way. Until that happens, I can always change my mind. I think we should say that "the vote of the heart" really and definitely occurs only when I cast a ballot. The choice truly and finally occurs only when the deed is done, but of course the decision is not just the external, mechanical conduct, which might be performed thoughtlessly. The decision is "internal," but it informs public conduct and is not separate from it.

Should we not say, likewise, that I have not truly predicated until I have made a public statement of some sort, at least until I have written it down on paper, even in private, or whispered it to myself? Isn't predicating somehow like voting? Does it really happen before I make a public statement? Everything is still somewhat tentative until that point, still an approach and not yet an arrival. Aquinas includes under the internal word not only simple concepts but also definitions, as well as judgments or enunciations, both positive and negative, and even arguments. How much of that can happen without the support of spoken speech?

How definite can an internal word be by itself? Even in our private thoughts, we play our thinking off against imaginary rehearsals, but we use imagined and incipient words to do so; words are fluttering about. What goes on in such rumination is fluid and indistinct, and it acquires whatever precision it has from the words and syntax that we employ. Words are the carriers or vehicles of identification, and how they function can best be brought out in comparison to picturing. A picture is a thing that presents another thing: it presents not just a resemblance, but the thing in its identity. Eisenhower is in his picture, presented in his individuality. "Being a general" is also presented in the picture, if Eisenhower is pictured in uniform or if he has a military look about him. But Eisenhower is also identifiable in his name, he is "in" the name, and he is there in a more crisp and definite manner than in his picture, because the name contains only him and not a lot of accidentals, which are there in the picture. "Being a general" is present in the word *general* (when it is being used appropriately), again in a crisp and definite manner, because *general* signifies that much and nothing else. Are Eisenhower and being a general also present in my mind, in internal words of some sort? Not apart from my mental imaging and my incipient use of words. They need the support of such phantasms and words for their identifiability. But the words have to be real words, that is, they have to be truly spoken and not parroted or mumbled; they have to be enlisted into syntax, recruited into grammar.[29] The *verbum vocis* is essential for the *verbum mentis* as its carrier.

One can, therefore, with Aquinas, distinguish between receiving an intelligible species (a thinkable look) and uttering an internal word. In the first step, we, through experience or instruction, become qualified to speak about the thing in question, and in the second step we actually speak about it, either by just naming the thing or defining it, or by saying something about it, or by arguing for the truth of what we have said. In performing these activities we occasionally declare ourselves as the ones doing them, but we do not declare ourselves as taking in the intelligible species. That occurrence is not an initiative of our own; it just happens to us if we are lucky, if we have a mind prepared, and if we pay attention. We show that it has happened by what we say and do. We do not even attach a name to the thinkable look; even naming a thing, entering it into a conversation, comes later, when we perform the first act of the intellect, the simple apprehension.

Are not all these activities and their constituted "products" made more tangible philosophically if we see them in their natural place, which is in the human conversation? Are not the internal words more verifiable if they are seen to be carried by spoken or at least imagined words? Are not the acts of intellect more easily distinguished if we see that they normally occur in response to others? The simple apprehension or the first act of the mind takes place when a speaker introduces a word into a conversation

---

[29] The book by Yves Floucat, *L'intime fécondité de l'intelligence*, defends Aquinas against the accusation of a crude representationalism. Floucat observes that Thomas was well aware of the metaphorical character of many of the words we use to speak about knowledge, that he insisted on the identity between the knower and the known, and that he held to an acceptable sense of representation in knowledge: "Far from being a substitute, a fac-simile, or a copy conforming to the object known, it [the species] is its abstracted *intentio*, that is to say, its intelligible form" (p. 49). He claims that a less satisfactory sense of representation was later introduced by Scotus (pp. 44–63). Floucat observes that Aquinas tends not to call the interior word a *sign* of the thing we know through it. Later commentators on Thomas introduced the notion of a "formal sign," and this, he says, was done in the unhealthy environment of modern epistemology. See pp. 143–53.

("Irredentism ...."). The speaker may need to define the word if his interlocutors do not know what it means; he goes back to a commonly understood genus and makes a specifying distinction, thus elaborating the simple apprehension he has brought about, but remaining within the first act of the mind. Then, after this interruption, he returns to the discussion and continues predicating and arguing, thus carrying out the second and third acts of intellect. This conversation needs to be escorted by thinking, of course; otherwise it quickly flounders and relapses into being mere voice and not speech, but the thinking is the inside dimension of something that is also outside.

And yet, conversation cannot be the whole story. Our minds are not emptied into public space. We need to think in solitude if we are to have anything distinctive to say. Josephine Jacobsen says about poets, "They work alone."[30] We must also turn away from others, because the conversational use of our words is not sufficiently under our own control; it is constricted by our interlocutors, by what they have to say and what they can directly understand. If poets are to charge words with the energy that they alone can give them, they need to separate themselves from the insistence of conversation. Jacobsen uses a photographic and hence visual analogy to show what happens when we speak an internal word, a word of the heart. She writes, "The poem's inception and execution is as secret as a film's development in a darkroom." A truly distinctive understanding can be initially verbalized only in the dim and gradual light of imagination; we develop our thoughts between conversations. Etymologically, *photograph* means sketching or writing with light, and we need background darkness for this to occur. But we cannot carry out this darkroom thinking without the vocabulary, images, and syntax that public discourse gives us. The conversation we carry on within ourselves is derived from our speech with others, and it is a preparation for what we will later have to say and show to them.

---

[30] Josephine Jacobsen, *The Instant of Knowing*, lecture given at the Library of Congress, May 7, 1973 (Washington, DC: Library of Congress, 1974), 5.

19

Conclusion, with Henry James

Categorial or syntactic structure makes it possible for us to rise from sensibility to reasoning and understanding. Philosophers have developed special words to name the various intellectual activities, such as *apprehension* and *judgment*. These words are used metaphorically at first. In the case of these particular terms, the original uses signify not mental activities but the bodily action of grasping something and the juridical action of declaring someone to be innocent or guilty. As time goes on and the philosophical problems become routine, the words take on the character of technical terms and we forget that they had a metaphorical beginning. We assume that they name obviously verifiable things, things that we can simply point out. We begin to think that the words have been devised in response to entities that we directly experience in our ordinary worldly involvements, as *apple* is devised to name an apple. In fact, the pre-philosophical overtone of such philosophical words is never entirely lost. Our access to a philosophical understanding of what it is to understand always remains closely tied to our pre-philosophical thinking, and all the words used in philosophy retain to some extent their pre-philosophical and pre-metaphorical significance. Philosophical language, furthermore, needs always to be revivified; we need to go back to the original meanings of the words and show how the words are tilted to function within the new stance introduced by philosophy. Attention to such linguistic transpositions makes us more aware of the distinctive character of philosophical thinking, which is always balanced on the edge of our more ordinary discourse.

Henry James on Simple Apprehension

To bring out this peculiarity of philosophical terms, I wish to draw attention to one of the ways that Henry James speaks about human understanding. His novels are highly sensitive to the nuances of human interaction, not only in regard to what people do toward and with one another, but also in regard to the way things show up for them. A term he often uses to name the event in which a human being "sees" something intellectually is *taking in*. This is not an established philosophical term, like *apprehension, judgment,* or *inference,* but it is especially effective in naming what we could call a categorial insight, an occurrence in which someone installs syntax into a situation that had been obscure and muddled, and thereby identifies what a thing is or what is going on. The person in question suddenly succeeds in putting things into relief, with the parts assembling themselves into a coherent and consistent whole and the nature of the issue being brought to light. To use the classical vocabulary, this event shows that the agent intellect has done its job and something has become understood. James's use of *taking in* stands halfway between ordinary and philosophical usage.

The term appears in many of James's novels, but it is especially prom-inent in *The Ambassadors.*[1] In this story, Lewis Lambert Strether, a man of fifty-five, is sent to Paris by the widowed Mrs. Newsome, of a wealthy New England family, to persuade her son Chadwick to return to the United States, to the city of Woollett, Massachusetts, to take over the family business and, more generally, to put his life in order. Strether finds Chad living happily and successfully in Paris, caught up in an interesting "complexity of relations,"[2] above all with one Madame de Vionnet. Strether gradually sees that Chad has been formed in Paris in a way that would have been impossible in Woollett. As events unfold, he begins to

---

[1] Henry James, *The Ambassadors* (New York: Norton, 1964). For a philosophical study of Henry James, see Robert B. Pippin, *Henry James and Modern Moral Life* (New York: Cambridge University Press, 2001). Pippin uses citations from James to very good effect. *The Ambassadors* is the final work treated in his book. He discusses many of the dilemmas of modernity, on both the large and the small scale, as they are expressed by James. One of the minor themes, for example, of considerable interest for phenomenology, is the contrast between the importance of advertising in modern life and the insubstantiality of the gadgets advertised (see pp. 165–6, and note 5 on p. 168).

[2] Ibid., 35. The same phrase is used in Henry James in *The Art of the Novel* (New York: Charles Scribner's Sons, 1934), 317, in the preface James wrote for the New York Edition (1909) of this work. James's description of how he conceived and composed *The Ambassadors* is itself an exercise in philosophical reflection, concrete and detailed. He says (p. 308) that the gist of the book "is that he [Strether] now at all events *sees;* so that the business of my tale and the march of my action ... is just my demonstration of this process of vision." Concerning the novel, he says, "I am able to estimate this as, frankly, quite the best, 'all round,' of my productions" (p. 309). On his own syntactic composition, he says, "These things continued to fall together, as by the neat action of their own weight and form, while their commentator scratched his head about them; he easily sees now that they were always well in advance of him" (p. 315). On p. 319, he speaks of "the intricate ins and outs of the compositional problem"; he says that "composition alone is positive beauty," and he momentarily laments "the dire paucity of readers ever recognizing or ever missing positive beauty."

doubt whether the return to America would be the decent thing for Chad
to do. He essentially fails in his mission on all counts. In the process he
forecloses possibilities of happiness that had opened up for him, both in
Europe (with Maria Gostrey) and in America. Strether repeatedly finds
that he is being used by people who know far more about what is going on
than he does and whose purposes he only belatedly discerns: "He had
allowed for depths; but these were greater."[3]

Throughout the novel, there are exchanges in which Strether, Chad,
and others discover certain things, and James often expresses this event by
using the term *taking in.* Describing the first meeting between Strether and
Maria Gostrey, James writes, "She paused while our friend took in these
things."[4] Later, it is Maria who comprehends a situation: "She had had
time to take in their companion's face; and with it, as such things were easy
for her, she took in all."[5] At another moment she succeeds in figuring out
the actions of a young man, Bilham, who is acting on Chad's behalf: "I
took him all in."[6] Sometimes the apprehension is not of a human
relationship but simply of a harmless event or a scenic view. Thus, Strether
"took in the two English ladies who had just creaked past them," and
Strether and Chad, walking out into the Avenue de l'Opéra, "had taken in
for a moment, through everything, the great clear architectural street."[7]
Sometimes the person takes in what someone else has said; Strether is told
of Madame de Vionnet's care for her daughter, Jeanne, and the role this
plays in the woman's relation with Chad, and "Strether took this in as they
slowly moved to the house."[8] At other times the perception is the person's
own: "She took him all in again."[9] In still other circumstances, someone
comes to an understanding based on what others want him to think;
toward the end of the book, when accounts have to be settled, Madame de
Vionnet says to Strether, "We've thrust on you appearances that you've had
to take in and that have therefore made your obligation."[10]

In a conversation with Mr. Waymarsh, another representative of the
Newsomes, Strether uses the term with a clever ambiguity, in a passage
where *taking in* can apply either to eating, and hence to the physical
assimilation of food, or to cognitive assimilation: "One does fill out some
with all one takes in, and I've taken in, I dare say, more than I've natural
room for."[11] Mr. Waymarsh, incidentally, is a good foil for Strether. He is

[3] James, *The Ambassadors*, 238.
[4] Ibid., 19.
[5] Ibid., 41.
[6] Ibid., 88.
[7] Ibid., 71 and 99.
[8] Ibid., 140.
[9] Ibid., 190.
[10] Ibid., 324.
[11] Ibid., 31.

unimaginative and his mind is sluggish, practically incapable of taking in anything at all: "[Strether] had never seen anyone less aware of anything than Waymarsh as he glowered at Chad. The social sightlessness of his old friend's survey marked for him afresh, and almost in an humiliating way, the inevitable limits of direct aid from this source."[12]

One of the best uses of our term occurs later in the story, during a critical conversation between Strether and Madame de Vionnet, who makes an important petition of him. The author then writes, "He took it all in, he saw it all together."[13] This is what syntax does. It does not just insert articulation into what we experience; it also draws a line around a whole: "he saw it all together." A continuous perception is unable to define a margin, but syntax can. Because it explicitly demarcates parts, it also determines where the context for those defined parts ends and where another whole begins. One could not have discrete parts without some sense of a whole. Sentences have periods or question marks; paragraphs have something like indentations; books have a title page and an index; a drama has a beginning, middle, and end; and lines in poetry sometimes end in rhymes, especially when they are meant to be recited and heard, not by the mind's tongue and ear but by the real ones. The introduction of syntax does not segment only a given proposition, but also the larger wholes in which the proposition finds its place. We become either able or unable to see it all together. There is another passage in the novel, however, where the parts do not fit into a whole because not all of them are registered. Describing a conversation between Strether and Chad, James says of the former: "Our friend took him in again – he was always taking him in and yet finding that parts of him still remained out."[14] Some parts are clearly there, but others are known to be absent, and so the configuration of those that have been defined remains inconclusive.

A triple use of the term is found at the peripety of the novel, when Strether, on an excursion into the countryside, prepares for supper at an inn at the side of a river ("an experiment in respect to dinner"; "something fried and felicitous").[15] He looks out over the water and sees two people, a man and a woman, together in a boat. The man, who is rowing, has his back to Strether, while the woman looks in his direction. The recognitions take place swiftly. First, Strether sees the woman as disturbed by a perception she has made and conveyed to her companion: "She had *taken in* something as a result of which their course had wavered,

[12] Ibid., 90.
[13] Ibid., 181.
[14] Ibid., 184. On parts and wholes, see p. 190, where Strether says, "I made it out but last night, putting various things together."
[15] Ibid., 302.

and it continued to waver while they just stood off." At this point still, even though she has recognized him and has been seen as such, Strether does not know who she is: "This little effect was sudden and rapid, so rapid that Strether's sense of it was separate only for an instant from a sharp start of his own." But the realization comes immediately: "He too had within the minute *taken in* something, *taken in* that he knew the lady whose parasol, shifting as if to hide her face, made so fine a pink point in the shining scene."[16] The lady, of course, is Madame de Vionnet, and the man is Chad, and the protagonist is now able to see it all together.

The interval between Madame de Vionnet's recognition and Strether's, the moment before the onset of syntax and insight in Strether's mind, is particularly well expressed in this passage. And Strether does not just recognize Madame de Vionnet; he also, concomitantly, recognizes that she has just recognized him. In fact, it is probably her recognition, more than her visible outline, that enables him to recognize her. Finally, what Strether is said to take in at the conclusion is not just who the woman is, but that he knows who she is.[17]

When we take something in, we identify a particular situation, event, or entity, but we do so by understanding what it is. We take it in not only as an individual but also as a kind, not only a *tode* but also a *ti.* Strether does not just identify the individuals; he also identifies what is going on. The thing is recognized for what it is, and we now understand, or at least think we understand, what is going on, and we can distinguish it from other things and events: it is a betrayal, a deception, a lapse into weakness, an act of generosity; or a tree, a spider, a shelter, a tribal ceremony; or perhaps something that still needs a name and that will get one, very likely, with the help of qualification or metaphor added to a familiar name. We take in the essence of something. We do so, however, not just in a single, isolated grasp, but within and underneath the articulations of syntactic structure.

[16] Ibid., 308. My italics.

[17] There is a similar recognition scene, also very intricate, in Chapter 16 of *The Wings of the Dove* (New York: Random House, 1937, part 1, pp. 317–21). Milly Theall, alone, is in the National Gallery in London. She overhears some people (three ladies) discussing something: "Handsome? Well, if you choose to say so. ... In the English style." At first she thinks they are talking about a painting, but then she understands that they are speaking about a man. She turns and sees that the person in question is Merton Densher ("these successions were swift"). Then she suddenly becomes aware that she herself is being "otherwise looked at," and by none other than Kate Croy, who is there with Densher. She achieves the categorial registration of linking the two. James describes the mixture of empty intentions, verbal expressions, and perceptions, both active and passive (looking and being looked at), and the identifications, both illuminating and embarrassing, that take place among these cognitive agents. There are many fine phrases in this passage. The three cloaks of the ladies are said to be "only thinkable as one," and James writes that "the predicament of course wasn't definite or phraseable," that is, it was not easily amenable to syntax. Densher's face, when recognized, is said to have had an "arresting power."

Taking in is more than merely receiving; it involves an initiative of the taker (an internal word), which occurs in the syntactic achievement that overlays the grasp of the intelligibility of the thing. *Taking in* is no less philosophical than *apprehending*, and the latter is no less dependent on the pre-philosophical usage than the former.

Metaphysics or Epistemology?

Much of what we have said in this book has dealt with speaking and thinking, and one might conclude that the book is an exercise in the theory of knowledge. I would rather say that it is a study in metaphysics, and to argue my case I appeal to the original metaphysician. Aristotle's *Metaphysics* is obviously a study of being as being. Its first chapter, however, does not speak immediately about being; it reflects on the fact that there is understanding in the world: not just perception and practical know-how, not just cognition for survival's sake, but understanding just for itself. The world includes the discovery even of things that cannot be used for any advantage by those who discover them. This knowledge for its own sake comes to be within the material universe, and the fact that it is there is one of the things that we should wonder about. The world is a marvelous and most interesting place, and most wonderful is the fact that it can be and is marveled at. The physics of nature ultimately makes a place for what John Archibald Wheeler calls observation and measurement, what Niels Bohr calls registration, and what Michael Oakeshott calls verdicts, all of which are part of intelligent life.[18]

The first sentence of the first chapter of the *Metaphysics* says that all men *by nature* (*physei*) strive or stretch out to know. What sort of "by nature" is this? The sentence is a link between the *Physics* and the *Metaphysics*, the book that was entitled by someone as being "beyond (*meta*) the physicals"; what kind of "beyond" are we dealing with here? The "beyond" is not simply the first cause or the prime mover, but also the context that is introduced when understanding comes into play, which is not just one of the processes of nature. The person who knows is a part of nature, but by nature and by virtue of reason (veracity) he stands on its margin; the achievement of truth is not just an event in the domain of cosmic forces; logic is not reducible to psychology. What we declare when we say we know or decide something is not just what nature has done in us; it is what *we* have done.

The universe had to be very finely calibrated for this emergence of a part of itself that could know the whole and know its own knowing. But, after all, it seems that the universe *has* been so attuned, thank you very

[18] On Wheeler and Bohr, see John Archibald Wheeler, with Kenneth Ford, *Geons, Black Holes and Quantum Foam: A Life in Physics* (New York: Norton, 1998), 338.

much. We *are* here. The arrangement is far more complex than Aristotle
could possibly have imagined. It involves not just elements and chemical
properties such as the hot and the cold, and the moist and the dry, which
were familiar to him, but also fields of force and various kinds of energy,
along with the most startling combinatorics of deoxyribonucleic and
ribonucleic acids, which come together luckily to provide a niche for this
kind of life and conversation. Without such a concourse no syntax could
have arisen.

Aristotle argues to a prime mover in Book 12 of the *Metaphysics*, but by
far the greatest part of the work deals with the activity of knowing and
with being as knowable. Much of the work examines what science and
wisdom are. It studies the substrate, form, and *telos* of entities, as well
as their actuality and potentiality, and it sees these principles both as
establishing substances and as making thinking possible. It studies
entities in their being and their truth, and it brings to light what enables
things to be disclosed in speech. Judgments and other kinds of disclosures are activities that yield syntactic wholes, and the constitution of
such wholes is not a merely natural or psychological process; it goes
"beyond physics" and establishes structures of appearance. The principle
of noncontradiction had to be justified in the *Metaphysics* and not in the
Physics or even the *De Anima*. Aristotle focuses on judgments, in which
"something is said of something," but measurements would be equally
deserving of analysis.[19] Equations also have a syntax, and they succeed
in manifesting things (even though they do not contain resources for
the declarative use of personal pronouns). If we wish to clarify them
philosophically, we should examine them in contrast with judgments.
Both predications and equations are truthful achievements, acts of
manifestation, and things show up through them. When we become
involved with them, we must take initiatives that are not prescribed by the
laws of nature or even by the properties of spacetime. The syntax of words
and numbers is different from the curvature of spacetime, which Wheeler
calls "the grammar of gravity."[20] It is discretely distinguished from space
and time, energy and matter. The human conversation is not a mere
continuation of the nature of things.

The declarative use of first-person pronouns is not just a linguistic
peculiarity but an emblem of what we are as datives of disclosure. The
study of being as being illuminates what we are as human beings, because
we are the kind of thing to whom being is exposed. Reciprocally, however,
the study of ourselves as agents of truth sheds light on what being is.

---

[19] See Robert Sokolowski, "Measurement," in *Pictures, Quotations, and Distinctions: Fourteen
Essays in Phenomenology* (Notre Dame, IN: University of Notre Dame Press, 1992), 139–54.
[20] John Archibald Wheeler, *A Journey into Gravity and Spacetime* (New York: Scientific
American Library, 1990), 68.

We could not get a glimpse of what it means for something to show up as true unless we got some inkling of what we are as the receivers of such disclosure. Aristotle frequently says in the *Metaphysics* that being and one (*on* and *hen*) are correlated with one another, but identity shows up to an identifier, and identification occurs in predication, in picturing and remembering, in experiencing something across presence and absence. It shows up especially when we identify ourselves declaratively by saying "I." This kind of intense identity sheds light on what identity as such can be, in both the living and the nonliving. The kind of life that incorporates intelligence clarifies what life is. We are, therefore, special, after all, in the way we are "selves." These are all issues in the philosophy of being. There is no such thing as epistemology separated from metaphysics.

Our scientific understanding of the world, along with the philosophical understanding that follows on it, is an apex of our cognition, but when reflecting on the place of reason in the world we should not overlook its practical forms. It is wondrous indeed that the cosmos contains a part that can discover something about the whole, but that same part also engages in more ephemeral and localized pursuits. It decides to fight or to flee, it gives and it takes, it befriends and betrays. It undergoes attachments and loss because it wants to be happy, and its syntax of action is no less subtle than the grammar of its speech. It carries out its actions through the understanding it has of the situation in which at the moment it finds itself, in response to the other agents and speakers who are involved with it. It can declaratively say "I" when engaged in such practical activity and such emotional involvements. It can use that sign design because its action is based on an understanding that occurs within articulated syntax. Moral syntax can be casual and relaxed, but it can also reach fierce intensity; even a brief encounter can be a transaction whose syntax gets so tangled that the protagonists destroy themselves – or almost destroy themselves – under the strain.[21]

We contemplate the cosmos that transcends human affairs, but we also enjoy contemplating the human exchanges that occur within it. They too, in their transience and apparent insignificance, can be part of the point of things. We contemplate them not only in philosophical treatises but also in things like the story of what Strether and Chad have done, the paintings of Giorgione and Sargent, and *Così fan tutte* and *Ariadne auf Naxos*. And high art is not the only way we theorize moral action; movies and country music are also vehicles in which we find moral situations and exchanges presented for our consideration. When we theorize action in such depicted ways, what we see will shape our own future action, which becomes conceivable for us

---

[21] See *Brief Encounter*, with Celia Johnson and Trevor Howard. There is a near-miss parallel between the conclusion of this movie and the climax of *Anna Karenina*.

through what we have taken in. Such understanding is not sought just for its own sake; it has an edifying (or a corrupting) effect on what we do.

Philosophical Language

Aristotle does not use the word *metaphysics*, but he does call his science "first philosophy" and the study of being as being, so he is aware of it as a distinct form of knowledge. He does not, however, have much to say about the kind of language that is used in this discipline.[22] Phenomenology has paid much more attention to the character of the philosophical viewpoint and to the language used in it. We have followed Thomas Prufer in calling this language transcendentalese, and we have emphasized the fact that philosophical discourse needs to adjust ordinary words when it incorporates them into its vocabulary. The philosophical attitude and speech exercised by phenomenology converge with Aristotle's first philosophy and his science of being as being. Each can shed light on the other.

One of the quirks of philosophical speech is that it seems almost trivially obvious and yet remains obscure. It uses words that seem to have an evident meaning, and it says things that seem unexceptionable, and yet the point of what it says is often elusive. The reason why philosophy has this perplexing quality is that the special perspective from which it speaks is not easily differentiated from other points of view. Philosophy strives to speak from a final context, a context beyond which there is no other, but most of the time its statements are understood as belonging to a partial context. They are taken as psychological or rhetorical, biological or physical, religious or prudential, instead of as belonging to the comprehensive view of the whole. This comprehensive view includes not only the whole of *things* but also the activity of *knowing* things and speaking about them; it includes the manifestation of things. The logic of parts and wholes takes on strange properties when it is applied to the most inclusive whole; the syntax has to be adjusted, and the meaning of words has to be troped. This modification in its language is often missed.

When one speaks philosophically about things, one speaks, first, with the utmost formality, and, second, about things in their being and their manifestation. Husserl expresses these two dimensions by saying that to enter the philosophical attitude one needs to carry out two procedures: the eidetic reduction, which moves from particulars to an eidetic form, and the transcendental reduction, which leads us to focus on being and manifestation as such. The transcendental reduction moves us out of the natural attitude, in which we pursue some particular kind of truth but do

---

[22] Aristotle has much to say about "analogous" terms or "*pros hen* equivocals," but his remarks do not make up a systematic description of philosophical language.

not think about truthfulness and disclosure as such.[23] Once the philosophical perspective has been attained, one can speak about the forms of manifestation and about the dative to whom things appear, as well as about things in their being and manifestability. One might use concrete examples in one's analysis, but the point of what one says is highly formal. One is not concerned with the particular, concrete features of things, but purely and simply with their being and their manifestation. The example one uses is not the terminus of analysis; the example is diaphanous; the listener must move through the example and reach the formality, and doing this may well strain the mind; we tend to stay with the tangible instance.[24]

For example, suppose one wished to speak philosophically about picturing. One would contrast being a picture with being a thing perceived, being pictured with being remembered, and being a picture with being a word. One might explore the kind of identity that exists in pictures. One might do all this while using a particular picture, such as Rembrandt's *Aristotle Contemplating the Bust of Homer*, as an example, but one would not be speaking just about that picture or about Dutch painting. One would be speaking about the formality of picturing and being pictured. The listener would have to think through the painting to the form that is being targeted, but the listener may well not be able to do so. He might very well take one's remarks as belonging to art history, or to psychology, or to aesthetics, but that would be to miss the point. It would be as though he took a geometrician to be speaking about the triangle drawn on the blackboard and not about the triangle as such. All these misinterpretations would sidestep the issues of being and truth, which need to be expressed on their own terms, by the use of a language adapted to this end. Again, someone might try to explain prehistoric paintings by saying that they were the work of shamans who experienced hallucinatory visions and tried to capture them by representing them on the walls and ceilings of caves. If true, this would be an interesting historical fact, but it would not be a philosophical account of picturing, because it does not clarify what the very dimension of picturing is. It tells a story when one wants a dimensional analysis.

---

[23] The two reductions, eidetic and transcendental, are treated and contrasted in many of Husserl's works. See *Cartesian Meditations*, trans. Dorion Cairns (The Hague: Martinus Nijhoff, 1977), §§34–36 for the eidetic, and §§7–15 for the transcendental. The interplay between the two reductions is discussed throughout *Ideas I.*

[24] The forms reached in philosophical discourse are different from the forms achieved in mathematics, whether in geometry or algebra. Examples have a role in mathematics, but they point beyond themselves. The square drawn on the blackboard is not the square the geometrician is speaking about; he is speaking about *the* square, and the listener has to make that transition.

As an example of how language is modified when it is used in first philosophy, consider the word *here*. In ordinary discourse, in the natural attitude, the term signifies the spot, large or small, where the speaker who uses the word is located. It is, necessarily, one site among many. The speaker can easily change his location, moving from this "here" to the spot that was formerly "there." But from the philosophical point of view, a more formal sense of *here* arises; we get to a "here" that is more inescapable. We get to the pure form of being here, one that is associated with the other pure forms at work in the being and the disclosure of things. When we theorize the speech-and-disclosure situation philosophically, we find that each speaker is involved in a kind of ultimate "here" wherever he goes; this kind of "being here" never changes. The same character belongs to the indexical *now*, which has been amply studied by Husserl in his work on inner time-consciousness and the living present, the *lebendige Gegenwart*. In the natural attitude, one "now" inexorably gives way to another. If we just wait a while, today will become tomorrow. But from the philosophical perspective, a sense of *now* arises that will always be with us, and from this perspective, tomorrow never comes; this tomorrow is always a day away.

Philosophical reflection discovers the pure form of being-here-and-now. This form is not just the center of our subjective awareness. It is involved in the existence of things. The crosshairs of the here and now target things in their actuality. The form of here and now is a kind of always, with everything else a sad waste extending before, after, and beyond. The form is also related to the structure of speech, with its indexicals and syntax as well as its declaratives. The declensions of place and time are related to the syntactic conjugations of words.

The pure indexical form of here-and-now, as a component of being and manifestation, can be studied in its relation to other forms, such as those of remembering and picturing, or the remembered and the pictured, as well as the forms of being identifiable as one, the forms of substantial change, the forms of predication, and the forms of the potential and the actual. It can be related to the speech act, and also to the "taking in" that one discusses in philosophy, the kind that does not involve consuming the thing that is known. One could also explore the "pure ego" (the dative of manifestation or the agent of truth), and one could show how the shape of bodily things is the primary property that they enjoy. Philosophy examines the network of such presentational and intentional structures and these principles of being. We do not and cannot live in these austere forms; we obviously do not live in the pure form of the here-and-now; none of us is a pure ego or a sheer dative; we live only in the world of the natural attitude, with its distributed heres and nows, and with you differentiated from me and we from "them"; but in philosophy we get to the formal structures that make the world a whole that is intelligible, which we can inhabit not just as bodies or animals but as agents of truth. Obviously, the terms *here* and *now* have been adjusted to fit this new context and perspective, but just as obviously listeners are going to be inclined to pull this new use of the terms back to the old ones, to the uses they have in the natural attitude, and philosophical statements using these terms will then appear obscure, like the dark utterances of Heraclitus.

Is it true that philosophy studies only the formal structures of manifestation? Doesn't it also try to get into the content of things? For example, isn't it interested in the differences between the living and the nonliving, or between human beings and nonhuman animals, or between politics and economics? Philosophy does examine these differences and these things, but it does so because they have different modes of appearing. Each of them has a formal structure of its own. Animals, for example, are not just complicated plants; they have dimension of appearance that plants do not have: more interiority, greater independence of their location, different kinds of responses and movement, different forms of identity. The differences between lions and zebras would be of less philosophical interest, except perhaps that one preys on other animals and the other does not, but this contrast also involves a structural difference in manifestation.

A Special Philosophical Term: *Eidos* or *Form*

I wish to focus on an especially troublesome issue in philosophy, along with its related terms. What I will now discuss involves the theme of the intelligibility of things, which we explored in Chapters 10 and 11, and it involves the term *eidos* or *form*. This word calls for a more refined analysis.

We have said that it is difficult to distinguish the philosophical perspective from the natural attitude and from other kinds of reflection, such as the psychological and the rhetorical. It is even more difficult to distinguish philosophical reflection from the kind of reflection that we introduced in Chapter 11, propositional reflection. In that chapter we drew the distinction between propositional and philosophical reflection. I would like to develop the point once more, and then apply it to the peculiarities of philosophical discourse.

We live our lives in the natural attitude. We live as agents of truth. We speak with others; we try to make things clear to them and to ourselves; we are honest or dishonest. As human beings, we do not just live a biological life; we live a life that involves thinking and truth. We are caught up in many enterprises and involvements, all of which engage our truthfulness in one way or another, and we also, very likely, have a sense of the whole of things, which we receive from our religion, our cultural tradition, our moral inheritance, and our own common sense. This sense of the whole is something like philosophy, but it probably is not very well articulated and not very clearly distinguished from our other opinions.

As we live in this natural attitude, one particularly significant distinction cannot help but surface for us: the difference between (1) the way things are and (2) the way they seem to be, or the way they are being presented by other people or by ourselves. Is there any human being for whom this distinction does not arise? The immature and those who are handicapped in certain ways do not make the distinction, but mature and normal people do. It establishes them as agents of truth, and it comes along with our ability to use syntax. Anyone who uses syntax, anyone who has been graduated from protolanguage to language, will inevitably have some sense of this distinction between being and seeming. The distinction must also have been made if we are to be able to use the first-person pronoun in a declarative way and to distinguish between what I think and what you think, between how things show up to me and how they show up to you, and between what I really think and what I just want to tell you.

The fact that we are able to make this distinction does not mean that we have been introduced to new entities of some sort. It means, rather, that we have become able to reflect in a new way on what we experience. This way of reflecting can be called "propositional reflection," as we have seen in Chapter 11. What happens in propositional reflection is that I do not merely accept the state of affairs that you articulate for me. Rather, I become critical. I take that state of affairs simply as being presented or proposed by you. I introduce a distinction between a state of affairs and a proposition, which is a state of affairs taken as proposed. This maneuver moves us into the domain of truth and verification. It allows us to quote others, because we can now distinguish what I say from what you or others say, and I can use my own voice to present what others say; I can manifest how the world looks to them. I can even make this reflective move toward what I myself have articulated in the world, and examine its correctness. This propositional reflection, however, with all its power and complexity, is not the same as philosophical reflection. It does not enable us to perform the wholesale examination of truth and disclosure as such.

Propositional reflection introduces a lot of words that are related specifically to it. The word *look* or *eidos* comes into play here, because we now distinguish between a thing and how it looks. The word *statement* or *proposition* comes into play, and so do *true* and *false*. Despite the amplification of our vocabulary that it enables, propositional reflection still does not allow us to enter into philosophy. Philosophical reflection comes later, and it sorts itself out only in contrast with propositional reflection.

Philosophy comes into play after we have already entered into the game of truth, and it looks at, marvels at, contemplates, and reflects on that game itself. It steps back one step further after we have already stepped back somewhat through our propositional reflection. When we enter into propositional reflection, we remain in the natural attitude and remain one of the contestants in the game of truth, the human conversation; we verify or falsify what we or others have said, and we engage in various ways of discovery and confirmation, both theoretic and practical. But when we enter into philosophical reflection, we lift ourselves above all this, and we adopt a stance from which all contention ceases and controversy turns to admiration, not because we know everything but because we *look at* the game of truth rather than play a part in it. If we really have made this move into philosophy, we know we are in a different dimension. We begin to speak transcendentalese. And just to draw the historical contrast: Machiavelli and Hobbes force the philosophical speaker or writer back into being one of the contenders in the natural attitude and the practical order. For them, ruling is the best life, not thinking, and the mind essentially governs and does not contemplate. In canceling the philosophical attitude, they cash out the theoretic life in order to buy the effective truth of things.

The word *eidos* appears within the scope opened up by propositional reflection. While living and speaking in the dimension that permits propositional reflection, I can ask, "How does this look to you?" I can also try to force a look or a form on you; I can try to bend your mind by speaking rhetorically about things and making you see them my way. But when I go beyond propositional reflection and enter the philosophical attitude, the word *eidos* (as well as its translations *look* and *form*) becomes troped. It becomes a name for *the* look of the thing, the thinkable look, the intelligibility of the thing. The term begins to function like the terms *here* and *now* when they are transposed into the philosophical vocabulary. The term *eidos* becomes highly formalized, and what it names can exist both in the thing that it determines and in those who know the thing. It can even be seen to exist in a picture of the thing, which will capture not only the shape of the subject but also its intelligibility. It can also be seen to exist in the name of the thing, and in the propositions in which the name is used.[25] The philosophical sense of *eidos* is more intensely concentrated than the sense of the term as it is used in the natural attitude, where it

---

[25] This would be the place to discuss Husserl's use of the word *noema*, which we mentioned in our chapter on Aristotle, but it would complicate my argument too much to discuss it in the text. For Husserl, *noema* is spoken only in transcendentalese, not in propositional reflection or in the natural attitude. It is used to name the world and all the things in it as the objective correlates of our noetic activities. When we adopt the phenomenological attitude and describe things as identities constituted by the various intentional acts, we carry out noematic analyses. Phenomenology also carries out noetic analyses, the counterparts or correlatives of noematic ones. Commentators on Husserl who try to identify the *noema* with sense go wrong here, because they do not distinguish phenomenological from propositional reflection. Sense or meaning is what propositional reflection targets, *noemata* are what phenomenological reflection targets.

signifies merely the appearance of things. Only from a philosophical viewpoint does it mean *the* intelligibility of the thing.

When we use the word *eidos* or *form* in the natural attitude, even when we engage propositional reflection, we distinguish the various locations the speakers occupy, and we distinguish the locations of the speakers from the locations of the things they talk about. If we talk about the thing's looks or its form, we assume that there must be some sort of copy of the thing in the sensory apparatus and the minds and brains of the persons who know the thing. But when we move into philosophical discourse, the words *eidos* and *form* have been troped, and issues like these, dealing with spatial differences and with copies, no longer apply. The intelligibility of a thing is not multiplied or copied. It is one and the same in its various existences. But to see this we must have gotten the point of philosophical speech, and have come to realize that it is not the simple discourse of the natural attitude. The form of a thing is a principle of its being, but a principle of a being is not a thing, and how it is different can be clarified by distinguishing the viewpoint from which it is named.[26] The "epistemological problem" is an aporia that seems insoluble because we do not appreciate clearly enough the peculiarities of transcendentalese and the philosophical stance from which it is spoken.

The Philosophical Voice and the Omniscient Narrator

Having discussed philosophical speech we can now discuss the philosophical voice. The philosophical speaker can be contrasted with many other voices, such as the speaker behind mathematics or biology, the political speaker, or the voice of religion. I will draw the contrast between the voice of the philosopher and the voice of the novelist. To make our treatment more specific, let us return to Henry James's *The Ambassadors* and consider, not one of the characters in the book, but the omniscient narrator, the voice that tells us what happens. Not all narrators in novels are omniscient; often one of the characters in the story will be the narrator, but our purposes are best served by the speaker who is not part of the cast.[27] He reports the events with contemplative detachment. He is omniscient, but there is a special reason why he knows everything: in the story, there is nothing to be known except what he tells us. The point needs clarification.

[26] I am grateful to John F. Smolko for highlighting the special character of principles of being (such as form and substrate; substance, property, and accident; potency and actuality; and, in medieval philosophy, essence and existence), and the distinctive manner in which they are named.

[27] In *The Art of the Novel* (p. 320), James speaks about the possibility of having made Strether the narrator of the novel: "Had I meanwhile made him at once hero and historian, endowed him with the romantic privilege of the 'first person' ... ."

Alistair Horne has written a biography of Harold Macmillan. He relates the fact that on June 22, 1944, Macmillan arrived in London from Italy to argue for an Allied thrust through the Ljubljana Gap as a way of routing the German forces and keeping the Russians from advancing more deeply into Central Europe.[28] We are not told where Macmillan slept on the night of June 22, 1944. However unimportant the event may be, the question can be asked, and there is an answer. Macmillan did sleep someplace, and we can find out where. Alistair Horne himself may not have known where Macmillan slept, so despite the extent of his knowledge he is not an omniscient narrator. No biographer is or can be. There will always be "other sides" to the things he talks about.

In *The Ambassadors*, we are told that in a conversation with Chad, "Strether paused in the act of pinning his necktie."[29] We are not told the color of the necktie. Does the narrator know its color? No; not because he is uninformed, but because there is nothing to know. There *is* no color of the necktie unless the author puts it in. The narrator is omniscient, not because he knows everything, but because there is nothing to know about the story except what he includes in the narrative. He is omniscient by fiat. A character in a novel or play possesses only those features that the writer gives him, and he enters into only those actions that the writer describes. Beyond that, the person has no identity and solicits neither reference nor sense. His being collapses into just what appears; he has no sides or profiles beyond those the author gives him. For Strether and Chad, as well as for Anna Karenina and Hamlet, *esse* and *manifestari* are equivalent. In an essay on the voice of poetry, Michael Oakeshott asks what Hamlet's normal bedtime was, and he responds, "Hamlet never went to bed: he exists only in the play, he is a poetic image composed of the words and actions which Shakespeare gave him, and beyond these he is nothing."[30]

Although the narrator is not one of the characters in the story, he still is a persona in the book. He does belong to the story as its narrator, and he is, therefore, a kind of fiction or something made. He could even use the first-person declarative to address the reader (who is also a kind of fiction), but he could not address a character in the story without breaking the spell. The narrator of *The Ambassadors* is Henry James. Henry James, however, is not just the narrator of that story; he has being apart from his manifestation as the storyteller. The narrator is "thinner" than Henry James, who is omniscient in regard to the story but not in regard to the world or even in regard to his own being, which has manifestations and

---

[28] Alistair Horne, *Harold Macmillan. Volume 1: 1894–1956* (New York: Viking, 1988), 219–20.

[29] James, *The Ambassadors*, 183.

[30] Michael Oakeshott, "The Voice of Poetry in the Conversation of Mankind," in *Rationalism in Politics and Other Essays*, new and expanded edition (Indianapolis, IN: Liberty Press, 1991), 519.

concealments apart from the story.³¹ We cannot even say that, strictly speaking, the author of the book is the narrator, because the author has properties that the narrator does not; the narrator as such does not receive royalties, and the same author could make one of his characters the narrator of the story.³² But although Henry James is not entirely the same as the narrator, he is identifiable with him, and he shares in the narrator's omniscience; he has written the book and has created the events and the persons, including the narrator. Incidentally, if the narrator of a particular novel were one of the characters in the story, he would not be transparent and would not be identifiable with the author, the maker of the story; he would have his own point of view and his own qualities, and hence would not see everything. He would be in the employment of the author but would not be identifiable with him.

The person who undertakes philosophical writing is similar to the omniscient narrator in that he enjoys a certain detachment from what he writes about. His philosophical writing is practically and politically uninvolved with the world he contemplates, just as the narrator is not one of the participants in the story he tells. Philosophy does not, as Machiavelli said it should, try to discover the *effective* truth of things; its excellence is of a different order. Philosophy contemplates and clarifies, but, if it truly is philosophy, it does not attempt to govern or contest. There is a human excellence beyond practical, political, and moral life, and it exercises its own kind of influence, more by exemplary than by efficient causation. It gets to things beyond ruling and rhetoric; it reaches its end and its proper good not by commanding or persuading but by the clarity of what it discloses. It nourishes a different kind of human life, which is so detached that one might complain that it is not appropriate for a human being: "But such a life would be mightier (*kreittōn*) than for a man, for it is not insofar as he is man that he will live so, but insofar as something divine is present in him."³³

The philosophical writer is also analogous to the narrator in the comprehensiveness of his vision, but the scope of philosophy is far wider. Nothing at all can be left out, in principle, from the purview of philosophy. It is not a partial science or a limited story, not even in regard to the writer or speaker himself. There is more to Henry James than being the narrator of the novel, and there are events in his life that he does not put into the

---

³¹ St. Augustine in the *Confessions* is anything but an omniscient narrator, but then he is not writing a story for readers like you and me. His narrative is addressed to his Creator, who is omniscient, but not in the manner of a narrator. Augustine asks his addressee to bring himself, Augustine, to light. This form of voice is very appropriate for theological writing.

³² The reader is likewise a fiction in the story, but he is also the human being who buys the book and sits down to read it, that is, to become the fictional reader. The reader as a fiction within the novel is "thinner" than the reader who buys the book.

³³ Aristotle, *Nicomachean Ethics*, X 7, 1177b26–8. (Ross translation, modified)

story he tells, but there is nothing in the philosopher that the philosophical writer does not wish to bring to light in the way he brings things to light, in their formality if not in their detail. There is no dimension of disclosure and action, not even the properties that belong to him as a philosopher, that he does not consider and reveal. It is true that the novelist will also present things in his story that reveal what it is to be a novelist, and to the extent that he does this, his writing verges on philosophy, but the story remains more closely tied to its incidents than philosophical writing remains tied to its illustrations. The philosophical writer uses examples and discards them (my anecdotes about Andrew the car salesman and Max Hastings the historian do not constitute a plot), but the novelist has to stay with the story, and the plot has to be sustained.

The philosopher is omniscient only formally and only in principle, that is, only potentially. People sometimes complain that a philosopher pretends to be a know-it-all, and that he tries to tell everybody else what they are doing: he tries, for example, to tell mathematicians what mathematics is, or the politician what politics is. But the complaint is unjustified. It is true that if someone presents himself as a philosopher, he will not be able to recuse himself from any philosophical question. He is called, in his profession, to address the whole of things and to show how parts differentiate themselves within the whole. He may, as an individual speaker, be unable to address a given issue, but he cannot say that his "field" does not address it. He may have to admit his own personal limitations in not being able to take it on, but he cannot say that philosophy does not deal with it. It would, for example, be unsuitable for someone to say, "I am a philosopher of language, but I need say nothing about moral conduct or political life." Such a person would be a scholar with an expertise, but not a philosopher. The potential omniscience of the philosopher is chastening, because, like Socrates, he is always aware that he does not know but is obliged to know.

A counterweight to philosophical "omniscience" lies in the fact that the philosophical writer addresses his readers as equals. The novelist does not treat his readers as equals; the reader of a novel is subordinated to the writer and narrator of the story. The writer of a story is almost despotic. The reader has to wait to find out what the writer will reveal to him, and he has to believe the storyteller. The reader of a philosophical text, by contrast, is simply being reminded of what he already knows. He is being helped to see the forms and principles that are already at work in his world and in himself as an agent of truth. The philosophical reader can even run ahead of the text or depart from it and formulate things on his own, and the philosophical author would be happy to see him do so, but the reader of a novel cannot run ahead and finish the story himself; it is logically or phenomenologically impossible for him; he has to wait and be told what happens. He is dependent on the author's revelation in a way that the philosophical reader is not. The narrator calls for faith, while the philosopher engages reason. In this respect, a novel is a monologue, while a philosophical text is a conversation. The philosophical reader does not simply listen and follow, but continuously evaluates and responds as he thinks on his own.

Last Reading

We conclude by returning to the issue with which we began this book, the declarative use of personal pronouns.

Mathematical equations do not provide any resources for declaratives. They are neither conversational nor predicational. Equations are "above" statements. They are more purely rationalized, so formal that they are not intellectually owned by anyone. They cannot be marked as appropriated; they are not somebody's opinion. At the other extreme, standing "below" statements are pictures, and they also do not give us any resources for the declarative use of the first person. If equations are more rationalized than spoken statements, pictures are less so. They include more sensibility than words do. Pictures cannot be declared in their own medium as being intellectually owned by someone: if a painter tried to declare himself by drawing a small picture of himself in the painting, how would we know that this image was a declaration and not part of what is being depicted? Pictures have signatures, but a signature on a painting is not a pictorial declaration; it is a written text, an intrusion of a verbal statement into the picture; a signature is not an image. A signature, furthermore, also differs from the prime instance of declaratives because it is written and not spoken; it is something like a delayed declarative, not one in actual speech, which appropriates what is being said at the moment it is being said. Pictures and signatures are not part of a direct conversation, in which declaratives are used to identify each of the interlocutors and the stands that they take; pictures and signatures, in regard to their temporality, are more like a letter written to someone. Also, a signature does not permit the modalities that declaratives allow. Neither equations, pictures, nor writing, therefore, can use a sign design to express the speaker as using that sign conversationally here and now.

A picture engages the essentials of the thing it depicts – it is, say, a picture of a man on horseback – but it also contains a lot of the accidentals that belong to the individual depicted: the clothing the man wears, the way his face is positioned, the color of the saddle. A picture cannot avoid asserting many accidental details, and it is not always clear what is essential and what is accidental in the image. What exactly is being said in the picture is, therefore, often unclear and suggestive.

A name contains an essential kind (*man* or *horse*), and in this respect it is like a picture, but it differs from pictures because it captures *only* the intelligibility or the essence, only the *eidos* of that thing. It leaves out *all* the particular accidentals, and so it introduces a sharp distinction between the essential and the accidental. Names are quintessential. Because they capture only the essential, words can be combined to make exact statements. When a speaker says something, he says *only* what he says. There may be some accidentals attaching to the words (the word might be spoken loudly, it might have a grating sound), but these are accidents of the words, not of what they signify. Words, in contrast with pictures, have "nothing to do" with the things they signify and no similarity to them (the word *robin* is not shaped like a bird, whereas the bird's image shows how it looks).[34] The accidentals that belong to the names do not contaminate the content of what is being said, which remains crystalline and purely intellectual, purely intelligible, so long as the words are being used thoughtfully. Statements, therefore, are crisp and clear, in principle at least, whereas pictures need interpretation, which is done in words.

The precise formulations that words permit serve as suitable substrates for declaratives, which express our appropriation of the particular syntactic whole that is expressed in the words. Without an exact statement at their base, our declaratives are insubstantial and merely apparent. There is nothing for them to appropriate. A declarative attached to a vague or meaningless statement would be like the phrase "It is true that ..." followed by a jumble of words that make no sense. In this case there is nothing to be true, and in the former we have nothing to declare.

In onomatopoeia, however, words take on some of the accidental features of what they designate. Words like *squeak, splash, bark,* and *buzz* resemble what they signify, but they still are words and can be embedded in syntax. If, however, in using them we begin to accentuate the resemblances, we drift closer to picturing and begin imitating the thing in question. For example, in playing a game with children we might begin by using the sound *buzz* as a word, and then turn the sound into an imitation of a bee; as we did so the syntax belonging to the word would drop away, leaving us with incantation rather than speech. Words have to stop imitating things if they are to become carriers of the intelligibility of the things and allow that intelligibility to be interwoven with others into a statement that we can appropriate by uttering a declarative. If we were to remain with the imitative dimensions of *buzz, splash,* and *squeak,* we would not be literally saying anything – although we might be depicting something – and we could not declare ourselves by using the word *I.* We

---

[34] See Edmund Husserl, *Logical Investigations*, trans. J. N. Findlay, ed. Dermot Moran (New York: Routledge, 2001), Investigation VI, §14a, volume 2, p. 220: "It is rather of the very essence of a significative intention, that in it the apparent objects of intending and fulfilling acts (e. g. name and thing named in their fully achieved unity) 'have nothing to do with one another'."

would be engaged in a more rudimentary manifestation. We might be expressing our feelings, but we would not be signaling any intellectual, syntactic composition. We could not be quoted by anyone else, but we could be imitated.

Words and their syntax carry out exact displays and allow us to distinguish among essence, properties, and accidentals. Our veracity unfolds in many forms of manifestation, which reach their climax in words and syntax. Words introduce us to equations (equations do not precede words), and words can be used to explain what is presented in a picture. They capture and carry the understandability of things, permitting us to make distinctions and to see that *this* is not *that*, and that therefore *this* has a necessity and substantiality, an entity, in itself. Through words we enjoy an articulated world in common and engage in reciprocal exchanges, whether moral, commercial, or political, in both friendship and, alas, enmity. By using them we take a stand among others, across space and time, and exercise and declare our own agency. Words allow us to live involved in light.

Bibliography

Abell, Catherine, and Gregory Currie. "Internal and External Pictures." *Philosophical Psychology* 12 (1999): 429–45.

Arendt, Hannah. *The Human Condition.* Chicago: University of Chicago Press, 1958.

Aristotle. *Aristotle's Prior and Posterior Analytics.* Edited by W. D. Ross. Oxford: The Clarendon Press, 1949.

On Memory and Recollection. In *On the Soul. Parva Naturalia. On Breath.* Translated by W. S. Hett. Loeb Classical Library. Cambridge, MA: Harvard University Press, 1957.

Problems. 2 volumes. Translated by W. S. Hett. Loeb Classical Library. Cambridge, MA: Harvard University Press, 1957 and 1961.

Aristotle's Metaphysics. Edited by W. D. Ross. 2 volumes. Oxford: The Clarendon Press, 1958.

Aristotelis Categoriae et Liber de Interpretatione. Edited by L. Minio-Paluello. Oxford: The Clarendon Press, 1961.

De Anima. Edited by W. D. Ross. Oxford: The Clarendon Press, 1961.

Aristotelis Ethica Nicomachea. Edited by I. Bywater. Oxford: The Clarendon Press, 1962.

Aristotelis Politica. Edited by W. D. Ross. Oxford: The Clarendon Press, 1964.

Nicomachean Ethics. Translated by David Ross. Revised by J. L. Ackrill and J. O. Urmson. New York: Oxford University Press, 1987.

Astington, Janet Wilde. *The Child's Discovery of the Mind.* Cambridge, MA: Harvard University Press, 1993.

Aubrey, John. *Aubrey's Brief Lives.* Edited by Oliver Lawson Dick. Ann Arbor: University of Michigan Press, 1957.

Bazán, Bernardo Carlos. "*Intellectum Speculativum:* Averroes, Thomas Aquinas, and Siger of Brabant on the Intelligible Object." *Journal of the History of Philosophy* 19 (1981): 425–46.

Bickerton, Derek. *Language and Species.* Chicago: University of Chicago Press, 1990.

Language and Human Behavior. Seattle: University of Washington Press, 1995.

Bloom, Paul. *How Children Learn the Meanings of Words.* Cambridge, MA: MIT Press, 2000.

Boethius. *The Theological Tractates and The Consolation of Philosophy.* Translated by H. F. Stewart and E. K. Rand. Loeb Classical Library. Cambridge: Harvard University Press, 1968.

Braine, David. *The Human Person: Animal and Spirit.* Notre Dame, IN: University of Notre Dame Press, 1992.

Brough, John B. "Translator's Introduction." In Edmund Husserl, *Phantasy, Image Consciousness, and Memory (1898–1925).* Dordrecht: Springer, 2005.

Burgess, Anthony. *Enderby Outside.* In *The Complete Enderby.* New York: Carroll & Graf, 1996.

Calvin, William H., and Derek Bickerton. *Lingua ex Machina: Reconciling Darwin and Chomsky with the Human Brain.* Cambridge, MA: MIT Press, 2000.

Changeux, Jean-Pierre. *The Physiology of Truth: Neuroscience and Human Knowledge.* Translated by M. B. DeBevoise. Cambridge, MA: The Belknap Press of Harvard University Press, 2004.

Churchland, Paul M. *The Engine of Reason, the Seat of the Soul: A Philosophical Journey into the Brain.* Cambridge, MA: MIT Press, 1995.

Conrad, Theodor. *Zur Wesenslehre des psychischen Lebens und Erlebens.* The Hague: Martinus Nijhoff, 1968.

Cowie, Fiona. *What's Within? Nativism Reconsidered.* New York: Oxford University Press, 1999.

Crick, Francis. *The Astonishing Hypothesis: The Scientific Search for the Soul.* New York: Charles Scribner's Sons, 1994.

Currie, Gregory, and Ian Ravenscroft. *Recreative Minds: Imagination in Philosophy and Psychology.* New York: Oxford University Press, 2002.

Davidson, Herbert A. *Alfarabi, Avicenna, and Averroes, on Intellect: Their Cosmologies, Theories of the Active Intellect, and Theories of Human Intellect.* New York: Oxford University Press, 1992.

Deely, John. *Four Ages of Understanding: The First Postmodern Survey of Philosophy from Ancient Times to the Turn of the Twenty-First Century.* Toronto: University of Toronto Press, 2001.

Descartes, René. *The Philosophical Writings of Descartes.* 3 volumes. Translated by John Cottingham, Robert Stoothoff, and Dugald Murdoch. New York: Cambridge University Press, 1984–91.

Dummett, Michael. *Frege: Philosophy of Language.* London: Duckworth, 1973.

Floucat, Yves. *L'intime fécondité de l'intelligence: Le verbe mental selon saint Thomas d'Aquin.* Paris: Pierre Téqui, 2001.

Frege, Gottlob. *Posthumous Writings.* Edited by Hans Hermes et al. Translated by Peter Long and Roger White. Chicago: University of Chicago Press, 1979. *Collected Papers on Mathematics, Logic, and Philosophy.* Edited by Brian McGuinness. New York: Basil Blackwell, 1984.

Garceau, Benoît, O.M.I. *Judicium: Vocabulaire, sources, doctrine de saint Thomas d'Aquin.* Paris: Librairie philosophique J. Vrin, 1968.

Gibson, James J. *The Senses Considered as Perceptual Systems.* Boston: Houghton Mifflin, 1966. *The Ecological Approach to Visual Perception.* Hillsdale, NJ: Erlbaum, 1986.

Harris, Paul L. *The Work of the Imagination.* New York: Blackwell, 2000.

Hastings, Max. *Overlord: D-Day and the Battle for Normandy.* New York: Simon and Schuster, 1984. *Armageddon: The Battle for Germany, 1944–1945.* New York: Knopf, 2004.

Heidegger, Martin. *Logik: Die Frage nach der Wahrheit.* Frankfurt am Main: Vittorio Klostermann, 1976.

Hobbes, Thomas. *De Homine.* In *Opera Philosophica quae Latine scripsit.* Edited by William Molesworth. Aalen: Scientia Verlag, 1961.
  The Elements of Law, Natural and Politic. Edited by Ferdinand Tönnies. London: Frank Cass, 1969.
  On Man. In *Man and Citizen.* Edited by Bernard Gert. Garden City, NY: Doubleday, 1972.
  Leviathan. Edited by Richard Tuck. New York: Cambridge University Press, 1996.
Horne, Alistair. *Harold Macmillan.* 2 volumes. New York: Viking, 1988 and 1989.
Hume, David. *A Treatise of Human Nature.* Edited by L. A. Selby-Bigge. Oxford: The Clarendon Press, 1960.
Husserl, Edmund. *Ideas: General Introduction to Pure Phenomenology.* Translated by W. R. Boyce Gibson. New York: Macmillan, 1931.
  Ideen zu einer reinen Phänomenologie und phänomenologischen Philosophie. Drittes Buch. Edited by Marly Biemel. Husserliana V. The Hague: Martinus Nijhoff, 1952.
  Analysen zur passiven Synthesis (1918–1926). Edited by Margot Fleischer. Husserliana XI. The Hague: Martinus Nijhoff, 1966.
  Formal and Transcendental Logic. Translated by Dorion Cairns. The Hague: Martinus Nijhoff, 1969.
  The Crisis of European Sciences and Transcendental Phenomenology. Translated by David Carr. Evanston, IL: Northwestern University Press, 1970.
  Experience and Judgment: Investigations in a Genealogy of Logic. Translated by James S. Churchill and Karl Ameriks. Evanston, IL: Northwestern University Press, 1973.
  Cartesian Meditations. Translated by Dorion Cairns. The Hague: Martinus Nijhoff, 1977.
  Logical Investigations. 2 volumes. Translated by J. N. Findlay. Edited by Dermot Moran. New York: Routledge, 2001.
Hyman, John. *The Objective Eye: Color, Form, and Reality in the Theory of Art.* Chicago: University of Chicago Press, 2006.
Jacobsen, Josephine. *The Instant of Knowing.* Lecture given at the Library of Congress, May 7, 1973. Washington, DC: Library of Congress, 1974.
James, Henry. *The Art of the Novel.* New York: Charles Scribner's Sons, 1934.
  The Wings of the Dove. New York: Random House, 1937.
  The Ambassadors. New York: Norton, 1964.
James, William. *Principles of Psychology.* 2 volumes. New York: Dover, 1950.
Kant, Immanuel. *Critique of Pure Reason.* Translated by Norman Kemp Smith. New York: St. Martin's Press, 1965.
Kass, Leon R. *The Hungry Soul: Eating and the Perfecting of Our Nature.* Chicago: University of Chicago Press, 1999.
Keller, Evelyn Fox. *Refiguring Life: Metaphors of Twentieth-Century Biology.* New York: Columbia University Press, 1995.
  The Century of the Gene. Cambridge, MA: Harvard University Press, 2000.
Klein, Jacob. *Plato's Trilogy.* Chicago: University of Chicago Press, 1977.
  Lectures and Essays. Edited by Robert B. Williamson and Elliott Zuckerman. Annapolis, MD: St. John's College Press, 1985.
Kretzmann, Norman. "Aristotle on Spoken Sound Significant by Convention." In *Ancient Logic and Its Modern Interpretations,* edited by John Corcoran, 3–21. Dordrecht: Reidel, 1974.

Lachterman, David Rapport. *The Ethics of Geometry: A Genealogy of Modernity.* New York: Routledge, 1989.

Leder, Drew. *The Absent Body.* Chicago: University of Chicago Press, 1990.

Leslie, Alan M., and Tim P. German. "Knowledge and Ability in 'Theory of Mind': One-Eyed Overview of a Debate." In *Mental Simulation: Evaluations and Applications,* edited by Martin Davies and Tony Stone, 123–50. Cambridge, MA: Blackwell, 1995.

Lonergan, Bernard, S. J. *Verbum: Word and Idea in Aquinas.* Collected Works of Bernard Lonergan, volume 2. Toronto: University of Toronto Press, 1997.

Luhrmann, T. M. "The Call of the Wild." *Times Literary Supplement,* January 25, 2002. Review of Michael Newton, *Savage Girls and Wild Boys: A History of Feral Children* (London: Faber and Faber, 2002).

MacIntyre, Alasdair. *Dependent Rational Animals: Why Human Beings Need the Virtues.* Chicago: Open Court, 1999.

Maclean, Charles. *The Wolf Children.* New York: Hill and Wang, 1997.

Macnamara, John. *A Border Dispute: The Place of Logic in Psychology.* Cambridge, MA: MIT Press, 1986.

Manent, Pierre. *La raison des nations: Réflexions sur la démocratie en Europe.* Paris: Gallimard, 2006.

Mann, Wolfgang Rainer. *The Discovery of Things: Aristotle's 'Categories' and Their Context.* Princeton, NJ: Princeton University Press, 2000.

Mansfield, Harvey C., Jr. *Machiavelli's New Modes and Orders: A Study of the 'Discourses on Livy'.* Ithaca, NY: Cornell University Press, 1979.

———. *Manliness.* New Haven, CT: Yale University Press, 2006.

Marbach, Eduard. *Das Problem des Ich in der Phänomenologie Husserls.* The Hague: Martinus Nijhoff, 1974.

Martin, Wayne M. *Theories of Judgment: Psychology, Logic, Phenomenology.* New York: Cambridge University Press, 2006.

McCarthy, Cormac. *Cities of the Plain.* New York: Vintage, 1998.

McGinn, Colin. *Mindsight: Image, Dream, Meaning.* Cambridge, MA: Harvard University Press, 2004.

Milbank, John, and Catherine Pickstock. *Truth in Aquinas.* New York: Routledge, 2001.

Mill, John Stuart. *On Liberty.* Edited by John Gray and G. W. Smith. New York: Routledge, 1991.

Modrak, Deborah K. W. *Aristotle's Theory of Language and Meaning.* New York: Cambridge University Press, 2001.

Newman, John Henry. *The Idea of a University.* Garden City, NY: Doubleday, 1959.

Noë, Alva. *Action in Perception.* Cambridge, MA: MIT Press, 2004.

———. "Real Presences." Forthcoming in *Philosophical Topics.*

Noë, Alva, and Evan Thompson. "Are There Neural Correlates of Consciousness?" *Journal of Consciousness Studies* 11 (2004): 3–28.

Oakeshott, Michael. *On Human Conduct.* Oxford: The Clarendon Press, 1975.

———. *Rationalism in Politics and Other Essays.* New and expanded edition. Indianapolis, IN: Liberty Press, 1991.

O'Callaghan, John P. *Thomist Realism and the Linguistic Turn: Toward a More Perfect Form of Existence.* Notre Dame, IN: University of Notre Dame Press, 2003.

Orwell, George. *1984.* New York: Signet Classics, 1961.

Owens, Joseph, C.Ss.R., *Cognition: An Epistemological Inquiry*. Houston, TX: Center for Thomistic Studies, 1992.

Paissac, Hyacinthe. *Théologie du Verbe: Saint Augustin et saint Thomas*. Paris: Cerf, 1951.

Parker, Andrew. *Seven Deadly Colours: The Genius of Nature's Palette and How It Eluded Darwin*. London: The Free Press, 2005.

Peifer, John Frederick. *The Mystery of Knowledge*. Albany, NY: Magi Books, 1964.

Perler, Dominik, editor. *Ancient and Medieval Theories of Intentionality*. Leiden: E. J. Brill, 2001.

Pinker, Stephen. *The Language Instinct: How the Mind Creates Language*. New York: William Morrow, 1994.

Pippin, Robert B. *Henry James and Modern Moral Life*. New York: Cambridge University Press, 2001.

Plato. *Republic*. Translated by G. M. A. Grube. Indianapolis, IN: Hackett, 1974.

Possidius. *Vita Sancti Aurelii Augustini*. Migne, *Patrologia Latina*, volume 32, columns 33–66.

Pritzl, Kurt, O. P. "Aristotle's Door." Forthcoming in a volume edited by Kurt Pritzl, at the Catholic University of America Press.

Prufer, Thomas. *Recapitulations: Essays in Philosophy*. Washington, DC: Catholic University of America Press, 1993.

Rabeau, Gaston. *Species. Verbum. L'activité intellectuelle élémentaire selon S. Thomas d'Aquin*. Paris: Librairie philosophique J.Vrin, 1938.

Schmidt, Robert W., S. J. *The Domain of Logic according to Saint Thomas Aquinas*. The Hague: Martinus Nijhoff, 1966.

Schore, Allan N. *Affect Regulation and the Origin of the Self: The Neurobiology of Emotional Development*. Foreword by James S. Grotstein. Hillsdale, NJ: Erlbaum, 1994.

Simon, Yves R. *A General Theory of Authority*. Notre Dame, IN: University of Notre Dame Press, 1980.

Slade, Francis. "Rule as Sovereignty: The Universal and Homogeneous State." In *The Truthful and the Good: Essays in Honor of Robert Sokolowski*, edited by John J. Drummond and James G. Hart, 159–80. Boston: Kluwer, 1996.

"Ends and Purposes." In *Final Causality in Nature and Human Affairs*, edited by Richard Hassing, 83–5. Washington, DC: Catholic University of America Press, 1997.

"On the Ontological Priority of Ends and Its Relevance to the Narrative Arts." In *Beauty, Art, and the Polis*, edited by Alice Ramos, 58–69. Washington, DC: Catholic University of America Press, 2000.

Sokolowski, Robert. *The Formation of Husserl's Concept of Constitution*. The Hague: Martinus Nijhoff, 1964.

Husserlian Meditations: How Words Present Things. Evanston, IL: Northwestern University Press, 1974.

Presence and Absence: A Philosophical Investigation of Language and Being. Bloomington: Indiana University Press, 1978.

Moral Action: A Phenomenological Study. Bloomington: Indiana University Press, 1985.

"Natural and Artificial Intelligence." In *The Artificial Intelligence Debate: False Starts, Real Foundations*, edited by R. Graubard, 45–64. Cambridge, MA: MIT Press, 1988.

Pictures, Quotations, and Distinctions: Fourteen Essays in Phenomenology. Notre Dame, IN: University of Notre Dame Press, 1992.

Introduction to Phenomenology. New York: Cambridge University Press, 2000.

"Friendship and Moral Action in Aristotle." *The Journal of Value Inquiry* 35 (2001): 355–69.

"Phenomenology of Friendship." *The Review of Metaphysics* 55 (2002): 451–70.

"Semiotics in Husserl's *Logical Investigations.*" In *One Hundred Years of Phenomenology*, edited by Dan Zahavi and Frederik Stjernfelt, 171–83. Boston: Kluwer, 2002.

"La grammaire comme signal de la pensée." Translated by Jocelyn Benoist. In *Husserl: La représentation vide*, edited by Jocelyn Benoist and J.-F. Courtine, 97–108. Paris: Presses universitaires de France, 2003.

"Visual Intelligence in Painting." *The Review of Metaphysics* 59 (2005): 333–54.

Christian Faith and Human Understanding: Studies in the Eucharist, Trinity, and the Human Person. Washington, DC: Catholic University of America Press, 2006.

"Discovery and Obligation in Natural Law." Forthcoming in a volume edited by Holger Zaborowski, at the Catholic University of America Press.

Spaemann, Robert. *Glück und Wohlwollen. Versuch über Ethik.* Stuttgart: Klett-Cotta, 1998.

Personen. Versuche über den Unterschied zwischen 'etwas' und 'jemand'. Stuttgart: Klett-Cotta, 1998.

Spruit, Leen. *Species Intelligibilis: From Perception to Knowledge.* Volume 1, *Classical Roots and Medieval Discussions.* Volume 2, *Renaissance Controversies, Later Scholasticism, and the Elimination of the Intelligible Species in Modern Philosophy.* Leiden: E. J. Brill, 1994 and 1995.

Stich, Stephen, and Shaun Nichols. "Folk Psychology: Simulation or Tacit Theory?" *Mind and Language* 7 (1992): 35–71.

Strauss, Leo. "The Living Issues of German Postwar Philosophy." In Heinrich Meier, *Leo Strauss and the Theologico-Political Problem.* Translated by Marcus Brainard. New York: Cambridge University Press, 2006.

Strawson, Peter F. *Freedom and Resentment and Other Essays.* London: Methuen, 1974.

Taylor, Charles. *Sources of the Self: The Making of the Modern Identity.* Cambridge, MA: Harvard University Press, 1989.

Thomas Aquinas. *Sancti Thomae de Aquino Opera Omnia.* Leonine Edition. Rome: Ex Typographia Polyglotta S. C. de Propaganda Fide, etc., 1882–. Volume 1, *In libros Perihermeneias expositio.* Volume 25, 1 & 2, *Quaestiones de quolibet.* Volume 43, *De principiis naturae, De unitate intellectus contra Averroistas, et alia.*

In Aristotelis librum De Anima commentarium. Turin: Marietti, 1948.

Summa theologiae. Pars Prima. Pars Prima Secundae. Turin: Marietti, 1950.

In duodecim libros Metaphysicorum Aristotelis expositio. Turin: Marietti, 1950.

Quaestiones disputatae. Volume 1. *De veritate.* Turin: Marietti, 1953.

Quaestiones disputatae. Volume 2. *De potentia. De anima. De spiritualibus creaturis. De unione Verbi Incarnati. De malo. Et alia.* Turin: Marietti, 1953.

Summa contra Gentiles. 3 volumes. Turin: Marietti, 1961–67.

S. Thomae Aquinatis Opera Omnia. Edited by R. Busa. Stuttgart-Bad Cannstatt: Fromann-Holzboog, 1980. Volume 1, *In quattuor libros Sententiarum.* Volume 6, *Lectio super evangelium Johannis.*

Thompson, D'Arcy Wentworth. *On Growth and Form*. New York: Dover, 1992.

Torrell, Jean-Pierre, O.P. *Saint Thomas Aquinas*. 2 volumes. Second edition. Translated by Robert Royal. Washington, DC: Catholic University of America Press, 1996 and 2003.

Travis, Charles. *Unshadowed Thought: Representation in Thought and Language*. Cambridge, MA: Harvard University Press, 2000.

Tugendhat, Ernst. *Ti kata tinos: Eine Untersuchung zu Struktur und Ursprung Aristotelischer Grundbegriffe*. Freiburg: Verlag Karl Alber, 1958.

Wheeler, John Archibald. *A Journey into Gravity and Spacetime*. New York: Scientific American Library, 1990.

 With Kenneth Ford. *Geons, Black Holes and Quantum Foam: A Life in Physics*. New York: Norton, 1998.

Whitaker, C. W. A. *Aristotle's 'De Interpretatione': Contradiction and Dialectic*. Oxford: The Clarendon Press, 1996.

White, Kevin. "St. Thomas Aquinas on Prologues." *Archivum Franciscanum Historicum* 98 (2005): 803–13.

Williams, Bernard. *Truth and Truthfulness: An Essay in Genealogy*. Princeton, NJ: Princeton University Press, 2002.

Index